THE MIEGUNYAH PRESS

This is number ninety-three in the
second numbered series of the
Miegunyah Volumes
made possible by the
Miegunyah Fund
established by bequests
under the wills of
Sir Russell and Lady Grimwade.

'Miegunyah' was the home of
Mab and Russell Grimwade
from 1911 to 1955.

Opus nunc denuò ab ipso Auctore recognitum, multisque locis castigatum, & quamplurimis nouis Tabulis atque Commentarijs auctum.

THE WORLD OF THE BOOK

DES COWLEY AND CLARE WILLIAMSON

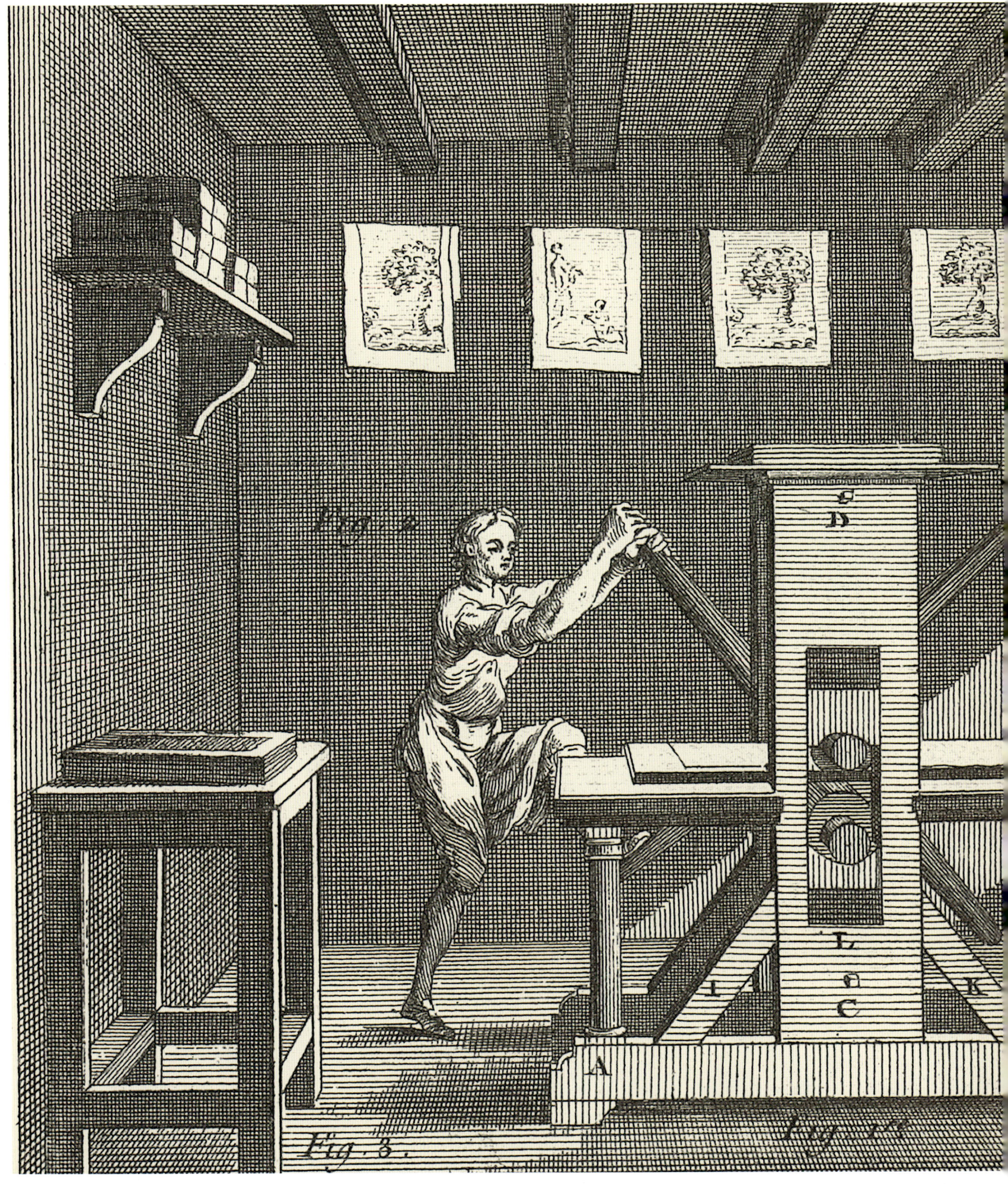

THE MIEGUNYAH PRESS
An imprint of Melbourne
University Publishing Limited
187 Grattan Street, Carlton,
Victoria 3053, Australia
mup-info@unimelb.edu.au
www.mup.com.au

Published in association with the
State Library of Victoria,
328 Swanston Street, Melbourne,
Victoria 3000, Australia
www.slv.vic.gov.au
www.mirroroftheworld.com.au

First published 2007
Text © State Library of Victoria 2007
Design and typography © Melbourne University
Publishing Ltd 2007
Illustrations © State Library of Victoria unless
otherwise noted.

This book is copyright. Apart from any use permitted under the *Copyright Act 1968* and subsequent amendments, no part may be reproduced, stored in a retrieval system or transmitted by any means or process whatsoever without the prior written permission of the publishers.

Every attempt has been made to locate holders of copyright and to seek other relevant permissions. If any omissions or errors are detected, the publishers invite relevant individuals or organisations to contact them to ensure that appropriate acknowledgement can be made in any future editions of this book.

Designed by Pfisterer + Freeman
Typeset in Adobe Garamond Pro and Matrix
by Pfisterer + Freeman
Printed in China through Australian Book Connection

National Library of Australia
Cataloguing-in-Publication entry

Cowley, Des.
The world of the book.

> Bibliography.
> Includes index.
>
> ISBN 9780522853780 (hbk.).
>
> 1. Books. 2. Book design. 3. Illustration of books.
> 4. Book industries and trade—History. 5. Popular culture—History. I. Williamson, Clare. II. Title.
> (Series : Miegunyah Press series. Series 2 ; no. 93).

002

FRONTISPIECE:
Abraham Ortelius
Theatrum Orbis Terrarum
Antwerp, Ant. Coppenium
Diesth, 1574

PREVIOUS PAGE:
Denis Diderot, editor
*Encyclopédie, ou,
Dictionnaire Raisonné
des Sciences, des Arts
et des Métiers*
Paris, Chez Briasson,
David l'Aîné, Le Breton,
Durand, 1751–72

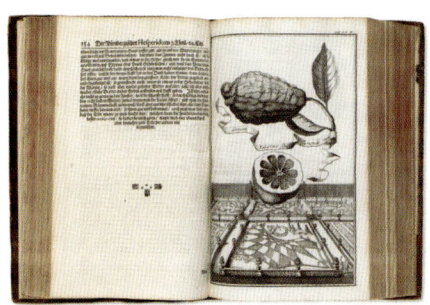

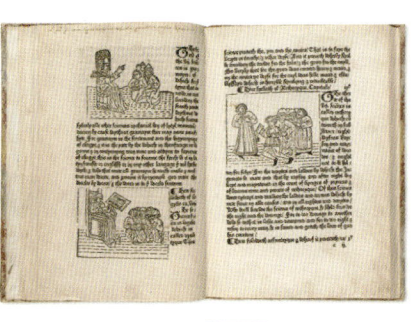

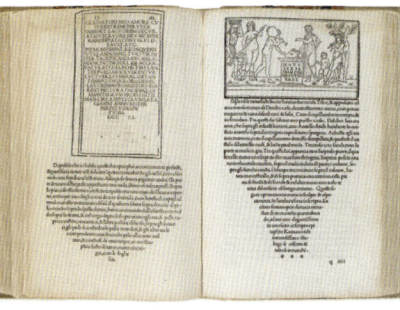
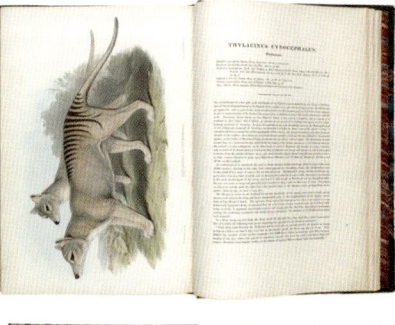

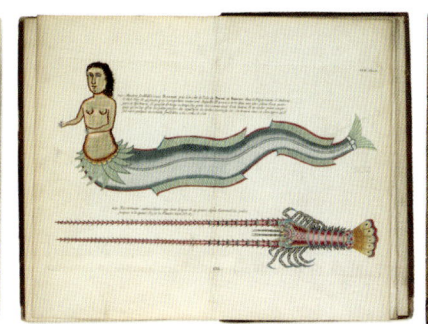

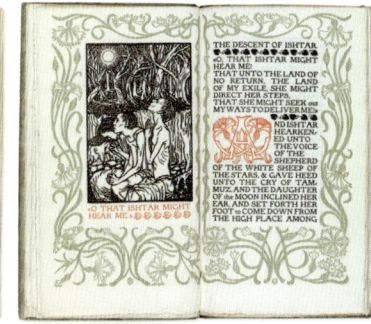

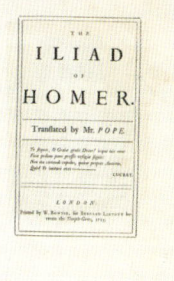
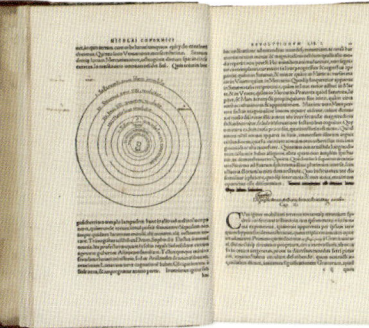
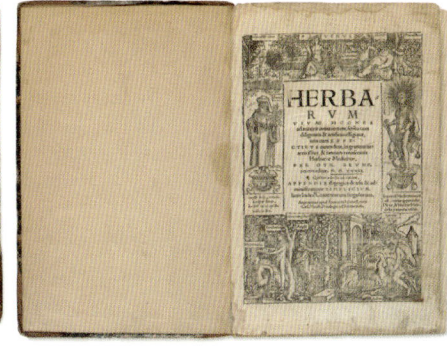
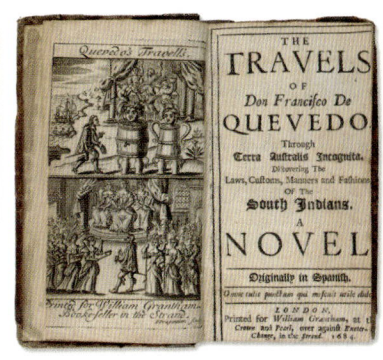

STEIN

KEROUAC

PENGUIN BOOKS

IT'S A
TTLEFIELD

GRAHAM
GREENE

UNABRIDGED

ULYSSES

BY

JAMES JOYCE

CONTENTS

Notes to the reader	x
Acknowledgements	xi
Introduction	xii

I. BOOKS AND IDEAS

The book before the book	3
The illuminated manuscript	9
The printed book	19
The sacred book	27
The world in a book	35
Books that changed the world	43

II. THE BOOK AND THE IMAGINATION

Literary foundations	53
Imaginary voyages	63
The modernist experiment: Joyce and his circle	71
The paperback revolution	79
The beat goes on	87
The popular imagination	93
Where imagination begins	105

III. EXPLORING THE WORLD

Venturing out	115
Other lands	125
Journeys into the past	133
Terra Australis	141
A closer look	151
The natural world	161

IV. THE ARTIST AND THE BOOK

The art of the book	173
The book in Edo Japan	181
The artist as illustrator	189
William Morris and the private press movement	201
Artists' books	211
Designing books	221
Picture credits	234
Further reading	236
Index	238

Notes to the reader

We respectfully advise Aboriginal and Torres Strait Islander peoples that this publication includes images and names of deceased persons.

Dates are indicated as BCE (Before the Common Era), which corresponds to the earlier term BC (Before Christ), and CE (Common Era), which corresponds to AD (Anno Domini).

The title of a work is given in its original language and with the spelling found on the book's title page. Titles and terms in languages that do not use Roman script, such as Arabic, Hebrew and Japanese, are given as Romanised transliterations.

The order of Japanese and Chinese names follows current convention, with the family name written first unless an individual generally uses the Western order of given name first in Western-language publications.

George Henry Mason
The Costume of China
London, printed for
W Miller by W Bulmer,
1800

Acknowledgements

This book has been made possible through the generous support of a great number of individuals and institutions. It marks another milestone for the State Library of Victoria in joint publishing with Melbourne University Publishing, in particular, The Miegunyah Press. The support of the Miegunyah Fund is gratefully acknowledged.

The library also owes a special thank you to Maria Myers AO, who generously supported this project.

We are particularly grateful to the following external advisers who generously read and provided valuable feedback on drafts of specific chapters or provided assistance with research into particular works:

Dr Abdul-Samad Abdullah, Senior Lecturer and Convenor of Arab and Islamic Studies, Asia Institute, University of Melbourne;
Richard Aitken, architect and garden historian;
Waleed Aly, Executive Committee Member of the Islamic Council of Victoria;
Dr Gary Hickey, Lecturer in Asian Art History, University of Melbourne;
Dr Fiona Hill, Islamic World Discovery Project and Almanar Consultancy;
Allison Holland, Curator, Prints and Drawings, National Gallery of Victoria;
Dr Helen Light, Director; Susan Faine, Curator–Collections; Sandra Khazam, Curator–Exhibitions; Jessica Rynderman, Collections Assistant, Jewish Museum of Australia;
Dr Hilary Maddocks, Fellow of the School of Culture and Communication (Art History), University of Melbourne;
Emeritus Professor Margaret Manion, School of Historical Studies, University of Melbourne;
Amelia McKenzie, Director, Asian Collections; and Mayumi Shinozaki, Librarian, Japanese Unit, Asian Collections, National Library of Australia;
Richard Overell, Rare Books Librarian, Monash University;
Kevin Patrick, comics historian;
Professor Abdullah Saeed, Sultan of Oman Professor of Arab and Islamic Studies; Director, Asia Institute; and Director, Centre for the Study of Contemporary Islam, University of Melbourne;
Susan Scollay, specialist in Islamic art and textiles;
Colin Wakefield, Deputy Keeper of Oriental Collections, Bodleian Library, University of Oxford.

Any errors that remain are entirely the responsibility of the authors.

We have been greatly assisted by many of our colleagues, both past and present, at the State Library of Victoria, who have undertaken research, written previous texts and provided valuable advice and support. In particular, we thank: Megan Atkins, Katrina Ben, Ann Carew, Miyuki Chikamatsu, Ian Cox, Katie Flack, David Harris, Gerard Hayes, Jean Holland, Brian Hubber, Shelley Jamieson, Jan McDonald, Catherine McFarlane, Kirstie McRobert, Anat Meiri, Susan Millard, Derrick Moors, Juliet O'Conor, Pam Pryde, Bev Roberts, Eve Sainsbury, Rachel Salby, Judith Scurfield, Sally Stewart, Edward Tadros, Sally Van Es and Zoe Velonis. We also extend our special thanks to Jane Rhodes for her expert coordination and unflagging support, and to Julia Church for her considered advice and assistance.

Except where noted, all photography has been undertaken by the Imaging Studio of the State Library of Victoria. For all of their care and professional expertise, we would particularly like to thank Adrian Flint, Erica Lauthier, Peter Mappin and Emilee Seymour. All books illustrated are from the collections of the State Library of Victoria unless otherwise acknowledged. We extend our thanks to the photographers of images supplied by other collections and owners.

We are grateful to the many authors, artists, publishers and copyright owners who generously gave permission for the reproduction of their work. Thanks in particular to the Chester Beatty Library, the Jewish Museum of Australia and the National Gallery of Victoria for permission to reproduce items from their collections. Many thanks also to Margot Jones for coordination of the copyright and permissions process.

We acknowledge the work of the following translators of quotes used in this book: Abdullah Yusuf Ali, Mildred Boyer and Harold Morland, Bradford Cook, Virginia Day, SCH de Dood, Robert Leslie Ellis and James Spedding, AH Gardiner, David Gerard, John F Healy, Harry Zohn, Frank Justus Miller, Mark Musa, Máire and Liam de Paor, and Frederik L Schodt.

We are very grateful to Melbourne University Publishing and the State Library of Victoria for giving us the opportunity to undertake this project. We would particularly like to thank Louise Adler, CEO, Melbourne University Publishing; Tracy O'Shaughnessy, Associate Publisher, The Miegunyah Press; and Felicity Edge, Managing Editor, Melbourne University Publishing. Thanks also to Bryony Cosgrove, consultant editor, Eugenie Baulch, Cinzia Cavallaro and to Hamish Freeman and Klarissa Pfisterer for their elegant design. At the State Library, we wish to acknowledge Anne-Marie Schwirtlich, CEO and State Librarian; Shane Carmody, Director, Collections and Access; Sue Hamilton, Director, Public Libraries and Communications; Shelley Roberts, Manager, Publications and Communications; and Robert Heather, Manager, Events and Exhibitions.

We would also like to thank the following for assistance and support: Dr Elaine Wright and Sinéad Ward, Chester Beatty Library; Margaret Dent and Brenda Runnegar, National Library of Australia; Alisa Bunbury, National Gallery of Victoria; Ken and Norma Cowley, Lin Tobias, and Ian and Jan Williamson.

Introduction

How to define the mysterious relationship we have with books. In his essay 'Unpacking My Library', Walter Benjamin invites the reader to join him 'among piles of volumes that are seeing daylight again after two years of darkness'. As he unpacks his books from their crates, he is filled with images and memories: of the cities in which he found them, Naples, Moscow, Paris, a musty book cellar in North Berlin; or the rooms where they had been housed, a student den in Munich, a room in Bern; and finally of his boyhood room, where his library began. For Benjamin, as for many of us, books are possessions that carry with them some fragment of our personal journeys. Their distinguishing trait is their transmissibility. They tell stories through the ages; they transmit our shared cultural memory.

The World of the Book celebrates the unique place of books in our lives. It provides a window into the history of book production, authorship and illustration, dating from the earliest developments of the written word through to contemporary graphic design. Rather than take a chronological approach, we have based the book around a number of themes and stories. We consider how books and writing first emerged, the way books have been the means by which we explore and know our world, and how they have liberated our imagination, enshrined religious beliefs and been catalysts for change. We also celebrate the sheer beauty of books and the ways in which artists have influenced their look and design from medieval times through to today.

In the world of books, no individual volume can ever hope to be all encompassing. This one draws largely upon the State Library of Victoria's rich holdings of more than two million books acquired over the past one hundred and fifty years. For Argentinean writer Jorge Luis Borges, a library was both paradise and labyrinth. It was in this same spirit that we approached the State Library's collections, as one might a vast book of stories, allowing the strengths of its collections to guide us. We first became involved with many of these stories as curators of the library's permanent exhibition *Mirror of the World: Books and Ideas*, which features many of the books contained in this volume. These range from a 4000-year-old cuneiform clay tablet to medieval manuscripts, lavishly illustrated books on ancient Egypt and botanical art, accounts of travels to distant lands, Japanese woodblock books, children's books, Beat literature and pulp fiction, graphic novels and artists' books. The list goes on.

The World of the Book is written by and intended for those who love and read books. Despite several decades of predictions about its imminent death, the book in our culture remains as vital and popular as ever, and more books are being produced and purchased now than at any other time in history. In a world where information is available via the touch of a button, publishers are increasingly producing books that are both innovative and desirable as objects. Books have always meant more to us than the information they carry. We engage with them intellectually, but also visually and sensually, drawn to their tactile and physical properties—paper, design, font, binding. The book has become emblematic of a personal and cultural identity that will not be easily replaced. We continue to attach value to the idea of books, and this value is abundantly represented in our ownership of them, in the way that we collect them, assembling them into personal and public libraries, great or small.

When Walter Benjamin finished unpacking all of his volumes from their crates, he allowed himself a brief moment to dwell upon the intimate relationship between a collector and his books: 'So I have erected one of his dwellings, with books as the building stones, before you, and now he is going to disappear inside, as is only fitting.'

Des Cowley and Clare Williamson

OPPOSITE:
Psalter-Hours
Liège, c.1270

> **All earthly existence must ultimately be contained in a book.**
> STÉPHANE MALLARMÉ, *THE BOOK: A SPIRITUAL INSTRUMENT*

Books are mirrors of many worlds: here and distant, past and present, real and imagined. Through text and image, they act as keepers of ideas, of knowledge and of stories. Since the earliest developments of writing, books have changed the world and enshrined the divine Word. They have been a primary means by which we have come to know ourselves and each other through the shared desire to collect and contain our knowledge of the world.

PART I BOOKS AND IDEAS

The Book BEFORE the Book

Man decays, his corpse is dust,
All his kin have perished;
But a book makes him remembered
Through the mouth of its reciter.

EGYPTIAN PAPYRUS FROM THE NINETEENTH DYNASTY, C. 1300 BCE

THE WRITTEN WORD CAN GRANT IMMORTALITY. WORDS LIVE ON AS REMINDERS OF PEOPLE'S DEEDS AND THOUGHTS. THROUGH THE WRITTEN WORD WE CAN CONNECT WITH SOME OF THOSE WHO WENT BEFORE US, VISIT THEIR CIVILISATIONS AND EXPERIENCE THEIR CULTURE.

Writing was the by-product of ancient societies' needs to communicate and document. As settlements developed and people organised themselves into farms and villages, ports and cities, temples and palaces, writing emerged as a method of recording the business transactions, employment arrangements and laws that governed daily life. The writing down of legends, proverbs, poems and even music soon followed, as the power of the word to preserve ideas as well as facts was increasingly recognised.

Writing developed independently in a number of cultures throughout the world. The oldest known script, and the one from which western writing systems emerged, was created by the Sumerians of Ancient Mesopotamia. The region of Mesopotamia, which equates to present-day Iraq and parts of Turkey and Syria, is often described as one of the world's cradles of civilisation. To date, the earliest archaeological evidence of writing from the area is contained within clay tokens dating back to the beginning of the Bronze Age around 3500 BCE. Incised with pictograms, these tokens were probably attached to sacks of goods and indicated the nature of the produce they held, such as barley or wheat. By 3300 BCE, these tablets provided further details, such as the quantities contained within. Two centuries later, an actual pictographic language was in use.

As the social structures and economic life of the Sumerians became more complex, their script developed new symbols to represent the syllables shared by the sounds of an increasing number of words. This would lay the foundations for alphabetic writing. As symbols became more abstract and refined, and as the demands for written documents increased, the need to write efficiently and clearly also grew. By around 2500 BCE, writing tools had developed from pointed reeds to wedge-shaped implements made from bamboo, wood, bone or metal. It is from this aspect that cuneiform writing derives its name, *cuneus* being the Latin word for 'wedge'. Marks were made by impressing a stylus into a tablet of damp clay that was baked in the sun. Symbols were also incised into stone cylinders that were then rolled and pressed into soft clay, generally to create seals denoting ownership or approval.

In use for three thousand years, cuneiform scripts spread throughout the region under subsequent empires and languages. The many thousands of tablets that survive today act as our library for the study of a number of civilisations including the Sumerian, Babylonian, Assyrian and Hittite. Akkadian has come down to us as the language of the Babylonians and the Assyrians, and was the major language to be communicated via the cuneiform script. Until these codes were

CUNEIFORM TABLET

This tablet records the delivery of taxes, paid in sheep and goats, in the tenth month of the forty-sixth year of Shulgi, second king of the Third Dynasty of Ur. Ur, located in southern Iraq, was the Sumerian capital for many centuries.

ABOVE:
Cuneiform tablet
Southern Mesopotamia,
c. 2050 BCE

OPPOSITE:
Egyptian
hieroglyphic script
From **Karl Lepsius**
Denkmäler aus Aegypten und Aethiopien
Berlin, Nicolaische Buchhandlung, 1849–59

deciphered relatively recently, other evidence such as temple ruins and statues remained mute and open to misinterpretation.

Henry Rawlinson is credited with cracking the cuneiform code. A young British officer stationed in Persia in 1835, Rawlinson was also a classics scholar and student of languages, including Persian. While at Behistun, in present-day Iran, he came across a vast wall of inscriptions carved into a rock face. Rawlinson determined that they were parallel texts in three different cuneiform languages: Old Persian, Elamite and Akkadian. He set about deciphering the first, Old Persian, before commencing work on the other two. Rawlinson established that the inscriptions comprised proclamations of Darius the Great, King of Persia from 522 to 486 BCE. While other scholars completed the decipherment of Elamite and Akkadian, it was Rawlinson who provided the vital key for unlocking cuneiform script.

At Nineveh, the capital of the Assyrian Empire, a library of around 25 000 tablets was discovered in the 1850s. Assembled by King Ashurbanipal (c. 668–627 BCE), this library was the first known to have been indexed and catalogued, and it included some of the best preserved copies of major texts such as the *Epic of Gilgamesh*. Another vast collection of tablets, dating back to 1800 BCE, was located in the mid twentieth century by archaeologists at Mari on the banks of the Euphrates in Syria. The contents of these two collections alone cover a broad range of subjects, including religion, geography, economics, medicine, astronomy and literature.

Mari was a powerful centre on the trade route between Syria and Mesopotamia from the third millennium BCE until its destruction by Hammurabi, King of Babylon, in c. 1750 BCE. The Code of Hammurabi is a 2-metre-high basalt stele, or monument. Outlining the laws of the Babylonian Empire, it dates from around this time and is one of the most important cuneiform artefacts to survive today. But the most famous piece of cuneiform writing to endure is the *Epic of Gilgamesh*.

The *Epic of Gilgamesh* recounts the legend of a mythical king of Uruk and is set in about 2700 BCE. Comprising 3500 lines, the earliest versions of the epic to have survived date to the Third Dynasty of Ur (2150–2000 BCE). The epic contains stories similar to the biblical accounts of temptation and flood, and its hero can also be likened to figures in Greek mythology such as Odysseus and Hercules. The *Epic of Gilgamesh* is recognised today as one of the world's earliest works of literature.

Within a century or two of the development of Sumerian cuneiform, hieroglyphic script emerged in Ancient Egypt. Earliest known examples date back to around 3100 BCE, and the script continued to be used until the fifth century CE. The term 'hieroglyph' derives from Greek words for 'sacred' and 'writing', as the script was associated with religious practice and the complex rituals required for an Egyptian's passage to the after life. Hieroglyphic writing is the language of the tomb and of the Book of the Dead, which recorded the prayers and charms required to protect the soul as it made this journey.

Egyptian hieroglyphs combined pictographic symbols with the phonetic or ideogrammatic, which were representative of an idea. Writing conferred power and was therefore originally restricted to the priestly, military and ruling classes.

As writing gradually spread throughout other sectors of Egyptian society, the symbols used became more simplified. By 600 BCE, demotic, a cursive script, was the primary writing system for everyday use. The famous Rosetta Stone, now held by the British Museum, bears a decree from the Pharaoh Ptolemy V (who reigned in 205–180 BCE), written in both hieroglyphic and demotic scripts. The fact that it also contained a parallel text in Greek assisted the decipherment of hieroglyphic script by the French archaeologist and linguist Jean-François Champollion in the 1820s.

As the Bronze Age gave way to the Iron Age around 1200 BCE, Phoenician civilisation developed along the coast of present-day Lebanon. The Phoenicians were great seafarers, and they incorporated and adapted ideas from a range of cultures throughout the Mediterranean. Phoenician writing had similarities to both cuneiform writing from Mesopotamia and Egyptian hieroglyphic writing, but it developed symbols for each consonant and, in the process, created the first truly alphabetic script. As the Phoenicians continued to trade with their neighbours throughout the region, their writing script was incorporated into Greek and also formed the basis for Aramaic, which in turn led to the development of Hebrew and Arabic.

The WORLD *of the* BOOK | 7

LEFT, TOP:
Greek papyrus
From *Greek Papyri in the British Museum*
London, British Museum, 1893

LEFT, BOTTOM:
Early Chinese picture writing
From **Henry Williams**
Manuscripts, Inscriptions and Muniments
London, Merrill & Baker, 1901

BELOW:
Mayan inscription
From **Agostino Aglio**
Antiquities of Mexico
London, Robert Havell and Colnaghi, 1831–48

OPPOSITE:
The Rosetta Stone
From **Henry Williams**
Manuscripts, Inscriptions and Muniments
London, Merrill & Baker, 1901

The Phoenician alphabet also provided, via Greek, a foundation for the Roman alphabet.

While many of the writing scripts known today have descended from Sumerian cuneiform, others derived from ancient Chinese script. Independent of developments in Mesopotamia, pictographic script emerged in China and, judging by early records, was already well developed by the second millennium BCE. Known today as 'oracle bones', the earliest surviving examples were incised into animal bones, which were used as divination tools.

As Chinese writing developed, phonetic and semantic elements were added to the original pictograms, resulting in thousands of symbols for objects and ideas. By 1400 BCE, more than 2500 characters were in use. In Japan, writing developed from the fifth century CE after contact with Chinese culture during previous centuries. Japanese script today combines Chinese characters (*kanji*) with symbols from two syllabic systems (*hiragana* and *katakana*), introduced around the ninth or tenth centuries.

Writing requires not only a script, but also a support that can record, transport and store the information contained within it. The clay tablets used in Mesopotamia were simple to produce and relatively durable unless dropped. Large quantities were difficult to store and transport, however, and the creation of long or complex documents was cumbersome. Papyrus emerged in Ancient Egypt as a practical support for writing. A paper-like material, it was produced from the stem of the papyrus plant, which grew in abundance in the Nile Delta. As papyrus would crack if folded, documents were generally rolled. Papyrus was adopted by the Greeks and Romans, who used it until around the second century CE. Papyrus documents could be easily transported, although they became brittle and decayed with age. As a result, many did not survive.

Our knowledge of the past depends on what survives from a culture and a place. As papyrus was subject to decay with age and destruction by fire, much of our information about Ancient Egypt has come down to us via the inscriptions and paintings preserved in tombs and on monuments. Ironically, the very flames that destroyed so many towns and villages in Ancient Mesopotamia preserved their histories, firing the hundreds of thousands of clay tablets stored in temple archives and libraries. Only a fraction of these have to date been deciphered, but the remainder will continue to reveal their secrets to future generations.

MAYAN INSCRIPTION

Mayan civilisation is distinguished by being the only pre-Columbian culture of the Americas to have had a developed writing system. The earliest evidence of Mayan hieroglyphic writing dates back to around 300 BCE, and it continued to be used for a century or two after Spanish colonisation in the sixteenth century. It is only since the mid twentieth century that decipherment of the hieroglyphs has advanced. Around eight hundred phonetic and pictographic symbols have been identified, each of which represents a syllable.

efunctox: qs de ho
care iussisti: i pace
none costituas et
ubeas esse conso
us venie largitor
humane salutis
ementiam tuam: vt n
ationis fratres, sor
s amicos et benefa
: qui ex hoc seculo
a maria semp vir
te cu omnib sctis
ue beatitudinis ᴐ
ire concedas. Ora
u deus oim condi
mptor aiab famu
oq tuax: remissi
bue pctox vt idu
a semp optaueri

The Illuminated MANUSCRIPT

You will make out intricacies, so delicate and subtle, so exact and compact, so full of knots and links, with colours so fresh and vivid, that you might say that all this was the work of an angel, and not of man.
GERALD OF WALES, TWELFTH CENTURY

BEFORE THE DEVELOPMENT OF THE CODEX BY THE ROMANS AROUND THE TIME OF THE FIRST CENTURY CE, TEXTS WERE INSCRIBED ONTO CLAY TABLETS OR SCROLLS OF PAPYRUS. THE WORD 'CODEX' LITERALLY MEANS A BOOK COMPOSED OF FOLDED SHEETS SEWN ALONG ONE EDGE AND BOUND BETWEEN COVERS OR BOARDS.

The codex offered distinct advantages over the scroll: it was easier to browse; its wooden boards protected it during transport; it could be better stored in a library; and unlike the scroll, both sides of its leaves or pages could be used. In particular, the development of the codex appears to have coincided with the rise of Christianity, and several early surviving biblical texts before 400 CE are in this form. It is possible that the more flexible and portable medium of the codex may have made it easier for Christians to transport and conceal texts outlawed by Roman authorities, as well as allowing them to differentiate their writings from the sacred books of Jewish scripture. By the fourth century CE, after the Emperor Constantine's conversion to Christianity, the parchment codex appears to have become the standard form throughout Europe for the production of manuscript texts.

The earliest codices were made out of papyrus from Egypt, and later from parchment or animal skin, which proved to be more durable and more easily procured in Europe. According to Roman historian Pliny the Elder, the method of treating animal skin to create a smooth textured surface for writing was developed at Pergamum (in present-day Turkey) in the second century BCE, during the reign of Eumenes II. The need for a new writing material arose at that time because the export of papyrus from Egypt was embargoed by King Ptolemy, who wished to prevent the library at Pergamum from rivalling that in Alexandria. In reality, parchment was probably in use much earlier than this. However, by the second and third centuries CE, parchment (*pergamena* in Latin, named after Pergamum, the city in which it was believed to have been first made), had become the standard material for the making of books.

Throughout the Middle Ages in Europe, from the fall of the western Roman Empire in 476 CE through to the Renaissance, the manuscript codex was the predominant form of the book. In the early Middle Ages, the majority of manuscripts were produced in scriptoria, the writing rooms of monasteries, and images of monks seated at their writing desks copying texts are commonly found in manuscripts of this period. Such activity by monastic scribes fostered the art of book production and helped preserve many ancient works that might otherwise have been lost. Illustrations began to appear in manuscripts from the late fourth century CE, but it was some time before the initials and letters of the script itself came to be embellished, often in silver and gold and glowing colours ground from costly materials. Such decoration was sometimes interpreted, especially in religious books used in church services, as 'lighting up' or 'illuminating' the sacred Word of God. Today, the term 'illuminated manuscript' refers to the decorated or illustrated handwritten book, whether this entails paintings in precious metals and vibrant colours or, more simply, drawings in pen and ink or coloured washes.

BOETHIUS

Boethius (c. 480–524 CE), a Roman scholar and statesman, composed *De Musica* in the early sixth century CE. It became the standard textbook on the theory of music throughout the Middle Ages and was still prescribed reading at the University of Oxford in the eighteenth century. The work consists primarily of diagrams and explanations about the relationship of music to mathematics, reflecting medieval thinking that music was a mathematical discipline. The manuscript provides an example of the Carolingian script, devised at the time of the Emperor Charlemagne in the late eighth and early ninth centuries.

TOP:
Boethius (Anicius Manlius Severinus Boethius)
De Musica
Northern Italy, eleventh century

BOTTOM:
Psalter-Hours
Liège, c. 1270

OPPOSITE, TOP:
Antiphonal
Paris, c. 1335–45

OPPOSITE, BOTTOM:
Book of Hours
(Use of York)
Bruges, late fifteenth century

PSALTER-HOURS

Psalters, like later Books of Hours, set out prayers and devotions for particular times of the day and the year. They also typically included a calendar. This Psalter was prepared in Liège in about 1270 and shows strong local features. Written in Latin and French in a Gothic script, it is richly illustrated with both religious and secular scenes. This book may have been prepared for the Béguines, a semi-religious women's order.

 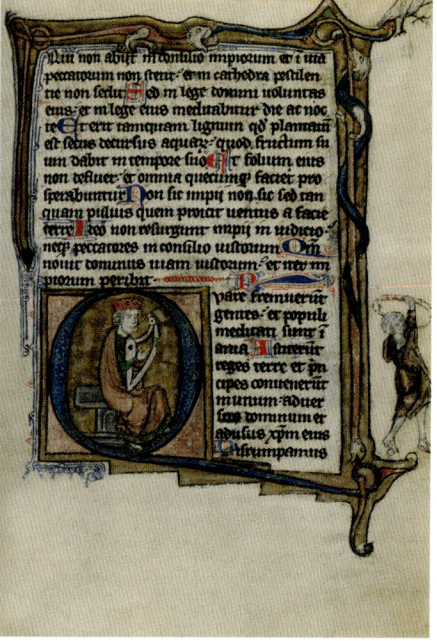

Many of the early works produced in monasteries are today renowned for their beauty, such as the Book of Durrow, the Lindisfarne Gospels and the Book of Kells. These gospel books, produced between the seventh and ninth centuries, feature rich ornamentation and abstract linear patterns modelled on Anglo-Saxon and Celtic metalwork of the period. They are referred to as 'insular manuscripts', having been produced in the monastic centres in Britain and Ireland.

In the early Middle Ages, private ownership of books was uncommon, and instead an emphasis was placed on the development of the communal monastery library. The focus on Christian books, or those thought relevant to the practice of Christianity, however, meant that much of the heritage of Greek and Roman writing was lost in Europe after the fall of the Roman Empire. This included significant works by writers such as Euclid, Archimedes and Ptolemy, which survived primarily in Arabic translations.

Before the ninth century, there was considerable variation in the kinds of scripts used in the writing of manuscripts. Those produced in Italy used capital letters that derived from the late Roman world, and may be compared with the inscriptions carved on ancient stone monuments. In Ireland, however, a distinction developed between the first letter of a passage, written in capital or majuscule, and subsequent letters, written in reduced size, or minuscule. One of the best-known examples of this style is to be found in the Book of Kells, which was written around 800 CE. In the late eighth and early ninth centuries, the educational reforms enacted by Emperor Charlemagne brought about the development of a standardised script for the writing of books that became known as the Carolingian script, or the Caroline minuscule. Charlemagne had a strong interest in books and engaged the services of a number of scholars at his court. One of the most notable was Alcuin, who came from York. It was Alcuin who

ANTIPHONAL

An antiphonal is a liturgical book, containing the antiphons and responsories sung in association with the psalms and readings of the Divine Office. This antiphonal was executed in Paris for the Royal Dominican Convent dedicated to St Louis, King of France, at Poissy. The library at Poissy was substantial and contained illuminated manuscripts of the highest quality. Its collection was dispersed at the time of the French Revolution.

BOOK OF HOURS (USE OF YORK)

Books of Hours (*Horae*) were designed as prayer books for private devotion. They usually contained the Hours of the Virgin to be said at the eight canonical hours of the day. This manuscript was produced in the city of Bruges, for a family in York, England. It is an unusually large example of a Book of Hours and was presumably designed for use in the family chapel, rather than for the owner's private worship. The book's calendar features twelve miniatures depicting the various 'labours' or activities engaged in over the course of a year. Illustrations such as these reveal much about daily life during the Middle Ages.

did much to inspire the revival of classical learning often referred to as the Carolingian Renaissance. From 796 onwards, he oversaw the scriptorium at St Martin's Abbey at Tours, which became the major centre for the production of Carolingian manuscripts. The script that emerged at the time of Charlemagne featured capitals, a clear, rounded lower-case minuscule, and spaces between words. It became the standard script used in the making of books in Europe until its replacement by the Gothic script around the mid twelfth century.

From the eighth to the eleventh century, the Islamic world was responsible for much of the development of intellectual knowledge. Working with the corpus of early Greek learning that had been preserved in these countries, Muslim scholars produced manuscripts that refined and extended Greek thought in the fields of mathematics, astronomy, botany and medicine. Private libraries and collectors also flourished, generating a greater demand for books than was to be found in Europe at that time. The Arab world also began to adopt the use of paper, which was first made in China, setting up a paper mill in Samarkand in the eighth century. According to the eleventh-century Arab historian al-Tha'alibi, the art of paper making was learned from Chinese prisoners captured at the battle of Tallas in 751. Damascus would later become a major centre for paper making, and it was from the Islamic world that the art first travelled to Spain, around the eleventh century, and then to the rest of Europe. Paper eventually replaced parchment after the introduction of printing in the mid fifteenth century.

The rise of universities in cities such as Paris, Bologna and later Oxford brought about an increased demand for books in the West, and manuscripts came to be made in commercial workshops or ateliers, rather than monasteries. The thirteenth century saw the rise of a flourishing book trade, with ateliers and stationers being responsible for the production and distribution

Details of Book of Hours (Use of York) Bruges, late fifteenth century

BELOW AND OPPOSITE:
Book of Hours (fragment)
France, c. 1430–40

BOOK OF HOURS (FRAGMENT)

This French manuscript is part of a Book of Hours and begins with a calendar, written in red and blue, with gold used as a highlight. The book is written in the one formal hand, in Latin and French. An early inscription in the book suggests that it was the property of M. Nicole Forissard, canon of the Sainte Chapelle at Dijon. Later inscriptions indicate that the book continued to be used in Dijon until the early nineteenth century.

of books. The increased secularisation of book production brought with it a growth in readership and a new focus on certain branches of knowledge that had been neglected in the West. As books ceased to be exclusively associated with monasteries, they were increasingly owned and traded by individuals, and came to serve a wider range of purposes. Aside from study and private devotion, books were made to entertain. Writing in the vernacular became more common, and wealthy patrons delighted in elaborate picture cycles devised to accompany the texts of popular histories, romances and tales of chivalry, such as those surrounding the legend of King Arthur.

The script that developed in the late Middle Ages is broadly known as Gothic, or 'blackletter' script. It became the model for the typefaces used by early German printers from the 1450s onwards. This script had the advantage that it could be written more quickly by scribes than the Carolingian minuscule, thereby facilitating the speedier production of books to meet growing demand. As well, its sharp, angular letters allowed more text to be written on each page, often in two columns, which reduced the amount of expensive parchment required. The increasing demand for books for private devotion brought with it the rise in popularity of specific prayer manuals for members of the laity. Best known of these is the Book of Hours, or *Horae*. By the fourteenth century, the Book of Hours had largely replaced the Psalter, or Book of Psalms, as the principal prayer book of the laity.

Manuscript production in the late Middle Ages involved a number of professional activities, from parchment maker to scribe, from illuminator to miniature painter, from binder to bookseller. Generally, page design was carried out at the preliminary stage, with spaces left before writing for the later inclusion of decoration. Scribes copied texts using quills commonly made of goose feathers. The designs for miniatures, decorated initials and borders were drawn onto the page and then coloured with pigments mixed from natural elements such as minerals or plants. Gold was often applied to the page as raised gold leaf, before the application of colour, or mixed as paint. At the final stage, the gatherings, or quires, of the book would be arranged in order and the volume bound, often between wooden boards covered in leather.

The production of finely crafted manuscripts flourished in centres throughout Europe in the fourteenth and fifteenth centuries. Books of Hours, in particular, were often lavishly illustrated with miniatures and illuminated in gold and expensive pigments, and they were prized as much for their beauty as for their textual contents. A Book of Hours typically contained devotional texts adapted for use by the laity, along with a calendar detailing the seasons and saints of the church year. Calendars were often illustrated with the signs of the zodiac and the agricultural and social activities appropriate for the time of year. By the late fifteenth century, particularly in France and the Netherlands, Books of Hours were being mass-produced for export, or for the general stock of stationers and booksellers. Their popularity points to the rise in literacy of the period and tells us much about the tastes of the patrons who commissioned them. Such books might confer status on an owner, and the very finest, such as the renowned *Très Riches Heures*, painted at Flanders by the Limbourg brothers between 1412 and

DE ALEXANDRO SIVE ALEXANDRINO. XXIJ.

ALEXANDER VEL ALEXANDRINVS nam incertum id quoq habetur, uirtutum merito uocatus est. Et cum contra indos pararet expeditionem, iusso Theodoto duce, Galieno iubente, poenas dedit, siquidem strangulatus in carcere captiuorum ueterum more perbibetur. Tacendum esse non credo quod cum de egypto loquor, uetus succedit hystoria: simul etiam Galieni factum: qui cum Theodoto uellet imperium proconsulare decernere, a sacerdotibus est prohibitus, qui dixerunt fasces consulares ingredi alexandriam non licere: cuius rei etiam Ciceronem cum contra Gabinium loquitur meminisse satis nouimus. Denique non extat memoria rei frequentare. quare scire oportet Herennium celsum uestrum parentem consulatum cupit, hoc quod desyderat non licere. Fertur enim apud memphim in aurea columna egyptijs esse literis scriptum. Tunc demum egyptum liberam fore, cum in eam uenissent romani fasces, et pretexta romanorum. quod apud Proculum grammaticum doctissimum sui temporis uirum, cum de peregrinis regionibus loquitur inuenitur.

DE SATVRNINO VIGESIMOTERTIO.

OPTIMVS DVCVM GALIENI TEMPORE sed a Valeriano dilectus Saturninus fuit. Hic quoq, cum dissolutionem Galieni pernoctantis in pubblicos ferre non posset, et milites non exemplo imperatoris sui, sed suo regeret, ab exercitibus sumpsit imperium, uir prudentie singularis, grauitatis insignis, uite amabilis, uictoriarum barbararum ubiq, notarum. Hic ea die qua est amictus a militibus peplo imperatorio, contione adhibita dixisse fertur. Commilitones bonum ducem perdidistis, et malum principem fecistis. Denique cum multa strenue in imperio fecisset, quod esset seuerior et grauior militibus, ab ysdem ipsis a quibus factus fuerat interemptus est. Huius insigne est, quod conuiuio discumbere milites ne inferiora nudarentur, cum sagis iussit, hyeme grauibus, estate perlucidis.

DE TETRICO SENIORE. XXIIII.

INTERFECTO VICTORINO ET EIVS FILIO mater eius Victoria siue Victorina Tetricum senatorem populi romani presidatum in gallia regentem ad imperium hortata, quod eius erat, ut plerique loquuntur, affinis, Augustum appellari fecit: filiumq eius Cesarem nuncupauit. Et cum

multa Tetricus feliciter se militum suorum imprudentia grauissimo principi, et statim ad Aurelianum se cum Aureliano nihil sumeret, senatorem populi romani omnes gallias rexerat, et Zenobiam Odenati uniano et Timolao, pudoquem triumphauerat nie, samni, lucanie, umbrie, piceni et flamicum non solum uiuere tus est, cum illum sepedo etiam imperatorem

DE TETRICO IVN

HIC PVER appellatus ta esset, in stea omnibus trimonio qu picus dicit semper insigni fuisse, neque quenq illi A latum Tetricorum domi contra usum metellinum utrinq pretextam tribue sceptrum, coronam cunc set Aurelianum dicunt

DE TREBELLIAN

PRVDENT Galieno fuereo luxuria ut iure timysauria priquem cum alij archipyr monetam etiam cudi ut

RIGHT:
Book of Hours
(Use of Paris)
Northern France,
c. 1510–20

BELOW AND OPPOSITE:
Scriptores Historiæ Augustæ
Florence, 1479

SCRIPTORES HISTORIÆ AUGUSTÆ

The *Scriptores* is a significant example of the Renaissance revival of classical literature. It consists of a series of biographies of Roman emperors from Hadrian to Numerian (117–284 CE), first composed in late antiquity, around 360 CE. This copy was commissioned by the Medici family, the great Florentine dynasty, and is executed in Latin in a formal humanist script written on fine parchment. The work contains eighty-one portraits of Roman emperors, although only the portrait of Hadrian is based on a known image.

1416 for Jean Duc de Berry, are masterpieces of medieval painting as well as of book production.

The Italian Renaissance brought with it a renewed interest in the classical world of Greece and Rome. Much of the knowledge that had been effectively lost to Europe in the early Middle Ages began to find its way into books produced in centres such as Florence, Padua and Venice. As early as the twelfth century, significant scientific and medical texts from the Graeco-Roman world had been sought by European scholars from centres of Arab learning in Spain and Sicily and translated into Latin for the first time. The scholar and poet Francesco Petrarch, one of the early founders of Italian Humanism, scoured the libraries of Italy in the first half of the fourteenth century in search of classical texts, unearthing little-known works by Cicero and Seneca. The fall of Constantinople to the Ottoman Turks in 1453 saw Byzantine scholars flee to Rome, bringing with them knowledge of early Greek learning. The Renaissance also brought with it a passion for book collecting, and the period saw the rise of a new class of bibliophiles, such as the Medici family in Florence, who built up large and important libraries of classical texts.

The intellectual movement in Italy that later came to be known as Humanism led to the development of a new script for use by Humanist scribes in their manuscripts. The Humanist, or Roman script, modelled its upper-case letters on those found on Roman ruins, while the lower case drew upon the earlier Carolingian script. This new script would directly influence the Roman typefaces of typographers, such as Nicolaus Jenson, and become the basis for scripts used today.

The introduction of printing in the mid fifteenth century did not see the manuscript replaced overnight. Indeed, manuscripts continued to be produced in Europe for a further fifty or sixty years after the development of the printing press. In particular, Books of Hours continued to be produced in this medium, and even when they came to be printed, they were often made to resemble manuscripts and contained hand-painted woodcuts in gold and glowing colours. Similarly, the earliest printed books commonly left spaces for the addition of painted initials at the heads of passages. The expense of replicating hand production, however, meant that, with time, the standard features of illuminated manuscripts—the decorated initials, the rubrication (use of red ink), the miniatures with their backgrounds in gold leaf—were dispensed with, and the majority of books came to be printed in black ink.

Despite being superseded by the printed book, the manuscript remains a touchstone of the past. Manuscripts have often survived in greater numbers than paintings or other objects from a particular place or period, and it is to the art and craft of anonymous scribes, illuminators, miniaturists, parchment makers and binders that we owe much of our knowledge of daily life in the Middle Ages.

n meū de manu philiſtinoʒ
ʒi pſm̃ meū. Venit eñ clamo
me. Cumq; aſpeꝛiſſet ſamuel
ñs dixit ei. Ecce vir quē dixeꝛã
te dñabitur pplo meo. Acceſſi
ul ad ſamuelẽ in medio poꝛ
ndica oꝛo michi: ubi eſt dom
ꝰ Et rñdit ſamuel ſauli dicens
ī vides. Aſcende ante me iɴ
in ut comedas mecū hodie ⁊ d
ꝛe mane: ⁊ oĩa que ſunt in coꝛ
icabo tibi · et de aſinis quas
ſterciꝰ pdidiſti: ne ſolicitus ſis
uete ſunt. Et cuius erũt optiã
ꝛl'? Nõne tibi et omni domu
is? Rñdes aūt ſaul ait. Nũqɴ
liꝰ iemini ego ſum de minima
ꝛl'· et cognacio mea nouiſſiꝑ
ũnes familias de tribu beɴy
Quare ergo locutꝰ es michi ſer
n iſtū? Aſſumes itaq; ſamuel
er puerū eiꝰ · introduxit eos iɴ
ū: et dedit eis locū in capite eo
t inuitati. Erãt eñ ipi triginta
ixitq; ſamuel coco. Da parte
edi tibi: et pꝛepi ut repones ſeo
pud te. Leuauit autem cocus a
et poſuit ante ſaul. Dixitq; ſa
Ecce qd̃ remanſit: pone ante t
ede: quia de induſtria ſeruati
quãdo pplm̃ vocaui. Et com

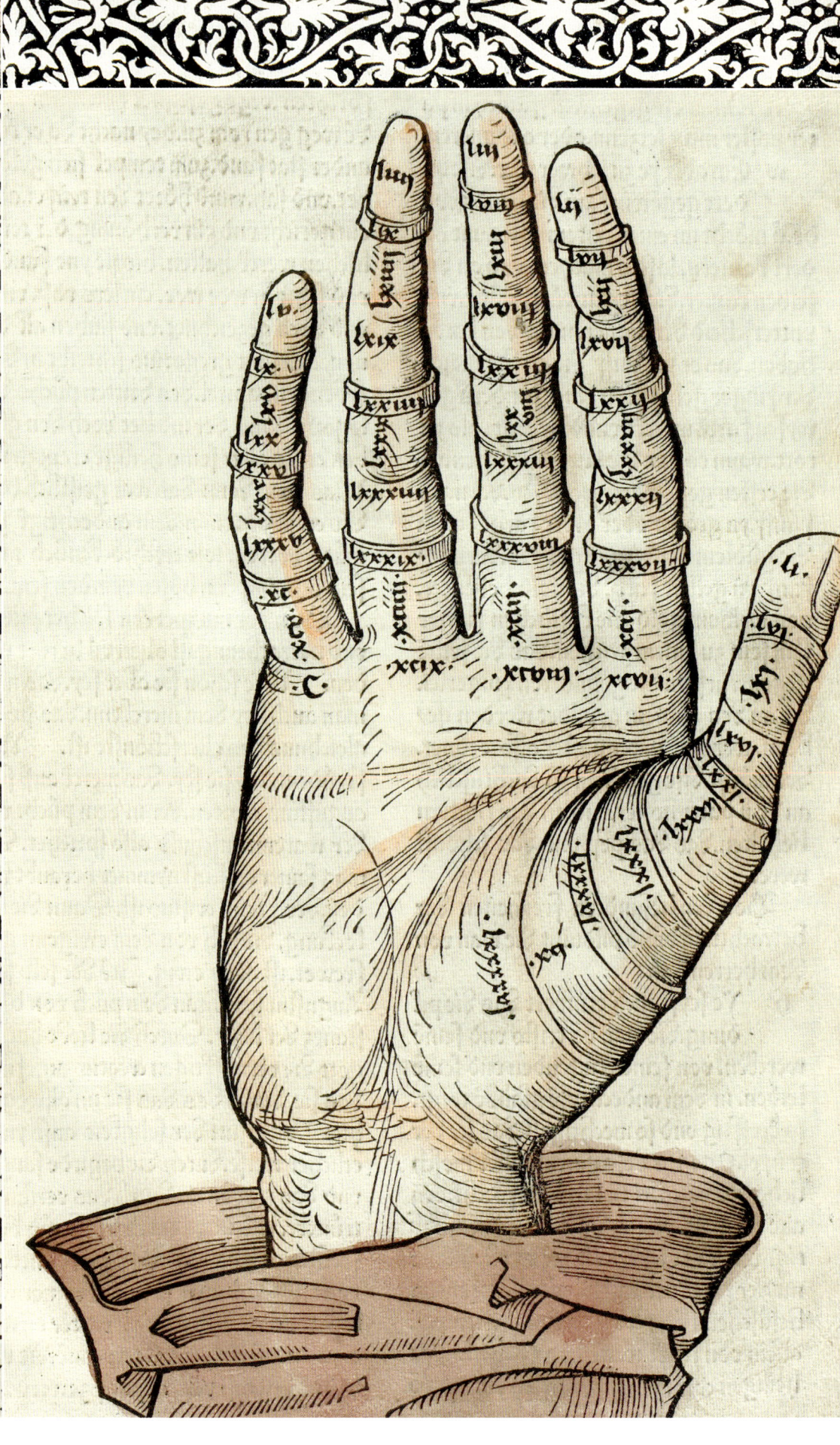

The PRINTED BOOK

The end of one epoch is the beginning of another.
An elite society gave way to a mass society.
LUCIEN FEBVRE, *THE COMING OF THE BOOK*

THE SHIFT FROM THE MANUSCRIPT BOOK TO THE PRINTED BOOK IN EUROPE REVOLUTIONISED THE WAY IN WHICH IDEAS AND KNOWLEDGE WERE MADE AVAILABLE TO AN INCREASINGLY LITERATE POPULATION. PRINTING WAS THE EARLIEST FORM OF MASS PRODUCTION, AND ITS RAPID SPREAD FROM GERMANY TO THE REST OF EUROPE IN THE SECOND HALF OF THE FIFTEENTH CENTURY CREATED A MASS AUDIENCE FOR THE PRINTED WORD. NO LONGER WAS KNOWLEDGE IN THE HANDS OF A FEW; IT WAS INCREASINGLY AVAILABLE TO ALL.

The story of printing began much earlier than the fifteenth century, and its origins were far from Europe. The method of printing images and text from single woodblocks, which came to be known as 'block book' printing, had been developed in China and Korea as early as the eighth century. There is also evidence of the use of moveable type made from wood and clay in China in the eleventh century, and the casting of individual characters in metal in Korea in the fourteenth century. Block books were produced in Europe by the mid fifteenth century, as were single devotional woodcut prints. The name most commonly linked to the invention of printing, however, is that of Johann Gutenberg, who developed the printing press and the technology of printing by means of moveable type in Mainz, Germany, around 1450. If Gutenberg was not the first to come up with the idea of moveable type, then he was certainly the first to perfect it for the mass production of printed text. Gutenberg and those who immediately followed him were responsible for a series of innovations—including moveable metal type, oil-based inks and the wooden hand press—that made the printing of books a commercially attractive and viable proposition.

Little is known of Johann Gutenberg's life, and no example of printing by him carries his name. From the thirty or so documents that have survived relating to him, we know that he was born at Mainz around 1400. By the late 1430s, a series of surviving court documents pertaining to a lawsuit indicate that he had borrowed substantial sums of money and was in possession of quantities of lead and a press. However, the development of printing by means of moveable type appears to have taken him a number of years, and it is uncertain exactly when he perfected the method for casting individual letters from metal. Such a process was fundamental to his invention, allowing a page of text to be assembled and printed from individual letters, which could then be reused to print further pages.

Gutenberg's earliest surviving specimens of printing include a series of papal indulgences allowing Catholics to seek pardon for their sins. The earliest to carry a date is from 1454. It is likely he began printing the work for which he is remembered, the 42-line Bible, around 1453, three years after he entered into a partnership with Johann Fust, from whom he borrowed eight hundred guilders to finance his new invention. This loan would be supplemented two years later by a further loan, also of eight hundred guilders.

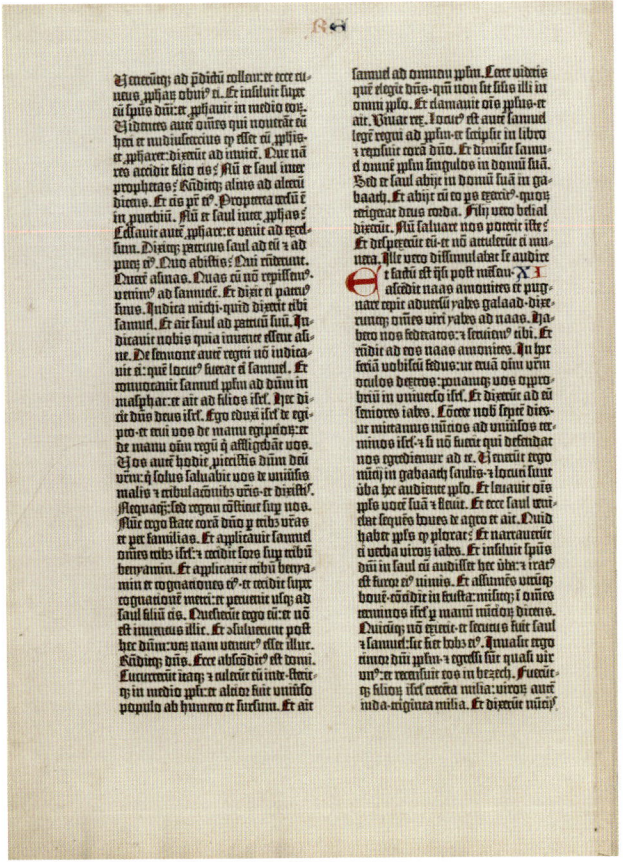

TOP, LEFT:
Leaf from Gutenberg Bible Mainz, Johann Gutenberg, c. 1450–55

TOP, RIGHT:
Portrait of Johann Gutenberg, engraved by Nicolas de Larmessin From **Jacques Ignace Bullart, editor**, *Academie des Sciences & des Arts*, Paris, 1682

Gutenberg's Bible was an ambitious project, comprising over 1200 printed pages bound in two large volumes. The text was printed in Latin in two columns of forty-two lines each, with titles, chapter headings, initials or rubrics being added by hand in the style of manuscript books. He printed about 180 copies, most on paper, which proved more suitable for the printing of large quantities, and some on vellum. In 1455, however, before he had completed the printing, Gutenberg was taken to court by Johann Fust for repayment of the original loan. When the court decided in Fust's favour, he was able to take control of Gutenberg's Bible, his type and press. He continued the business in partnership with his future son-in-law, Peter Schoeffer, who had been an assistant to Gutenberg. While Gutenberg would later acquire another press and more type, his subsequent contribution to printing history was minimal in the period before his death in 1468.

Johann Fust and Peter Schoeffer's first book was a large Psalter, or Book of Psalms, printed at Mainz in 1457. It was the first book to be printed in colour, featuring red and blue initials, and the first to include a date and printer's name. After Fust's death from the plague, contracted while on a visit to Paris in 1466, Schoeffer continued as a printer, publishing some 130 titles before being succeeded in the business, after his death in 1502, by his son Johann.

Fust and Schoeffer made no mention of Gutenberg in their books. One of the earliest references to Gutenberg's role in the birth of printing appeared in the so-called Cologne Chronicle, published in that city in 1499 by Johann Koelhoff. It records a statement by Koelhoff's master, Ulrich Zell, the first printer of Cologne, that Johann Gutenberg, a citizen of Mainz, was the inventor of printing, and ascribes a date of 1450 for the introduction of moveable type. When Schoeffer's son Johann printed his German edition of Livy's history of the Romans in 1505, he, too, acknowledged Gutenberg's role in the birth of printing: 'The wondrous art of printing was invented finally by the ingenious Johannes Gutenberg, 1450 years as it is counted from the birth of Our Lord Christ, and thereafter improved and made permanent by the diligence, cost and labour of Johannes Faust [sic] and Peter Schoeffer at Mainz'.

Between 1460 and 1465, Albrecht Pfister, in Bambourg, Germany, was producing the first books from moveable type to contain woodcuts. By the end of the decade, printing had spread to the major cities of Europe, including Rome, Venice and Paris. In England, William Caxton set up his press in London in 1476, becoming the country's first printer. Caxton had travelled to Bruges as a young man in the mid 1440s and spent the next thirty years on the continent. The exact means by which he gained his knowledge of printing are unknown, but it was most probably in Cologne in the early 1470s at the workshop of the type founder and printer Johann Veldener. He first set up a press in Bruges, where he printed, probably in 1473, the first book in English,

ABOVE:
Myrrour of the World
London, William Caxton,
c. 1490

LEFT:
William Caxton's
printer's device
Myrrour of the World
London, William Caxton,
c. 1490

MYRROUR OF THE WORLD

Myrrour of the World was printed in England by William Caxton c. 1481 and again, c. 1490, and is one of the first illustrated books printed in that country. It is an English translation of *L'Image du Monde*, which in turn was chiefly derived from the medieval Latin text *Imago Mundi*. The *Myrrour of the World* is an encyclopedic work covering geography, economics, music, cosmography, zoology, meteorology and astronomy. While translating the work, Caxton added a prologue and postscript, and included material of English interest, such as noting Oxford and Cambridge as centres of learning.

Sexta etas mūdi
Sexta etas mūdi
Foliū C
NVREMBERGA

Die linck hand.
Die recht hand

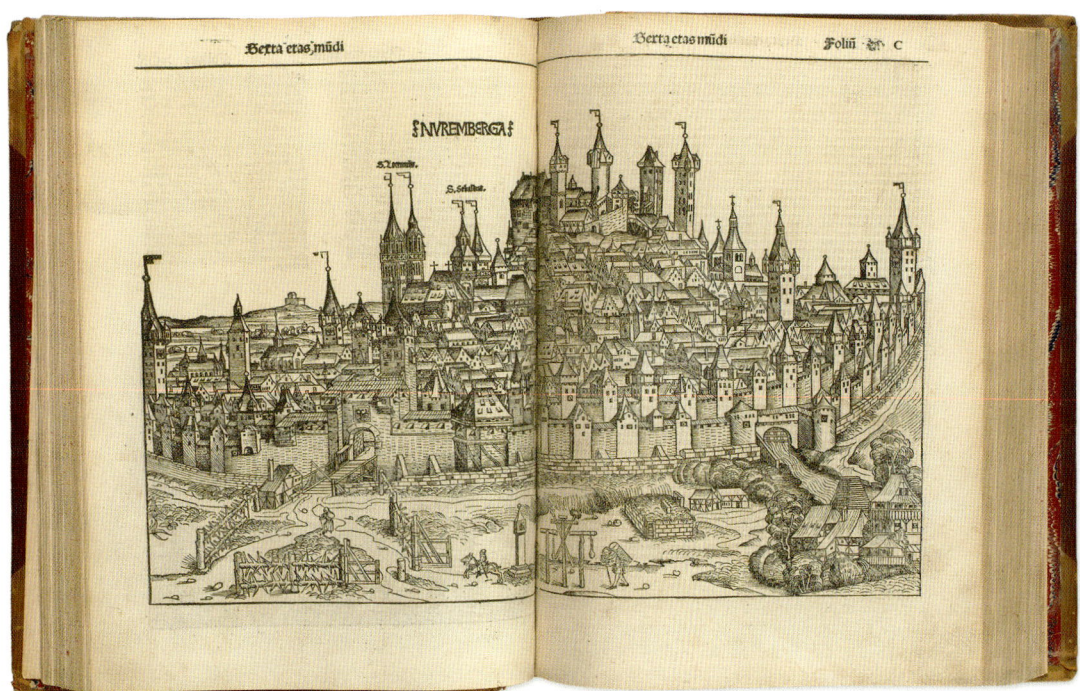

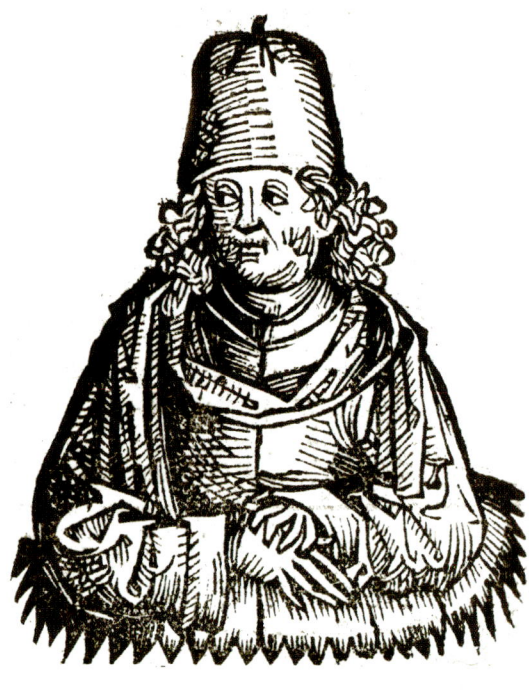

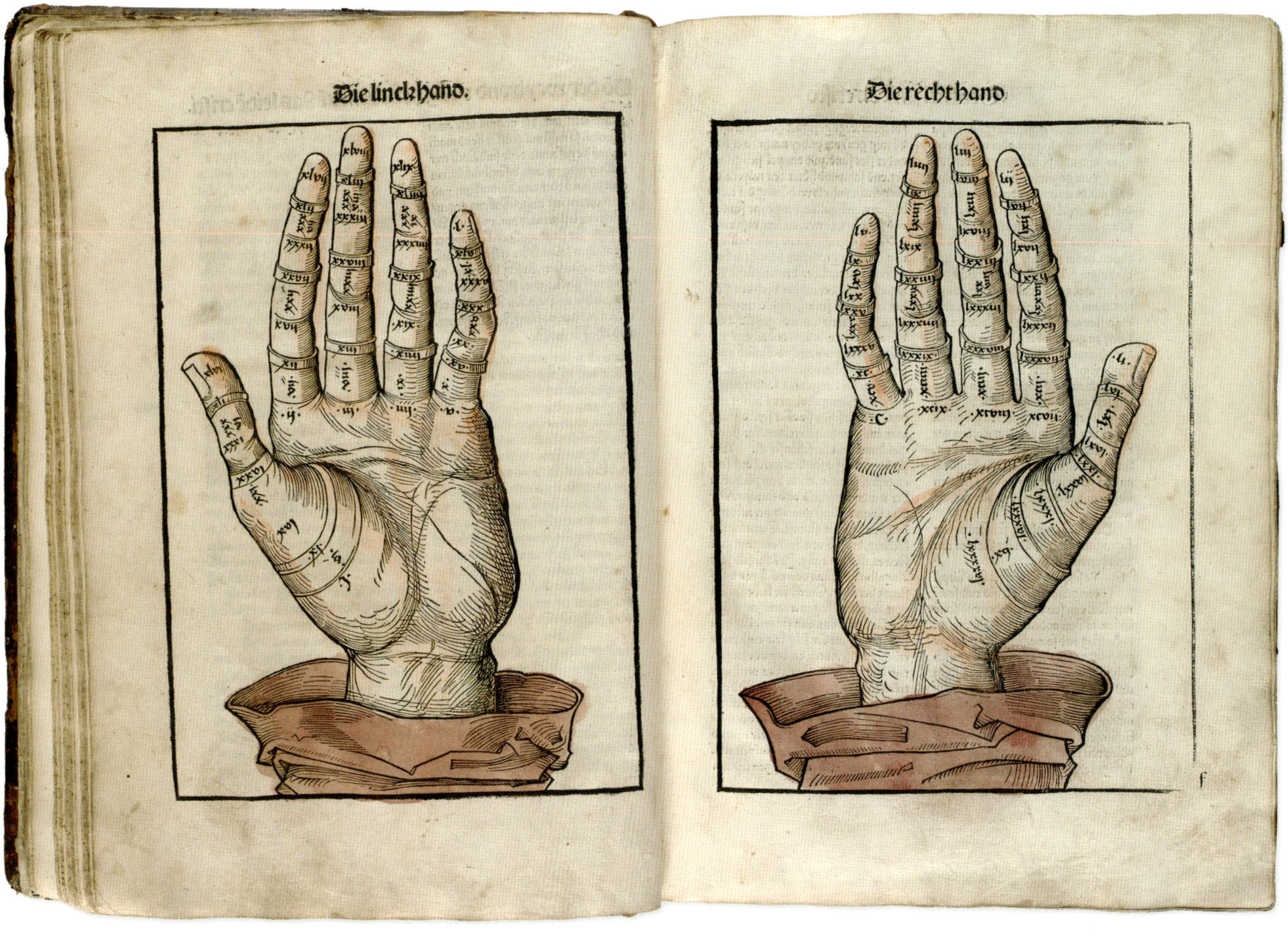

a translation of Raoul Lefèvre's chivalrous romance *Receuils des Histoires de Troye*, which he had made several years earlier for Edward IV's sister, Margaret of York. After returning to England and setting up his workshop in the vicinity of Westminster Abbey, Caxton embarked on the printing of more than a hundred books, including the first printing of Chaucer's *Canterbury Tales* (c. 1476) and one of the first illustrated books printed in England, *Myrrour of the World* (1481).

While Latin remained the dominant language of early books, printing in the vernacular was commonly used for popular or literary tales. Caxton, however, was significant for producing his books almost entirely in English. Out of his hundred or so surviving works, about seventy were published in English. His books contributed to the emergence of a standard written language at a time when numerous dialects were in use. In terms of printing quality, his books lacked finesse, and they pale against the productions of his German contemporaries. Unlike most printers, however, his interests were predominantly literary. He translated many of the texts he published, frequently adding his own prefaces and epilogues, and popularised them for an English readership.

In Germany, the cities of Augsburg and Ulm became important centres for the production of illustrated books. The woodcut books printed in the 1470s by Günther Zainer, of Augsburg, and Johann Zainer, of Ulm, have been described by William Morris as 'second to none'. But it was Nuremberg, where Anton Koberger set up a large-scale workshop in 1470, that became the centre of early German printing. Koberger's operation combined printing, publishing and bookselling, and at one time he ran twenty-four presses operated by over a hundred staff, the largest in Germany at that time.

Koberger's most ambitious publication was the *Liber Chronicarum* (1493), or the Nuremberg Chronicle, the most lavishly illustrated book of the fifteenth century. It contained 1809 illustrations, printed from 645 blocks, by Michael Wolgemut, the leading German artist of his day, and his stepson Wilhelm Pleydenwurff. These woodcuts depicted the major cities of Europe, along with numerous portraits of kings and rulers, and biblical scenes. The young Albrecht Dürer, who was Koberger's godson, was apprenticed to Wolgemut's workshop for four years from 1486 to 1490, and possibly had a hand in the illustrations.

The first edition, in Latin, took nineteen months to complete, and was so popular that a German edition followed within six months.

Koberger's other great book, the *Schatzbehalter* (1491), was written by Stephan Fridolin, a Franciscan friar at Nuremberg. Fridolin's meditations on the life of Christ were lavishly illustrated by Michael Wolgemut, whose ninety-six full-page woodcuts are considered his finest achievement.

Early printing in Germany and England featured the use of Gothic typefaces. However, printers in Italy, and later France, began to develop Roman typefaces modelled on the Humanist script found in Italian Renaissance manuscripts. While Roman type had first been cut in Strasbourg in 1467, it was the Roman typefaces designed by French-born Nicolaus Jenson that proved influential in Roman type being adopted by Italian printers. In 1458, Jenson was sent to Mainz by King Charles VII to learn the new art of printing. From there he took his craft to Venice, which was the centre of Renaissance printing at the time. Though Jenson was a printer of books, producing some 150 during his time in Venice, his fame rests on the series of Roman typefaces he designed, which became widely imitated and served as inspiration for later typographers such as Claude Garamond.

German printer and typecutter Erhard Ratdolt was also active in Venice during the period 1476–82, before returning to his native Augsburg. Ratdolt's best-known work was his printing of Euclid's *Elementa Geometriae* (1482), which contained around four hundred mathematical and geometrical diagrams, the first book to do so. Ratdolt's printing is especially admired for the fine borders, initials and ornamentation included in his books.

Venice's greatest printer was Aldus Manutius, who arrived in the city in about 1490 and set up his printing house soon after. Manutius was an admirer of classical Greek literature and wanted to save it from further loss by committing it to type. Prior to his venture, most Greek literature was only known in Latin translation. Employing both Humanist scholars and Greek compositors, Manutius's Aldine Press began to issue scholarly, pocket-sized editions in Greek of classics by Aristophanes, Sophocles, Herodotus, Euripides and others, before branching out to include Latin classics by authors such as Virgil and Pliny. His type designer, Francesco Griffo, developed the first italic script for use in these editions, as well as a Greek typeface and fine Roman types.

OPPOSITE, TOP:
Hartmann Schedel
Liber Chronicarum
(Nuremberg Chronicle)
Nuremberg, Anton Koberger, 1493

OPPOSITE, BOTTOM:
Stephan Fridolin
Schatzbehalter
Nuremberg, Anton Koberger, 1491

BELOW:
Euclid
Elementa Geometriae
(Elements of Geometry)
Venice, Erhard Ratdolt, 1482

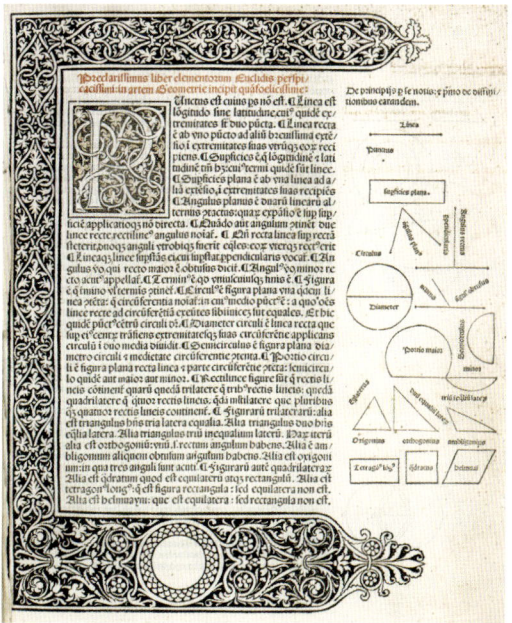

EUCLID

Euclid was the most important mathematician in antiquity. His *Elementa Geometriae* (Elements of Geometry) is a compilation of early Greek mathematical knowledge. This first printed edition is based on Adelard of Bath's twelfth century translation from Arabic to Latin, and is the first work on mathematics to be illustrated with diagrams. Euclid's work formed the basis of geometric theory until the development of non-Euclidean geometry in the nineteenth century. Over a thousand editions of the work have been issued.

In 1499, Manutius printed what is considered one of the finest illustrated books ever published, the *Hypnerotomachia Poliphili*. The work is renowned for the sheer beauty of its typographical design and layout, and the way that it integrates the Roman type designed by Griffo with the book's 174 woodcuts. Authorship of the narrative, which concerns an allegorical search by Poliphili for his lost lover Polia, has been attributed to Francesco Colonna, a Dominican monk who lived in Venice. Colonna's name is revealed by taking the first letter of each of the thirty-eight chapters to spell out *Poliam frater Franciscus Columna peramavit*, meaning 'Brother Francesco Colonna loved Polia tremendously'. Poliphili's love for Polia takes him on a fabulous journey through history, revealing his great knowledge of architecture and landscape design, as well as engineering, painting and sculpture.

The artist who worked on the illustrations for *Hypnerotomachia* is unknown, though the designs have variously been attributed to Andrea Mantegna, Fra Giocondo, Vittore Carpaccio and Gentile Bellini. Recent research has identified the illuminator Benedetto Bordon as the likely artist responsible for them. The woodcuts are drawn with a clean line, and the generous use of space on the page contrasts dramatically with the overall angular density of German woodcuts of the period, giving the illustrations a modern look. There is an almost perfect meeting of illustration and typography, with some pages reproducing images, such as a goblet, purely by means of type. It has been argued that the *Hypnerotomachia* was responsible for the shift in France, in the first quarter of the sixteenth century, from Gothic to Roman typefaces. Its influence can be seen in the work of early sixteenth-century French printers, such as Geofroy Tory. Tory's elegant Book of Hours, the first edition of which appeared in 1525, exhibits the same use of architectural space in its woodcut designs, along with Aldine-influenced Roman typography.

In the first fifty years after Gutenberg, printing presses were operating in virtually every significant urban centre in Europe, and up to eight million books were printed. This figure far exceeds the number of manuscripts produced by scribes in Europe during the preceding thousand years. While there have been many revolutions in human history, it is arguable that the printing revolution, at least in Europe, wrought the most enduring changes. For the past five hundred years, it has been the principal means by which ideas have flourished. Unlike the preceding period, when knowledge was in the hands of a few, the introduction of the printed book allowed for the dissemination of ideas on an unprecedented scale. It allowed the Renaissance to flourish, along with the Reformation. It encouraged the widespread rise of literacy and the growth of scientific endeavour. It was the first form of mass communication, which would give rise to popular culture. It seems fitting, therefore, that the oldest digital archive of books, Project Gutenberg, founded in 1971 with the aim of making important texts freely available to everyone in the world, should have taken its name from the inventor of the printing press.

RIGHT:
Horae in Laude Beatiss, Virginis Mariae, ad Usum Romanum (Book of Hours)
Paris, Geofroy Tory, 1531

OPPOSITE:
Francesco Colonna
Hypnerotomachia Poliphili
Venice, Aldus Manutius, 1499

The Sacred Book

In the beginning was the Word and the Word was with God and the Word was God.
JOHN 1:1

BOOKS ARE CENTRAL TO MANY OF THE WORLD'S RELIGIONS. THEY ARISE FROM ORAL TRADITIONS IN WHICH THE DIVINE WORD IS RECEIVED AND RECITED, LEARNED AND WRITTEN DOWN SO THAT IT IS PRESERVED FOR AND SHARED WITH FUTURE GENERATIONS. THESE HOLY BOOKS ARE VENERATED AS SACRED OBJECTS IN THEMSELVES, TO BE TREATED WITH RESPECT AND CEREMONY. CONCEPTS OF BEAUTY ARE ALSO FUNDAMENTAL TO MOST RELIGIOUS TEXTS, EXPRESSED IN THE POETRY OF THEIR WORDS AND THE DECORATION OF THEIR PAGES.

All great religious texts have influenced the development of language and literature in the cultures from which they have emerged. In ancient Sumerian civilisation, temples were the centres of learning, some housing vast libraries of clay tablets that recorded hymns and religious epics as well as the more prosaic transactions of daily economic life. In Egypt, the development of papyrus enabled the production of Books of the Dead, which would ensure their owners' safe passage to the afterlife.

One of the oldest surviving religions with a literary tradition is Hinduism. Its teachings are enshrined within a range of scriptures known as Vedas ('knowledge' in Sanskrit), which provide guidance for spiritual life. These range from the *Rigveda*, dating to around 1400 BCE, to the *Upanishads*, which were composed around 1000–500 BCE.

The Vedas have been passed down both orally and in written form and continue to provide the basis for Hindu religious thought and philosophy. Sections of the Vedas are learned and recited today as a demonstration of religious faith. Religious codes of conduct (*dharma*) are also at the heart of the great Indian epic the *Mahabharata*, composed from around 400 BCE and traditionally attributed to the legendary priest and teacher Vyasa ('compiler'). The *Mahabharata* continued to evolve over the next eight hundred years, one of the later additions being the *Bhagavad-Gita*, or 'Song of the Lord'. The *Bhagavad-Gita* is especially sacred to followers of Krishna but is also celebrated today as a major work in the history of world literature.

Buddhism originated in northern India, now Nepal, with the teachings of the Buddha Siddhartha Gautama, who lived around the sixth to the fourth century BCE. Early Buddhist literature developed in a range of ancient Indian languages, particularly Pali and Sanskrit. The *Tipitaka* (in Pali) or *Tripitaka* (in Sanskrit) refers to a canon of Buddhist scripture, the contents of which has varied within the schools of Buddhism. The oldest collection comprises the doctrines and discourses of Theravada Buddhism, which is now dominant in Sri Lanka, Burma, Thailand, Laos and Cambodia. Composed in the first five hundred years of Buddhism, the *Tipitaka* includes the teachings ascribed to Buddha himself. From the first century CE, Mahayana Buddhism developed

The Torah being presented to the congregation
From **Jean-Frédéric Bernard**, editor
Cérémonies et Coutumes Religieuses de Tous les Peuples du Monde
Amsterdam, 1723–43
Engraving by Bernard Picart

BELOW:
Gautama Buddha in an early nineteenth century illuminated manuscript
From **Ananda K Coomaraswamy**
Mediaeval Sinhalese Art
Broad Campden, UK, Essex House Press, 1907–08

in India and now predominates in China, Korea, Japan and Tibet. Well-known texts to have been added by Mahayana Buddhism include the Diamond Sutra, Lotus Sutra and the Heart Sutra.

The earliest Buddhist manuscripts known to survive were written on birch bark; dating back to the first or second century CE, they were found near the border of Pakistan and Afghanistan in the late twentieth century. Buddhism was closely associated with the development of the book throughout much of Asia. Paper had been invented in China around the second century BCE and was used as the material for scrolls from the first or second century CE. With the spread of Buddhism, paper and the scroll format were introduced to Korea and Japan from the fourth to the sixth century. Block printing was the next book technology to be developed in China, and from there it was disseminated to other Buddhist cultures. Some of the earliest known examples of printing include the Buddhist charms ordered by the Japanese Empress Shotoku around 764 and a copy of the Diamond Sutra printed in China in 868.

A sacred book is at the heart of each of the three great monotheistic religions practised today. These are the Torah in Judaism, the Bible in Christianity and the Qur'an in Islam. Indeed, the centrality of a book to each of these faiths is represented by various terms. For example, the word 'Bible' originates from the Greek *biblion*, or 'book', and 'Qur'an' can be translated from Arabic to mean 'recitation'. *Am HaSefer* is a Hebrew term that refers to followers of the Jewish faith as 'people of the book'. The Qur'anic phrase *ahl al-kitab* also translates literally as 'people of the book' and refers in Islam to those of other faiths who have received earlier revelations, particularly Jews and Christians.

Judaism, Christianity and Islam are known as Abrahamic religions as all three recognise Abraham as an important prophet. Jews and Christians each adhere to the collection of books that are known in Judaism as the Tanach (which includes the Torah) and referred to in Christianity as the Old Testament. The Christian Bible also contains the New Testament, which includes the gospel accounts of Jesus's life as well as letters and

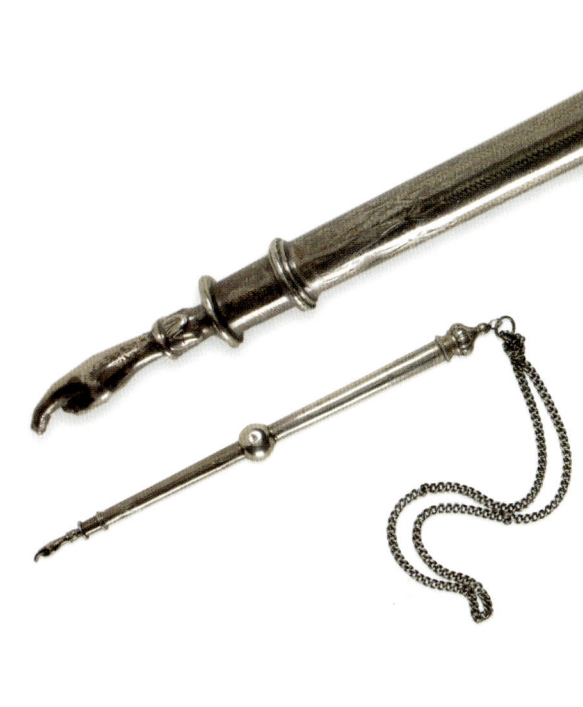

ABOVE, LEFT:
Sefer Torah
Eastern Europe, mid nineteenth century
Collection: Jewish Museum of Australia, Melbourne

ABOVE, RIGHT:
Yad, or pointer, with which to read the Torah
Collection: Jewish Museum of Australia, Melbourne

scriptures relating to the early years of Christianity. The Qur'an recognises the revelations given to the earlier prophets, including Moses and Jesus, and includes stories such as the Garden of Eden and Noah's Ark (with some narrative differences). While Jesus is seen in Islam as a major prophet who will come again, Muslims regard Muhammad as the last of the prophets and his revelations as superseding those that preceded him.

Within these three religions, adherents worship and study the sacred texts of their faiths through public recitation as well as private reading. In Judaism and Islam, the book itself is literally the Word of God and must be reproduced without alteration and handled carefully according to religious law.

Judaism is the oldest of the three religions and dates back approximately four thousand years to the time of Abraham, regarded as the father of the Hebrew people. At its core is the Torah (Instruction or Law), also known as the Pentateuch (Greek for 'five containers') or the 'five books of Moses': Genesis (*Bereshit*), Exodus (*Shemot*), Leviticus (*Vayikra*), Numbers (*Bamidbar*) and Deuteronomy (*Devarim*). The Hebrew titles are derived from the first significant word in each book—for example, *bereshit* means 'in the beginning'. Together with the books in the *Nevi'im* (Prophets) and the *Ketuvim* (Writings), the Torah forms part of the Tanach. The Torah represents the covenant between God and the Jewish people, as revealed to Moses at Mount Sinai. As such, its significance to Jewish religious, political, cultural and social life cannot be overstated.

Before the introduction of printing to Europe in the fifteenth century, Jewish texts were written by hand on parchment scrolls, and this form continues to be central to religious observance. The *Sefer Torah*, which is a manuscript Torah scroll written in Hebrew, is the only form appropriate for public reading in the synagogue. Its production is governed by strict guidelines that have remained unchanged over time. As the Talmud (which interprets Jewish law) commands, 'Prepare a beautiful *Sefer Torah* written in good ink with a fine pen by an expert *sofer* [scribe]'. The scroll must be produced from the skin of a kosher animal—that is, one killed in the ritual manner. The writing implement and ink must contain no metal as this is the substance of weapons, which take away life. The Torah gives life, as expressed in the verse 'It is a tree of life' (Proverbs 3:18) which is recited when the Torah is returned to its housing, the Holy Ark, during a service in the synagogue.

When a reader reads from the Torah, a *yad*, or pointer, in the shape of a hand with extended forefinger is used to protect the parchment from human contact. Torah scrolls that have become worn with age are ritually buried in consecrated ground so that the Word of God is not destroyed.

As every word of the Torah has sacred meaning, great care must be taken to transcribe the text word for word and letter for letter. This process has ensured that these texts have remained unchanged, demonstrated in the matching of contemporary versions to those in the Dead Sea Scrolls, discovered in 1947 and containing Hebrew scriptures dating back to the first century CE. The scribe must speak each word before writing it and, before writing the name of God, must state 'I am writing in the name of God for the holiness of His name'.

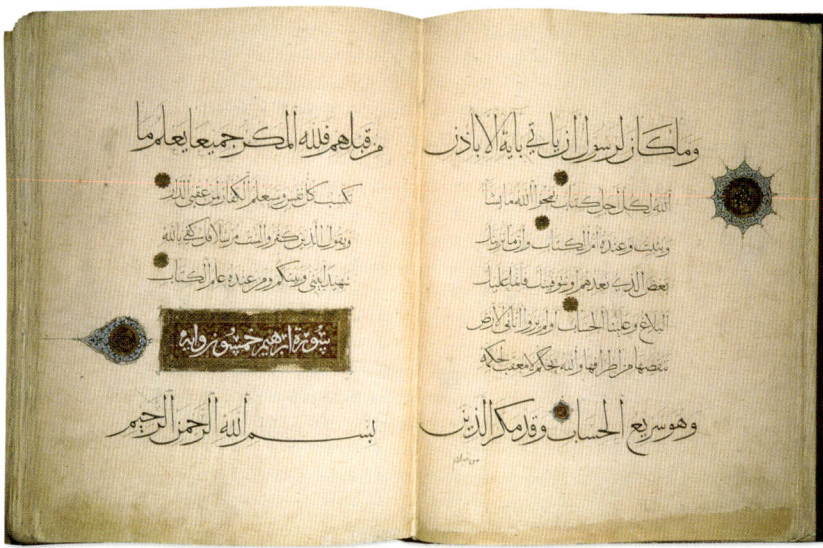

BELOW, LEFT:
Devotees reciting from a Qur'an at the tomb of Sultan Mahmud of Ghazna in Afghanistan
From **James Rattray**
Scenery, Inhabitants and Costumes of Afghaunistan
London, Hering & Remington, 1848

BELOW, RIGHT:
Qur'an fragment (Chapters 2:4–66:2)
Likely produced in Baghdad, early fourteenth century
Rayhan script
Collection: Chester Beatty Library, Dublin

A *Sefer Torah* is unadorned, so that only the Word of God is present. While the Torah itself is not decorated, its housings within the synagogue are often objects of great beauty, in accordance with the *hiddur mitzvah*, or divine commandment to 'decorate holiness'. These elements include the *mitpachat*, which is a mantle used to cover the Torah between readings, an ornamental breastplate and the Holy Ark.

With the introduction of printing to Europe, copies of the Torah and other Jewish texts began to be printed and bound as codex books. While the manuscript scroll continued as the only appropriate form for use in the synagogue, this new and more portable format enabled the dissemination of texts for private study, particularly among the growing Jewish diaspora throughout Europe. Today, the Torah is available in mass-printed editions, known as the *Chumash*, and is often published in the original Hebrew with an accompanying translation into the language of the reader. Such translations, however, do not have the same religious import as the *Sefer Torah* because, unlike the *Sefer Torah*, they are not handwritten in Hebrew and are therefore not recognised as the literal Word of God.

Throughout the Islamic world, the central role of the Qur'an in the life of all Muslims is witnessed by the practice of reading and reciting from it every day. The Qur'an is regarded as the sacred Word of Allah (Arabic for God), revealed to the Prophet Muhammad through the intermediary of the Archangel Gabriel. These revelations took place over twenty-three years from 610 to 632 CE, when Muhammad was living in Mecca and then Medina, in present-day Saudi Arabia. Islam has no ordained priests, and the Qur'an urges all Muslims to read so that they may study and know the sacred text for themselves:

'Proclaim! [or read!] And thy Lord is Most Bountiful,—
He Who taught (the use of) the pen,—
Taught man that which he knew not.'
(Qur'an 96:3–5)

Like the Jewish Torah, the text of the Qur'an is fixed as the unalterable Word of God. Revealed in Arabic, any translations into other languages are accepted as interpretations only. These may be used for personal reference but, for all Muslims, only the Qur'an in Arabic may be used for worship, whether public or private. As the language of Islam, Arabic has spread beyond the Arabian Peninsula to countries throughout the world, wherever there are Muslim populations.

The Qur'an is a book to be recited. During Ramadan, Muslims recite all 114 *surahs*, or chapters, of the Qur'an from beginning to end. One who succeeds in the remarkable act of memorising the whole Qur'an is known as a *hafiz*. Recitation competitions are regularly held throughout the world, and children, including those of non-Arabic speaking background, often excel.

As the words of the Qur'an are sacred, so are the materials on which these words are written. A Muslim is expected to undertake a ritual ablution before touching the Qur'an. The book must never come into contact with the ground or anything unclean and is often protected by a covering, which can range from a simple cloth to an ornate leather binding and satchel. While most Muslims today use printed copies of the Qur'an for their daily prayer and study, manuscript versions continue to be highly valued as works of art made in God's honour.

As writing is a crucial means by which the Word of God is conveyed and venerated, Arabic calligraphy has developed as a major form of artistic expression. As well as being used in the production of ornate manuscript Qur'ans, the calligraphic arts can be seen in the inscription of Qur'anic verses in Islamic architecture, metalwork and ceramics. A number of distinct calligraphic scripts have developed over the centuries, many of which continue to be practised throughout different regions of the Islamic world today. The first of these is the angular *kufic* script, named after the town of Kufah in Iraq, where it was developed in the early decades of Islam. Over subsequent centuries, a range of cursive scripts developed from *kufic*. Six of these in particular were established as the classical styles of writing: the *muhaqqaq*,

QUR'AN

This Qur'an is in the *maghribi* script that developed in North Africa and Spain and spread south to West Africa. The term *maghribi* derives from the Arabic word for 'west' and is therefore used to refer to scripts developed in the western part of the Islamic world. This Qur'an is housed within a separate blind-tooled leather cover and a leather satchel, enabling it to be kept close during the owner's travels and protecting the sacred Word of God from coming into contact with the ground or any unclean surfaces.

TOP:
Leather satchel and cover to house Qur'an
West Africa, c. mid nineteenth century

BOTTOM:
Qur'an
West Africa, c. mid nineteenth century

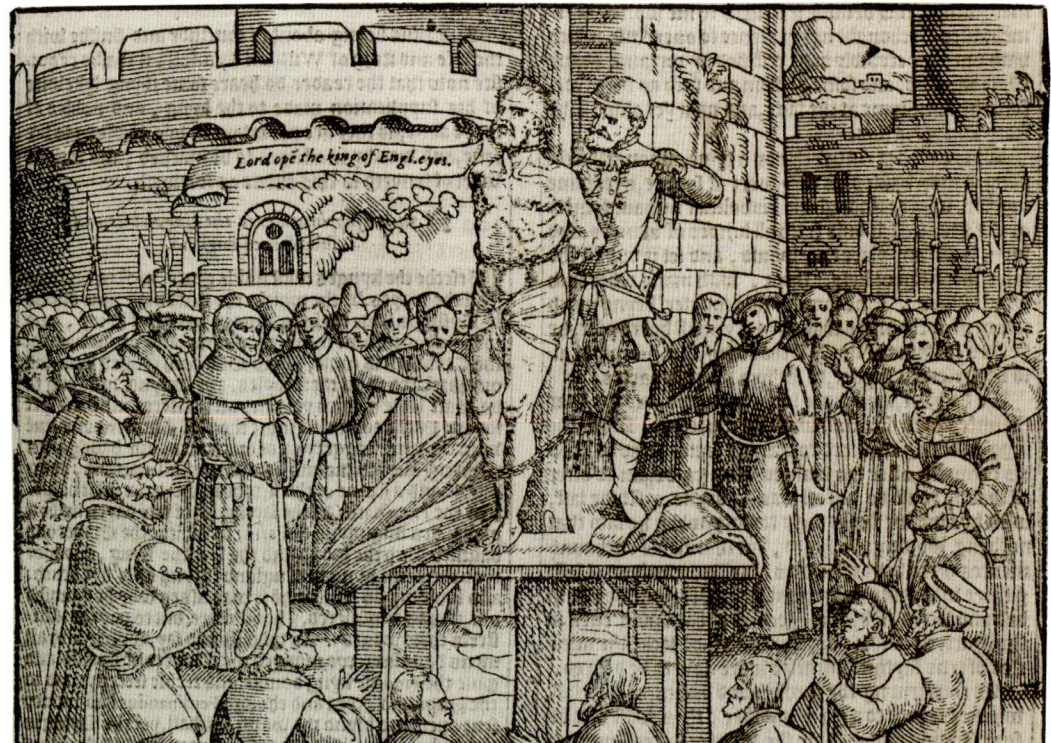

FOXE'S BOOK OF MARTYRS

Commonly known as Foxe's Book of Martyrs, this work was a key text in the Protestant movement of Elizabethan England. This woodcut depicts William Tyndale uttering the words 'Lord, open the king of England's eyes' as he is burned at the stake in 1536 for having translated the Bible into English.

LEFT:
The martyrdom of William Tyndale
From **John Foxe**
Actes and Monuments of these Latter and Perillous Days, Touching Matters of the Church
London, printed by John Daye, 1570

OPPOSITE, LEFT:
The Holy Bible, Conteyning the Old Testament, and the New (the King James Bible)
London, Robert Barker, 1611

OPPOSITE, RIGHT:
Bible (German)
Nuremberg, Anton Koberger, 1483

rayhan, *thulth*, *naskh*, *tawqi'* and *riqa'*. As Islam spread, the flowing *nasta'liq* script developed in Persia, the *maghribi* in North Africa and Spain, and the *divani* under the Ottoman Turks.

Printing technologies were late in being adopted in Islamic cultures. Not only was calligraphy seen as being integral to representing the Word of God, but the flowing style and changing letter forms of Arabic script, depending on each letter's position within a word, did not readily lend themselves to casting in moveable type. There is evidence of some Qur'ans being printed as early as the tenth century using the block printing method, in which a woodblock was carved for each page. These were in the minority, however. The introduction of lithography in the nineteenth century enabled the reproduction of the cursive and decorative elements of Arabic script and ornament, although these mass-produced copies could never match the sacred nature of a manuscript Qur'an.

While the Torah and the Qur'an have remained unchanged for centuries, the history of the Christian Holy Bible is one of translation and interpretation. The early Christian Church compiled its Bible from the Jewish Tanach (which it called the Old Testament) and a new body of writings, the New Testament. The canon of twenty-seven books that today comprises the New Testament was set in the fourth century when the Church selected these from a greater number of first- and second-century Christian texts.

The first Christian Bibles were in Koine Greek, the common dialect of the postclassical Greek language. The Old Testament was based on the Septuagint, the Greek translation from the Hebrew undertaken in Alexandria, Egypt, between the third and second centuries BCE. The various books of the New Testament were originally written in Greek or translated from Aramaic, believed to be the language spoken by Jesus. Greek versions of the Bible continued to serve the churches in the Byzantine East, while various translations into Latin began to be made for churches in the Rome-focused West. In the fourth century CE, Pope Damasus I commissioned Jerome to make a definitive Latin translation from the original Hebrew and Greek texts. This would become known as the Vulgate Bible and would serve as the official Bible text for the Roman Catholic Church for centuries to come.

During the Middle Ages, various sections of the Bible were translated from Latin into a range of vernacular languages across Europe. In Britain the desire for a Bible that was more accessible and that used the language of the people provoked enormous opposition from the Church. In the late fourteenth century, Oxford scholar John Wycliffe argued that the Bible alone should be the basis for religious devotion and that all adherents, therefore, should have direct access to its contents. Together with fellow scholars, he produced the first complete English translation of the Bible in 1382. As hundreds of manuscript copies began to circulate, the Church responded vehemently. Wycliffe's Bible was banned and many of his supporters were arrested, tortured and executed. But despite an edict in 1412 that all copies be burned, a remarkable 170 copies remain in existence today.

The history of the Bible entered a new phase with the introduction of Gutenberg's printing press, and it is not coincidental that the Bible was the first significant work to be printed. While Gutenberg's Bible was a printed edition of the Latin Vulgate, the ability to produce books in their thousands would soon have a profound impact on the availability of the Bible in other languages. In 1522, Martin Luther published his German translation of the New Testament, and in 1534 the complete Bible. As well as its role in the reformation of the Church, Luther's Bible marked a turning point in German literature and influenced the development of the German language.

In 1524, scholar and theologian William Tyndale left England, where the political and religious climate made it impossible to produce and distribute a Bible in English. He settled in Cologne, one of the great centres for printing at the time, and completed his translation of the New Testament from the original Hebrew and Greek. Fleeing to the city of Worms after pressure from the Catholic Church, he had 18 000 copies of two English editions printed during the next three years. These were printed in a small and

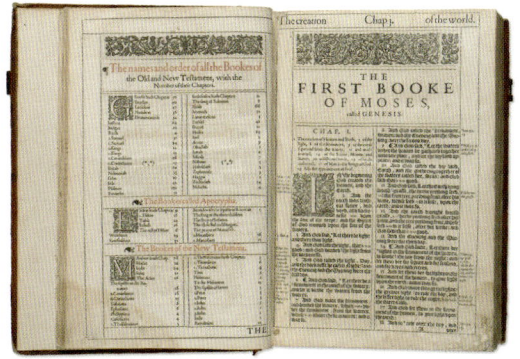

easily concealable size, six thousand of which were secretly imported into England. These were immediately banned, and any seized copies were destroyed. Only two complete copies of Tyndale's Bible survive today, and Tyndale himself was captured and burned at the stake. But his Bible was a book that changed the world. His version introduced a huge array of new phrases such as 'let there be light' and 'my brother's keeper', which would provide the basis for the King James Bible. The groundswell for an English Bible could no longer be stopped.

By the end of the sixteenth century, there were so many English versions in existence that it became imperative for the Church of England to produce one authorised text. To this end, King James I inaugurated a new translation, undertaken by fifty-four translators over an intensive seven-year period. The King James Bible was issued in 1611 and, despite a range of subsequent translations through to today, has remained the best known and most popular version ever since. It is a landmark in the history of the English language, inspiring generations of poets and writers, from John Milton through to Emily Dickinson and TS Eliot.

All sacred texts have profoundly influenced the art, literature and culture of the peoples to whom they belong. The words of these texts today reach global audiences through electronic as well as traditional manuscript and printed versions. But although it is now possible to download the complete Qur'an to one's mobile phone or to receive podcasts of the Torah, these holy books will continue to be venerated in their original forms because they enshrine the Word of God.

BIBLE (GERMAN)

This is the first German-language Bible to be printed in Nuremberg. It was printed by Anton Koberger, who had the typeface cut especially for the work. The book contains more than one hundred woodcuts, the style of which influenced later German biblical illustration, including Albrecht Dürer's *The Apocalypse*, printed in 1498.

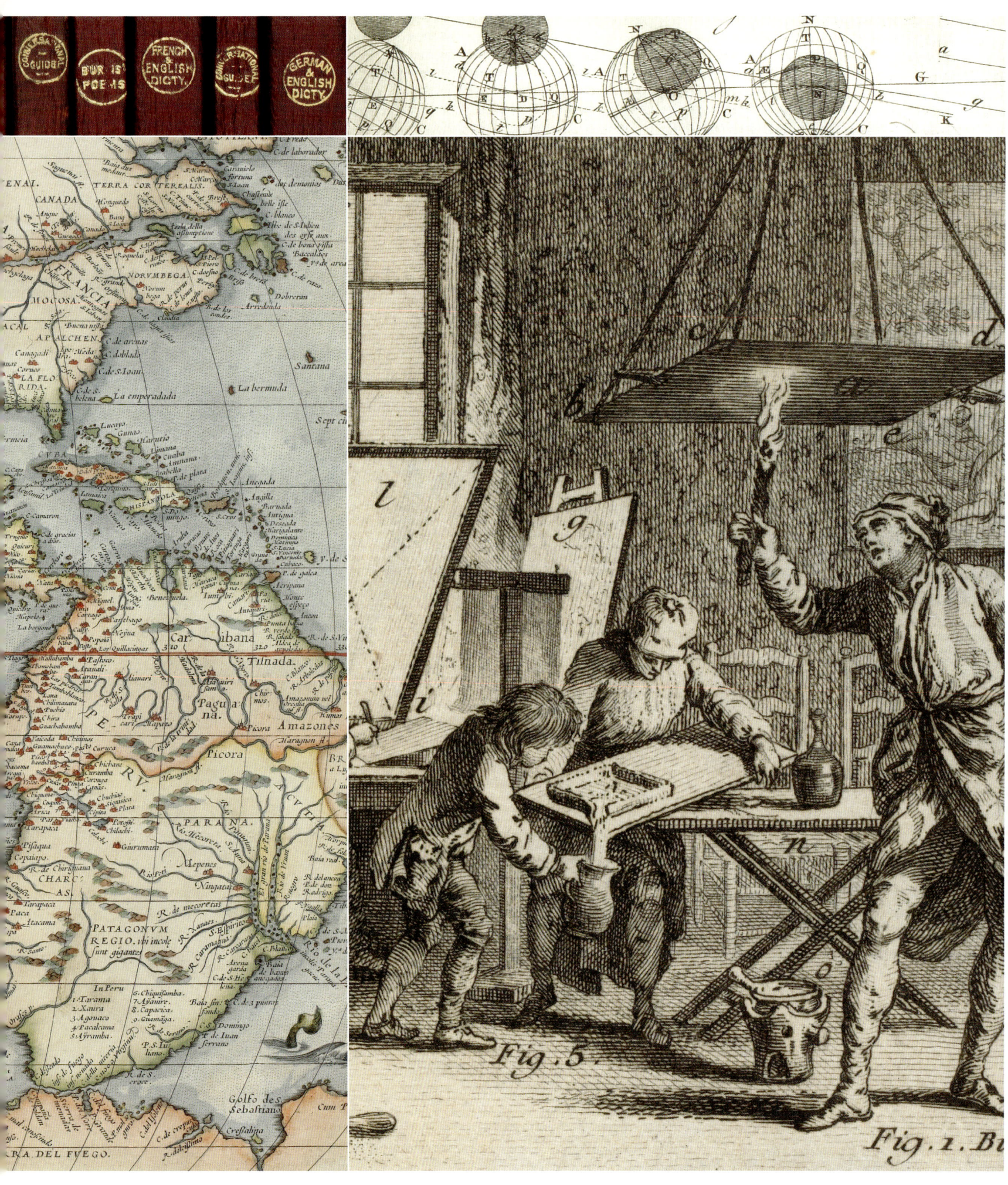

The WORLD in a Book

Encyclopedia. n. s. The circle of sciences; the round of learning.

SAMUEL JOHNSON, *A DICTIONARY OF THE ENGLISH LANGUAGE*

THROUGHOUT THE HISTORY OF THE BOOK, THE ATTEMPT TO COLLECT AND CONTAIN THE WORLD'S KNOWLEDGE HAS BEEN AN ONGOING ENTERPRISE. THE WORLD'S OLDEST LIBRARIES TRIED TO AMASS AND CONTAIN THE SUM OF RECORDED HUMAN KNOWLEDGE AT A TIME WHEN SUCH A FEAT SEEMED POSSIBLE.

The fabled Library of Alexandria, founded by the Ptolemies in Egypt around the start of the third century BCE, attempted to collect all Greek knowledge and learning of the day, along with translations of Assyrian, Persian, Egyptian and Jewish literature. The library was said to be particularly strong in the works of Homer. Estimates of the number of scrolls that resided there vary from several hundred thousand to upwards of half a million.

Stories abound regarding the library's methods of acquiring manuscripts. One states that all visitors to the city were forced to surrender their manuscripts, which were then copied by official scribes before being returned. So accurate were these copies that visitors sometimes unwittingly departed the city carrying the copy rather than the original, which had been deposited in the library. Scholars were encouraged to make use of the library, and prominent among them were the Greek mathematician Euclid and the philosopher Eratosthenes, who first calculated the circumference of the earth. Sources concerning the library's fate are sketchy; it is likely the eventual destruction by fire occurred as a result of several military engagements in the city, from Julius Caesar's conquest of Egypt in 48 BCE to the Emperor Aurelian's suppression of a revolt in Alexandria in 270 CE.

Greek philosopher Plato founded his academy in Athens in 387 BCE, and it became the centre for Greek learning, operating for nine centuries. The Greeks used the terms *enkuklios*, meaning 'circular', and *paideia*, meaning 'education', and together they referred to the 'circle of knowledge'. The two words were first joined by Sir Thomas Elyor in 1531, when he coined the term 'encyclopaedia' in his book *Bok of the Governour*. Elyor defined it as 'that lernynge whiche comprehendeth all lyberall science and studies', and it was thereafter adopted by lexicographers to mean a reference work that contains all branches of knowledge or one that treats a specific branch comprehensively.

Greek and Roman writers compiled a number of encyclopedic works, not all of which survived. It is estimated that Roman writer Marcus Terentius Varro (116–27 BCE), who was called by Cicero the 'most learned of the Romans', composed over seventy works during his life, including an encyclopedia of the arts, and an illustrated dictionary of Greek and Roman biography. Pliny the Elder's *Historia Naturalis* was the first encyclopedia of natural history, composed in the first century CE. After the fall of the Roman Empire, much of this Greek and Roman knowledge was lost to Europe, sometimes surviving only in Arabic translations, where it formed the basis of early Arabic encyclopedias, such as al-Farabi's ninth-century *Mafatih al-Ulum*.

In medieval times, knowledge was limited to small groups and related to particular cultural or geographic areas. The earliest compendiums sought to collate historical and scientific knowledge of the world into a single volume. The major encyclopedia of the medieval period in Europe was compiled by Vincent of Beauvais, a thirteenth-century Dominican friar. Little is

known of his life, but it is believed he lived for a time at the Dominican monastery founded by Louis IX of France at Beauvais in Picardy and received royal patronage. His work *Speculum Majus* (The Great Mirror) consists of three parts: *Speculum Naturale*, *Speculum Doctrinale* and *Speculum Historiale*. A fourth part, entitled *Speculum Morale*, is considered to be by a later hand. Vincent's encyclopedic work was produced for use within a narrow religious community, as a preaching manual for friars, rather than for scholars or theologians. He adopted the modern practice of employing assistants and researchers, dispatching young monks to monastery libraries throughout France to gather information. Typical of early encyclopedias, his work was largely a collection of extracts from earlier authors, including Latin, Greek, Arabic and Hebrew writers. Vincent's *Speculum Majus* was a vast compendium, running to almost 10 000 chapters, of all knowledge of the Middle Ages: 'things that have been made or done or said in the visible or invisible world from the beginning until the end, and even things to come'.

The history of the book is rife with ambitious projects whose aim was nothing less than to encompass the world within a book. The encyclopedia, the dictionary and the atlas all endeavour to capture and describe the world in a variety of ways, to contain all knowledge, or all the words of a language, or all the lands and seas, within the covers of a single volume or set of volumes. The *Liber Chronicarum* or 'Chronicle of the World', better known as the Nuremberg Chronicle after the German city in which it was first printed in 1493, attempted to record all knowledge of the world from creation up to the year of its publication. Encompassing history, geography, religion and myth, it is a virtual encyclopedia of Europe in the fifteenth century. The chronicle's compiler, Hartmann Schedel, was a leading Humanist scholar and physician in Nuremberg who had amassed a considerable library, including some 370 manuscripts, many of which he had copied himself, and six hundred printed books. His text drew heavily upon biblical sources, as well as the work of classical authors such as Pomponius Mela and Gaius Julius Solinus. Like many encyclopedic works, the growth of new knowledge soon outstripped its contents. Columbus's voyage to the Indies, which reshaped the map of the world, took place a year before the publication of the Nuremberg Chronicle, rendering its view of the world outmoded. In many ways, the chronicle stands as a crowning achievement of the past, a reflection of a medieval world soon to be eclipsed by Renaissance scholarship.

When we compare the world map in the *Liber Chronicarum* with the one in Abraham Ortelius's atlas of 1570, the distinctions could not be more dramatic. In less than eighty years, the European view of the world had more than doubled to encompass the Americas and the Pacific.

Ortelius's *Theatrum Orbis Terrarum* is considered to be the first true atlas of the world in that it sought to contain all knowledge of the world's cartography in a book. In its first edition, it combined sixty-nine of the most reliable and up-to-date maps available, printed at uniform size and arranged in a logical order, accompanied by Ortelius's text. Significantly, Ortelius also appended a bibliography or *Catalogus Auctorum*, an uncommon practice at that time, listing eighty-seven significant cartographers, including those whose maps were sourced for the atlas. The *Theatrum* was published at the port city of Antwerp during a formative period of European voyages of discovery, and its publishing success saw it reprinted four times in its first year of publication. Over the next forty years, beyond Ortelius's death in 1598, his atlas was regularly revised and expanded to take into account new geographical discoveries, and by 1612 it included 167 maps and had been printed in forty-two editions.

While some compilers of encyclopedic works in the fifteenth and sixteenth centuries tried to gather the sum of the world's knowledge in a book, others, such as Georgius Agricola, compiled definitive treatises on a single subject. Agricola's *De Re Metallica*, published in twelve books in

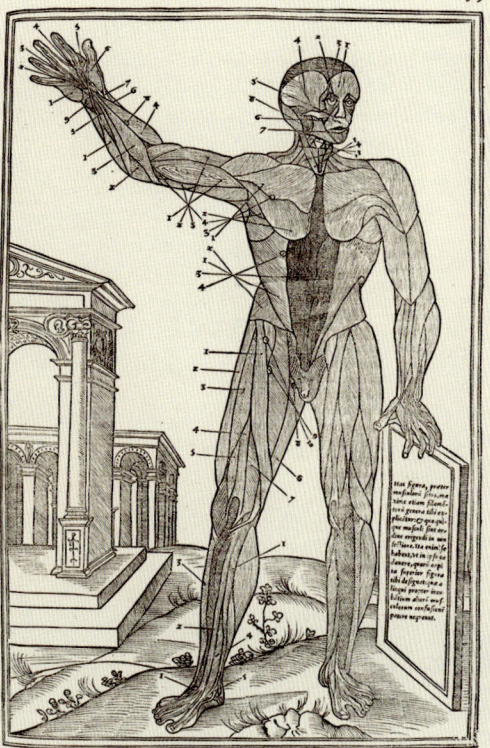

CHARLES ESTIENNE

Early anatomical atlases, such Andreas Vesalius's *De Humani Corporis Fabrica* (1543) and Charles Estienne's *De Dissectione Partium Corporis Humani* point to the growth in sixteenth-century knowledge about the human body and its workings. Estienne began work on his illustrated atlas in 1530, but publication was delayed when a lawsuit was brought against him by surgeon and artist Étienne de la Riviére, who demanded credit for the dissections upon which the woodcuts were based.

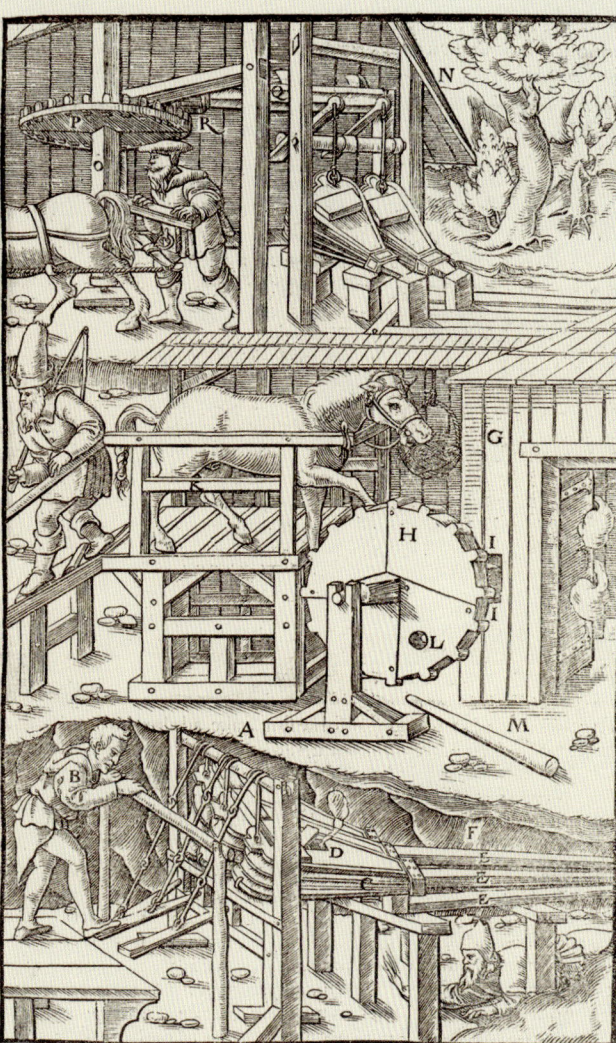

ABOVE:
Charles Estienne
De Dissectione Partium Corporis Humani
Paris, Simonem Colinaeum, 1545

LEFT:
Georgius Agricola
De Re Metallica
Basel, J Froben & N Episopius, 1556

OPPOSITE, LEFT:
Hartmann Schedel
Liber Chronicarum
(Nuremberg Chronicle)
Nuremberg, Anton Koberger, 1493

OPPOSITE, RIGHT:
Abraham Ortelius
Theatrum Orbis Terrarum
Antwerp, Ant. Coppenium Diesth, 1574

Fig. 2
Fig. 3
Fig. 4
Fig. 5
Fig. 1. Bis

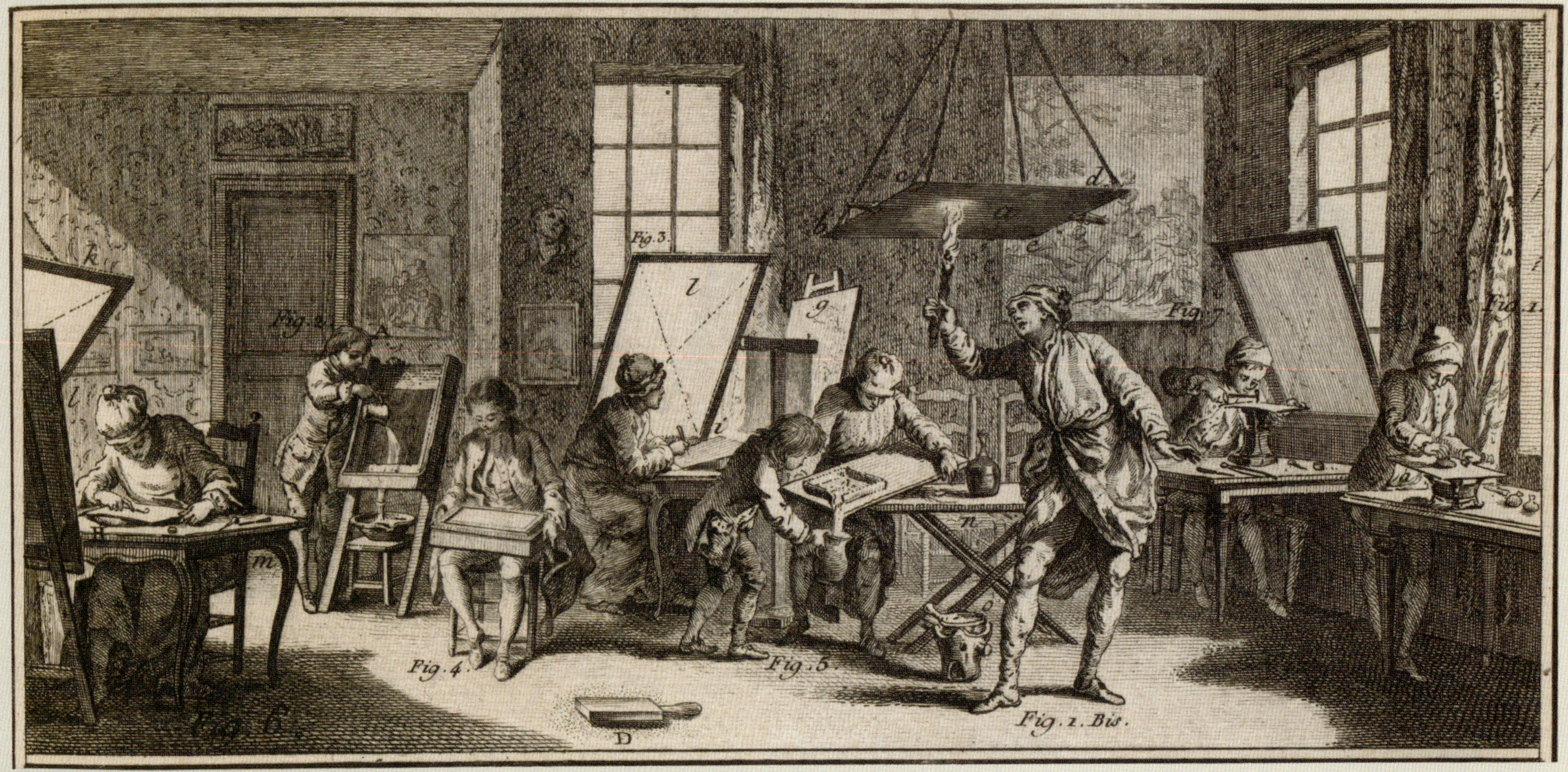

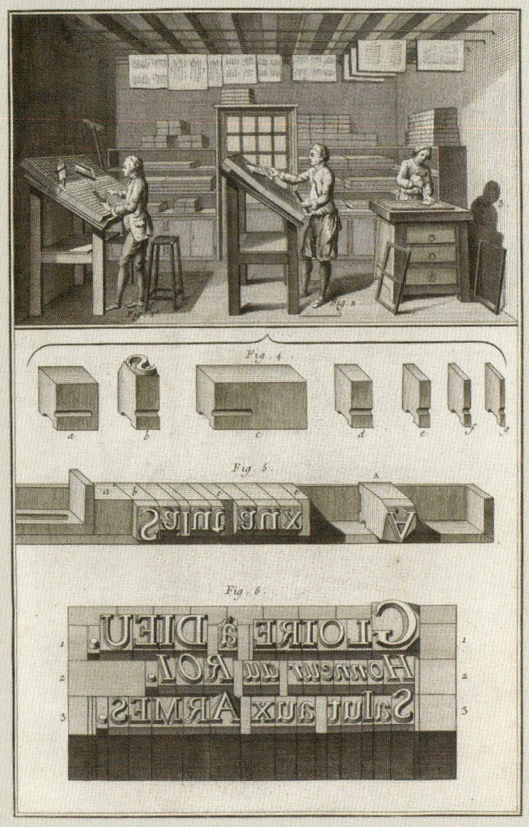

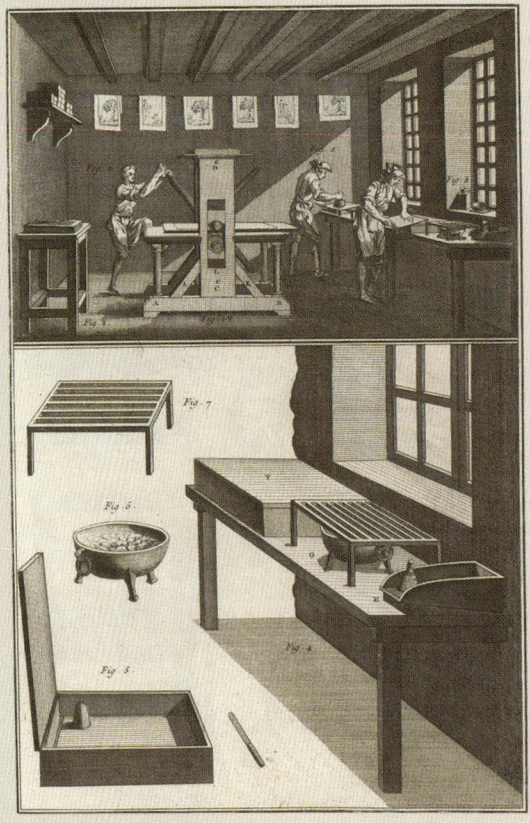

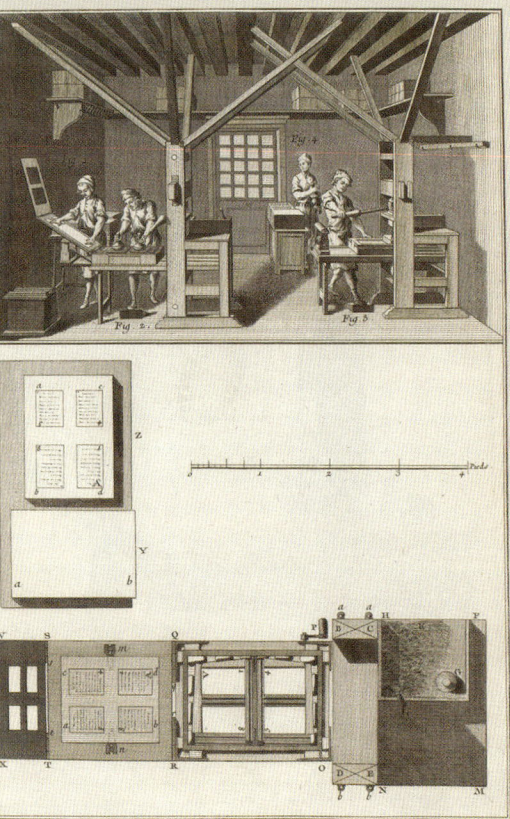

OPPOSITE:
Denis Diderot, editor
Encyclopédie, ou, Dictionnaire Raisonné des Sciences, des Arts et des Métiers
Paris, Chez Briasson, David l'Aîné, Le Breton, Durand, 1751–72

RIGHT:
L'Encyclopédie Méthodique ou par Ordre de Matières par une Société de Gens de Lettres, de Savants et d'Artistes
Paris, Chez Panckoucke, 1782–1832

L'ENCYCLOPÉDIE MÉTHODIQUE

A revised and enlarged edition of Denis Diderot's *Encyclopédie*, arranged as a series of separate subject volumes, was published by Charles Panckoucke in 1782–92, and continued by Henri Agasse in 1792–1813 and by Mme la veuve Agasse in 1813–32. All told, this massive revision of Diderot's work ran to 206 volumes, comprising over 120 000 pages, with more than five thousand illustrations.

The Age of Enlightenment in Europe in the eighteenth century brought with it a renewed enthusiasm for categorising and classifying the world's knowledge into an authoritative intellectual system. Reason and rationality were applied to the process of organising new learning in the sciences and the arts into an ordered and objective set of universal principles, and nowhere was this more apparent than in the creation of the great French *Encyclopédie*, edited by Denis Diderot. The work's genesis came about when publisher André Le Breton approached Diderot with a proposal to translate Ephraim Chambers's *Cyclopedia, or Universal Dictionary of Arts and Sciences* (1728) into French. Diderot soon convinced Le Breton, however, to conceive instead of an entirely new work, one that would bring together all the great writers and new knowledge of the day into a single, vast encyclopedic work.

Diderot's co-editor on the project was the mathematician Jean Le Rond d'Alembert, who would resign before completion of the work after Jesuit authorities, infuriated by the work's secular bias, petitioned the government to withdraw the publishing privilege for the project. His withdrawal left the task of overseeing its completion to Diderot, who at the same time contributed innumerable entries of his own. The resulting *Encyclopédie, ou, Dictionnaire Raisonné des Sciences, des Arts et des Métiers*, published over a 21-year period between 1751 and 1772, was a vast, collaborative project by a French 'society of men and letters'. It contained contributions from more than 140 writers, including Voltaire and Rousseau, on subjects as diverse as alchemy, coffee, morals, parricide and volcanoes. In particular, its emphasis on technology and the mechanical arts made known many specialist craft and artisan practices to a wider audience for the first time. The *Encyclopédie* was published in twenty-eight volumes, including seventeen of text comprising some 70 000 articles, and eleven volumes of engraved illustrations. So painstakingly detailed are the numerous engraved plates that it is almost possible to recreate eighteenth-century industrial life from them alone. The *Encyclopédie* reflected Diderot's anti-establishment views, so much so that, on several occasions, the government attempted to suppress publication of the work, and the later volumes were published in clandestine fashion. Diderot's *Encyclopédie* has rightfully been considered the greatest intellectual accomplishment of the French Enlightenment.

1556, brought together all knowledge about Renaissance mining and metallurgy. His real name was Georg Bauer, but he used the Latinised version, Georgius Agricola, for his writings. Much of *De Re Metallica* was based on his first-hand observations of mining centres, firstly at Joachimsthal (now Czechoslovakia), where he lived for several years, and later at Chemnitz (now Germany). The work embraced everything on the subject, from assaying and smelting, through to use of machinery and equipment and the administration of mines. As a medical doctor, Agricola also included information on diseases and accidents common to miners, as well as means to prevent such occurrences. The book was illustrated with over 292 woodcuts, based on drawings made by Blasius Weffring, depicting the procedures and machinery explained in the text. Agricola is often cited as the father of mineralogy and *De Re Metallica* remained the standard book on mining and metallurgy for over two hundred years.

MIDGET LIBRARY

Miniature books were a novelty that proved popular in the late nineteenth century. Their proliferation was, in part, made possible by advances in printing technology such as photo-lithography. The *Midget Library* comprised twelve miniature reference books, including a Bible, Qur'an, English, French and German dictionaries, a volume of Robert Burns's poems, and an alphabet of birds and animals. Glasgow publisher David Bryce & Son was particularly known in the late nineteenth and early twentieth centuries for the production of miniature books.

ABOVE:
Midget Library
Glasgow, David Bryce & Son, c. 1895

BELOW:
Samuel Johnson
A Dictionary of the English Language
London, printed by W Strahan, for J & P Knapton, T & T Longman, C Hitch & L Hawes, A Millar, and R & J Dodsley, 1755

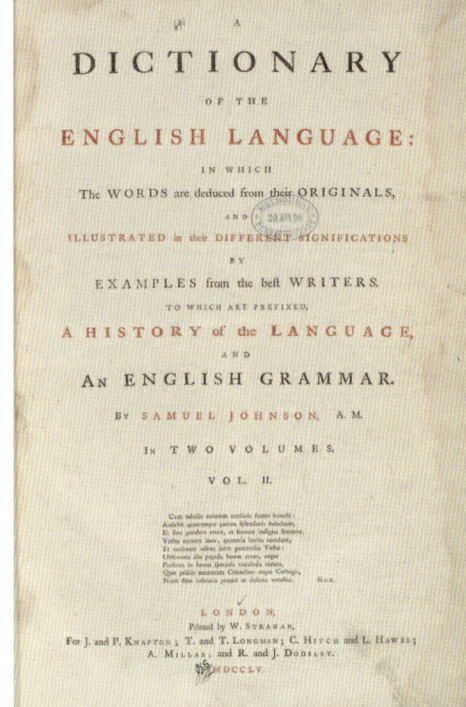

If Diderot's *Encyclopédie* was remarkable in the way it drew upon the considerable talents of France's elite philosophers and writers, then Dr Samuel Johnson's *A Dictionary of the English Language* (1755) seems all the more remarkable for its being the work of one man. Johnson was initially commissioned by a group of London publishers in 1746 to produce a dictionary of the English language. Although he estimated the work would take three years, it eventually took eight to produce. The massive two-volume dictionary contained over 42 000 words, with the definitions being illustrated by over 100 000 quotes from English authors. Johnson, who received a mere £575 for his work, noted in his preface: 'Among these unhappy mortals is the writer of dictionaries … Every other author may aspire to praise; the lexicographer can only hope to escape reproach'. Although not the first English dictionary, Samuel Johnson's would deservedly become the most famous, providing the basis for all modern dictionaries until it was superseded by the *Oxford English Dictionary*, published between 1884 and 1928.

The resounding success of Diderot's *Encyclopédie* inspired Scottish printer Colin Macfarquhar and engraver Andrew Bell to create their own English-language encyclopedia, which would reflect the new era of scholarship and enlightenment. They hired 28-year-old William Smellie to edit the work, which was to be arranged alphabetically and 'compiled upon a new plan in which the different Sciences and Arts are digested into distinct Treatises or Systems'. Within a couple of years, Smellie had composed and compiled 2500 pages of entries drawn from prominent authors, including John Locke, Voltaire, Benjamin Franklin and Samuel Johnson, all unacknowledged. The first *Encyclopædia Britannica* was issued in a hundred weekly parts, later bound into three volumes, between 1768 and 1771. When the first part, a pamphlet-sized booklet, was put on sale in Edinburgh, it was greeted with little interest, but persistent marketing generated sales of three thousand copies of the first edition, enough to justify a new edition. A second edition, in ten volumes, was published between 1774 and 1784, and a third edition, the first to include contributions by outside writers, in 1797. While generally thought of as a British icon, the *Britannica* was taken over by American interests in the 1920s.

The first electronic version of *Encyclopædia Britannica* appeared in 1993. Since then, the growth of the internet has redefined the process of systematically gathering and organising knowledge within the covers of a bound book. The internet is an ever-evolving 'web' of information from a seemingly infinite range of both reliable and unreliable sources. As electronic sources enable data to be stored, searched and retrieved through a multitude of access points and search terms, it seems inevitable that dictionaries and encyclopedias will be among the first texts to disappear from traditional printed book form.

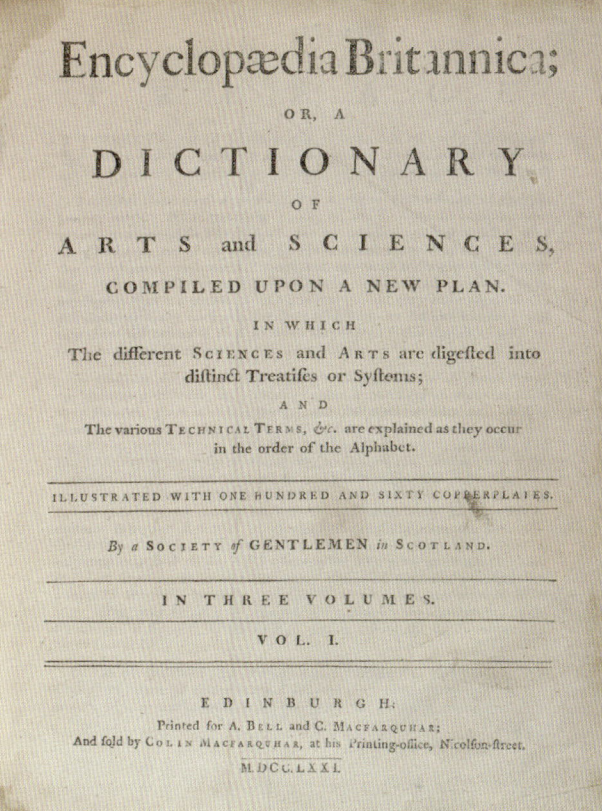

Encyclopædia Britannica, or, a Dictionary of Arts and Sciences, Compiled upon a New Plan in which the Different Sciences and Arts Are Digested into Distinct Treatises or Systems; and the Various Technical Terms, etc., Are Explained as they Occur in the Order of the Alphabet by a Society of Gentlemen in Scotland
Edinburgh, printed for A Bell & C Macfarquhar, and sold by C Macfarquhar, 1771

Books that CHANGED the World

It is well to observe the force, virtue, and consequences of discoveries which are nowhere more conspicuous than in those three which were unknown to the ancients, namely, printing, gunpowder, and the compass. For these three have changed the whole face and state of things throughout the world.
FRANCIS BACON, *NOVUM ORGANUM*

BOOKS HAVE ALTERED THE COURSE OF HISTORY. EMBODYING POLITICS AND IDEOLOGY, PHILOSOPHY AND RELIGION, ART AND SCIENCE, BOOKS ENABLE NEW IDEAS TO TRAVEL VAST DISTANCES AND TO REACH MANY MINDS, PROFOUNDLY INFLUENCING THE WAY WE SEE OURSELVES, EACH OTHER AND THE WORLD AROUND US.

If asked to nominate the ten most influential books of all time, no two individuals would present exactly the same list. Books likely to appear on many lists, however, might be the Bible and the Qur'an, the complete works of William Shakespeare, Karl Marx's *Das Kapital*, and titles as diverse as Plato's *Republic* and Simone de Beauvoir's *The Second Sex*. Such a list would also vary greatly according to the moment at which the question was asked and the personal experience and cultural background of the person answering the question.

The power, even danger, of the printed word and its ability to change the world are reflected in the censorship, banning and destruction that have occurred for almost as long as the existence of books themselves. One of the earliest records of book destruction details the burning of books in China in the third century BCE under orders from the Qin Emperor Shi Huangdi. While the extent of the destruction is open to debate, it is generally accepted that the burned works were by scholars who opposed the Qin view of history and philosophy. Books that have been considered a threat to authority, order or faith have been targeted ever since. Significant instances include the regular mass destruction of non-Catholic texts in medieval and Renaissance Europe. In the 1490s alone, five thousand Arabic texts and six thousand Hebrew texts were burned in separate events during the Spanish Inquisition. In Italy, manuscripts by writers such as Dante, Ovid and Boccaccio were burned in the famous 'Bonfires of the Vanities', which took place in Florence in the 1490s at the command of the religious zealot and Dominican friar Girolamo Savonarola.

Political change has also been the catalyst for the destruction of books. Bolshevik Russia, Nazi Germany and communist China during the Cultural Revolution were all settings for book burnings. Recent atrocities against books occurred during the civil war in Bosnia and during the assault on Iraq by Coalition forces, both events leading to the burning and looting of irreplaceable collections of books, manuscripts and archives.

In addition to acts of physical destruction, the fear of books is also witnessed in the regular censorship and banning of titles that are perceived as challenging the prevailing morals of their day. From the Spanish Inquisition, with its *Index Librorum Prohibitorum* (Index of Prohibited Books) to the McCarthyist era in the United States, governments, educational institutions and even libraries themselves have regularly controlled the material available to their reading publics. Famous works to have been banned at different times include the Bible and the Qur'an, Geoffrey Chaucer's *Canterbury Tales*, Thomas Paine's *Age of Reason*, James Joyce's *Ulysses*, Salman Rushdie's *Satanic Verses* and, ironically, Ray Bradbury's *Fahrenheit 451*, which itself deals with the burning of books. The latest books to face bans in the West are those deemed to promote terrorism.

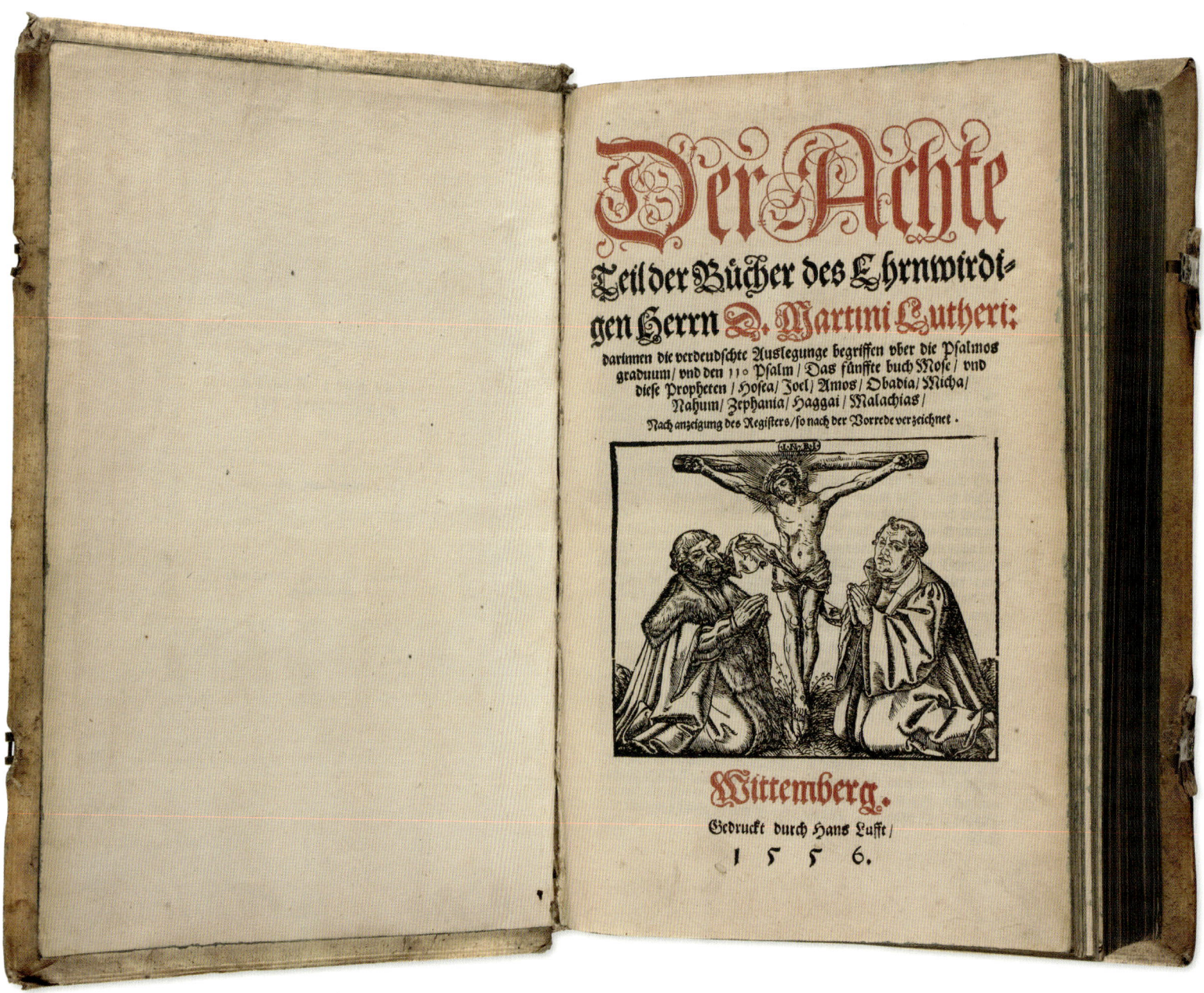

MARTIN LUTHER

Martin Luther
Der Achte Teil der Bücher des Ehrnwirdigen Herrn D Martini Lutheri
Wittenberg, Hans Lufft, 1556

Martin Luther was one of the most influential religious thinkers in the history of the Christian Church in Europe. Luther took advantage of the newly developed printing technologies to spread his ideas widely, most particularly in his famous 'Disputation on the Power and Efficacy of Indulgences' of 1517. Known more commonly as the '95 Theses', this document accused the Catholic Church of abusing its powers and ultimately triggered a series of protest movements that led to the Protestant Reformation. The title page shown here is from the eighth volume of Luther's collected works, published in the decade following his death in 1546.

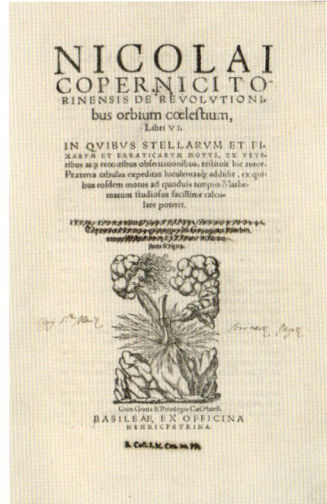

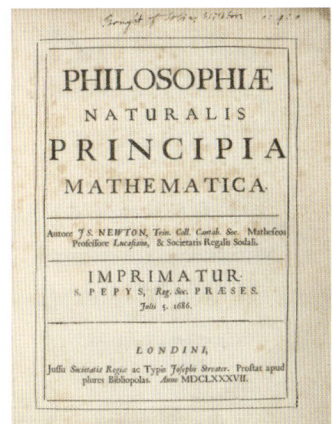

LEFT, TOP:
Nicolaus Copernicus
De Revolutionibus Orbium Coelestium
Basel, 1566

LEFT, BOTTOM:
Sir Isaac Newton
Philosophiae Naturalis Principia Mathematica
London, Joseph Streater for the Royal Society, 1687

ABOVE:
Galileo Galilei
Dialogo Sopra i Due Massimi Sistemi del Mondo, Tolemaico e Copernicano
Florence, Giovanni Battista Landini, 1632
This frontispiece, by Stephano Della Bella, depicts, from left to right, the three great astronomers of different eras: Aristotle, Ptolemy and Copernicus.

One of the earliest scientific texts to have been banned, but which radically changed our understanding of the universe and our place within it, was Nicolaus Copernicus's *De Revolutionibus Orbium Coelestium* (On the Revolutions of the Celestial Spheres). First printed in 1543, the year of his death, it presented Copernicus's discovery of a heliocentric solar system, in which the planets rotate around the sun. This radical theory contradicted the Church's belief that the earth, God's creation, was at the centre of the universe. Seventy years after Copernicus's death, the astronomer and physicist Galileo Galilei continued to argue for the heliocentric theory. As a result, the Inquisition placed Copernicus's book on the *Index Librorum Prohibitorum* in 1616, and a papal decree in 1620 demanded alterations to the text in ten specific places. These alterations are visible in surviving copies today, and Copernicus's book was not removed from the *Index* until 1835.

Galileo's own treatise, *Dialogo Sopra i Due Massimi Sistemi del Mondo, Tolemaico e Copernicano* (Dialogue Concerning the Two Chief World Systems, Ptolemaic and Copernican), published in 1632, also attracted the ire of the Catholic Church. While Copernicus had developed his heliocentric theory by mathematical means, Galileo confirmed it through his development and use of the telescope. After initially permitting its publication so long as Galileo presented his theories as hypothetical, the Church then called Galileo before the Inquisition in 1633, accused him of heresy and banned his text. Galileo was placed under house arrest, where he remained until his death.

The Age of Enlightenment, which began in the seventeenth century, was more receptive to new scientific theories. One work from this period that would change the world was Isaac Newton's *Philosophiae Naturalis Principia Mathematica* (The Mathematical Principles of Natural Philosophy). First published in 1687, Newton's *Principia* continues to underpin contemporary theories of dynamics. It outlines Newton's three laws of motion and his theory of universal gravitation. These theories enabled him to explain the movements of planets, moons and comets within the solar system, the behaviour of the earth's tides and the precession of the equinoxes.

A book that profoundly influenced scientific, religious and philosophical thought was Charles Darwin's *On the Origin of Species by Means of Natural Selection* (1859). A naturalist and geologist, Darwin began to formulate his theories of evolution during the survey expedition of the HMS *Beagle* to the South Pacific, South America and Australia in 1832–36. It would be another twenty years before he would publish his ideas, but when *Origin of Species* first appeared, all 1250 copies sold out almost overnight. Its thesis that humans and animals had evolved from a common ancestry caused widespread controversy among the scientific and religious communities, but the work continued to be a bestseller, selling more than 20 000 copies by the time of Darwin's death in 1882.

94 TRAITTÉ DE LA PEINTVRE

Comment on doit composer vn animal feint & chimerique.
CHAP. CCLXXXVI.

Vovs sçauez qu'on ne peut representer vn animal s'il n'a des membres, chacun desquels soit en quelque sorte vn peu semblable à ceux d'vn autre animal ; donc si vous voulez faire qu'vn animal feint semble naturel, soit par exemple vn serpent, prenez pour la teste celle d'vn mastin, ou de quelque braque, & y mettez les yeux d'vn chat, les oreilles d'vn porc-epy, le museau d'vn levrier, les surcils d'vn lyon, les costez des temples de quelque vieux cocq, & le col d'vne tortuë d'eau.

Ce qu'il faut faire pour que les visages ayent du relief auec de la grace.
CHAP. CCLXXXVII.

Dans les ruës qui regardent au couchant, le soleil estant à son midy, & les parois esleuées à telle hauteur, que celle qui est tournée au soleil ne vienne point à refleschir sa lumiere sur les corps ombreux, il seroit bien auantageux que l'air n'eust point de clarté pour lors, car on verra les deux costez des visages participer de l'obscurité de leurs parois opposites, & ainsi les carnes du nez, & toute la face tournée à l'embouchure de la ruë sera esclairée, par lequel effect l'œil qui sera au milieu de l'embouchure de cette ruë, verra ce visage bien esclairé en toutes les parties qui se trouuent au droict de luy, & les costez vers les parois couuerts d'ombres, à quoy se joindra encore la grace des ombres noyées insensiblement, & ne monstrant aucun finiment d'ombres trenchées : ce qui prouiendra à cause de la longueur des rayons du jour ; lequel passant par entre les toicts des maisons, & penetrant entre les parois, vient frapper sur le paué de la ruë, & rejallist par vn mouuement refleschy dans les lieux ombreux des testes, & les teint legerement de quel-

que lumiere, & la longueur de la lumiere susdite du jour, marquée par les bords de toicts, auec toute sa plenitude, laquelle est sur l'embouchure de la ruë esclaire presque jusques à la naissance des ombres qui sont sous l'object

DE LEONAD DE VINCI 95

de la face, & en continuant ainsi de suitte, se va changeant en clarté, jusques à ce qu'elle soit arriuée sur le menton auec vn ombre insensible de tous les costez : comme par exemple, si cette lumiere estoit A. E. elle void la ligne F. E. de la lumiere qui esclaire jusques sous le nez, & la ligne C. F. esclaire seulement jusques sous la levre, & la ligne A. H. s'estend sous le menton, & en ce lieu-là le nez demeure fort esclairé, parce qu'il est veu de toute la lumiere A. B. C. D. E.

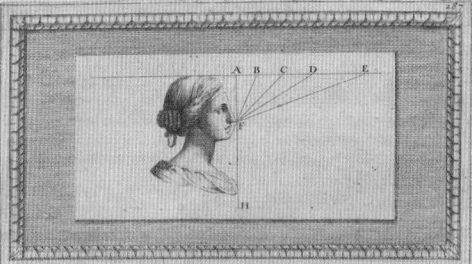

Pour détacher & faire sortir les figures hors de leur camp.
CHAP. CCLXXXVIII.

Vovs deuez placer vostre figure dans vn champ clair si elle est obscure, & si elle est claire mettez-là en vn champ obscur, & si elle est claire & obscure, faites rencontrer la partie obscure sur vn champ clair, & la partie claire sur vn champ obscur.

De la difference des lumieres selon leur diuerse position.
CHAP. CCLXXXIX.

Vne petite lumiere fait de grandes ombres & terminées sur les corps ombreux, & tout au contraire les grandes lumieres font sur les mesmes corps ombreux de petites ombres & confuses dans leurs termes, quand la petite & forte lumiere sera enfermée & comprise dans la grande & moins puissante, comme le soleil dans l'air, au moins la plus foible ne tiendra lieu que d'vne ombre sur les corps qui en seront esclairez.

Qu'il faut euiter la disproportionalité jusques aux moindres parties en vne composition. CHAP. CCXC.

C'est vne tres-grande ineptie, mais ordinaire à beaucoup de peintres, de faire (par exemple) vn bastiment, & d'autres telles parties de composition,

---

Leonardo da Vinci
Traitté de la Peinture de Leonard de Vinci
Paris, Jacques Langlois,
1651

LEONARDO DA VINCI

Leonardo da Vinci had planned to write three major books—on painting, anatomy and architecture—but none were completed by the time of his death in 1519. His pupil Francesco Melzi, who inherited his manuscripts and drawings, later compiled Leonardo's thoughts and ideas into publishable form. The illustrations for the work were executed by French artist Nicolas Poussin.

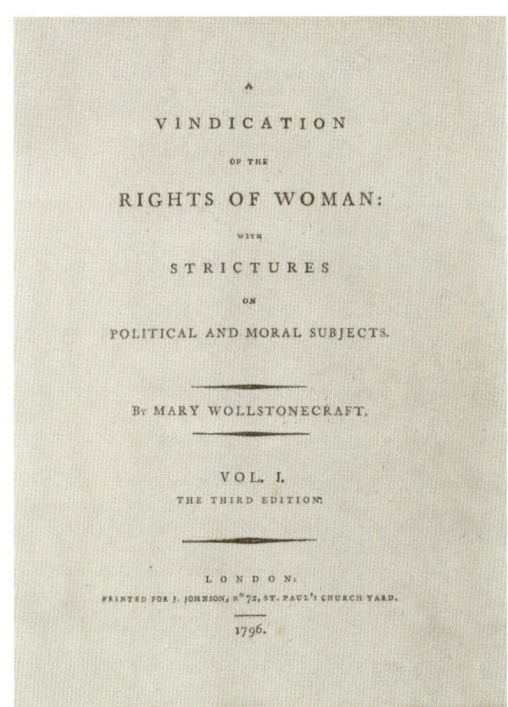

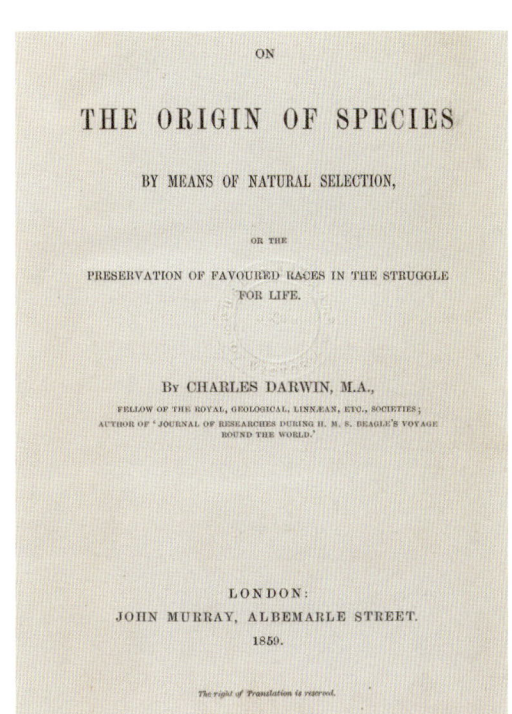

ABOVE, LEFT:
Mary Wollstonecraft
A Vindication of the Rights of Woman
London, J Johnson, 1796

ABOVE, MIDDLE:
Charles Darwin
On the Origin of Species
London, John Murray, 1859

ABOVE, RIGHT:
Karl Marx
Das Kapital: Kritik der Politischen Oekonomie, vol. 1, Hamburg, Meissner, 1872

BELOW:
Sigmund Freud
Gesammelte Schriften
Vienna, Internationaler Psychoanalytischer Verlag, 1924–34

In addition to conveying scientific discoveries and new areas of knowledge about the physical world, books are central to the dissemination of new ideologies, political theories and social movements. Two influential works in the development and spread of communism are Karl Marx's *Das Kapital* and *Quotations from Chairman Mao Tse-tung*. Marx's seminal work, *Das Kapital: Kritik der Politischen Oekonomie* (Capital: a Critique of Political Economy) was a cornerstone in the foundation of the communist movement as well as modern socialism through its assertion of the importance of economic factors in history. Though Marx intended *Das Kapital* to be a comprehensive history of capitalism as well as a critique of its failings, he had published only the first volume of his great work when he died. The second and third volumes were edited and published by Friedrich Engels, and a fourth by Karl Kautsky.

Commonly known as 'The Little Red Book', *Quotations from Chairman Mao Tse-Tung* (Zedong) was first published in May 1964. The work was compiled from Mao's speeches and writings by Lin Biao, one of Mao's key military commanders and party leaders. Lin Biao saw the *Quotations* as a means of inspiring soldiers of the Red Guard at the time of the Cultural Revolution. The first English edition, issued by the Foreign Languages Press in Beijing, appeared in 1966. It is estimated that up to five billion copies have subsequently been printed in over five hundred different editions and fifty languages, including Norwegian, Swahili and Esperanto.

One of the movements to have changed the world's social landscape forever, particularly in the West, is feminism. Two groundbreaking and highly influential works, written almost two centuries apart, are Mary Wollstonecraft's *A Vindication of the Rights of Woman* and Germaine Greer's *The Female Eunuch*. Written amid the intellectual fervour of the French and American revolutions, Wollstonecraft's feminist manifesto was published in 1792, a year after her *A Vindication of the Rights of Man*. Its passionate arguments for social and political reform caused a great stir. One prominent English critic called Wollstonecraft 'a hyena in petticoats', but the book was an immediate bestseller. During the nineteenth century, disapproval of Wollstonecraft's unorthodox personal life caused many feminists to reject her ideas. But from the 1890s her work became influential in the developing women's

SIGMUND FREUD

Sigmund Freud is generally known as the 'father of psychoanalysis'. His theories of the unconscious, of dreams and of psychosexual development continue to be intensely debated but have had a profound influence on psychology, sociology, feminism and cultural studies. *Gesammelte Schriften* (Collected Writings) was the first compilation of Freud's writings and includes all of his major texts within its twelve volumes. This first volume includes *Studien über Hysterie* (Studies in Hysteria), a groundbreaking treatise written with Freud's scientific partner, physician Josef Breuer, and first published in 1895.

Simone de Beauvoir
Le Deuxième Sexe
Paris, Gallimard, 1949
(1961 printing)

Nelson Mandela
I Am Prepared to Die
London, Christian Action
Publications, 1970

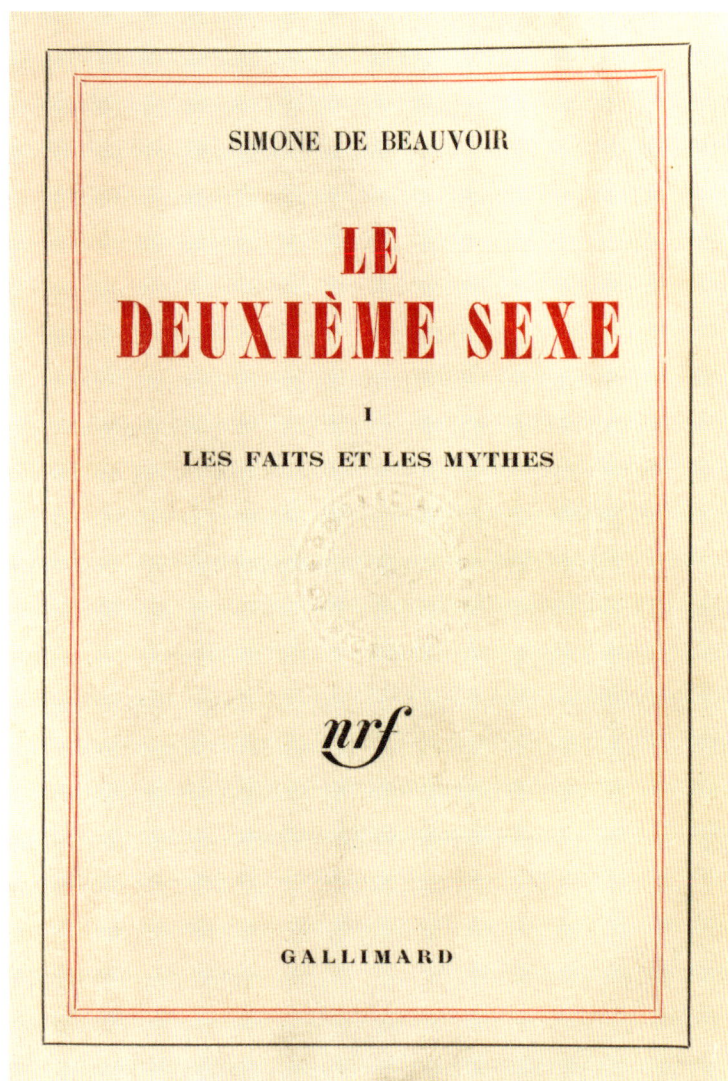

SIMONE DE BEAUVOIR

'One is not born but becomes a woman.' French feminist, novelist and existentialist philosopher Simone de Beauvoir's *Le Deuxième Sexe* (The Second Sex) is a foundational text in feminist literature. In it she deconstructs the notion of the 'eternal feminine' and argues that women have suffered by being perceived historically and culturally as the inferior 'Other'.

NELSON MANDELA

'I am prepared to die' were the closing words of Mandela's statement at the commencement of his trial on charges of sabotage in April 1964. Mandela was already incarcerated, serving a five-year sentence for crimes of leaving the country illegally and incitement to strike. The 1964 trial resulted in a sentence of life imprisonment. Mandela's powerful statement garnered support from individuals and organisations across the world, creating a momentum for change that ultimately brought about an end to apartheid in South Africa. Mandela was released from prison in 1990 and was awarded the Nobel Peace Prize in 1993.

  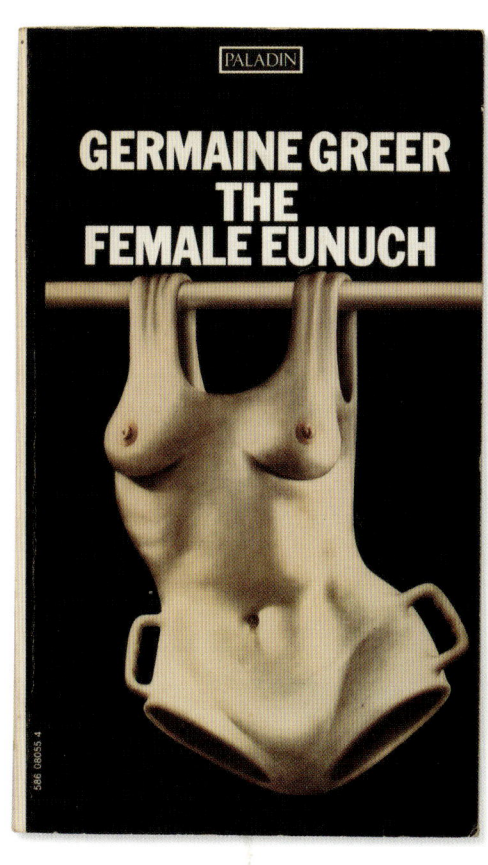

movement, and it is now recognised as a significant work in feminist and intellectual history.

Within six months of the release of Germaine Greer's *The Female Eunuch* in 1970, it was being reprinted monthly and had been translated into eight languages. Its analysis of attitudes towards women and its call for an end to sexual repression placed *The Female Eunuch* at the centre of twentieth-century feminism for many years. Stories abound of copies being kept hidden beneath brown paper covers and of being hurled at husbands. Germaine Greer's ideas antagonised as many readers as they inspired, but the work continues to be published, sold and read throughout the world.

Critic and theorist Marshall McLuhan summed up the power of the word and communication with his influential phrase 'the medium is the message'. His ideas were published in 1967 as *The Medium is the Massage*, a photo-essay that continues to resonate today with its bold graphic design by Quentin Fiore and McLuhan's short punchy texts. According to McLuhan's son, the word 'massage' in the title was a printer's mistake, but when McLuhan saw it, he exclaimed, 'Leave it alone! It's great, and right on target'. McLuhan was prophetic in recognising that our future lives would be lived in a global village of communication networks, 'a brand new world of allatonceness'. For him, the form by which we communicate would, in the future, carry a greater weight than the content of the communication.

This raises the question of who or what has changed the world: the books or the people who wrote them? Some revolutionary figures, such as Karl Marx, chose to communicate with their mass audiences through their books. Others, such as Martin Luther King, will be remembered for their impassioned speeches at public rallies rather than the books that also carried their ideas. From Plato and Machiavelli through to Einstein and Freud, however, books have been the vehicle by which radical ideas have continued to travel throughout the world long after their authors have passed away.

ABOVE, LEFT:
Marshall McLuhan and Quentin Fiore
The Medium is the Massage
Harmondsworth, UK, Penguin, 1967
Cover photograph by Tony Rollo

ABOVE, CENTRE:
Mao Zedong
Quotations from Chairman Mao Tse-Tung
(bilingual edition) Beijing, Foreign Languages Press, 1967 (later printing)

ABOVE, RIGHT:
Germaine Greer
The Female Eunuch
London, Paladin, 1971

For myth is at the beginning of literature, and also at its end. JORGE LUIS BORGES, *DREAMTIGERS*

From the earliest known myths and legends to postmodern fiction, books hold the world's stories. They are also keys that unlock inner worlds. The greatest authors and texts act as literary milestones, signposts marking the collective journeys of the imagination. At their most fundamental level, books allow us to imagine ourselves as other than who we are.

PART II | THE BOOK AND THE IMAGINATION

THE MES HIS TH

Mi ritrouai per una selua oscura,
Che la diritta uia era smarrita,

Literary FOUNDATIONS

Midway along the journey of our life
I woke to find myself in a dark wood,
for I had wandered off from the straight path.
DANTE, *DIVINE COMEDY*

THROUGHOUT HISTORY, LITERARY WORKS HAVE TRANSCENDED THE PLACE AND CULTURE OF THEIR ORIGIN. THEIR UNIVERSAL THEMES SPEAK ACROSS CULTURES, ACROSS LANGUAGE AND ACROSS TIME. EPICS SUCH AS *GILGAMESH*, *BEOWULF*, THE *MAHABHARATA* AND HOMER'S *ILIAD* CONTINUE TO HOLD OUR IMAGINATION THOUSANDS OF YEARS AFTER THEIR CREATION.

Great narratives are retold and reinterpreted by each new generation, refashioned for television, film and the internet. When we watch Baz Luhrmann's *Romeo + Juliet* we marvel at how Shakespeare, writing four hundred years ago, could know our hearts so well. The Coen brothers' film *O Brother, Where Art Thou?* lifts Homer's Odysseus up from Ancient Greece and sets him down in America's Depression-era deep south. In these ways, literary works will continue to cast a spell, just as they did when they first entered the world.

The earliest narratives were recounted orally and only later recorded in written form. The Indian epic the *Mahabharata* had its origins in myths and legends dating back thousands of years. Over the centuries, its tales of gods and men were passed down by generations of priests and musicians, synthesised by around 400 CE into a monumental poem of more than 100 000 stanzas. Through the actions and the battles of the Pandava and Kaurava cousins, the *Mahabharata* explores philosophical, ethical, moral and religious themes. It also contains the *Bhagavad-Gita*, an immensely significant religious text that considers the nature of God through a dialogue between Prince Arjuna and his friend Krishna. Together with the *Ramayana*, the second great Indian epic, the *Mahabharata* is at the core of Hindu belief, and continues to exert a powerful influence on Indian literature and culture today.

Poetry and philosophy have been central elements of Chinese literature since ancient times. One writer to have transcended both time and place is the Taoist philosopher Lao-tzu. As the proverbs in his *Tao-te Ching* were transmitted orally for centuries, it is difficult to date his work or, indeed, to establish whether Lao-tzu (which can be translated as 'Old Master' or 'Old Masters') was an individual or a number of authors. First-century BCE accounts state that Lao-tzu was a contemporary of Confucius and that both lived around the sixth century BCE; however, many scholars date the *Tao-te Ching* to the fourth or third centuries BCE. Over the centuries, this work has influenced painters, calligraphers, poets and garden designers, not only in China but also in Japan, Korea, Vietnam and the West.

Japan is widely considered to have witnessed the creation of the world's first novel. *Genji monogatari* (Tale of Genji) was written in the eleventh century by a lady of the Japanese imperial court known as Murasaki Shikibu. The name 'Murasaki', taken from a character in the novel, was probably given to the lady by

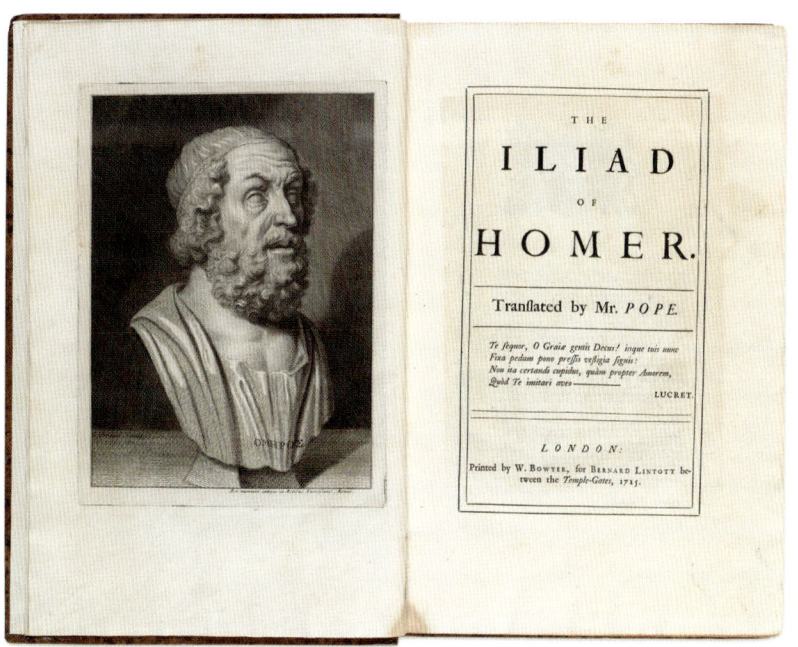

HOMER

Homer's epics have been translated into English since the seventeenth century. English poet and satirist Alexander Pope issued his translation of the *Iliad* in six parts between 1715 and 1720. It was a great commercial success, enabling Pope to survive on the proceeds of his writing alone. He followed this up in 1725–26 with a translation of the *Odyssey*, done in collaboration with William Broome and Elijah Fenton, both poets and Greek scholars. While perhaps more celebrated today for his own compositions, such as *The Rape of the Lock*, Pope regarded these translations of Homer's epics as among his greatest achievements.

ABOVE:
The Iliad of Homer
Translated by Alexander Pope
London, printed by W Bowyer for Bernard Lintott, 1715–20

OPPOSITE:
Murasaki Shikibu
Genji monogatari utaejo
(Poem and picture album of the Tale of Genji)
Manuscript concertina album, mid seventeenth century
Collection: Chester Beatty Library, Dublin

others at court. The Tale of Genji recounts the romantic adventures, both within and outside the court, of Prince Genji, a handsome and cultured son of the emperor. Its themes of love and lust, loyalty and family reveal much about attitudes to women, marriage and court life of the time, but the novel continues to speak to contemporary audiences through reinterpretations in film, opera and even *manga* (Japanese comics).

Around the time that the Tale of Genji was composed, another work that would endure for centuries was created in Persia. The *Rubáiyát of Omar Khayyám* is a collection of poems by astronomer, scientist and poet Omar Khayyám (1048–1131). 'Rubáiyát' derives from the Arabic word for 'four': all of the poems are quatrains, that is, four lines in length. The *Rubáiyát* was introduced to readers of English when writer Edward Fitzgerald published his translation in 1859; it has since been translated into a range of other languages.

Western literature traces much of its origins back to Ancient Greece: to the works of poets and playwrights such as Aeschylus, Sophocles, Euripides and Aristophanes, and to the epic poems of Homer, in particular. The *Iliad* and the *Odyssey* are epics in both scale and concern. Little is known of their author, or indeed whether the poems were composed by multiple authors. They are thought to have been written by a blind Greek poet who lived around the ninth or eighth centuries BCE. Drawn from earlier oral traditions, these accounts trace the final year of the Trojan War, in the *Iliad*, and the long journey home of its hero, Odysseus, in the *Odyssey*. The epics' universal themes—of the violence as well as the tedium of war, of love and loyalty, of good and evil—provided a basis for education in Ancient Greece, and they continue to be studied and enjoyed today.

In the first century BCE, Homer's epics inspired Virgil, regarded as Rome's greatest poet, to write his masterpiece the *Aeneid*. From the tale of Aeneas, a Trojan character in the *Iliad*, Virgil created his celebrated founding myth of the origins of Rome. Virgil's *Aeneid* would in turn inspire Dante to compose the work considered to be the foundation of Italian literature: *La Divina Commedia* (Divine Comedy). In this poem of a hundred cantos, written between 1306 and 1321

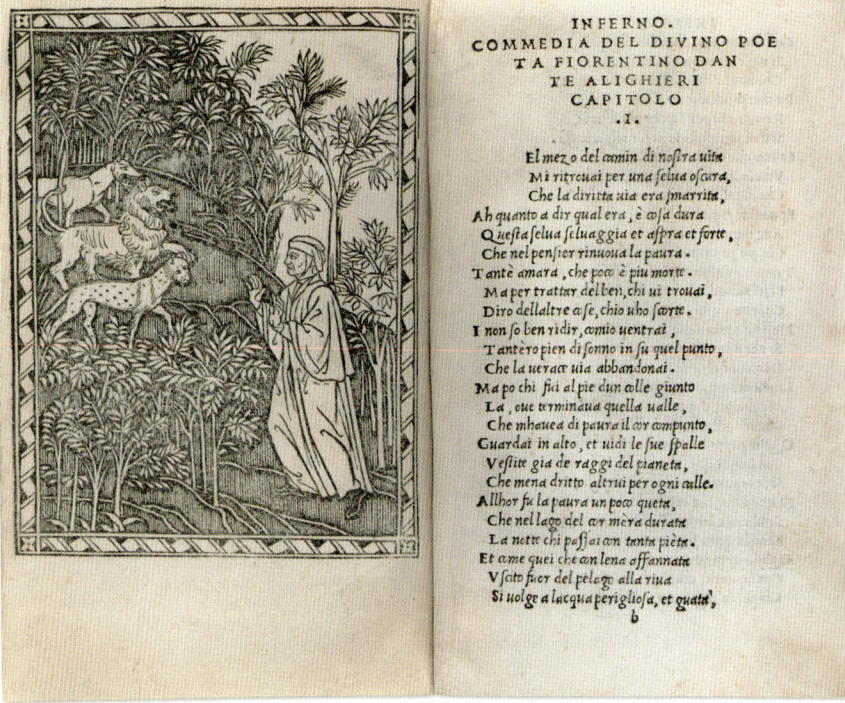

in vernacular Italian rather than Latin, Virgil acts as Dante's guide through hell and purgatory, after which Dante is guided through heaven by his dead lover, Beatrice. Dante's tale of the transience of human life, destiny and eternity paved the way for Italian as a literary language and heralded the work of Renaissance writers such as Petrarch and Boccaccio.

A pillar in the foundation of English literature is the epic poem *Beowulf*. Generally considered to have been composed in the eighth century, *Beowulf* is written in Old English. Its narrative is set around the sixth century and recounts the adventures of its eponymous hero as he travels through the Germanic lands of Scandinavia. This was a period of Anglo-Saxon migration to England, and it was the dialects of these peoples, together with Norse languages, from which Old English originated. Consisting of 3182 lines, *Beowulf*'s content is known from an untitled tenth-century manuscript now held by the British Library. *Beowulf* was championed by JRR Tolkien, and its influence can be seen in his writings, particularly *The Hobbit*. The story of *Beowulf* has also been adapted into a range of forms including comics, games, heavy metal music and a rock opera, and its hero has appeared in episodes of the television programs *Star Trek* and *Xena: Warrior Princess*.

The medieval period was a time of chivalry. Travelling musicians and troubadours of the courts sang and recited tales of knights bold, maidens fair and dragons slain. The most famous of these were the tales of King Arthur, who is believed to have lived around the fifth or sixth century. Myths and legends recounting the events of his life were transmitted orally until around the twelfth century, when the Arthurian romances were popularised by writers including Geoffrey of Monmouth in England and Chrétien de Troyes in France. But it was William Caxton's printing of Sir Thomas Malory's *Le Morte d'Arthur* in 1485 that made the tales of Arthur more widely known in the English-speaking world. Subsequent reinterpretations of the Arthurian legends have ranged from Alfred Tennyson's *Idylls of the King* (1859–85) and Richard Wagner's *Parsifal* (1882) to the 1960s musical and film *Camelot*.

Malory's *Morte d'Arthur* was just one of many literary works made popular in England by the introduction of printing there by Caxton in 1476. One of Caxton's first, and most significant, publications was Geoffrey Chaucer's *The Canterbury Tales*. Unfinished at the time of Chaucer's death in 1400, these often bawdy accounts of pilgrims on their way to Canterbury were, nonetheless, already popular in manuscript

ABOVE, LEFT:
Virgil
Opera
Venice, Augustinum de Zannis de Portesio, 1519

ABOVE, RIGHT:
Dante (Dante Alighieri)
Commedia di Dante
Florence, Filippo Giunti, 1506

OPPOSITE, TOP:
Geoffrey Chaucer
The Workes of Geffray Chaucer: Newly Printed, with Dyvers Workes Never in Print Before
London, T Godfray, 1532

OPPOSITE, BOTTOM:
Sir Thomas Malory
The Birth, Life and Acts of King Arthur … Le Morte d'Arthur …
London, JM Dent, 1927

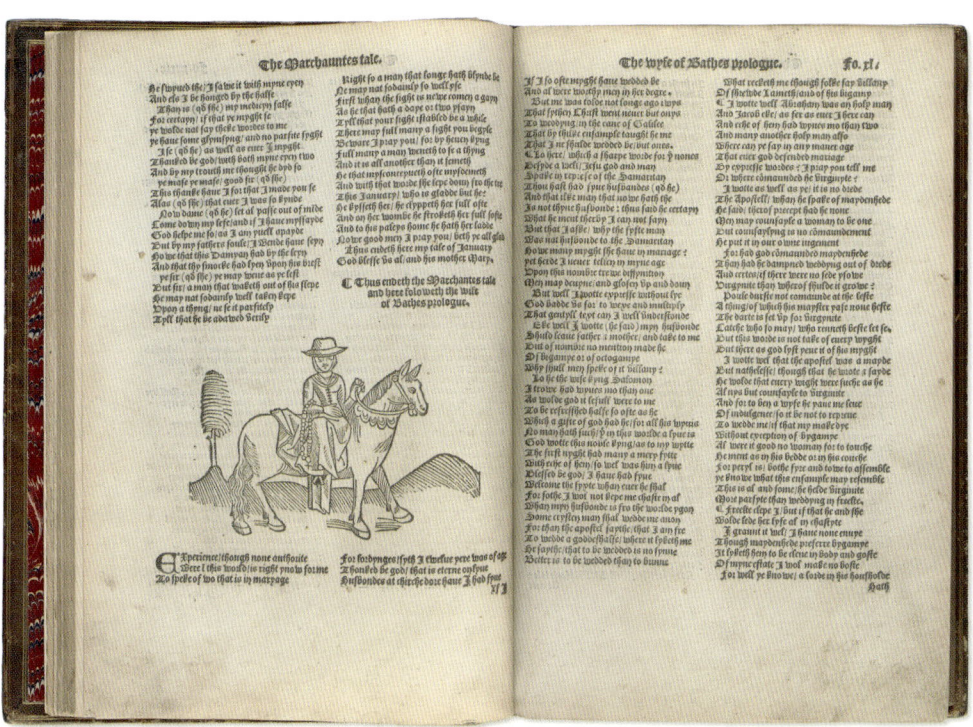

GEOFFREY CHAUCER

This volume was the first edition of Chaucer's collected works. The editor, William Thynne, was chief clerk of the kitchen of Henry VIII, a position that allowed him access to library collections across England to source the forty-one pieces selected for inclusion in the book. The woodcut illustrations throughout were reproduced from the same blocks used by William Caxton for his second edition of *The Canterbury Tales*, printed in 1483.

SIR THOMAS MALORY

JM Dent's deluxe edition of Malory's *Le Morte d'Arthur* was first published in 1893–94. It presents the text as it appeared in William Caxton's original printing of 1485 but with modern spelling applied. The work is richly decorated with full-page illustrations, borders and initials by Aubrey Beardsley, a relatively unknown young artist at the time.

SEBASTIAN BRANT

The *Ship of Fooles* was a bestseller. Originally published in German as *Das Narrenschiff* in 1494, then in Latin in 1497, this English edition was published in 1570. Sebastian Brant's poem, an allegory about fools on a ship bound for a 'fool's paradise', presents many human follies and vices as a warning to the general public to amend their ways. The woodcut illustrations made the work accessible to an illiterate audience, thereby ensuring a wide reception.

Sebastian Brant
Stultifera Navis …
The Ship of Fooles
London, John Cawood, 1570

The Ship of Fooles.

The earth, the sea, and euery thing of nought,
Yet of some fooles the cause hereof is sought,
Which labor also with curiositie,
To knowe the beginning of his diuinitie.

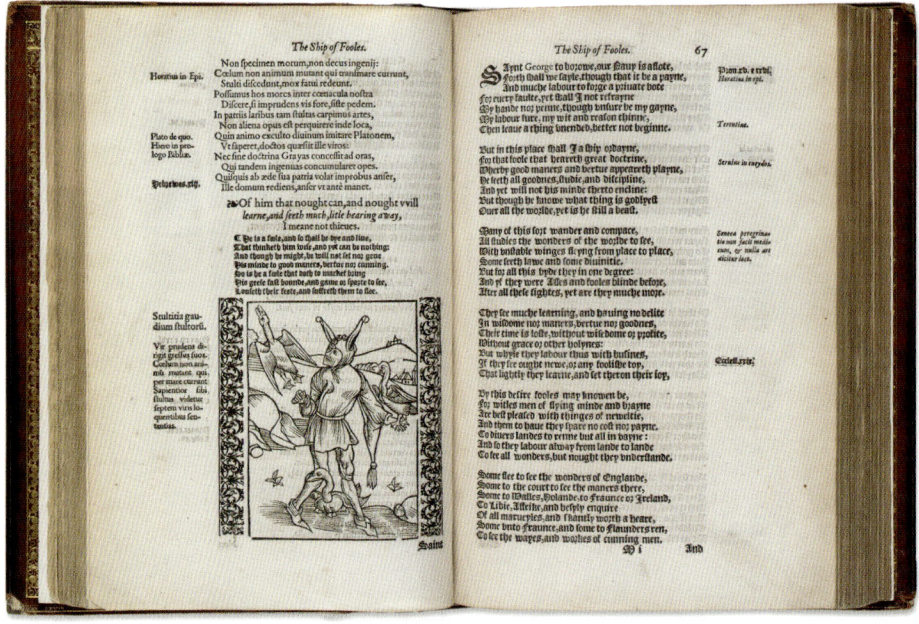

Miguel de Cervantes
Vida y Hechos del Ingenioso Cavallero Don Quixote de la Mancha
Amberes, Geronymo & Juan Bautista Verdussen, 1672–73

form by the time Caxton published his printed version. Written in Middle English, Chaucer's tales have always had broad appeal through their use of humour and their themes of love, greed, deception and the foibles of human nature.

Miguel de Cervantes's *Don Quixote* is often referred to as one of the first modern novels. Published in two parts (1605 and 1615), *Don Quixote* is the tale of small-time landowner Alonso Quixano. Quixano convinces himself that he is the knight Don Quixote as he travels through peasant Spain with his longsuffering companion Sancho Panza. A satire of chivalric life, *Don Quixote*'s great popularity helped establish the modern Spanish language and has remained in print ever since. It has inspired not only other writers but also artists such as Pablo Picasso and the composer Richard Strauss, as well as giving us expressions such as 'quixotic' and 'tilting at windmills'.

The Elizabethan era of the sixteenth century was a period in which the literary arts flourished. Poetry and drama, in particular, developed in the hands of writers such as Edmund Spenser, Sir Philip Sidney and Christopher Marlowe. No other writer, however, would alter the course of Western literature more than William Shakespeare. The scope of his output, generally accepted by scholars today to be thirty-eight plays, 154 sonnets and other poems, is disproportionate to his enormous influence. While his plays' themes of love, betrayal, family ties and power are universal, it is in the development of the English language that Shakespeare has had the greatest impact. He introduced thousands of new words and phrases, such as 'budge an inch', 'ill-tuned' and 'what the dickens'. Western literature would go on to have its Goethes and Voltaires, its Swifts and Wordsworths, its Austens and Whitmans, its Joyces and Steins. But none would usurp Shakespeare's place in the literary canon. To quote his contemporary Ben Jonson, Shakespeare 'was not of an age, but for all time'.

WILLIAM SHAKESPEARE

The First Folio of Shakespeare's plays was published in 1623, seven years after his death. It was compiled from unauthorised versions by John Heminge and Henry Condell, two actors of the King's Men company of actors, to which Shakespeare had also belonged. The First Folio remains the only surviving source from the time for many of Shakespeare's plays. This Second Folio, published in 1632, included John Milton's first published poem, 'An Epitaph on the Admirable Dramaticke Poet, W. SHAKESPEARE', which appeared anonymously. The well-known portrait of Shakespeare, included as a frontispiece to the first and subsequent folios, was made by artist Martin Droeshout.

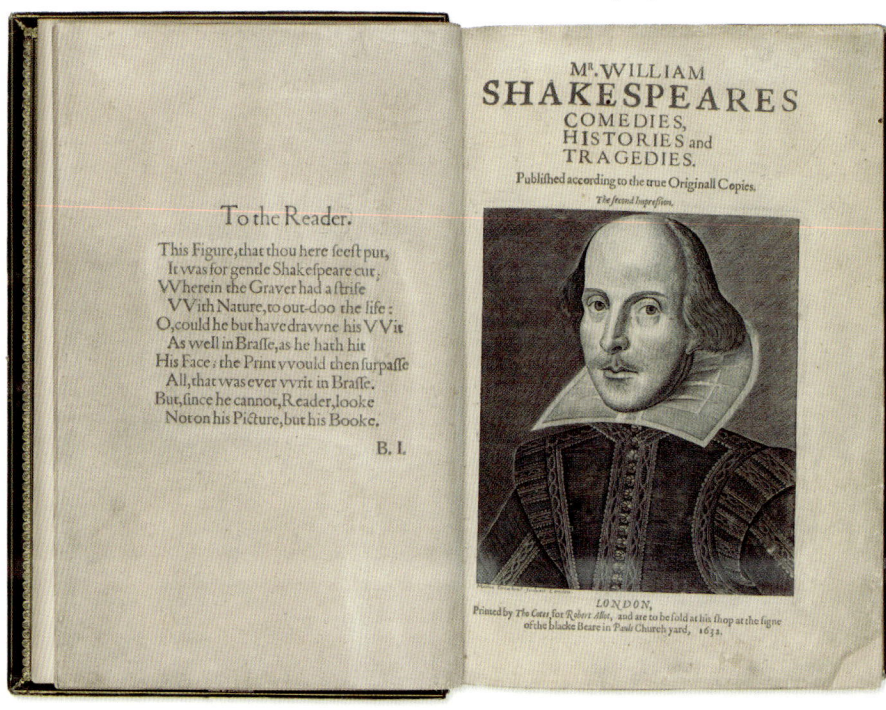

William Shakespeare
Mr William Shakespeares Comedies, Histories and Tragedies. Published According to the True Originall Copies, the Second Impression
London, Tho. Cotes for Robert Allot, 1632

JOHN MILTON

John Milton's epic poem about man's fall from grace and the battle between God and Satan was first published in 1667. The 11 000-line poem originally comprised ten books, but by the second edition of 1674 Milton had revised and restructured the poem into twelve books. At the urging of his publisher, the second edition also included prose arguments at the head of each book to assist the reader. The 1688 edition shown here was the first to be illustrated and included dramatic full-page engravings to introduce each book.

John Milton
Paradise Lost: a Poem in Twelve Books
London, printed by Miles Flesher for Richard Bently and Jacob Tonson, 1688

OPPOSITE:
Detail of *Paradise Lost*

Imaginary VOYAGES

I could frequently distinguish the Word Yahoo, which was repeated by each of them several times; and altho' it was impossible for me to conjecture what it meant; yet while the two Horses were busy in Conversation, I endeavoured to practice this Word upon my Tongue.
JONATHAN SWIFT, *GULLIVER'S TRAVELS*

LONG BEFORE THE SOUTHERN HEMISPHERE WAS CHARTED, IT WAS A PLACE FOR THE IMAGINATION. WHEN THE GREEK GEOGRAPHER PTOLEMY, WRITING IN THE SECOND CENTURY CE, POSITED THE THEORY OF A GREAT SOUTHERN CONTINENT TO COUNTERBALANCE THE WEIGHT OF THE LANDMASSES IN THE NORTHERN HEMISPHERE, HE UNWITTINGLY CREATED A LITERARY SPACE FOR STRANGE CREATURES, MONSTERS AND CIVILISATIONS THAT INVERTED THE NATURAL ORDER. THE ONE-EYED, HEADLESS OR BIG-FOOTED BEINGS THAT INHABIT THE PAGES OF THE NUREMBERG CHRONICLE (1493) RESIDED IN THE DARKEST CORNERS OF THE IMAGINATION, A WORLD OF MYTH AND TRAVELLERS' TALES BEYOND THE THEN KNOWN WORLD.

The cartographers and mapmakers of the fifteenth and sixteenth centuries depicted this vast southern continent as lying to the south of Africa and the Americas, and spanning the Pacific and Indian oceans. In Abraham Ortelius's world atlas of 1570, *Theatrum Orbis Terrarum*, it is called 'Terra Australis Nondum Cognita', though on other contemporary maps it is more commonly shown as 'Terra Australis Incognita'. Is it any wonder that its presence proved a fertile breeding ground for fiction writers? To them it was like a blank canvas, giving free rein to the imagination.

The literary genre of 'imaginary voyages' to the southern oceans first began to appear in the early seventeenth century, in the wake of the great sea voyages of Sir Francis Drake, Thomas Cavendish and others. The genre remained popular with readers through to the end of the eighteenth century, when the voyages of James Cook forever laid to rest the belief in a great southern landmass other than New Holland, first charted by the Dutch in the 1600s. Jonathan Swift's *Travels into Several Remote Nations of the World* (1726), or *Gulliver's Travels*, remains the best known of the many fictional accounts set in the southern oceans, his island of Lilliput being situated somewhere in present-day South Australia.

In many cases, these fictions were little more than thinly disguised attacks on political systems in Europe. By using the convention of the shipwrecked sailor who finds himself washed up on unknown shores, a writer was free to plead openly the virtues of an alternative society encountered there, even if it just so happened that its political systems and moral orders inverted the natural state of things back home.

The earliest imaginary account set in *Terra Australis Incognita* is Bishop Joseph Hall's *Mundus Alter et Idem*, published anonymously in Latin in 1605. It tells the story of an Englishman, Mercurius Britannicus, and his travels through the four main regions of the newly discovered *Terra Australis*: Crapulia, the land of gluttons and drunkards; Lavernia, the land of thieves; Fooliana, the land of fools; and Viraginia, the land of women. Hall's *Mundus* is a satirical attack on the ordered world of London society, and is believed to have influenced Swift's *Gulliver's Travels*.

LEFT:
Hartmann Schedel
Liber Chronicarum (Nuremberg Chronicle)
Nuremberg, Anton Koberger, 1493

BELOW:
Joseph Hall
Mundus Alter et Idem, Sive Terra Australis Antehac Semper Incognita
Utrecht, Joannem à Waesberge, 1643

The Travels of Don Francisco de Quevedo: Through Terra Australis Incognita (1684) purported to be a translation of an old Spanish manuscript, in which all that remained of the author's name was Don Q–. In fact, it was a cheap, pirated adaptation of Hall's *Mundus*. Such use of anonymous or vague authorship, or fictitious details, on the title pages of imaginary voyages was common, and protected authors from political reprisal.

Zaccaria Seriman's *Viaggi di Enrico Wanton alle Terre Incognite Australi* (Voyage of Enrico Wanton to Terra Australis Incognita), first published in Venice in 1749, recounts the voyage of an Englishman, Henry Wanton, to an unknown Austral land. There, he comes across a highly refined society of monkeys who share all of the trappings of civilised Europe. The book's claim to having been translated from the English is false, and to this date there has never been an English edition of the work. The book's Spanish translator, Joaquin de Guzmán y Manrique, took it upon himself in 1778 to add two entirely new volumes to Seriman's original story, satirising Spanish customs and manners.

Many imaginary voyages drew upon real accounts for their veracity. Peter Longueville's *The Hermit, or, the Unparalled Sufferings and Surprising Adventures of Mr Philip Quarll, an Englishman* (1727) sees its hero shipwrecked on a small island off the coast of Mexico for more than fifty years. Immensely popular with the English reading public, it borrowed shamelessly from the published accounts of William Dampier, as well as Daniel Defoe's *The Life and Strange Surprizing Adventures of Robinson Crusoe* (1719). Defoe's novel had been influenced by an earlier fiction, Henry Neville's *The Isle of Pines, or, a Late Discovery of a Fourth Island near Terra Australis* (1668). Neville's imaginary voyage recounts the

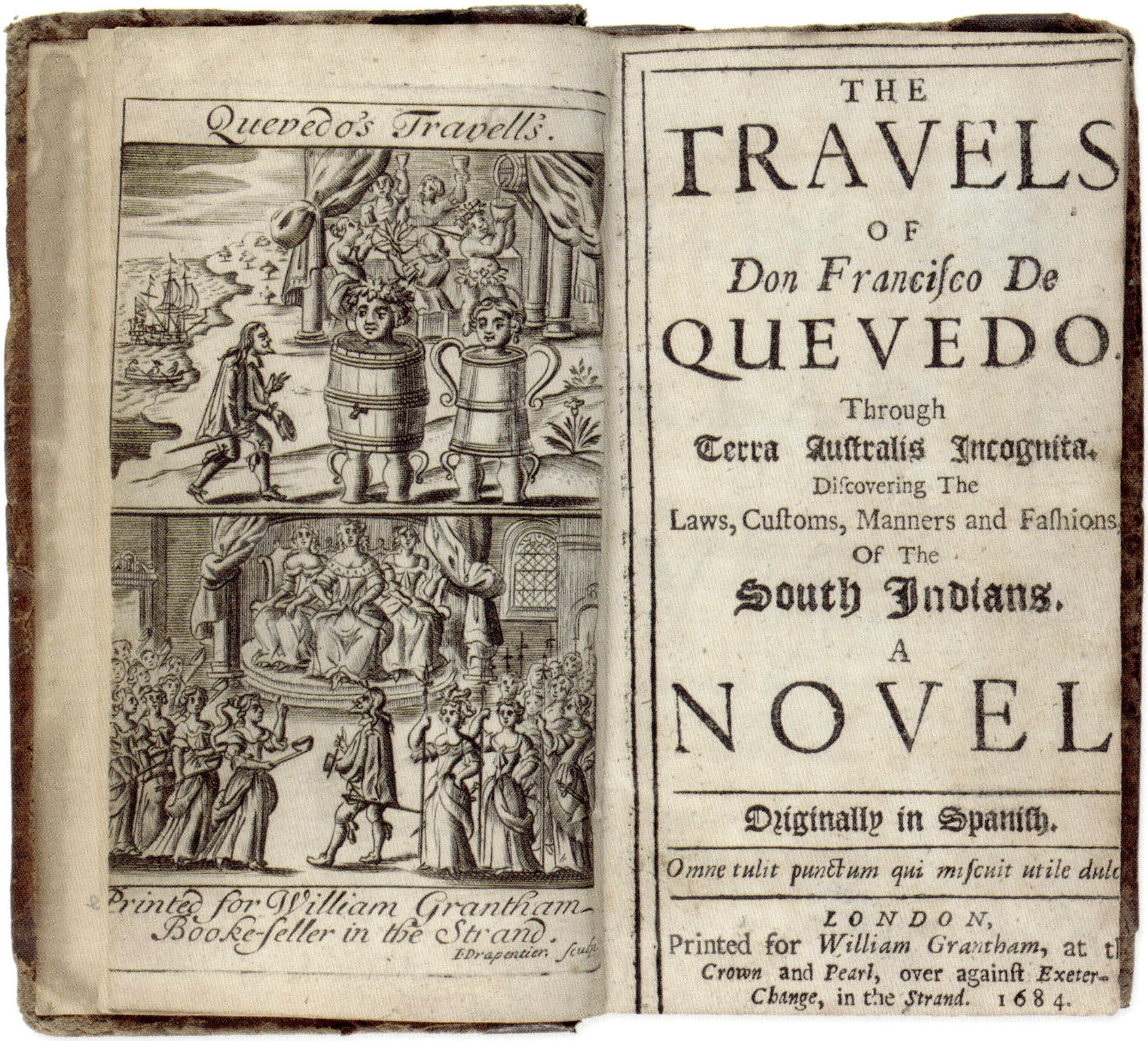

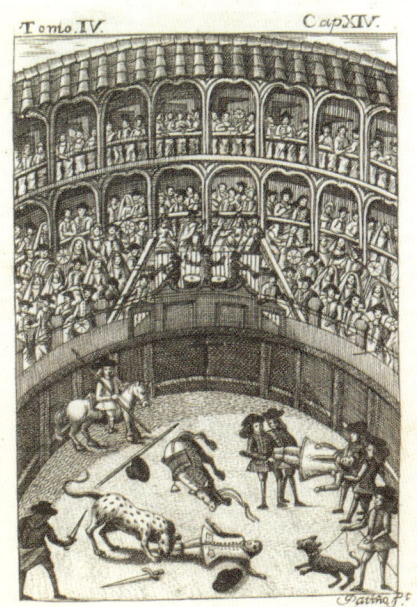

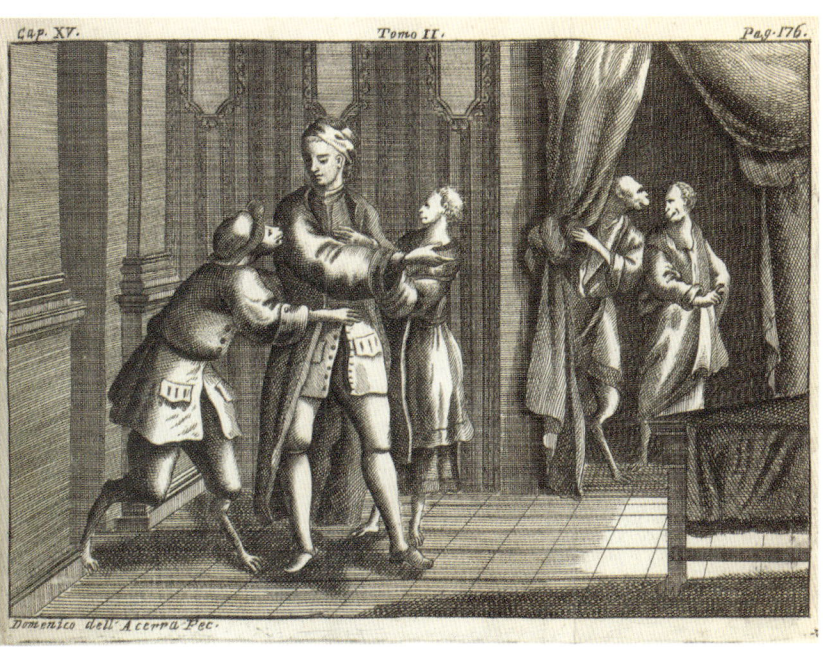

THE
TRAVELS
OF
Don Francisco De
QUEVEDO
Through
Terra Australis Incognita.
Discovering The
Laws, Customs, Manners and Fashions
Of The
South Indians.
A
NOVEL
Originally in Spanish.
Omne tulit punctum qui miscuit utile dulc
LONDON,
Printed for William Grantham, at t
Crown and Pearl, over against Exeter-
Change, in the Strand. 1684.

The Travels of Don Francisco de Quevedo: through Terra Australis Incognita
London, printed for William Grantham, 1684

FAR LEFT:
Zaccaria Seriman
Viaggi di Enrico Wanton a las Tierras Incognitas Australes
Madrid, Don Antonio de Sancha, 1778

LEFT:
Zaccaria Seriman
Viaggi di Enrico Wanton alle Terre Incognita Australi
Naples, Presso Alessio Pellecchia, 1756

RIGHT:
Peter Longueville
The Hermit, or, the Unparalled Sufferings and Surprising Adventures of Mr Philip Quarll, an Englishman
Westminster, T Warner and B Creake, 1727

BELOW:
Henry Neville
The Isle of Pines, or, a Late Discovery of a Fourth Island near Terra Australis
London, printed for Allen Banks and Charles Harper, 1668

story of the shipwrecked George Pine, who along with four women, is cast away on an island near the coast of *Terra Australis Incognita*. Within fifty-nine years, a flourishing community of 1789 descendants resides on the island, but this sudden influx of population sees Pine's original paradise descending into disorder.

Gabriel de Foigny's *La Terra Australe Connue* (1676) has shipwrecked sailor Jacques Sadeur plucked from the sea by a winged monster and dropped onto the shores of *Terra Australis*, a land of 'fourscore and 16 millions' population situated between South America and South Africa. Foigny's 'Australiens' are hermaphrodites who have abolished sexual relations altogether. Sadeur, by good fortune a hermaphrodite himself, is accepted into their community after being found naked upon its shores. Having rejected the pleasures of the body, the society Sadeur encounters appears rational and harmonious. The fact that author Foigny was himself a defrocked priest with a history of sexual miscon-

duct no doubt says much about the novel's underlying themes. It is also notable that the earliest English translation of Foigny's work, published in 1693, anglicised 'Terre Australe' to 'Australia' and its inhabitants 'Australiens' to 'Australians', the first recorded use of these terms.

Denis Vairasse d'Allais's *L'Histoire des Severambes* makes reference to seventeenth-century Dutch landings on the west coast of Australia, including the wreck of the *Vergulde Draeck* there in 1656. The fictional Captain Siden sails on that ship, but the subsequent fate of the 380 shipwrecked castaways mirrors François Pelsaert's brutal account of the wreck of the *Batavia* on the Abrolhos Islands, off the west Australian coastline, in 1629. The first part was published anonymously in English in 1675, prior to the full work appearing in French in 1677–79. The author's preface claimed the account to be factual, based on papers given to him by Captain Sidens on his deathbed, and early readers and reviewers seem to have been taken in by it. *Severambes* influenced

Gabriel de Foigny
Sehr Curiöse Reise-Beschreibung Durch das-Neu-Entdeckte Südland
Dresden, Johann Jacob Wincklern, 1704
A German edition of Foigny's account of the adventures of shipwrecked sailor Jacques Sadeur.

Swift's *Gulliver's Travels* and, in an odd twist, appeared in 1727 in an English translation as a third volume to Swift's novel, published the previous year.

The anonymous *Voyage de Robertson aux Terres Australes* (1766) also mined factual sources. The fictitious author Robertson claims to have sailed with Francis Drake to South America on the *Elizabeth* in 1585. Put in charge of a small cutter and seeking landfall, he is blown off course during a storm and discovers a new continent, Australia, to the west of Chile, peopled by a virtuous society. In fact the work was an attack on the French government of the day, and is said to have inspired William Penn to found an ideal society in North America.

Simon Tyssot de Patot's *Voyages et Avantures de Jacques Masse* (c. 1714) is also set off the coast of Chile, where sailor Masse is shipwrecked on a southern continent 60 degrees longitude and 44 degrees latitude. Travelling inland he discovers a peaceful and organised utopia, a *Terra Australis* described as 'a plentiful fruitful country, a land of blessing and peace'. The early editions of the work are famed for their fictitious title pages, with five separate editions all carrying a date of 1710, though in all likelihood none was printed in that year. Tyssot de Patot was a Huguenot freethinker who lived much of his life in the Netherlands, and his work openly criticised the Christian Church and its beliefs. By predating the book's real publication, the publisher helped insulate himself against possible reprisal for the book's anti-religious sentiments, in effect claiming it had been in the public domain for several years already.

Perhaps the strangest imaginary voyage set in the southern oceans is Restif de la Bretonne's *La Découverte Australe par un Homme-Volant* (1781) or 'The discovery of Australia by a flying man'. Restif de la Bretonne's work describes an imaginary voyage by flying machine to a fictitious Australia. The hero of the novel, Victorin, travels to the land of Metapatagonia, an antipodean world where everything turns out to be a mirror image of Europe: the language is back-to-front French, and inhabitants wear hats in the shape of shoes. A prolific writer and well-known shoe fetishist, Restif de la Bretonne published more than two hundred works, many based on his own libertine life. He was reviled as a pornographer in his day, and his books earned him the epithets 'the Rousseau of the gutter' and 'the Voltaire of the chambermaids'.

From the time it first appeared on the charts of early mapmakers, the land of *Terra Australis Incognita* proved itself to be a fertile place for the speculative dreams and utopias of European writers. After the great voyages of Captain Cook in the late eighteenth century, there remained little of the Southern Hemisphere left for the European literary imagination. Later writers such as Jules Verne turned their imagination elsewhere—to the moon, the centre of the earth, or under the sea, giving rise to literary genres such as science fiction and fantasy.

LEFT:
Nicolas Edmé Restif de la Bretonne
La Découverte Australe par un Homme-Volant
Leipzig, et se trouvé à Paris, 1781

OPPOSITE:
Denis Vairasse d'Allais
Historie der Sevarambes
Amsterdam, Timotheus ten Hoorn, 1682

the Waves
Virginia Woolf

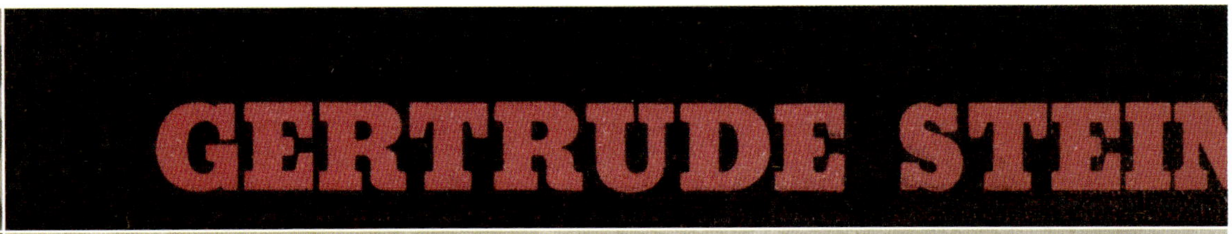
GERTRUDE STEIN

WYNDHAM
LEWIS

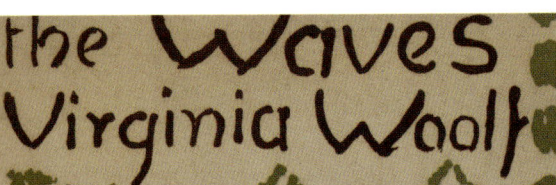

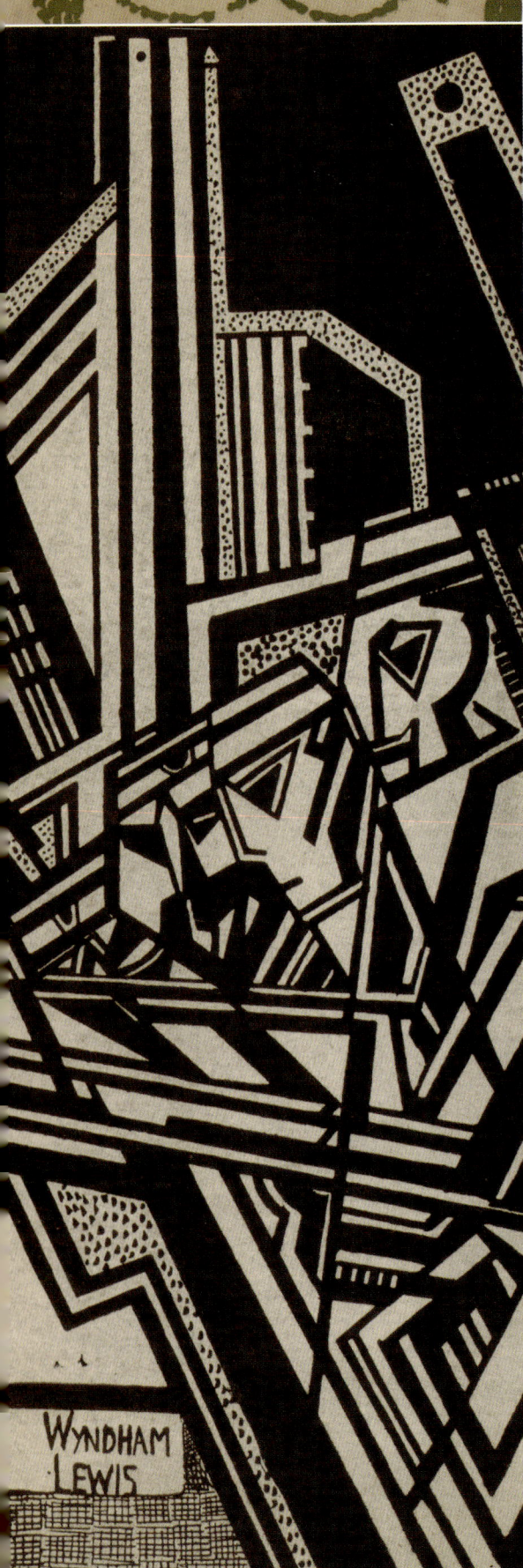

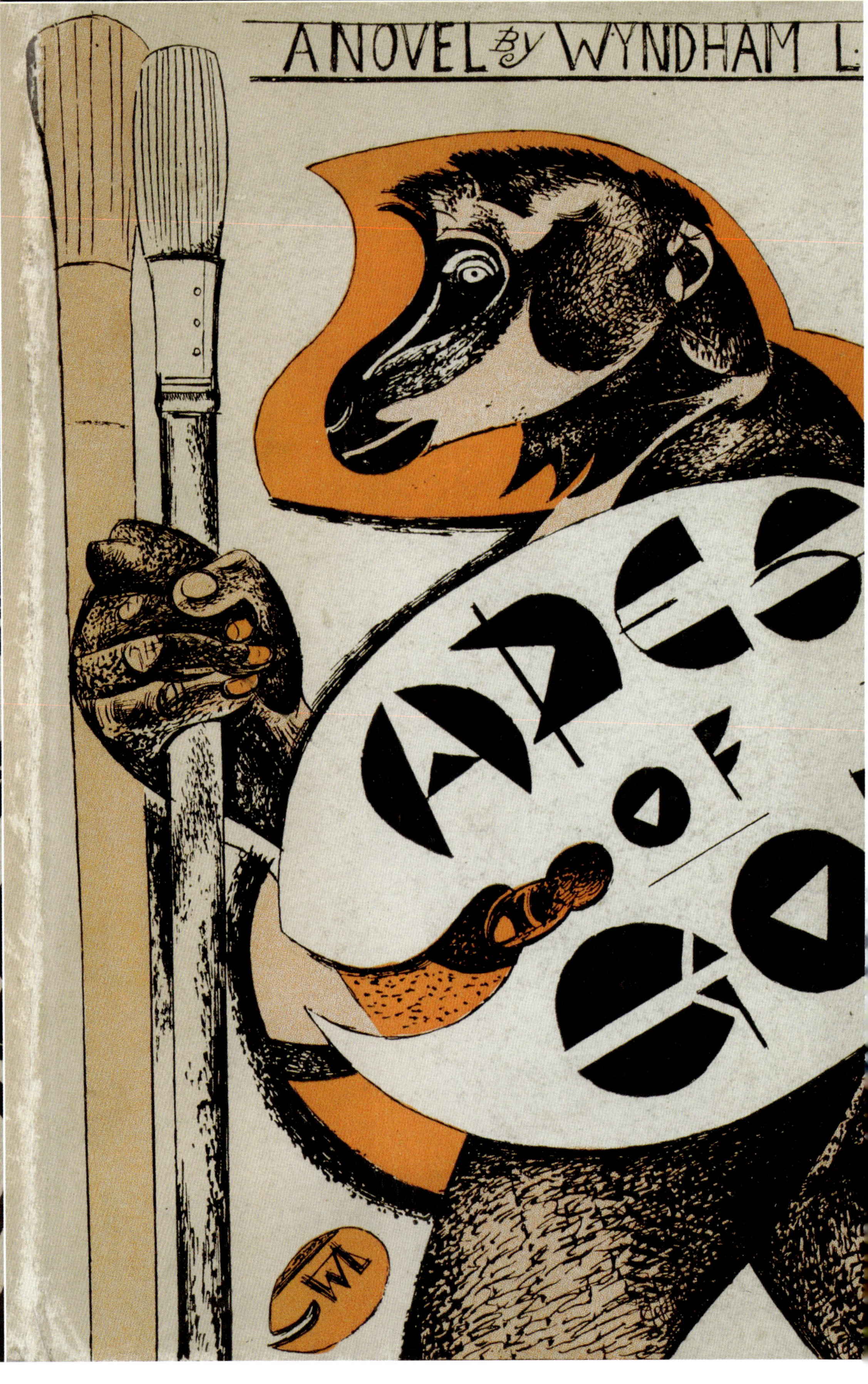
A NOVEL By WYNDHAM
APES
OF

The Modernist EXPERIMENT: Joyce and His Circle

I can't go on. I'll go on. SAMUEL BECKETT, *THE UNNAMABLE*

THE EXTRAORDINARY SOCIAL CHANGES BROUGHT ABOUT BY INDUSTRIALISATION AND URBANISATION IN THE LATE NINETEENTH CENTURY SET THE SCENE FOR A DRAMATIC REVOLUTION IN THE ARTS. PAINTERS SUCH AS PAUL CÉZANNE, GEORGES-PIERRE SEURAT, CAMILLE PISSARRO AND OTHERS BEGAN QUESTIONING THE PREVAILING REALISM OF THE TIME, OFFERING INSTEAD A PERSPECTIVE THAT WAS BOTH SUBJECTIVE AND UNCERTAIN. THEIR PAINTERLY INSIGHTS PAVED THE WAY FOR THE RADICAL EXPERIMENTS IN COLOUR AND FORM INITIATED BY PABLO PICASSO AND HENRI MATISSE IN THE FIRST DECADE OF THE TWENTIETH CENTURY.

While imaginative literature initially lagged behind these innovations, it would emerge from the bloodied trenches of World War I radically altered. In the face of such unimaginable destruction and loss of life, literature would rarely again speak in a unified voice. In future, poets and writers would look as much to Friedrich Nietzsche's dictum 'God is dead' or to Sigmund Freud's 'royal road to the unconscious' as they previously had to the nineteenth-century realism of Charles Dickens or Honoré de Balzac.

Almost a century after it was first issued in 1914, Wyndham Lewis's *Blast* magazine still looks strikingly modern. With its daring approach to design and typography, it was intended by Lewis as a shot across the bow of literary romanticism. In its place, *Blast* offered what he termed 'the Poetry which is the as yet unexpressed spirit of the present time, and of new conditions and possibilities of life'. The prevailing sense of futility that followed the traumatic events of World War I gave rise to a wave of literature that rejected the logical arrangement of ideas and narrative, instead favouring juxtaposition, repetition, collage and fragmentation. Lewis's own bitterness and antipathy towards London's cultural establishment would later manifest itself in his satirical novel *The Apes of God* (1930), a thinly veiled attack on the Bloomsbury group, among others, that caused a furor in literary and artistic circles.

The work that forever changed the landscape of English poetry, TS Eliot's 'The Waste Land', first appeared in October 1922 in the inaugural issue of the London literary magazine *The Criterion*. It appeared in the American magazine *Dial* the following month. The original manuscript of eight hundred lines was edited by Eliot's friend Ezra Pound, and Eliot subsequently dedicated it to him. Loosely structured around the legend of the Holy Grail, the 433-line poem expressed the disillusionment and sense of hopelessness that prevailed in postwar London. It was issued in book form in 1923 in Britain by Leonard and Virginia Woolf at their Hogarth Press in an edition of 450 copies with the text handset by Virginia.

The Hogarth Press, set up by the Woolfs in 1917, championed a number of modernist writers.

Over a thirty-year period, the press issued some five hundred titles, including the work of Gertrude Stein, TS Eliot, Katherine Mansfield, Vita Sackville-West and Sigmund Freud. The Hogarth Press also published Virginia's own books, many featuring dust-jacket designs by her sister Vanessa Bell. Her novels, beginning with *The Voyage Out* in 1915, and her many essays distinguished her as a tireless experimenter with literary form as well as a social commentator. Her essay 'A Room of One's Own' (1929), with its simple statement 'a woman must have money and a room if she is to write fiction' would become a mantra for later feminist writers. In her novels *To the Lighthouse* (1927) and *The Waves* (1931), Woolf dispensed with linear narrative altogether, embracing instead the interiority of her characters' lives.

If there was a big bang of literary modernism, then it came with the publication of James Joyce's *Ulysses*, the plot of which takes place on a single day in Dublin, 16 June 1904. After having been turned down by other publishers, *Ulysses* was issued by Sylvia Beach, American owner of the Paris bookshop Shakespeare and Company. She published it in Paris in February 1922, in an edition of a thousand copies. The first British edition, from the Egoist Press, was issued in London later that same year in an edition of two thousand copies, of which a thousand were destined for the United States. Due to the novel's explicit sexual content, its initial reception was marred by censorship. Five hundred copies of the Egoist Press edition were burned by New York post office authorities. The press issued a further five hundred in 1923, of which 499 were seized by British customs authorities. The work remained banned in the United States and the United Kingdom until 1934 and 1936 respectively.

BELOW, LEFT:
Wyndham Lewis
Apes of God
London, Arthur Press, 1930

BELOW, MIDDLE:
TS (Thomas Stearns) Eliot
The Waste Land
London, printed and published at the Hogarth Press, 1923

BELOW, RIGHT:
Virginia Woolf
The Waves
London, Hogarth Press, 1931

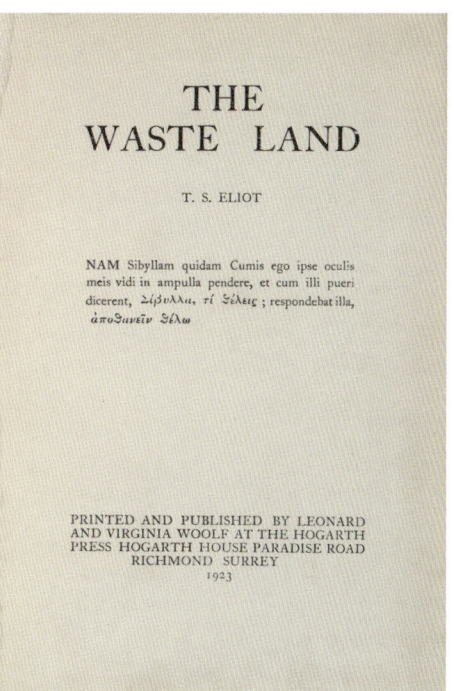

OPPOSITE:
Wyndham Lewis, editor
Blast: a Review of the Great English Vortex
no. 2
London, John Lane, 1915

ULYSSES

BY

JAMES JOYCE

OPPOSITE AND BELOW, LEFT:
James Joyce
Ulysses
Paris, Shakespeare and Company, 1922
Copy number 25 of the special issue of a hundred copies of the first edition printed on Dutch handmade paper and signed by Joyce

Joyce's next work, an ambitious project he first called *Work in Progress*, would push the boundaries of literary experimentation even further. The first episode, *King Roderick O'Conor*, was drafted by Joyce in March 1923; subsequent fragments and episodes were published over the next fifteen years in avant-garde magazines, such as Eugene and Maria Jolas's *Transition*, and as booklets *Anna Livia Plurabelle* (1930) and *Haveth Childers Everywhere* (1930). Negative feedback on the work, including from friends such as Ezra Pound, led Joyce to encourage supporters to publish a book of essays in its defence. The 1929 publication *Our Exagmination Round his Factification for Incamination of Work in Progress* included essays arguing the work's merits by Samuel Beckett and William Carlos Williams. Beckett's essay 'Dante...Bruno.Vico..Joyce', his first published work, set out the principal tenet of modernist literature: 'what is said in it is indissolubly linked with the manner in which it is said, and cannot be said any other way'. Joyce's novel was finally completed in 1938 and published the following year as *Finnegan's Wake*, his last and most complex book.

Though never achieving Joyce's literary fame, the American Gertrude Stein's radical prose pieces were, in their own way, the equal of Joyce's experiments. In place of Joyce's linguistic virtuosity, she laid emphasis on syntax and rhythm. She rejected standard literary structures and instead used repetition and abstraction to record what she called a 'continuous present'. Stein settled in Paris in 1904, and her salon at 27 Rue de Fleurus became a haven for avant-garde artists and writers of the day, including Georges Braque, Guillaume Apollinaire and, later, Ezra Pound and Ernest Hemingway. She came up with the term 'Lost Generation' to describe the expatriate Americans living in Paris at the time. Her *Portraits and Prayers* (1934) is a collection of 'word-portraits' of members of her Paris circle including Paul Cézanne, Henri Matisse, Pablo Picasso and Erik Satie. Stein's 'portraits' were the literary equivalent of cubist paintings, her fragmentary and repetitive phrases evocations of her own experience of her subjects rather than recognisable depictions of the individuals themselves.

According to Joyce biographer Richard Ellmann, Stein and Joyce met only once, at a party given in Paris by Eugene Jolas. The two, it turned out, had little to say to one another. Stein is said to have been annoyed at the fuss made in literary circles upon publication of *Ulysses*. She had composed her own experimental masterwork *The Making of Americans* some years before the appearance of Joyce's book. But her nearly thousand-page novel was not finally published until 1925, three years after *Ulysses*, when Robert McAlmon's Contact Editions issued it in Paris in an edition of five hundred copies. Stein purposely drew attention to the novel's true place in the modernist timeline by adding a statement to the title page to the effect: 'Written by Gertrude Stein 1906–1908'. *The Making of Americans* was not officially published in the United States until 1934, and only then in a heavily truncated version. Despite her pioneering style and the influence she exerted on a number of Paris-based writers of the period, in particular the early stories

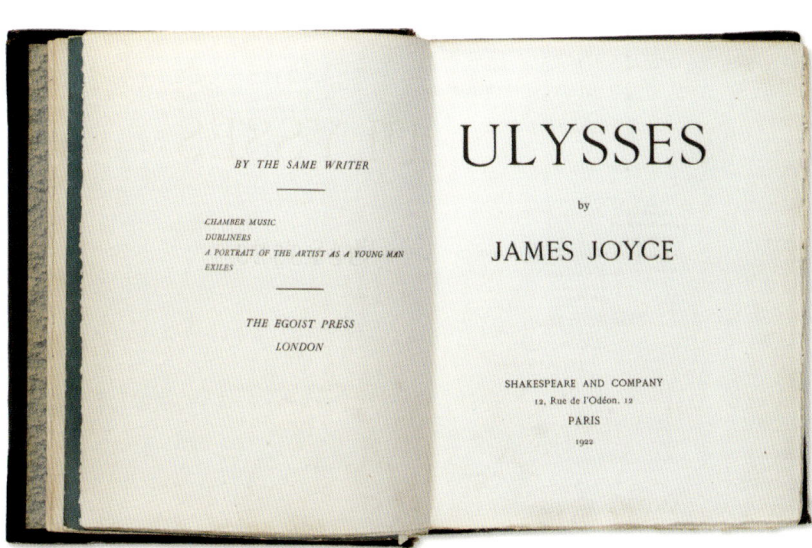
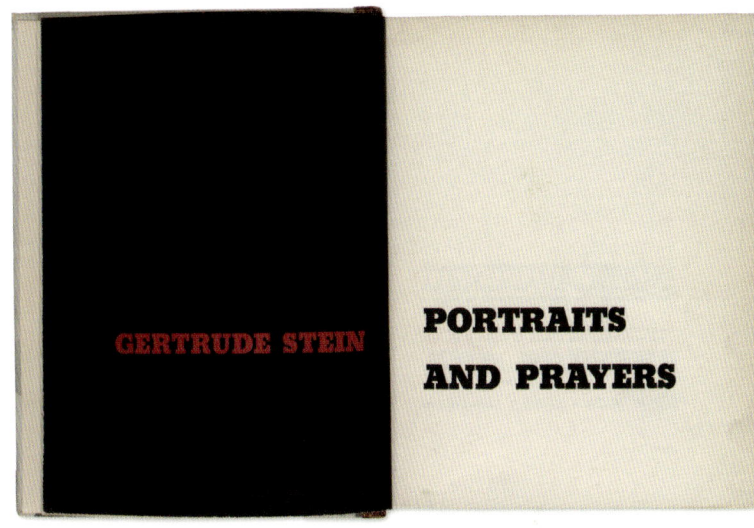
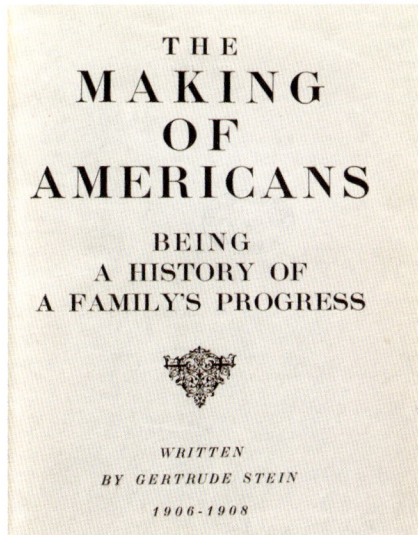

ABOVE:
Gertrude Stein
The Making of Americans
Paris, Contact Editions, 1925

ABOVE, RIGHT:
Gertrude Stein
Portraits and Prayers
New York, Random House, 1934

RIGHT:
Ezra Pound
*Section: Rock–Drill
85–95 de los Cantares*
London, Faber and Faber, 1957

FAR RIGHT:
Ezra Pound
The Cantos
London, Faber and Faber, 1954

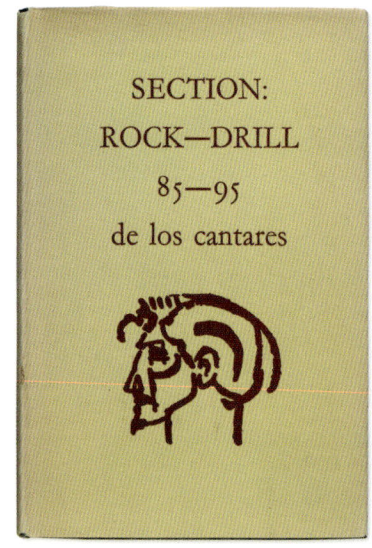
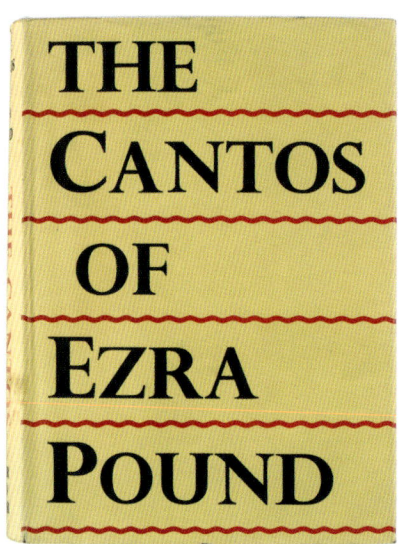

and novels of Ernest Hemingway, Stein remains best known for the relatively conventional *Autobiography of Alice B Toklas*, her only genuine bestseller, and for her immortal phrase 'a rose is a rose is a rose is a rose'.

When critic Hugh Kenner first met the American poet Ezra Pound in St Elizabeth's Hospital in Washington in 1948, he said of the experience, 'I suddenly knew that I was in the presence of the center of modernism'. Kenner had already begun a doctorate on Joyce, but after meeting Pound and reading his *Pisan Cantos*, he decided he had found a more interesting subject. Kenner's assessment of Pound's role in the early development of modernism was accurate, for here was a man who had founded the Imagist movement in London in 1910, who had first coined the term 'vortex' to describe the English art and literary scene, who had edited the first drafts of Eliot's 'The Waste Land', who had brokered the serialisation of Joyce's *Ulysses* in Margaret Anderson's *Little Review* magazine, and who had actively championed and assisted the careers of so many other writers, including William Carlos Williams, HD (Hilda Doolittle), Marianne Moore and Robert Frost. For more than thirty years, Pound laboured on his epic poem *The Cantos*, issued in books from the 1920s through to the 1960s. His later fame was tarnished by a series of broadcasts he made during World War II from Italy, where he had moved in 1924, in support of Mussolini. The broadcasts led to his eventual arrest on charges of treason, but back in the United States he was deemed unfit to face trial on grounds of insanity and was instead incarcerated at St Elizabeth's Hospital from 1946 to 1958. Upon his release, he returned to Italy, declaring the United States to be a 'lunatic asylum'. Like Joyce's *Finnegan's Wake*, Pound's *Cantos* stand at the peak of modernist literature, begging the question: where to from here?

If there is a defining writer who straddles modernism and postmodernism, it is Samuel Beckett. The stark landscape that Vladimir and Estragon awake to in *Waiting for Godot* heralds a new age. Beckett had first met James Joyce in Paris in 1928, and the two became close friends. Joyce's influence on the young writer can be seen clearly in Beckett's early fictional works *More Pricks than Kicks* (1934) and *Murphy* (1938). But Beckett's decision in the 1940s to turn his back on the rich rhetoric of his native Irish tongue and compose his works in French freed him from the shadow of Joyce. Henceforth, he would write without style, slowly stripping away the layers of meaning from the world around him until all that was left was silence. Regardless of the uncertainty Joyce, Woolf, Pound, Stein and Eliot brought to literature, it still took a measure of surety and belief to erect the great edifices of modernism: *Ulysses*, 'The Waste Land', *The Cantos*. When Vladimir and Estragon utter their final words, it is clear that the last vestiges of that certainty have vanished forever:

Vladimir: Well? Shall we go?
Estragon: Yes, let's go.
They do not move.

Samuel Beckett
Waiting for Godot
London, Faber and Faber, 1956

Samuel Beckett
Imagination Dead Imagine
London, Calder and Boyars, 1965

Murder COMPLETE AND UNABRIDGED

PENGUIN BOOKS

THE PLEASANTNESS AT THE [BEL]LONA CLUB

D[O]ROTHY L. SAYERS

THE CORONATION OF HAILE SELASSIE

EVELYN WAUGH

70

The PAPERBACK Revolution

The Penguin books are splendid value for sixpence, so splendid that if the other publishers had any sense they would combine against them and suppress them.

GEORGE ORWELL, NEW ENGLISH WEEKLY, 1936

ALTHOUGH THE ADVENT OF THE PAPERBACK CAN BE TRACED TO THE NINETEENTH CENTURY, IT WAS PENGUIN FOUNDER ALLEN LANE WHO TRULY REVOLUTIONISED ITS PLACE IN PUBLISHING HISTORY WITH THE LAUNCH OF HIS PAPERBACK IMPRINT IN 1935.

Lane was managing director of The Bodley Head publishing firm at the time. The idea of launching an attractive line of affordable paperback reprints of fiction and nonfiction came to him after a weekend visit to Exeter to meet Agatha Christie. Lane was struck by the lack of cheap reading matter available to him at the train station on his return trip, and back in London began formulating his plan for a new line of inexpensive but quality paperbacks.

The first Penguins, priced at sixpence, went on sale on 30 July 1935. They included Ernest Hemingway's *A Farewell to Arms*, Agatha Christie's *The Mysterious Affair at Styles* and Dorothy Sayers's *The Unpleasantness at the Bellona Club*. The designs for the covers were simple but effective: blue for biography, green for crime, orange for fiction. They were intended, as Lane said, to 'be bought as easily and as casually as a packet of cigarettes' and 'to fit the normal male pocket or the normal feminine handbag'. Lane's plan was ambitious. To keep costs down, he needed to sell around 17 000 copies of each title to break even. The venture, however, was an instant success. Within the first ten days, Lane sold more than 150 000 Penguins and went on to sell three million copies in the first year of operation.

Lane's use of design was innovative and eye-catching, though clearly indebted to the look of Albatross paperbacks in Germany. Lane was opposed to illustrated covers, and adopted the colour grid as a dignified alternative. The first Penguin books were designed by Edward Young, the firm's 21-year-old office junior. Young was also responsible for the first version of the Penguin logo, after having been despatched by Lane to the London Zoo to sketch a penguin. The fact that the distinctive colour bands and penguin logo took equal billing on the covers with the author and title created an instantly recognisable brand.

By 1936, Penguin was a separate company, having severed ties with The Bodley Head, and its operations were being overseen by Allen Lane and his two brothers, Richard and John. The following year, Lane moved the firm to new premises on the Bath Road, Harmondsworth, from where Penguin would operate for the next sixty years.

While the initial Penguins were reprints sourced from other publishers, Lane's Pelican imprint, launched in 1937, began issuing the first Penguin originals. The series was intended as a nonfiction imprint designed to explore contemporary social issues. In the same year, Lane also launched the incongruous Penguincubator, a vending machine that dispensed Penguin books, at Charing Cross railway station.

Thereafter, the imprints proliferated: King Penguins, Puffins, Penguin Modern Painters,

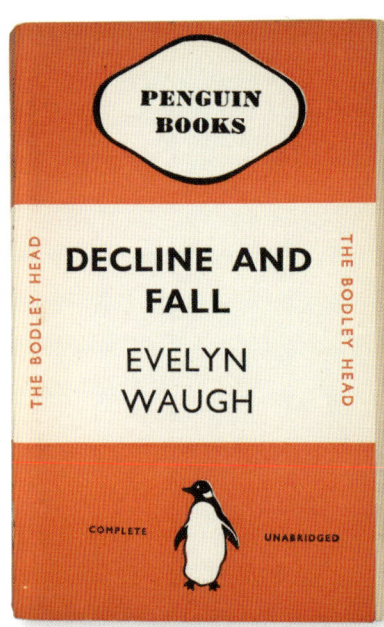
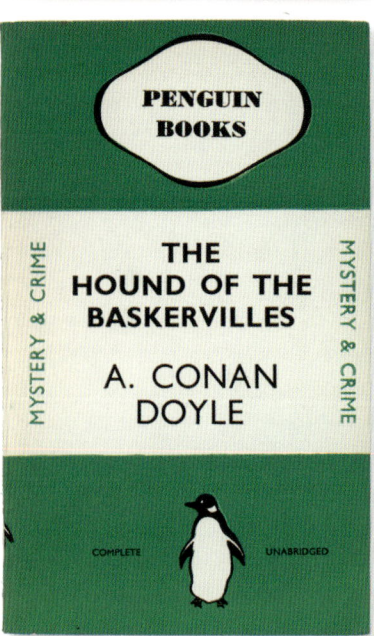

TOP ROW:
Ernest Hemingway
A Farewell to Arms
London, Penguin, 1935

Dorothy L Sayers
The Unpleasantness at the Bellona Club
London, Penguin, 1935

Evelyn Waugh
Decline and Fall
London, Penguin, 1937

MIDDLE ROW:
A Conan Doyle
The Hound of the Baskervilles
London, Penguin, 1937

Antoine De Saint-Exupéry
Night Flight
Harmondsworth, UK, Penguin, 1939

Agatha Christie
The Mysterious Affair at Styles
London, Penguin, 1935

BOTTOM ROW:
Aldous Huxley
Crome Yellow
London, Penguin, 1936

Dashiell Hammett
The Thin Man
London, Penguin, 1935

Graham Greene
It's a Battlefield
Harmondsworth, UK, Penguin, 1940

OPPOSITE:
William Faulkner
Light in August
Harmondsworth, UK, Penguin, 1960

Monica Dickens
Joy and Josephine
Harmondsworth, UK, Penguin, 1958

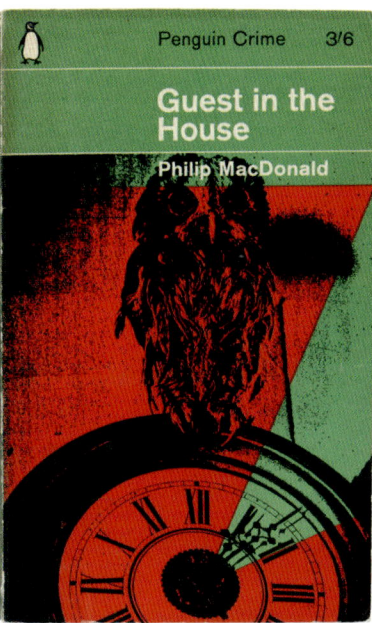

John Bingham
Murder Plan Six
Harmondsworth, UK,
Penguin, 1964
Cover design by
Sheila Perry

Stanley Ellin
Dreadful Summit
Harmondsworth, UK,
Penguin, 1964
Cover design by
Germano Facetti

Philip MacDonald
Guest in the House
Harmondsworth, UK,
Penguin, 1964
Cover design by
Germano Facetti

AEW Mason
The House of the Arrow
Harmondsworth, UK,
Penguin, 1960
Cover design by
Romek Marber

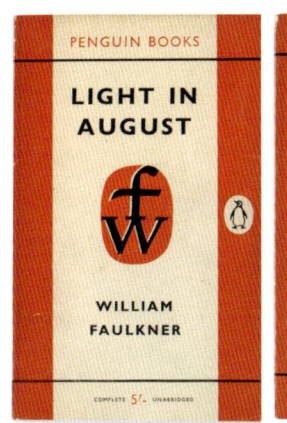
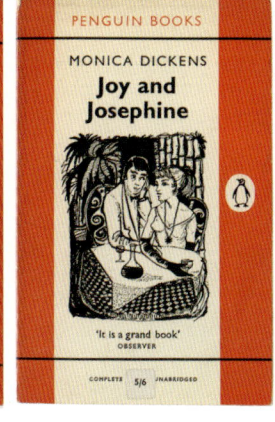

JAN TSCHICHOLD

Jan Tschichold began work on a vertical grid for Penguin covers in 1948 to replace the original horizontal bands. His successor, Hans Schmoller, introduced the design, which allowed space for illustrations, in the early 1950s.

Penguin Poets, and many others. In 1946, the firm launched its Penguin Classics series with EV Rieu's translation of Homer's *Odyssey*, a title that went on to sell some three million copies. Rieu became editor of the Classics series and aimed to present the general reader with 'readable and attractive versions' of Greek, Latin and European classics. To achieve this, he often looked to literary writers such as Robert Graves and Dorothy Sayers for translations, believing their versions avoided 'the archaic flavour and the foreign idiom that renders so many existing translations repellent to modern taste'.

Lane's paperback model did not go unnoticed. In America, paperback imprints such as Pocket Books, Avon, Dell and Ballantine began appearing in the late 1930s and 1940s. Unlike Penguins, they featured eye-catching illustrations on the covers, and were designed in a way that put them more in competition with pulp magazine publishers than with Penguin's more literary and innovative style.

Penguin's commitment to the design and look of its titles was further strengthened by the appointment in 1947 of German typographer Jan Tschichold. Lane was well aware of the need to raise the typographic and design standards of Penguins to keep pace with newly emerging paperback competitors. After having failed to entice Oliver Simon, of the Curwen Press, to take up the position, he accepted Simon's advice to seek out Tschichold, the foremost typographer of his day. Tschichold had been a pioneer and advocate of the asymmetrical and modern style of the 'new typography' in the 1920s, but by the late 1930s he had begun to re-embrace a more classical style suited to Lane's vision for Penguin books.

Upon taking up his appointment at Penguin, he set about overhauling everything from the familiar Penguin logo to the firm's stationery and business cards, implementing standardised design principles across the company's many paperback series and titles.

Tschichold's desire for a uniform typography and format led him to develop the 'Penguin Composition Rules', a four-page document that detailed the design and typographic conventions to be used for all Penguin titles. Underlying these rules was a flexible, horizontal grid system that unified the look of the covers and spines of all titles in the Penguin series. Tschichold strove most of all, during his brief tenure at Penguin, to create a balance and harmony between the many elements that made up a Penguin paperback.

Tschichold left Penguin in 1949, but not before recommending his successor, typographer Hans Schmoller, at that time an employee at the Curwen Press. Schmoller further modified Tschichold's grid system from horizontal to vertical, allowing space for illustrations while at the same time adhering to the original 1930s colour scheme.

In 1961, Italian art director Germano Facetti was appointed head of design to reinvigorate the look of Penguins. He commissioned striking new designs that modernised the look of Penguin Crime, Penguin Classics and other series. Facetti's use of talented young designers such as Romek Marber, Derek Birdsall, Alan Fletcher and Roger Main saw a shift away from the identifiable branding of the original 1930s Penguins. David Pelham's bold 1972 cover design for *A Clockwork Orange*, or his images of pop-culture detritus emblazoned on the covers of the 1970s editions of

JG Ballard's novels, would have been unthinkable in Lane's early days at Penguin.

Though Facetti left the firm in 1972, the fruits of his bold initiatives can be seen in the 1980s work of designers Mike Dempsey and Ken Carroll for the revived King Penguin series. The various Milan Kundera titles issued under the imprint, featuring striking cover illustrations by Andrzej Klimowski, deserve their classic status.

Unlike most paperback publishers, Penguin, from the outset, demonstrated a commitment to typography as an element of cover design. With the recent revival of interest in letterpress and letter forms, ironically generated in an electronic age, this commitment was reaffirmed in the Great Ideas series, published in 2004. Created by a number of designers, including David Pearson, Phil Baines and Catherine Dixon, the cover of each uses type and decorative borders that suggest the period in which the text was written. The Great Ideas series has received numerous design awards and has sold more than two million books.

For their seventieth anniversary in 2005, Penguin issued a set of seventy Pocket Penguin paperbacks featuring classic Penguin authors, from F Scott Fitzgerald and Virginia Woolf

BELOW, LEFT:
Anthony Burgess
A Clockwork Orange
Harmondsworth, UK,
Penguin, 1972
Cover design by
David Pelham

BELOW, RIGHT:
Milan Kundera
The Farewell Party
Harmondsworth, UK,
Penguin, 1984
King Penguin series
Cover illustration by
Andrzej Klimowski

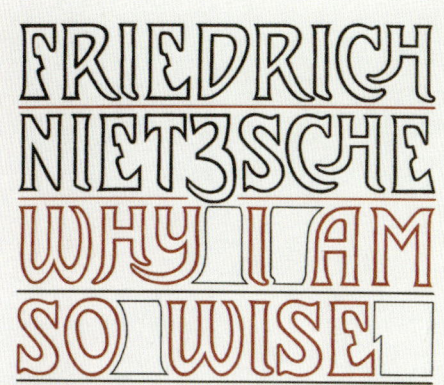

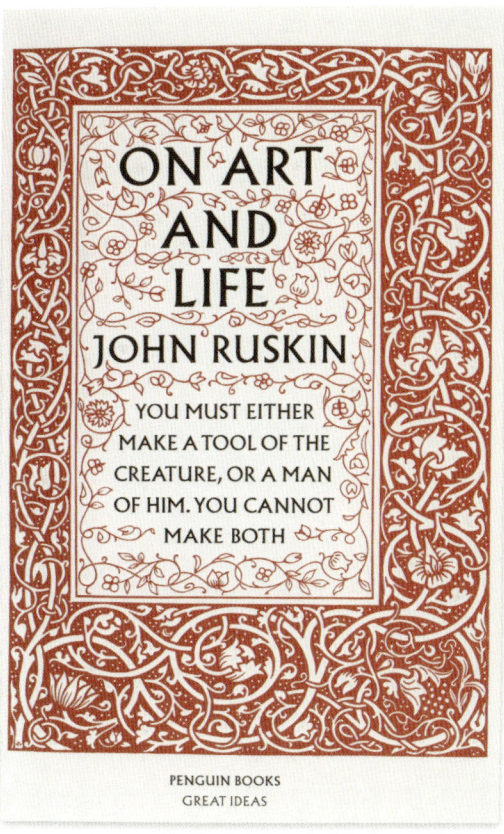
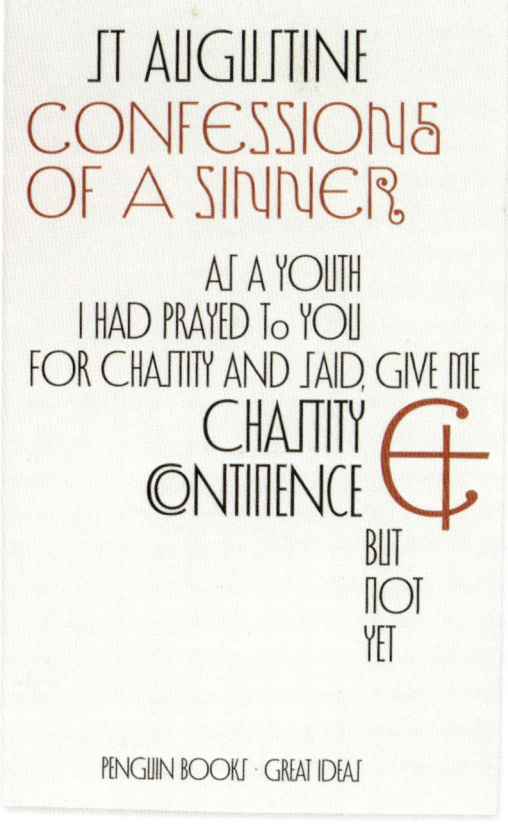

ABOVE, LEFT TO RIGHT:
Friedrich Nietzsche
Why I Am So Wise
London, Penguin, 2005
Penguin Great Ideas series
Cover design by
Phil Baines

Sigmund Freud
Civilization and Its Discontents
London, Penguin, 2005
Penguin Great Ideas series
Cover design by
David Pearson

Jonathan Swift
A Tale of a Tub
London, Penguin, 2005
Penguin Great Ideas series
Cover design by
David Pearson

RIGHT:
John Ruskin
On Art and Life
London, Penguin, 2005
Penguin Great Ideas series
Cover design by
David Pearson

FAR RIGHT:
St Augustine
Confessions of a Sinner
London, Penguin, 2005
Penguin Great Ideas series
Cover design by
Catherine Dixon

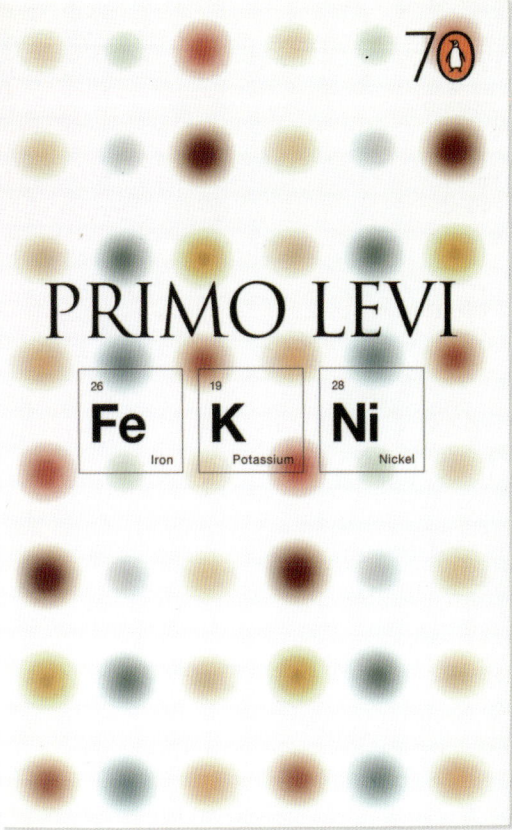

OPPOSITE, TOP,
LEFT TO RIGHT:
Antony Beevor
Christmas at Stalingrad
London, Penguin, 2005
Pocket Penguin series
Cover artwork by
Nathan Burton

Jonathan Safran Foer
The Unabridged Pocket Book of Lightning
London, Penguin, 2005
Pocket Penguin series
Cover artwork by
Ruslana Lyzchicko

Evelyn Waugh
The Coronation of Haile Selassie
London, Penguin, 2005
Pocket Penguin series
Cover artwork by
Andrew Smith

OPPOSITE, BOTTOM,
LEFT TO RIGHT:
Ali Smith
Ali Smith's Supersonic 70s
London, Penguin, 2005
Pocket Penguin series
Cover artwork by
Kate Gibb

John Updike
Three Trips
London, Penguin, 2005
Pocket Penguin series
Cover artwork by
Romek Marber

Primo Levi
Iron, Potassium, Nickel
London, Penguin, 2005
Pocket Penguin series
Cover artwork by
Jim Friedman

through to Zadie Smith and WG Sebald. The design idea was the brainchild of John Hamilton and Jim Stoddart, who came up with the novel idea of using seventy different designers, each charged with the mission to design their cover within seven days for £70.

In an age where a publishing company's backlist struggles for attention in an increasingly crowded marketplace, Penguin has turned to design as a means of persuading readers to revisit classic books. Nowhere is this more apparent than with the two recent initiatives: Penguin Graphic Classics and Penguin Designer Classics. The Graphic Classics feature covers by leading graphic novelists: Art Spiegelman illustrates Paul Auster's *New York Trilogy* while Chris Ware provides a mini comic strip for the cover of Voltaire's *Candide*.

The Penguin Designer Classics were issued in 2006 to celebrate sixty years of Penguin Classics. Leading international designers were invited to select a favourite title, and were then given complete freedom to design the work. Video artist Sam Taylor-Wood's stark and minimal photographic portrait of a young man graces F Scott Fitzgerald's *Tender is the Night*; graphic design partnership Fuel (Stephen Sorel and Damon Murray) look to Russian Constructivism for their take on Dostoyevsky's *Crime and Punishment*; and shoe designer Manolo Blahnik gives Flaubert's *Madame Bovary* a playful and sexy new look. It is hard to imagine anyone actually reading these editions; they are in many ways a triumph of design over content. Published in limited editions of a thousand copies, and priced at £100, the five titles that comprised the first series of Penguin Designer Classics sold out worldwide upon release. A far cry from Allen Lane's sixpenny paperbacks, the revolution has come full circle.

BELOW, LEFT TO RIGHT:
Fyodor Dostoyevsky
The Idiot
London, Penguin, 2006
Penguin Designer Classics series
Cover design by Ron Arad

F Scott Fitzgerald
Tender is the Night
London, Penguin, 2006
Penguin Designer Classics series
Cover design by Sam Taylor-Wood

DH Lawrence
Lady Chatterley's Lover
London, Penguin, 2006
Penguin Designer Classics series
Cover design by Paul Smith

Fyodor Dostoyevsky
Crime and Punishment
London, Penguin, 2006
Penguin Designer Classics series
Cover design by Fuel

Gustave Flaubert
Madame Bovary
London, Penguin, 2006
Penguin Designer Classics series
Cover design by Manolo Blahnik

ABOVE:
Paul Auster
The New York Trilogy
New York, Penguin, 2006
Penguin Graphic Classics series
Cover design by Art Spiegelman

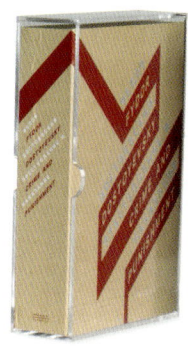

NAKED LUNCH

early poems
Allen Ginsberg

Jack Kerouac
Scattered Poems

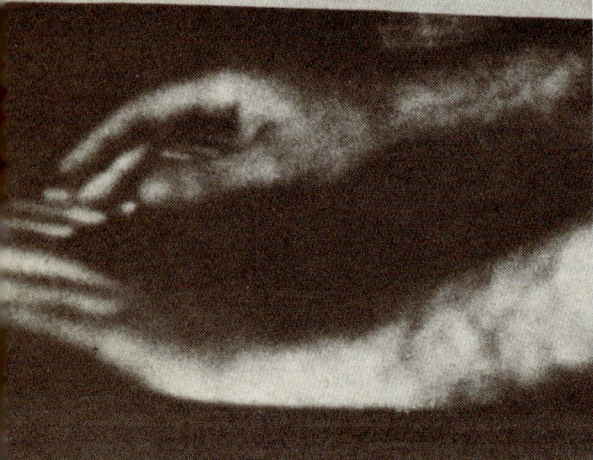

The BEAT Goes On

I saw the best minds of my generation destroyed by madness,
starving hysterical naked,
dragging themselves through the negro streets at dawn looking for
an angry fix ... ALLEN GINSBERG, HOWL

BEAT LITERATURE BURST ONTO THE AMERICAN LITERARY SCENE IN 1956 WITH THE PUBLICATION OF ALLEN GINSBERG'S EPIC POEM 'HOWL'. GINSBERG DEDICATED *HOWL AND OTHER POEMS* TO HIS FRIENDS JACK KEROUAC, WILLIAM BURROUGHS AND NEAL CASSADY. 'HOWL' WAS FIRST RECITED BY GINSBERG AT THE LEGENDARY 'SIX POETS AT SIX GALLERY' READING, HELD ON 7 OCTOBER 1955, AN EVENT FICTIONALISED IN KEROUAC'S 1958 NOVEL *THE DHARMA BUMS*, WHERE HE CALLED IT 'THE NIGHT OF THE BIRTH OF THE SAN FRANCISCO POETRY RENAISSANCE'. IT IS SAID THAT GINSBERG WEPT UPON FINISHING HIS READING OF 'HOWL' THAT NIGHT, AS DID POET KENNETH REXROTH, WHO HOSTED THE EVENING.

The term 'Beat' predates Ginsberg's poem, having reputedly been introduced by Kerouac in the late 1940s, and given further currency by novelist John Clellon Holmes's *New York Times* article of 1952, 'This is the Beat Generation'. While the original derivation was meant to describe a postwar *beaten* generation, Kerouac and Ginsberg later emphasised the 'beatific' or visionary aspects of the term. The Beats initially heralded from New York, but came to be synonymous with San Francisco after poet Lawrence Ferlinghetti and Peter Martin opened the City Lights bookstore there in 1953. The bookstore, named after Martin's *City Lights Magazine*, became a haven for writers and artists. Soon afterwards, Ferlinghetti founded his City Lights Books, issuing the first of the titles, including Ginsberg's *Howl*, in the famed Pocket Poets series. Ginsberg's poem, which has never been out of print, was first published in November 1956 in an edition of 1000 copies, and sold for 75 cents.

In looking to save costs, Ferlinghetti had *Howl* printed in England. While the first printing passed through US customs without incident, 520 copies of the second printing were seized upon entry into the United States by the San Francisco Collector of Customs, Chester MacPhee, on the grounds of obscenity. Reacting to the poem's language and blatant homosexual references, MacPhee declared, 'You wouldn't want your children to come across it'. To circumvent the jurisdiction of customs, Ferlinghetti had a third printing of 2500 copies done in the United States, which went on sale at City Lights bookstore. Customs soon after cleared the seized copies, but not before Ginsberg's poem had come to the attention of Captain William A Hanrahan of the San Francisco Police, who filed obscenity charges against Ferlinghetti for selling the book. Though Ferlinghetti was eventually cleared of all charges, the ensuing trial generated enormous publicity for Ginsberg, who was then relatively unknown outside his small coterie, and ensured rapid sales for the book. To meet the demand, Ferlinghetti embarked on a fourth printing of 5000 copies in October 1957. Since then, *Howl* has gone on to sell upwards of a million copies, a startling figure for a book of poems.

Beat literature's defining moment, however, came in 1957 with the publication of Jack Kerouac's novel *On the Road*, a semifictionalised account of a road trip he made across America in the late 1940s with friend Neal Cassady, immortalised in the novel as Beat hero Dean Moriarty. Aside from appearing in many of Kerouac's later works as Cody Pomeray, Cassady is also referenced in Ginsberg's *Howl*, and has walk-on parts in Tom Wolfe's *Electric Kool-Aid Acid Test* and Hunter S Thompson's *Hell's Angels*. Though Cassady was never a literary writer, Kerouac cited his prolific letter writing as an influence on his own style.

Kerouac claimed to have typed *On the Road* onto a 120-foot-long (37-metre) scroll, made up of rolls of tracing paper taped together, in three weeks in 1951. This feat later led to novelist Truman Capote's famous damning remark: 'That's not writing, that's typing'. Kerouac used the scroll as a means of composing his text without breaking his thoughts at the end of each page. He intended the novel's spontaneous and rhythmic prose to be the literary equivalent of jazz improvisation. Kerouac, along with Ginsberg, had frequented clubs such as Minton's Playhouse in New York in the postwar years, and there they'd witnessed the birth of bebop in the late-night jam sessions led by Charlie Parker and Dizzy Gillespie. Ginsberg later claimed that *Howl* was influenced by Lester Young's classic jazz composition 'Lester Leaps In', while Kerouac's *On the Road* portrayed his characters 'bowed and jumping' before a phonograph listening to 'a wild bop record … called The Hunt with Dexter Gordon and Wardell Gray blowing their tops before a screaming audience'. Kerouac's essay 'Essentials of Spontaneous Prose' emphatically proclaimed 'no periods separating sentence-structures' but instead 'the vigorous space dash separating rhetorical breathing (as jazz musician drawing breath between outblown phrases)'.

Kerouac had initially begun writing *On the Road* in 1949, at his mother's house, soon after returning from his cross-country trip with Cassady. But he was dissatisfied with early drafts of the novel. He found sudden inspiration in a long letter sent to him by Cassady the following year, which became known in Beat folklore as the 'Joan Anderson letter' or simply the 'Joan letter'. Cassady's letter was a 23 000-word non-stop verbal outpouring written over three days while he was high on Benzedrine. Kerouac's use of the scroll was, in part, an attempt to emulate Cassady's high-speed style of composition, and he accordingly armed himself with supplies of Benzedrine, coffee and cigarettes for the duration of his marathon writing session.

Kerouac's novel found immediate success with the reading public, and the fictional Dean Moriarty provided the lasting model for the Beat archetype. *San Francisco Chronicle* journalist Herb Caen coined the term 'Beatnik' in late 1957, after the launch of the Russian sputnik into space in October that year. While the ensuing cliché of the goateed, beret-wearing, bongo-playing Beatnik had little to do with Kerouac's book, it would define the Beats for much of middle America, reaching an apotheosis in US popular culture with the character Maynard G Krebs in the television series *The Many Loves of Dobie Gillis*, which went to air in 1959.

Kerouac and Ginsberg had met William Burroughs in New York in 1943–44. Burroughs's first book, *Junkie, Confessions of an Unredeemed Drug Addict*, was published in 1953 as an Ace Books pulp paperback under the name William Lee. It sold for 35 cents and, although ignored by reviewers, went on to sell more than 100 000 copies in its first year. Burroughs's second published novel, the acclaimed *Naked Lunch*, was written in a hotel room in Tangiers, Morocco, between 1954 and 1957. While living there, Burroughs was visited by Ginsberg and Kerouac, and they helped him to put the hundreds of pages of text he had accumulated into some sort of order. When ten episodes of the novel were published in the first issue of *Big Table* in 1959, the magazine was impounded by the Chicago Post Office. The resulting trial, however, brought Burroughs's novel to the attention of Maurice Girodias, the famed Paris-based publisher of literary erotica, who brought it out as part of his Olympia Press Traveller's Companion series. Burroughs claimed to have no memory of writing *Naked Lunch* and stated that its title was suggested by Kerouac: 'NAKED Lunch—the frozen moment when everyone sees what is on the end of every fork'. The book's US publication in 1962 triggered a landmark obscenity trial that changed America's approach to the censorship of literary works. Henceforth, the concept of obscenity in American law was redefined to exclude works of 'artistic merit'.

Allen Ginsberg
Howl and Other Poems
San Francisco, City Lights
Pocket Bookshop,
1956 (4th printing, 1957)

William Burroughs
The Naked Lunch
Paris, Olympia Press,
1959

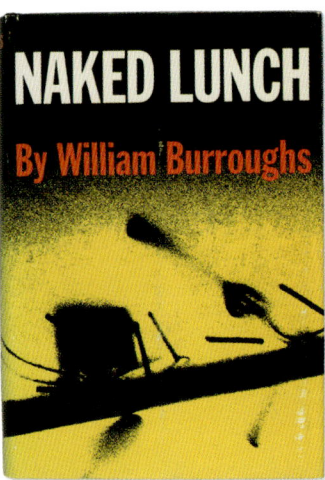

William Burroughs
Naked Lunch
New York, Grove Press,
1962

William Burroughs
The Naked Lunch
London, John Calder in
association with Olympia
Press, 1964

Jack Kerouac
On the Road
London, Andre Deutsch,
1958 (1959 impression)

 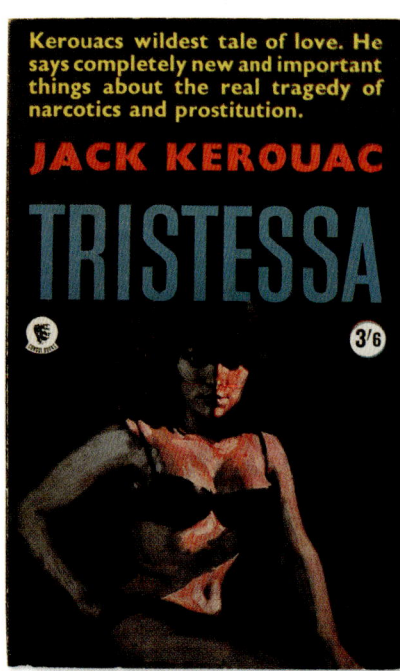 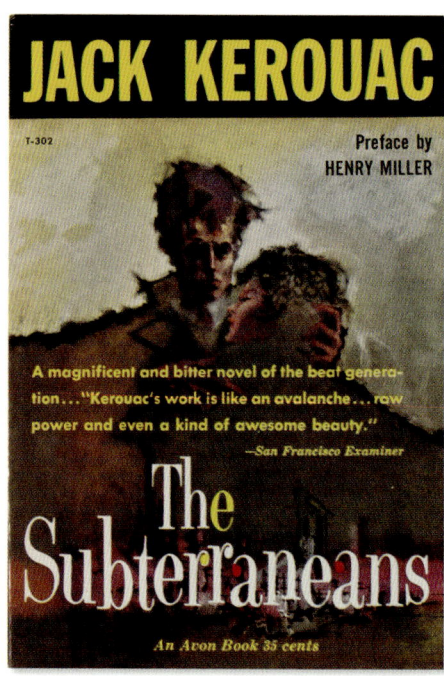

FROM LEFT TO RIGHT:
Jack Kerouac
The Dharma Bums
London, Pan Books, 1962

Jack Kerouac
Tristessa
London, World Distributors, 1963

Jack Kerouac
The Subterraneans
New York, Avon, c. 1959

By the start of the 1960s, Beat writers found themselves in high demand, the subject of national stories in *Time* and *Newsweek*. Publishers were quick to capitalise on the rise of a new postwar youth culture, and cheap paperbacks, espousing the new 'hipster' philosophy, proliferated. The cover of the Pan pulp paperback of Kerouac's *Dharma Bums* (1962) said it all: 'Fighting, drinking, scorning convention, making wild love—zany antics of America's young Beats in their mad search for kicks'. The jacket blurb to the 1963 British pulp edition of Kerouac's *Tristessa* described the novel's plot in prose that must surely have pained the author: 'the heart-breaking story of Tristessa, a girl of throat-stopping Aztec loveliness'. Even Hollywood got in on the act, firstly with Charles Haas's 1959 B-movie *The Beat Generation*, which centred on a police hunt for a serial rapist through the 'Beatnik' coffee dens of Los Angeles, and then with MGM's 1960 film version of Kerouac's *The Subterraneans*, starring George Peppard and Leslie Caron.

The reality was not always so glamorous. Kerouac was dead by 1969, aged forty-seven, from a life of heavy drinking. The previous year, his friend Neil Cassady had been found in a coma by a railroad track in Mexico and died shortly afterwards, aged forty-one. The Beat torch would be carried on by Gregory Corso, Michael McClure, Gary Snyder, Lawrence Ferlinghetti and others. Ginsberg remained a vital presence in American poetry, winning the National Book Award for Poetry for *The Fall of America: Poems of these States 1965–1971* (1972). But it was Burroughs who, up until his death in 1997, refused to be pigeonholed. His final years included everything from appearances in Nike ads and on MTV to collaborations with musicians like Tom Waits and Sonic Youth and film director Gus van Sant.

Despite their burgeoning popularity in the 1960s, many Beat writers, to their credit, continued to publish with small and independent publishers, such as Ferlinghetti's City Lights and Ted and Eli Wilentz's Corinth Books in New York. An adherence to the prevailing counterculture, combined with a natural flair for publicity, guaranteed Beat literature its permanent cult status.

TOP:
Jack Kerouac
Scattered Poems
San Francisco, City Lights Books, 1971
(1980 impression)

Jack Kerouac
Book of Dreams
San Francisco, City Lights Books, 1961

BOTTOM:
Allen Ginsberg
Empty Mirror: Early Poems
New York, Corinth Books, 1970

William Burroughs
Early Routines
Santa Barbara, Cadmus Editions, 1982

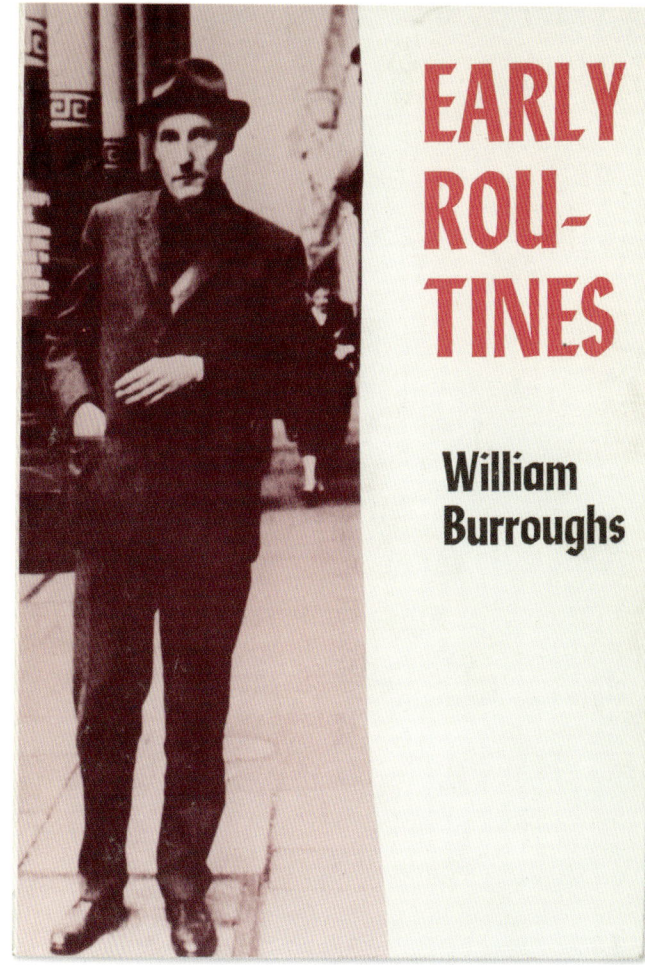

The POPULAR Imagination

*Comics are an international language.
They can cross boundaries and generations.
Comics are a bridge between cultures.*

TEZUKA OSAMU

SINCE ANCIENT TIMES, LITERATURE HAS SERVED TO INSPIRE, EDUCATE, TRANSPORT AND AMUSE. WHILE SOME WORKS ENDURE FOR THEIR TIMELESS THEMES, THEIR IMPACT ON LANGUAGE AND THEIR OBSERVATIONS ON HUMANITY, OTHERS HAVE BEEN CREATED PRIMARILY TO ENTERTAIN IN THE MOMENT.

Throughout the twentieth century, comics and pulp fiction have traditionally fulfilled this role of popular entertainment. However, the diversification of comics in recent decades and the emergence of the graphic novel have seen a blurring of distinctions between the literary and the popular, and the playful and the profound.

Comics are generally understood as stories told through sequential panels of images and related text that is presented as either caption or direct speech. Some historians regard Ancient Egyptian hieroglyphics as antecedents of the comic genre. The term 'comic', however, dates from the nineteenth century, and it is from this period that we recognise more direct precursors to the genre as we know it today.

Political cartoons figured strongly in many nineteenth-century newspapers. In the West, these drew on an earlier tradition of caricature by artists such as William Hogarth, James Gillray and George Cruikshank. In 1841, the British satirical weekly magazine *Punch* was launched, modelled on the French magazine *Le Charivari*, which had begun a decade earlier. Comic imagery was a major feature of both magazines, and *Punch* made one of the first uses of the term 'cartoons' to refer to its humorous drawings.

Political cartoons were generally single panels of image and text. Comic strips, which presented a sequential narrative through a series of panels, appeared first as separate magazines in the 1880s and then as strips in newspapers from the 1890s. One of the first newspaper strips was RF Outcault's *Hogan's Alley*, which appeared in US papers from 1895. This strip soon became known as *The Yellow Kid*, named after its lead character, and was one of the first comics to make use of the speech balloons that are integral to most comics today. *The Yellow Kid*'s enormous popularity boosted sales of its various host newspapers and encouraged the development of similar comic strips for other papers. It also heralded the role that the United States would play as a primary producer of comics throughout most of the twentieth century. The comics industry also flourished in Europe and Britain. Long-running twentieth-century titles included *Les Aventures de Tintin* from Belgium and *Beano* from the United Kingdom.

From the 1920s, comic strips began to diversify beyond the literally 'comic' to include content drawn from pulp, or genre fiction, of the time such as adventure or war stories and science fiction. One of the most famous, and long-running, of these was *Tarzan*, based on Edgar Rice Burroughs's novel, which first appeared in *All-Story Magazine* in 1912. The strip was originally drawn by Harold (Hal) Foster and first appeared in US and Canadian newspapers on 7 January 1929. The first science fiction strip was also released on that day: *Buck Rogers in the Year 2429 AD*, written by Philip Francis Nowlan and drawn by Dick Calkins. *Buck Rogers* also had its origins in pulp, Nowlan's story first appearing in *Amazing Stories* in 1928. The double debut of these two newspaper strips is often credited with heralding the 'Golden Age' of comics from the 1930s to the 1950s.

During this 'Golden Age', comic publishing diversified from newspaper strips to the comic book format that we recognise today. The first series of comic books was *Famous Funnies*, published in America by Dell from 1934. But it was the superhero titles from DC Comics that would really influence the future of the genre. The first issue of DC's *Action Comics* was released in 1938, starring Superman. An array of superhero characters soon followed, including DC's Batman and Wonder Woman, and Captain America, published by Marvel Comics (then known as Timely Comics).

While the so-called 'pulp' genre of fiction had been in existence since the 'penny dreadfuls' of nineteenth-century Britain, it also came to the fore in America during the 1920s and 1930s. There was considerable crossover of both authors and subjects between pulp fiction and comics. The term 'pulp' refers to the cheap wood pulp papers on which these popular and affordable romance, western, crime, science fiction and war novels were printed. Produced as small-format magazines, pulps featured glossy colour covers with titles such as *Kitten You're a Killer* or *Cosmic Calamity* and illustrations of heroic fighter pilots, tough cowboys, hard-nosed detectives or wayward women.

Individual issues of popular pulp titles could sell hundreds of thousands of copies. Many pulp fiction series were centred around, and named after, a particular character, the first and most famous being *The Shadow*, which was written by Walter B Gibson under the pseudonym of Maxwell Grant and was issued for nearly twenty years from 1931. Other famous characters whose exploits were serialised were Doc Savage, the Phantom Detective and the Lone Wolf. Pulp was also hugely popular in Europe from the 1920s, significant genres being the French *fantastique populaires* and the Italian *gialli*, both of which continue to be very popular today.

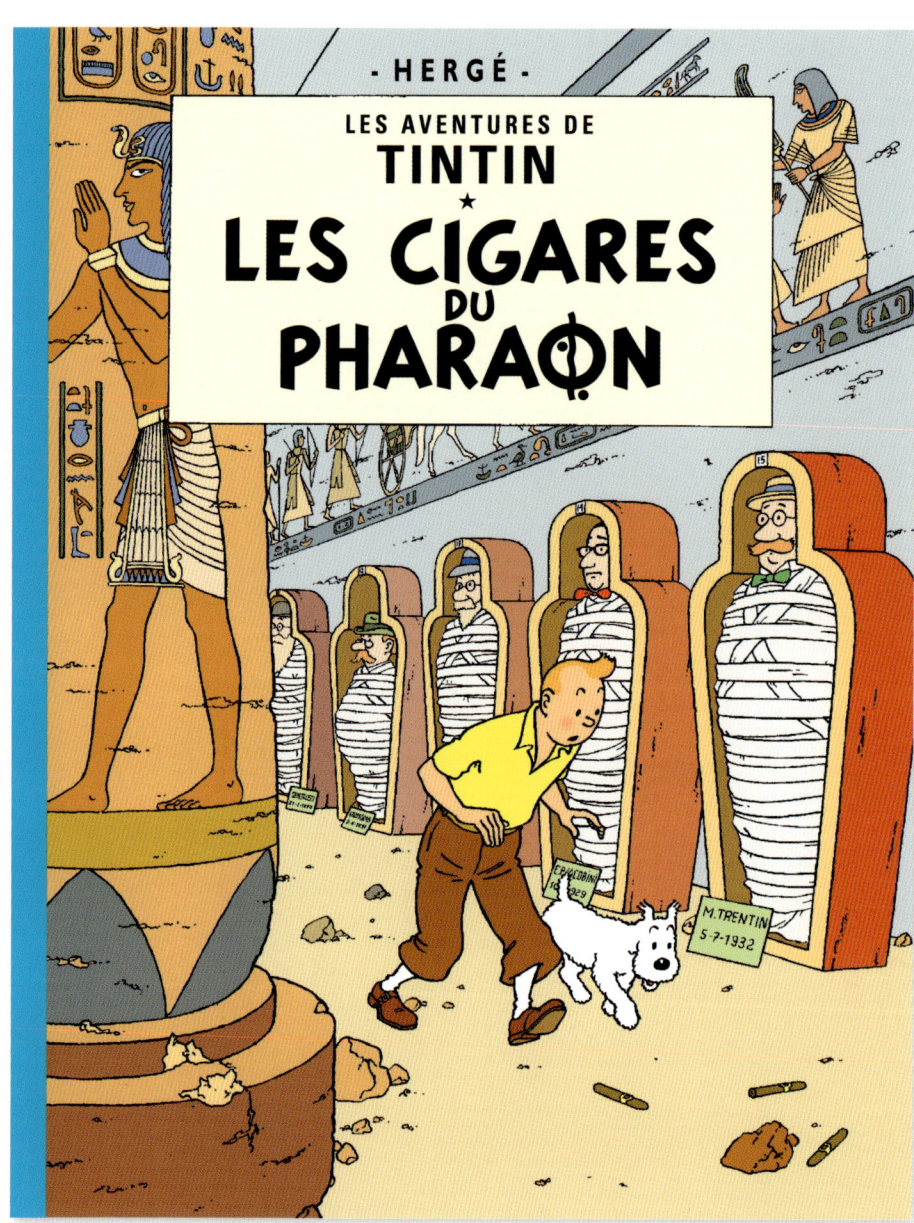

HERGÉ

Hergé's *Les Aventures de Tintin* first appeared as a comic strip in the Belgian newspaper *Le Vingtième Siècle* in 1929, and has since been celebrated in books, film, television and postage stamps. The young reporter Tintin and his trusty terrier Snowy feature in twenty-three comic book adventures, which take them as far afield as Europe, South America, the former Soviet Union, Asia, the Middle East and the moon. The storylines reflect Hergé's interest in culture, archaeology, science and politics. The Tintin series has been translated into more than fifty languages, including Latin and Mongolian.

Hergé (Georges Remi)
Les Aventures de Tintin: les Cigares du Pharaon
Paris-Tournai, Casterman, 1979

ABOVE, LEFT:
Buck Rogers Special,
no. 13
Melbourne, Southdown Press, c. 1950–52

ABOVE, RIGHT:
John Dixon, cover artist
The Phantom Commando
no. 3
Sydney, Horwitz, 1959

Maurice Bramley
The Phantom Commando
no. 8
Sydney, Horwitz, 1962

96 | The POPULAR Imagination

STANLEY PITT

Stanley Pitt was one of Australia's most successful comic artists of the 1950s. He originally created *Silver Starr and the Flameworld* for Sydney's *Sunday Sun* newspaper from 1946 to 1948. *Silver Starr* was then published as a black-and-white comic book from 1949 until the early 1950s. In 1956 a second series commenced but did not survive beyond the first issue. This single issue was printed in colour, reflecting the experimentation by publishers at a time when the comic book industry was under threat from the new medium of television.

Stanley Pitt
Silver Starr,
no. 1
Sydney, Apache Comics,
c. 1956

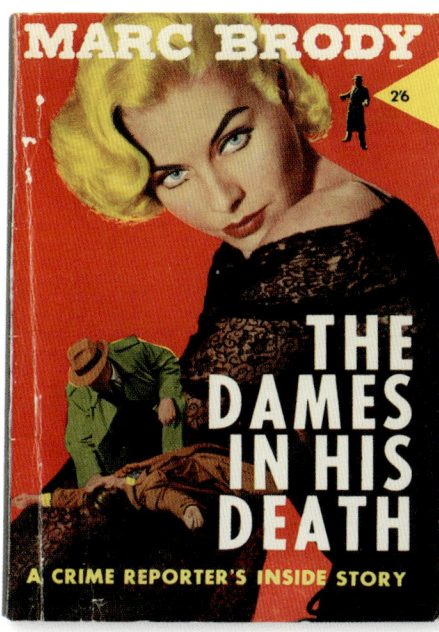
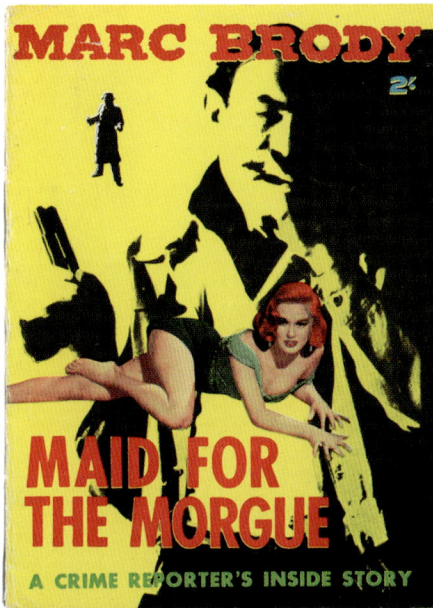

A selection of Australian pulp fiction covers from the 1950s
Titles by Marc Brody, Carter Brown, and Paul Valdez published by Horwitz, Sydney.
Larry Kent titles published by Cleveland, Sydney.

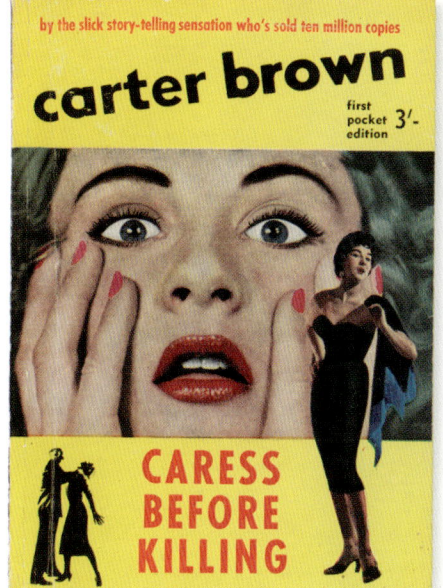
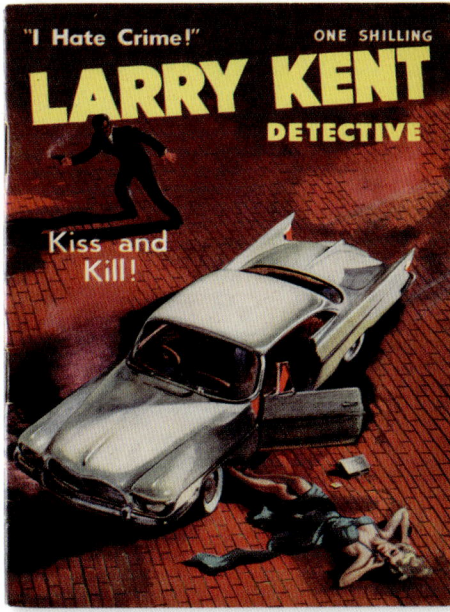

KT McCall
The Lady's a Decoy
Sydney, Horwitz, 1957

KT MCCALL

The authors of pulp crime were almost all male. One significant Australian exception was KT McCall, 'Crime fiction's best selling woman author', as her covers proclaim. A glamorous portrait on the reverse was captioned 'Meet KT McCall. Blonde, beautiful and with brains— a combination that has taken KT into the front of the world's highest paid women crime writers'. KT McCall was in fact a pseudonym for the collaboration between writers Audrey Armitage and Muriel Watkins, and McCall's so-called portrait was that of a professional model.

In the United States, the popularity of pulp magazines began to decline during the 1940s. This was largely due to increased production costs resulting from paper shortages during World War II, but also to the growing popularity of comic superheroes, who always overcame their enemies and thus cheered up wartime audiences. By the late 1940s, however, even these superheroes had had their day, and comic sales flagged.

While pulp fiction and comics were declining in the United States, in Australia they were entering their most popular phase. Australian readers had already developed an appetite for American pulps and comics when wartime restrictions on the import of these publications came into force. Australian publishers rushed to satisfy the demand, commissioning local writers and artists to produce pulps and comics at unprecedented rates.

Some comics, such as *Kokey Koala*, celebrated their local origins; however, Australian-made pulp fiction tended to mimic the US titles that had been so popular. Written by journalists using American-sounding pseudonyms, their stories as well as their covers continued to be set on the mean streets or in the wild west of the United States. Sydney publishers such as Horwitz Publications and Cleveland Publishing Company led the way, putting together stables of writers capable of producing books to order.

The Larry Kent stories, which can lay claim to being the longest running pulp crime series in Australian publishing history, were initially inspired by *I Hate Crime*, a popular radio series of the early 1950s. By the time Cleveland published the final one in 1983, more than four hundred Larry Kent titles had been issued. While the majority of the Larry Kent stories carry no attributions of authorship, some seventy titles are credited to Don Haring, an American writer resident in Australia. Others are believed to have been the work of Des R Dunn, a Queensland author who also wrote numerous westerns for Cleveland.

Between 1955 and 1960 Horwitz issued eighty-two novels by intrepid crime reporter Marc Brody. A back cover biography claimed, among other things, that Brody was 'married to a former ballet dancer of the Bodenweiser group'. In real life Marc Brody was WH Williams, an Australian journalist and editor of the Melbourne *Truth*. Williams also published war novels with Horwitz under his own name.

Carter Brown was one of the most prolific—and certainly the most popular—of Australia's pulp crime writers. Between 1954 and 1984, author Alan Yates, publishing with Horwitz under the pseudonym Carter Brown, wrote more than three hundred novels. It has been estimated that more than eighty million books had been sold by the time of his death in 1985. Yates also published scientific thrillers under the name Paul Valdez, and westerns under the names of Tex Conrad and Tod Conway.

With the growing popularity of television in the 1950s, US demand for comics and pulp fiction went into decline. Publishers such as EC Comics began to produce comics for the newly identified consumer called the 'teenager'. These darker works combined the subject matter of pulp with the graphic imagery and rapid-fire dialogue of comics. They soon attracted the ire of mainstream America for their perceived corruption of young minds. After a number of US Senate hearings, the comics industry embarked on a period of self-censorship. Sales slumped, however, as comics lost much of their edge.

In the 1960s, American comics had to either conform to the moral code or operate completely outside it and survive on the margins. Mainstream comics made a successful return to the superhero genre by creating characters, such as Marvel's Spider-Man, who still possessed unearthly powers but also now expressed human emotions like fear and self-doubt. On the alternative front, one of EC's titles was *Mad*, which parodied the comic genre as well as contemporary America. *Mad*'s subversive humour provided inspiration for a generation of comic artists, most notably Robert Crumb. Crumb's *Zap Comix* first appeared on the streets of San Francisco in 1967, its new spelling as well as its political satire, sexual explicitness and celebration of drug culture heralding a genre that would become known as underground 'comix'.

While the fortunes of comics were waxing, waning and being reinvented in the West, *manga* (comics) burgeoned in Japan after World War II. The cultural origins and social role of Japanese *manga* are distinct from those of comics elsewhere. Unlike the West, where visual and textual art forms have generally evolved separately, Japan has a strong tradition of combining the two. This approach has been used both to entertain and to convey a diverse array of literary, philosophical and cultural concepts and stories, just as *manga* does today. As a result of this diversity, *manga* is created for and read by an enormous variety of distinct audiences in Japan,

Robert Crumb
'Mr Natural' from *Odds and Ends* London, Bloomsbury, 2001

from the children and youth with whom we associate mainstream comics in the West, to businessmen and women, sports enthusiasts and young mothers. The variety of *manga* genres is seemingly infinite, ranging from art *manga*, baseball *manga*, Buddhist *manga* and cooking *manga* through to gambling *manga*, golf *manga*, horror *manga*, motorcycle *manga* and beyond.

The origins of *manga* can be seen in a number of earlier cultural forms in Japan. Comic imagery can be traced back many centuries to forms such as *emakimono*, or picture scrolls. *Emakimono* are horizontal in format, and their stories unfurl in sequences of images and text running from right to left. By the late eighteenth century, *kibyōshi*, so named for their yellow covers, were a very popular literary genre. These mass-produced books were often satirical in nature and presented adventure stories and moral tales through the combination of words and pictures.

The term *manga* was first coined in 1814 by the renowned artist Katsushika Hokusai in reference to his fifteen volumes of humorous figures and sketches from everyday life. Later in the nineteenth century, after a period of relative isolation, Japan entered a period of rapid modernisation in which it consciously studied and incorporated ideas from the West. The subsequent dialogue between two distinct cultures would lead to the unique nature of *manga* as we know it today.

Japanese artists were exposed to new forms of comic imagery introduced by foreigners who had recently taken up residence in the major cities. These included satirical engravings in *Japan Punch*, modelled on the British *Punch* and produced by foreign residents for fellow expatriates. British- and US-style newspaper strips began to be incorporated into Japanese newspapers in the 1920s. However, it would be the period following World War II that would witness the development and explosion of *manga* as a dynamic new cultural form.

US troops stationed in Japan in the 1940s brought with them countless numbers of comic books, and the bold and colourful images and dramatic tales of heroic adventures were a revelation to Japanese readers and comic artists alike. One of these artists was Tezuka Osamu (1928–1989), now universally acclaimed as the father of *manga*. Over a career of more than forty years, Tezuka produced six hundred *manga* and sixty animations. He continuously shaped both forms with his innovations in visual expression and dramatic subject matter, which ranged from the tales of a robot boy called Tetsuwan Atomu (Astroboy) to the life of Buddha.

Tezuka had a great interest in both Japanese and Western cinema. Techniques he introduced to *manga* include cinematic framing, dramatic action and the use of graphic lines to signify speed or motion. Tezuka also introduced the idea that a comic could be hundreds of pages in length and present the complex inner life of its characters within a detailed narrative. Tezuka nurtured and inspired future generations of *manga* artists, and his influence continues to be felt.

Manga today makes up almost 40 per cent of book and magazine sales in Japan, and popular titles such as the boys' magazine *Shonen Jump* can sell up to three million copies. Mass-produced in black and white or with one additional colour, they are inexpensive to purchase and almost as ephemeral as the daily newspaper. Rather than suffering the fate of Western comics, which faded with the advent of television and cinema, *manga* has remained a dominant form of popular culture in Japan and provides the inspiration for many of the country's television programs and animation films.

In Japan, as in the West, a new form to emerge from the comic genre in recent decades has been the graphic novel. *Gekiga*, or 'dramatic pictures', began to appear in Japan from the 1950s as an alternative to mainstream *manga* magazines, which were then aimed primarily at children. *Gekiga* presents more adult subject matter and realistically depicts the human form and facial expressions rather than using the exaggerated eyes and cartoon-like figures of children's *manga*. Originally selling outside mainstream channels, *gekiga* soon developed a strong following, and its characteristics have been incorporated into and have helped create the diversity of *manga* today.

The graphic novel in the West also arose from the development of a new generation of older readers who had grown up with comics and who now sought a graphic form that would continue to capture their imaginations in adulthood. The term 'graphic novel' was coined in 1978 by American comic artist Will Eisner. Eisner had been producing comics for forty years (including the very successful *The Spirit*) and he developed the term to distinguish his book of four stories, *A Contract with God and Other Tenement Stories*, from what readers generally understood to be comics. Eisner continued to write graphic novels until his death in 2005, and his *A Contract with God* has never gone out of print.

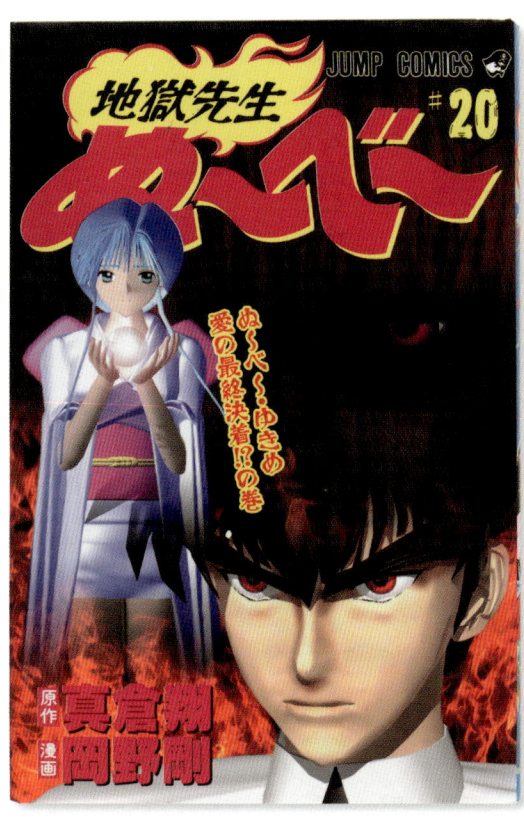

Shō Makura and Takeshi Okano
Jigoku sensei nūbē
no. 20
Tokyo, Jump Comics,
Shūeisha, 1997

TEZUKA OSAMU

Buddha is one of Tezuka Osamu's *manga* masterpieces and his longest work. It was originally issued in serialised form between September 1972 and December 1983, and from 1974 was published in eight volumes. Tezuka used the comic form of *manga* to communicate complex philosophical concepts such as fate, suffering and transcendence to a broad audience of both children and adults. While Buddha is at the heart of the work, he does not appear until the end of the first volume. The account of his life is placed within a broader narrative of imagined characters, whose experiences represent the concepts embodied in Buddha's teachings.

Tezuka Osamu
Buddha
vol. 7
Tokyo, Ushio Shuppansha, 1994

DANIEL CLOWES

Daniel Clowes is considered one of the leading US comic artists of his generation. His 1998 graphic novel *Ghost World* was made into a movie in 2001. *Ice Haven* presents the various misfit residents of an imagined small town, described by *Time* magazine as 'another of his hilariously slightly off-center worlds that have a vague sense of dread about them. Kind of like where you live'.

DIABOLIK

Diabolik is a long-running and hugely popular *giallo*, or pulp series, in Italy. The eponymous anti-hero was created by sisters Angela and Luciana Giussani in 1962. They continued to author the monthly series until the 1980s after which the writing was largely taken over by Patricia Martinelli. A number of artists have created the graphic imagery for the series over the years, most significantly Sergio Zaniboni. This issue was illustrated by Emanuele Barison and Pierluigi Cerveglieri.

ABOVE:
Daniel Clowes
Ice Haven
New York, Pantheon Books, 2005

RIGHT:
Patricia Martinelli and Mario Gomboli
Il Grande Diabolik: per la Testa di Diabolik
Milan, Astorina, 2003

Art Spiegelman
Maus II: a Survivor's Tale: and Here my Troubles Began
New York, Pantheon Books, 1991

The year 1986 marked another turning point for the graphic novel. In that year, two very different but seminal works were published: Frank Miller's *Batman: the Dark Night Returns* and Art Spiegelman's *Maus: a Survivor's Tale*. Published by DC Comics, Miller's *Batman* reintroduced readers to the dark character who had featured in the original 1930s comics and who had been largely forgotten in the widespread popularity of the more light-hearted television series. Miller's novel was aimed at adult readers, and its literary sensibility and noir tone, as well as its presentation as a series of four books, had a profound impact on both comic and graphic novel genres.

When Art Spiegelman won a Pulitzer Prize in 1992 for *Maus*, the ability of the graphic novel to express powerful themes was confirmed. Spiegelman used the comic strip form to 'speak the unspeakable' in his biographical story about his parents during the Holocaust. Depicting Nazis as cats and Jews as mice, Spiegelman created a multilayered narrative that recounted the traumatic experiences of his parents together with his own desire, as a second-generation Holocaust survivor, to come to terms with these events and to relate to his father.

Over the past twenty years, graphic novels have witnessed a rapid shift from the margins to the mainstream of literary publishing. Japanese *manga* has also reached the shelves of bookstores in the West, providing new inspiration and imagery for artists and readers alike. Graphic novelists today are experiencing greater recognition through awards such as the *Guardian* newspaper's First Book Award, presented to Chris Ware in 2001 for his novel *Jimmy Corrigan, the Smartest Kid on Earth*. And others, such as Dan Clowes (*Ghost World*), Alan Moore and Eddie Campbell (*From Hell*), Harvey Pekar (*American Splendor*) and Frank Miller (*Sin City* and *300*) are seeing their works reach new audiences by being adapted for cinema. Distinctions between the literary and the popular, the comic and the novel, mainstream and marginal, seem set to blur further in this ever-diversifying field.

CHRIS WARE

Although *Jimmy Corrigan* first appeared as a syndicated strip in US newspapers, author and artist Chris Ware conceived it, from the outset, as a lengthy narrative. The work combines innovative comic book art, hand lettering and graphic design to tell the story of Jimmy Corrigan, a boy with the face of a disappointed old man, and his relationship with his absent father. Ware has stated that he drew inspiration from 'original advertising drawings done for a Depression-era Chicago cosmetics firm where all the typography was hand done with a brush and white ink'.

Chris Ware
Jimmy Corrigan, the Smartest Kid on Earth
London, Jonathan Cape, 2001

Where IMAGINATION Begins

'... what is the use of a book,' thought Alice, 'without pictures or conversations?'
LEWIS CARROLL, *ALICE'S ADVENTURES IN WONDERLAND*

BOOKS FOR CHILDREN ARE A MAJOR PART OF CONTEMPORARY PUBLISHING THROUGHOUT THE WORLD. IT IS HARD TO IMAGINE A TIME WITHOUT THEM, BUT THEY ARE A RELATIVELY NEW PHENOMENON.

For thousands of years, children as well as adults listened to myths and fables for entertainment and for education. The first books specifically for children in the English-speaking world emerged during the Renaissance. These were alphabet books and primers, designed to instruct children from the privileged classes to learn to read and to become responsible adults. The earliest of these, in use from the fifteenth to the nineteenth century, were known as 'horn books': paddle-shaped objects designed to fit the hands of small children so that they learned as they played. The first horn books featured the letters of the alphabet in upper and lower case, incised into timber panels. Later versions consisted of the alphabet, vowel and consonant combinations, numbers, the Lord's Prayer and words of moral instruction. These were printed onto paper that was mounted onto panels of timber, ivory, leather or silver. The text was then protected by a transparent layer of animal horn, hence the term 'horn books'. By the late eighteenth century, these were joined by battledores—folded cards that contained short stories, fables and illustrations as well as the alphabet lessons of the horn book.

Children's primers conveyed religious and moral lessons along with literacy skills. One of the most significant of these, *The New-England Primer*, was first printed in North America in 1690. Its popularity quickly spread, with editions also becoming available in England, and it remained in print until the nineteenth century. Puritans believed that an inability to read enabled Satan to keep people from the teachings of the Scriptures. Each letter of the alphabet was introduced with a religious phrase and a woodcut illustration. It also included a range of prayers, religious verses and moral themes such as piety and duty to one's parents.

Another early book of instruction, from the late eighteenth century, *The Christmas-Box, or, the Golden Play-Thing for Little Children* by 'Nurse Truelove', summed up the intentions of such books for children in its subtitle: 'by which they may learn the Letters soon as they can speak, and know how to behave so as to make every body love them'. James Janeway also encouraged children to mend their wicked ways in his *Token for Children: Being an Exact Account of the Conversion, Holy and Exemplary Lives, and Joyful Deaths of Several Young Children*, first published in 1672.

By the seventeenth century, education in Europe began to spread to the middle classes with the establishment of elementary schools run by the state. The first children's picture book was also published at this time: Johann Amos Comelius's *Orbis Sensualium Pictus* (The Visible World in Pictures), published in Nuremberg in 1658. An illustrated dictionary with entries relating to the sciences, humanities and religion, the original version in Latin and German was quickly followed

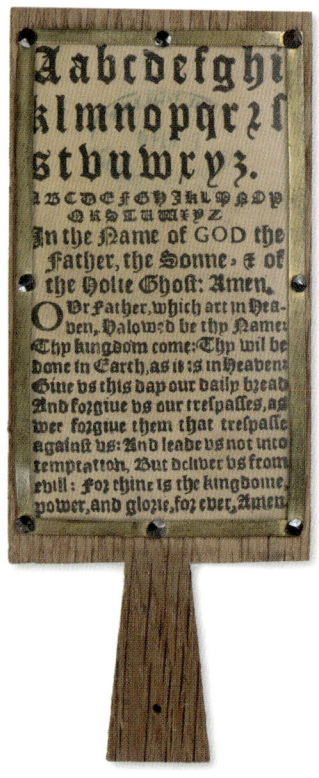
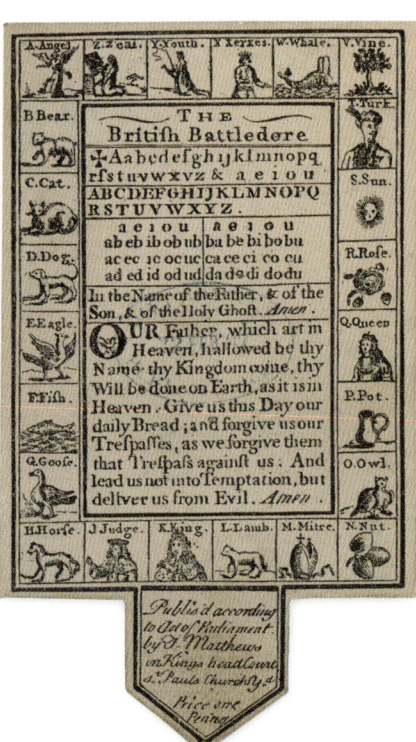
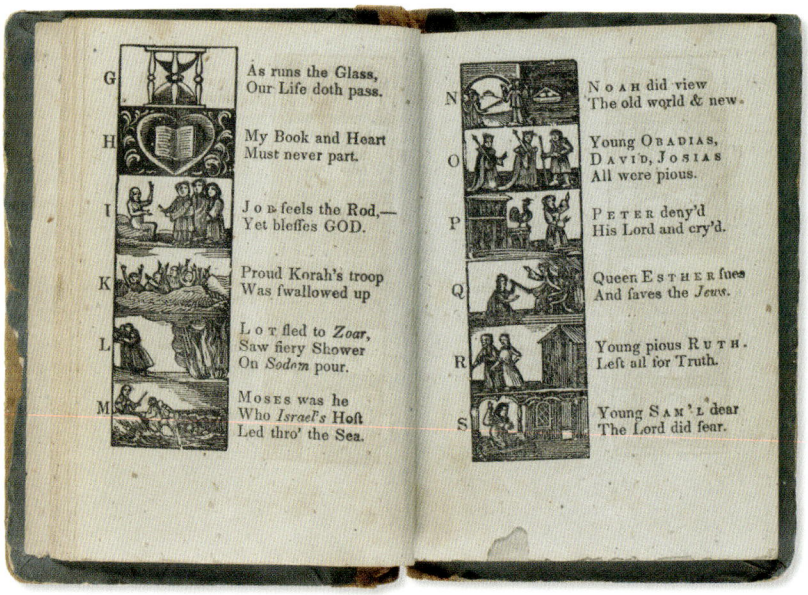

LEFT:
Facsimile horn book
From *History of the Horn-book*
London, Leadenhall Press, 1896

MIDDLE:
Facsimile battledore
From *History of the Horn-book*
London, Leadenhall Press, 1896

RIGHT:
The New-England Primer
Hartford, Connecticut,
Ira Webster, 1843
(1850 printing)

by multilingual editions in English, Italian and French. John Newbery's *A Little Pretty Pocket-Book* (1744) contains games, nursery rhymes and fables, and is often described as the first pleasure book for children. Newbery, a London bookseller and publisher, used a very early form of marketing to promote sales—the book was sold with a ball for boys and a pincushion for girls. His *History of Little Goody Two-Shoes* (1765) was also a favourite for many years.

Fairytales, nursery rhymes and fables have always been popular with children and were handed down orally before the production of books. *Aesop's Fables* was a perennial favourite, the first English edition of which was printed by William Caxton in 1484. Jean de La Fontaine's interpretations of the fables in the late seventeenth century were extremely popular, and were translated from French into many languages. The French poet Charles Perrault was one of the first to collect and publish fairytales. His *Histoires ou Contes du Temps Passé* (1697) included on its frontispiece *Contes de ma Mère l'Oye* ('Tales of Mother Goose'). It included the tales of such characters as Cinderella, Puss in Boots, Sleeping Beauty and Little Red Riding Hood but none of the nursery rhymes later associated with Mother Goose. These appeared in John Newbery's publication *Mother Goose's Melody* in 1781. In 1835, Hans Christian Andersen began publishing his fairytales in the first of many volumes he would issue over subsequent decades.

In Germany, Jacob and Wilhelm Grimm published their *Kinder-und Hausmärchen* (Childhood and Household Tales) as a series between 1812 and 1822. These first appeared in English the following year as *German Popular Stories* with illustrations by the renowned caricaturist George Cruikshank. Sourced from a range of oral traditions but infused with the Grimms' own social ideologies, these tales have been reinterpreted, studied and enjoyed for two centuries.

The nineteenth century was a golden age for children's books in England. Greater literacy coincided with technological innovations in printing and illustration that enabled the production of highly visual works on a mass scale. Mechanical or pop-up books also became easier to produce and were very popular throughout this period. Illustrators played an increasingly important role in books for children, and their names were used as well as those of the authors to promote sales, as they continue to be today.

Important children's books published in the latter part of the nineteenth century and throughout the twentieth century are too numerous to mention; however, one of the great works is Lewis Carroll's *Alice's Adventures in Wonderland* (1865). Written under a pseudonym by the Reverend Charles Dodgson, this work was originally produced in manuscript form in 1864 as a gift for Alice Liddell, the young daughter of HG Liddell, Dean of Christ Church at the

ABOVE:
Child holding horn book
From *History of the Horn-book*
London, Leadenhall Press, 1896

OPPOSITE:
Walter Crane
Puss in Boots
London, George Routledge and Sons, 1873

PUSS IN BOOTS.

A MILLER lay dying,—he made his last will;
He left his three sons his cat, ass, and mill:
To the eldest the mill, to the second the ass;
The third had the cat, and he cried out, "Alas!
I must starve now, unless I take Pussy to eat!"

OPPOSITE:
Edmund Dulac
Sindbad the Sailor and Other Stories From the Arabian Nights
London, Hodder and Stoughton, 1918

RIGHT:
Lewis Carroll
Alice's Adventures in Wonderland
London, Macmillan, 1898
Illustrated by John Tenniel

BOTTOM:
Mother Goose: The Old Nursery Rhymes
London, William Heinemann, 1913
Illustrated by Arthur Rackham

University of Oxford. Titled 'Alice's Adventures Underground', it included original illustrations by Dodgson himself. When it was published in a commercial edition the following year, Dodgson's illustrations were replaced by those of *Punch* magazine cartoonist John Tenniel. While many great artists have illustrated subsequent editions of this timeless favourite, Tenniel's illustrations continue to have iconic status.

Edmund Evans was a major figure in children's book illustration of the time. A master printer, he developed the 'toy book'—picture books with few pages but lavishly illustrated with full-colour wood engravings. Evans worked with publishers to commission illustrations from major artists including Walter Crane, Kate Greenaway and Randolph Caldecott. Walter Crane drew artistic inspiration from William Morris's Arts and Crafts movement as well as Japanese *ukiyo-e* woodblock prints. As an illustrator he viewed a book as a single work with multiple elements, regularly designing the title page, covers, endpapers and text as well as the illustrations themselves.

At the turn of the twentieth century, processes such as wood engraving were superseded by colour photographic processes. These enabled the reproduction of a whole range of imagery, from Beatrix Potter's delicate watercolours to the dramatic scenes painted by Arthur Rackham and Edmund Dulac for deluxe editions of children's books. Not all twentieth-century children's books were produced in large format or with lavish colour. AA Milne's *Winnie-the-Pooh* has remained a favourite for many children, as well as adults, since it was first published in 1926. Ernest H Shepard's modest pen-and-ink drawings perfectly

captured the foibles as well as the endearing qualities of Christopher Robin (based on Milne's son) and his toys Pooh, Piglet, Tigger and Eeyore as they ventured into the Hundred Acre Wood.

Other significant children's books to appear throughout the twentieth century were Jean de Brunhoff's tales of Babar the Elephant (first published in French in 1931, then in English in 1933) and the many works of Theodor Geisel, better known as Dr Seuss. Maurice Sendak's *Where the Wild Things Are* (1963) would determine much of the look and format of picture books as we know them today. With its economy of words and the conveying of a narrative through bold, full-page imagery, *Where the Wild Things Are* was an instant success and has remained in print ever since.

It is impossible to consider children's books today without mention of JK Rowling's Harry Potter. Although the series has been the subject of debate about its literary merits and perceived promotion of witchcraft and the dark arts, there has never been a publishing phenomenon quite like it. The books have been read in more than sixty languages by millions of children and adults alike.

In the early years of the twenty-first century, the range of fiction and nonfiction titles for children and young adults is as diverse as that for adults. As well as the picture books with simple narratives for young children, there are now picture books with complex social themes aimed at older readers. Literary genres continue to expand and now encompass a broad range of culturally specific audiences and age groups throughout the world. Children's authors today attract great followings, and their books continue to transport children to worlds that can only be imagined.

LEGENDS OF MOONIE JARL

Indigenous culture in Australia has a strong tradition of stories transmitted orally over thousands of years. Since the arrival of Europeans, some of these stories have been recorded in print but often from a non-Indigenous perspective. *The Legends of Moonie Jarl* is the first collection of stories for children told and illustrated by members of the community to whom the stories belong—the Badtjala people of the Fraser Island–Maryborough region in Queensland. Its images act as story maps and are presented with image keys and text to assist cultural interpretation.

ABOVE, LEFT:
Wilf Reeves, writer
Olga Miller, artist
The Legends of Moonie Jarl
Brisbane, Jacaranda Press, 1964

ABOVE, RIGHT:
AA Milne
Detail from
Winnie-the-Pooh
London, Methuen, 1926
Illustrated by Ernest H Shepard

RIGHT, TOP:
Maurice Sendak
Where the Wild Things Are
London, The Bodley Head,
1963 (1967 printing)

BOTTOM, LEFT:
Jean de Brunhoff
Babar's Travels
London, Methuen, 1935

BOTTOM, RIGHT:
Shaun Tan
The Lost Thing
Melbourne,
Lothian, 2000

JEAN DE BRUNHOFF

The tales of Babar the young elephant were first created by Cécile de Brunhoff and told to her children. In collaboration, her husband Jean then wrote and illustrated the first of many stories, *L'Histoire de Babar* (The Story of Babar), published in 1931. Six more Babar stories soon followed, and the series was continued by the de Brunhoffs' son, Laurent, after Jean's death. The Babar stories were translated into English, beginning with the first volume in 1933, and millions of copies in French and English have since been sold.

SHAUN TAN

In his picture book about a child's discovery of a huge machine-like thing, Shaun Tan explores notions of difference and belonging, conformity and creativity, humanity and mechanisation. He collages text and painting over a background of pages from physics and engineering textbooks. Tan's images propose an unknown and fantastic world while also paying homage to a range of artists such as Edward Hopper, Jeffrey Smart and John Brack.

Following the light of the sun, we left the Old World.
CHRISTOPHER COLUMBUS

Books reflect our desire to know the world—to see it, to classify it and to make sense of it. As well as documenting the past, books have always recorded the new. From scientific discoveries to journeys to new lands, books enable ideas and information to be shared across the globe.

PART III EXPLORING THE WORLD

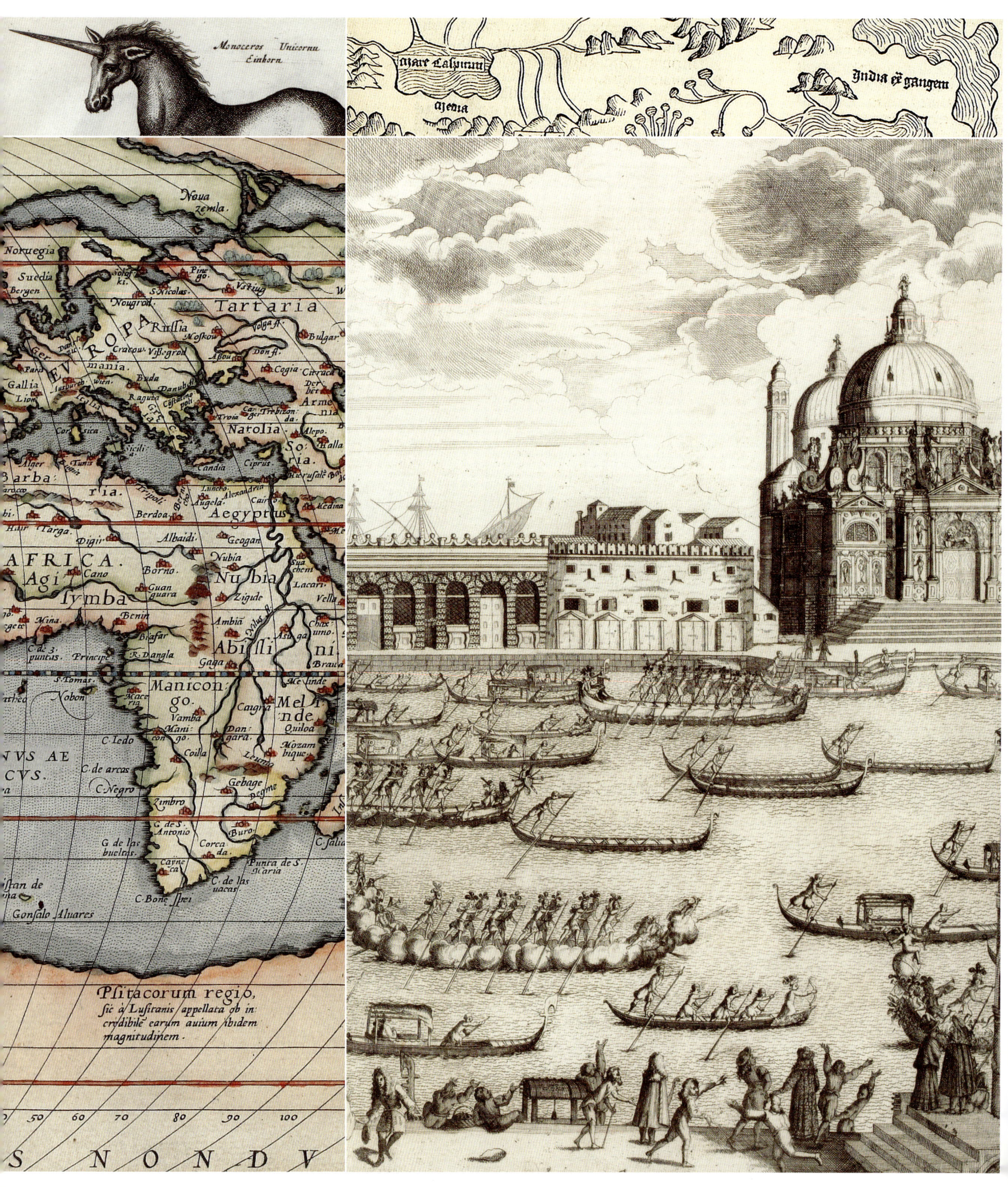

VENTURING
Out

There will come an age in the far-off years,
When Ocean shall unloose the bonds of things,
When the whole broad earth shall be revealed ...
SENECA, MEDEA

WHEN GREEK GEOGRAPHER PTOLEMY, WRITING IN ALEXANDRIA, EGYPT, IN THE SECOND CENTURY CE, COMPILED ALL THAT WAS KNOWN OF THE WORLD AT THE TIME OF THE ROMAN EMPIRE, HIS TREATISE *GEOGRAPHIA* SET IN PLACE MANY OF THE CONVENTIONS USED IN MODERN CARTOGRAPHY. PTOLEMY OVERLAID A GRID ON HIS WORLD MAP, ASSIGNING COORDINATES TO SOME EIGHT THOUSAND GEOGRAPHIC PLACE NAMES HE KNEW. HIS WORLD MAP SPANNED 180 DEGREES LONGITUDE, FROM THE CANARY ISLANDS TO CENTRAL CHINA, AND ROUGHLY 80 DEGREES LATITUDE, FROM THE ARCTIC TO THE EAST INDIES AND AFRICA.

Ptolemy's *Geographia* drew upon earlier sources of information, such as the geographer Marinos of Tyre, and Roman and Persian gazetteers. Ptolemy's general theories, like much knowledge from the Graeco-Roman world, were largely lost during Europe's Middle Ages. The thirteenth-century Byzantine scholar Maximos Planudes claims to have discovered, through much toil, a copy of the work, which he notes had disappeared for many years. This copy was most likely the source for the earliest surviving manuscript copies, produced around 1300. From that time on, it appears that Ptolemy's *Geographia* circulated rapidly in Europe, and its translation into Latin around 1406 by Jacopo d'Angelo enhanced its reputation as the single most important work on cartography at the time of the Renaissance. The first printed edition appeared in Venice in 1475, and the first with printed maps in Bologna in 1477. It became common practice for later, fifteenth-century editions to alter and add to the book's maps regularly as new information came to hand.

In discussing the problem of depicting a spherical earth on a sheet of paper, Ptolemy demonstrated both awareness that the world was round and also that his world map outlined far less than was known to exist. His underestimation of the size of the earth would later lead Christopher Columbus to believe he could reach Asia by sailing west from Spain. The earliest Ptolemaic maps often depicted a landlocked Indian Ocean, with Africa joined to Asia. Such depictions gave rise to the concept of a vast landmass in the southern oceans, believed to counterbalance the landmasses in the Northern Hemisphere. As the earliest European navigators set sail in the late fifteenth century, and the outlines of Africa and the Americas became known, this speculative landmass was pushed south, and was routinely depicted on sixteenth- and seventeenth-century maps as a vast southern continent circling the globe, known as *Terra Australis Incognita*.

But Ptolemy's interests were not limited to cartography. His *Almagest* drew together astronomical knowledge of the heavens from Greek and other sources, in particular the work of Greek astronomer Hipparchus, who, in the second century BCE, compiled the earliest star chart.

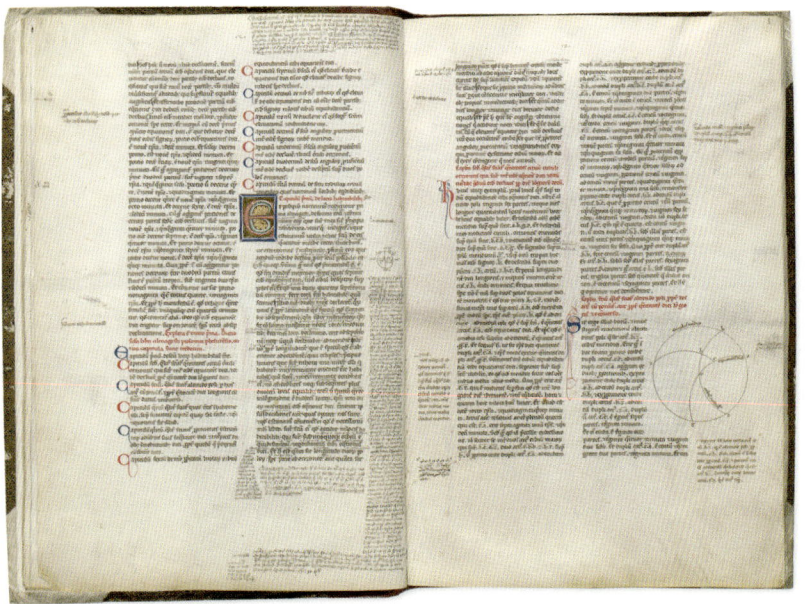
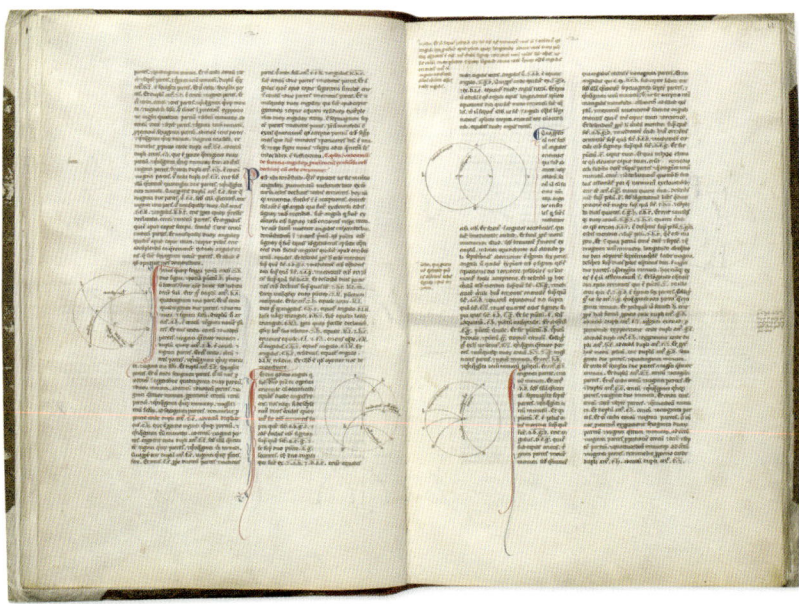

Ptolemy
Almagest
Italy, c. thirteenth century

In the *Almagest,* Ptolemy catalogued more than a thousand stars and outlined a geocentric model of the universe, with the earth at the centre of all the heavenly bodies.

The original title of Ptolemy's work on astronomy was the *Syntaxis*, but it is better known as the *Almagest*, a corruption of its Arabic title. It was lost to Europe in the Middle Ages, but survived in Arabic translations, where it proved influential during the great phase of Islamic astronomy between 900 and 1200 CE. In the twelfth century, the *Almagest* was translated from Arabic into Latin by Gerard of Cremona, an Italian scholar who travelled to Toledo, a centre of Arabic learning at the time, to devote himself to Latin translations of Arabic scientific literature. It was via his translation that Ptolemy's astronomical theories re-entered European thought, where they would hold sway until Copernicus proposed his heliocentric model, with the sun at the centre, in 1543.

The reintroduction of Ptolemy's work, along with other Greek and Roman texts, into Renaissance Europe set the scene for an explosion of knowledge about the world: its landscapes, peoples, natural history and wider cosmography. Hartmann Schedel's Nuremberg Chronicle of 1493 included a Ptolemaic world map showing only the outlines of Europe, northern Africa and India. Less than eighty years later, when Abraham Ortelius published his atlas *Theatrum Orbis Terrarum* (1570), the extent of the known world had more than doubled to embrace the Americas and the Pacific Ocean. In between these two books, the first European voyages of discovery had been undertaken—by Bartolomeu Dias, Vasco da Gama, Columbus, Magellan—and a narrative of new lands, exotic peoples and wondrous creatures had begun to be constructed in European literature and imagination.

Stories of strange and monstrous beings inhabiting the outermost edges of the world had long been in circulation. Greek historian Herodotus, writing in the fifth century BCE, included references to one-eyed peoples and to those with feet like goats residing in mountainous regions. Roman historian Pliny the Elder's natural history books, compiled in the first century CE, included commentaries on monstrous races in far, distant lands. The tenth-century Anglo-Saxon text known as *Wonders of the East* recycled these tales. Medieval manuscript copies featured illustrations of men with eyes and mouths in their chests and of dog-headed men known as cynocephali. Their reappearance as a series of woodcuts in the Nuremberg Chronicle attests to the continuing presence of monstrous peoples in European folklore into the Renaissance period, and to the fact that knowledge of unfamiliar regions relied as much upon myth and hearsay as it did upon accurate description.

Before the fifteenth century, travel books illustrated from life were not the convention. It was common practice for artists to depict scenes of which they had no first-hand experience. Representations of people, towns and landscapes in books tended to be both stylised and symbolic, as in the Nuremberg Chronicle, where the same woodcut was used to illustrate the cities of Mainz, Bologna and Lyon. Bernhard von Breydenbach's *Peregrinatio in Terram Sanctam* (1486), a record of his journey to the Holy Land in 1483–84, was significant for featuring first-hand topographic

BERNHARD VON BREYDENBACH

Breydenbach, a wealthy canon of the cathedral at Mainz, Germany, travelled to the Holy Land in 1483–84. He was accompanied by the artist Erhard Reuwich, who produced the map and six views included in the book. Breydenbach's is considered the first illustrated travel book to be printed, and the first to include topographic views drawn from life.

ABOVE:
Bernhard von Breydenbach
Peregrinatio in Terram Sanctam
Speier, Germany,
Peter Drach, c. 1502

LEFT:
Hartmann Schedel
Liber Chronicarum
(Nuremberg Chronicle)
Nuremberg, Anton Koberger, 1493

Abraham Ortelius
Theatrum Orbis Terrarum
Antwerp, Ant. Coppenium
Diesth, 1574

Pieter van der Aa
Icones Arborum, Fruticum et Herbarum
Leiden, c. 1720

PIETER VAN DER AA

Pieter van der Aa was a prolific Dutch publisher of maps and atlases. He was born in Leiden, the Netherlands in 1659, and was apprenticed to the bookselling trade at age nine, later starting his own business as a publisher at twenty-three. For the next fifty years, he published a large number of atlases and illustrated works, two of them running to twenty-seven and twenty-eight volumes respectively and containing more than three thousand maps and plates. He regularly recycled the work of earlier cartographers, caring little for the originality of his own works.

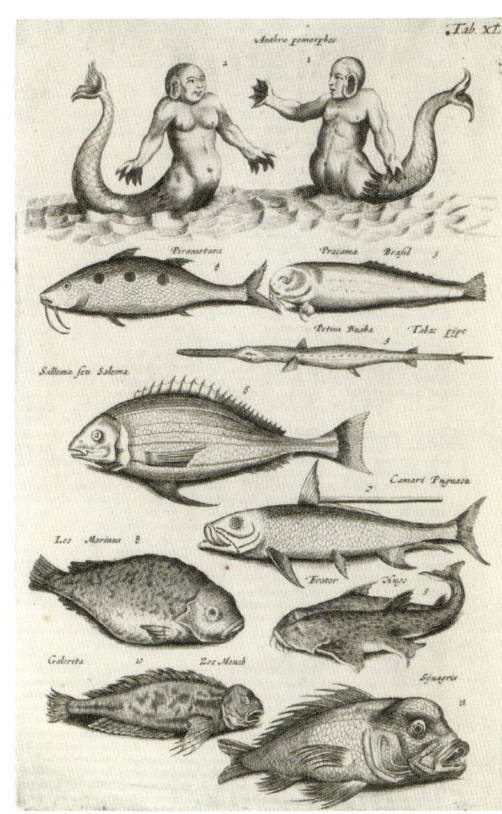

views by an artist, Erhard Reuwich, who accompanied him on his travels.

The illustrated botanical exotica of Pieter van der Aa's *Icones Arborum, Fruticum et Herbarum* (c. 1720), a work that drew liberally upon the accounts of Jan Huyghen van Linschoten's travels to the Portuguese East Indies in the 1580s, show that for many readers of the period, the real and the imaginary coexisted. The rigorous dividing line between fact and fiction, so central to the scientific revolution of the seventeenth century, was yet to be defined in the popular domain. Fantastical illustrations and stories were unquestioningly borrowed and recycled by writers from earlier accounts, where they intermingled with the everyday. Scottish writer John Johnston's seventeenth-century books on quadrupeds and marine life, which freely plundered the pioneering natural history works by Konrad Gesner and Ulissi Aldrovandi, featured striking engravings by Swiss artist Matthäus Merian of unicorns, mermaids and winged beasts, alongside Dürer's well-known rhinoceros. Early herbals commonly displayed male and female mandrake plants, which were believed to emit horrible screams when uprooted. Edward Topsell's *History of Four-Footed Beasts and Serpents* (1658) promulgated as accepted wisdom that weasels give birth through their ears and that unicorn horn is a cure for poison.

ABOVE, LEFT:
John Johnston
Historiae Naturalis de Quadrupedibus
Amsterdam, Joannem Jacobi fil. Schipper, 1657

ABOVE, RIGHT:
John Johnston
Historiae Naturalis de Piscibus et Cetis
Amsterdam, Joannem Jacobi fil. Schipper, 1657

RIGHT:
Edward Topsell
The History of Four-Footed Beasts and Serpents
London, printed by E Cotes, for G Sawbridge, T Williams and T Johnson, 1658

EDWARD TOPSELL

Edward Topsell, a Church of England clergyman, published his *Historie of Foure-Footed Beastes* in 1607. It drew heavily on Konrad Gesner's *Historiae Animalium* (1551–63), taking all the woodcuts directly from it. In 1608 he issued *Historie of Serpents*. These two works were later combined into a single volume in 1658 by John Rowland, twenty years after Topsell's death. It is considered an early example of employing the scientific method, even though much of the information was based on classical references that we now know to be mythical.

ROBERT HOOKE

Robert Hooke was responsible for designing a compound microscope and illumination system, one of the best microscopes of his day. He used magnifying lenses to make detailed observations of insects, plant life and such everyday things as cork or bird feathers. *Micrographia* was a record of these detailed observations, illustrated with Hooke's own superb drawings. The famous diarist Samuel Pepys claimed he stayed up until 2 a.m. one night reading Hooke's book, which he called 'the most ingenious book that I ever read in my life'.

BELOW, LEFT:
Robert Hooke
Micrographia, or, some Physiological Descriptions of Minute Bodies Made by Magnifying Glasses
London, printed by J Martyn and J Allestry, 1665

BELOW, RIGHT:
Johannes Hevelius
Selenographia
Gdansk, Poland, printed by Andreas Hünefeld, 1647

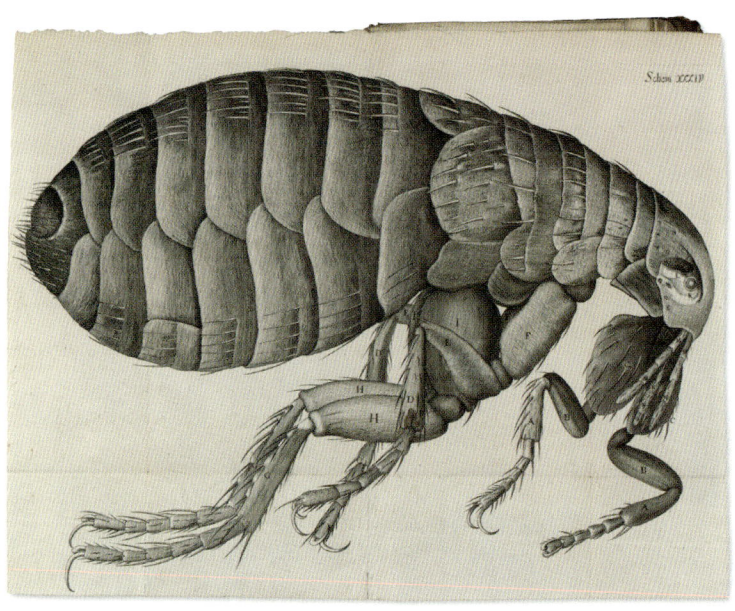

While the fantastic continued to be represented in accounts of newly discovered lands long after Europe's Renaissance, the spirit of scientific enterprise had nevertheless begun. In the wake of Copernicus and Galileo, astronomers like John Flamsteed, using telescopes that enabled more accurate observation, directed their attention to the furthest heavens. Flamsteed plotted the night skies in his *Atlas Coelestis* (1729) with accuracy unimaginable in Galileo's day. Johannes Hevelius's *Selenographia* (1647), lavishly illustrated by his own hand, provided the first descriptions of the moon, while around the same time English scientist Robert Hooke cast his gaze in very different directions. His *Micrographia* (1665), the result of the earliest use of the compound microscope, described and illustrated everyday microscopic organisms such as fleas and mites.

When we look at these early works of scientific inquiry, we can perhaps understand the confusion between the real and the imagined. Would Hooke's engraving of a common mite, or the craters of Hevelius's moon, have looked any less fantastical to a seventeenth-century viewer than the winged dragons or many-headed hydra to be found in Johnston's catalogue of serpents?

Setting out from their ports in the Mediterranean and beyond—Lisbon, Cadiz, Amsterdam, Bristol—European sailors brought home stories of extraordinary new lands. When, in the 1520s, Magellan's crew first reported a race of giants residing on the southern tip of South America, the concept seemed entirely credible to those back home. Magellan's name for these people, the Patagones, lent itself to the region, Patagonia. Subsequent reports from the voyages of Francis Drake and others confirmed these sightings, with some accounts claiming to have seen dead bodies nearly 4 metres long. The giants of Patagonia remained in the European imagination for 250 years, until the late eighteenth century. Their continued presence within a wider narrative of discovery reinforces the sense of adventure and wonder Europeans must have felt upon glimpsing these new lands for the first time.

JOHANNES HEVELIUS

Johannes Hevelius was born in Gdansk, Poland. He was the first person to depict the moon in a realistic manner with craters and plains, and was the founder of the science of selenography, or lunar cartography. Hevelius built his own observatory, carried out his own observations, ground his own lenses and made his own telescopes. He also drew and engraved all the illustrations in this book, which was first published in an edition of around a thousand copies. Tragically, Hevelius's observatory, containing all his instruments and much of his work, was burnt down in 1679, a blow from which he never recovered.

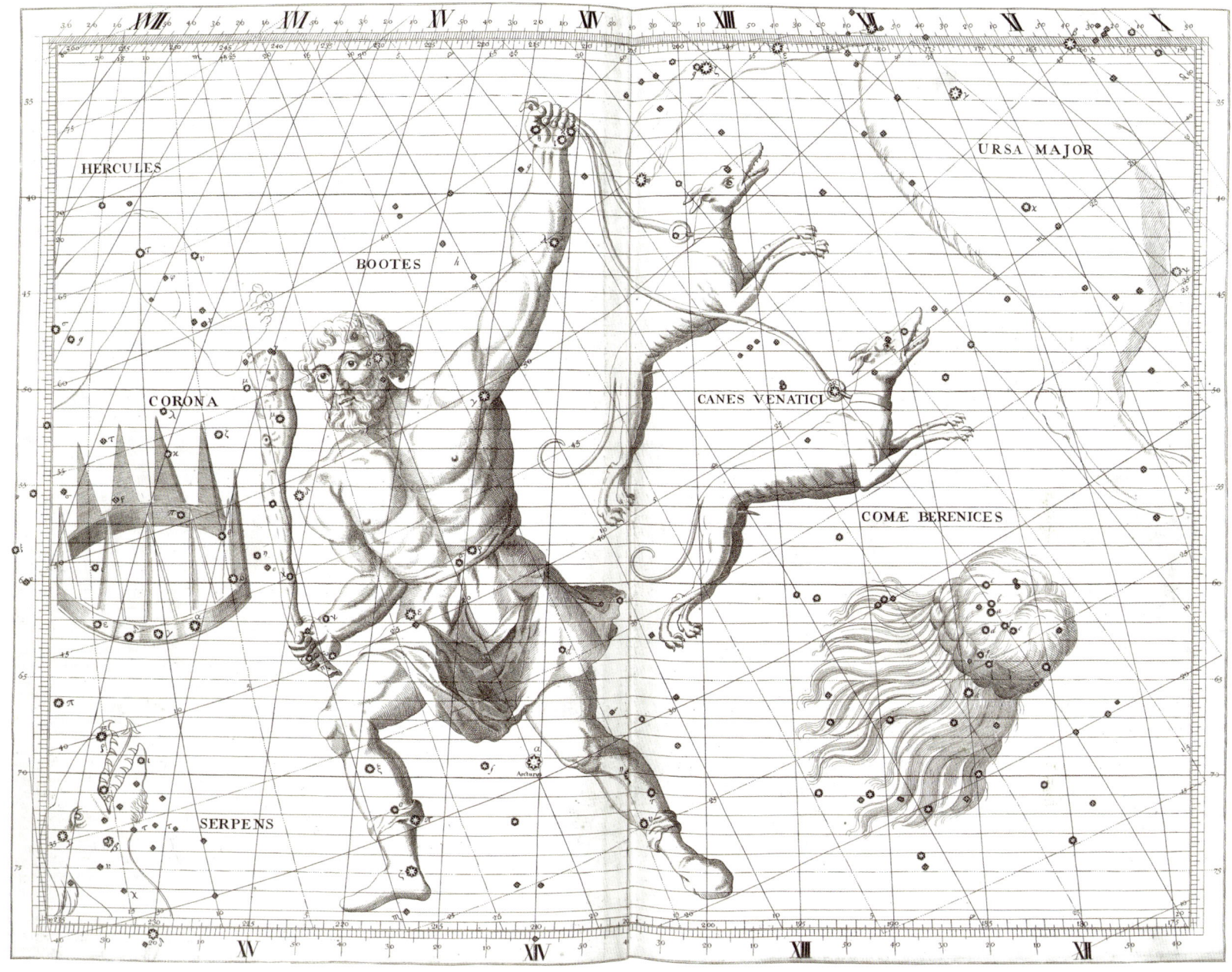

JOHN FLAMSTEED

John Flamsteed left school at a young age due to illness and taught himself astronomy from home. In 1675, he became the first royal astronomer at the newly built observatory at Greenwich. His catalogue of stars and his celestial atlas, which took more than twenty years to produce, were published after his death by his widow and set a new standard for astronomical scholarship. Flamsteed had previously fallen out with Isaac Newton and Edmond Halley after they pushed for premature publication of his work. Despite Flamsteed's objections, four hundred unauthorised copies of his incomplete observations were published by Prince George of Denmark in 1712. Flamsteed retrieved three hundred and burned them.

John Flamsteed
Atlas Coelestis
London, 1729

Other LANDS

There at last it lay, the bourn of my long weary pilgrimage, realizing the plans and hopes of many and many a year.

RICHARD BURTON, *PERSONAL NARRATIVE OF A PILGRIMAGE TO EL-MEDINAH AND MECCAH*

THE GREAT SEA VOYAGES OF THE FIFTEENTH TO EIGHTEENTH CENTURIES OPENED UP THE WORLD TO THE WEST LIKE NEVER BEFORE. THESE EUROPEAN EXPEDITIONS TO ASIA, THE MIDDLE EAST, AFRICA, THE AMERICAS AND THE PACIFIC WERE GENERALLY DESPATCHED WITH COLONIAL OR ECONOMIC IMPERATIVES IN MIND, BUT EXPLORERS ALSO RETURNED WITH TALES OF EXOTIC LANDS, AS WELL AS NEW SKILLS AND KNOWLEDGE FROM THOSE WHOM THEY ENCOUNTERED.

With new maps drawn, trade routes established and colonial outposts founded, a new wave of overland travellers embarked on discoveries of their own, gathering new information about the cultures, beliefs and everyday lives of the inhabitants they met.

While some travellers found themselves in new lands as members of military expeditions or trading parties, others were keen adventurers who had the passion and also the means to travel with the requisite retinue of guides, porters and cooks. While such journeys were difficult enough for men, a number of intrepid women also ventured across the globe, among them Lady Jane Digby, to the Middle East, and Mary Kingsley, to Africa.

Many travellers' accounts were published in lavishly produced volumes which were avidly collected and studied by a wealthy and educated elite of 'armchair travellers'. From the eighteenth century onwards, illustrations were increasingly incorporated into these publications, enhancing their ability to convey information to the reader.

The Spanish and Portuguese had been the first Europeans to discover new trade routes and establish powerful empires across the globe. They were followed by the Dutch, the French and the British, who all established colonies that would provide economic wealth and power for centuries to come.

With its major trading settlement at present-day Jakarta in Indonesia, the Dutch East India Company was the wealthiest company in the world in its day. Arnoldus Montanus drew on original manuscripts written by employees of the company, as well as other published sources, to compile his *Gedenkwaerdige Gesantschappen*, or 'Memorable Embassies' (1669). With its descriptions of the cities, nature, religions and customs of Japan, this book was the first major work on that country published in the West, and the Dutch were in a unique position to produce it. After being open to European traders and missionaries for nearly a hundred years, Japan had closed its borders to most foreigners by the mid seventeenth century. The only Westerners allowed to enter Japan for the next two hundred years were Dutch traders, and they were generally restricted to the man-made island port of Dejima at Nagasaki. There was great fascination in Europe with this little known land, and Montanus's work was translated into English and German within a year of its original publication by Jacob van Meurs.

TOP:
Arnoldus Montanus
Gedenkwaerdige Gesantschappen
Amsterdam, Jacob Meurs, 1669

BOTTOM:
Melchisédech Thévenot
Relations de Divers Voyages Curieux
Paris, de l'imprimerie de Jacques Langlois, 1663

PHILIPP FRANZ VON SIEBOLD

Philipp Franz von Siebold was one of the first Europeans to study Japanese life and culture in detail. A doctor as well as a naturalist, he was stationed at the Dutch trading base at Nagasaki from 1823. He facilitated the exchange of valuable information between the two cultures, introducing Western medical practices to Japan and educating European readers about Japanese arts, customs, history and its natural environment.

RIGHT:
Philipp Franz von Siebold
Nippon: Archiv zur Beschreibung von Japan
Leiden, 1852

BELOW:
George Henry Mason
The Costume of China
London, printed for W Miller by W Bulmer, 1800

Van Meurs also issued Montanus's work on the Americas as part of his series on world geography. Montanus was a staunchly Calvinist minister as well as a classicist, and because he never actually left Holland, his works are infused with his own speculations and biases.

French scientist and orientalist Melchisédech Thévenot published his *Relations de Divers Voyages Curieux* in 1663. The work is a compilation of French translations of previously published accounts of exploration and of a number of other unpublished manuscripts. Richly illustrated and with numerous maps, it describes discoveries throughout the Middle East, the East Indies and the Pacific. It includes one of the first printed maps to show Abel Tasman's charting of the Australian coastline in 1644. This inclusion is particularly rare for a French publication of the time because the Dutch tightly controlled knowledge and activity surrounding trade in the region of the East Indies.

China fascinated travellers in the eighteenth century. The trading port of Canton (present-day Guangzhou) was one of the few centres open to outsiders at that time and was of great interest to visitors. One of them was British Major George Henry Mason, who visited in 1789. His *Costume of China* (1800) contains sixty colour plates depicting different members of Chinese society in the dress and environment typical of their trade or class. The original illustrations were undertaken by the studio of Cantonese illustrator Pu Qua, who specialised in works for sale to western visitors. As he pointed out in his introductory text, Mason's publication was aimed at the growing market of book buyers fascinated by the 'domestic and mechanical habits of an original and remote nation'. His was one of a series of costume books published by William Miller around this time. In addition to works on Turkey, Austria, Spain, Italy and the Russian Empire, Miller also published *The Costume of Great Britain* (1805).

THOMAS DANIELL

Thomas Daniell was known as an 'artist-adventurer' because of his extensive travels throughout India. Travelling with his nephew William, Daniell arrived in Calcutta in 1786. Between 1788 and 1793 they made three tours of the country, supplementing their income by restoring paintings in the possession of European residents. Daniell's *Oriental Scenery* presented 144 views of landscapes and monuments in a series of large-scale deluxe volumes. This work was so popular with both Indian and European patrons that a smaller quarto edition was also issued.

ROBERT MELVILLE GRINDLAY

Robert Grindlay was seventeen years old when he arrived in Bombay in 1803 to join the East India Company's Native Infantry. A self-taught artist, he produced many sketches of daily life in India, from which these hand-coloured aquatints were made.

TOP:
Thomas Daniell
Oriental Scenery: Twenty-Four Views in Hindoostan
London, Thomas Daniell, 1797

RIGHT:
Robert Melville Grindlay
Scenery, Costumes and Architecture Chiefly on the Western Side of India
London, R Ackermann, 1826–30

ABOVE:
Alexander Russell
The Natural History of Aleppo
London, GG and J Robinson, 1794
(2nd edition)

With its depictions of potters, tanners, brewers and knife grinders, many of its subjects were arguably as foreign to its readership as those from lands distant and unknown.

Following the wave of military and archaeological expeditions, the Middle East and, in particular, the Holy Land became an area of great interest to travellers and readers during the eighteenth and nineteenth centuries. While many publications, such as those of traveller and artist David Roberts, focused on the temple ruins and other reminders of the region's archaeological past, others examined the daily life and culture of its contemporary inhabitants. *The Natural History of Aleppo* (1756) by Alexander Russell is one such example.

Scottish brothers Alexander and Patrick Russell lived in Aleppo, in modern-day Syria, during the mid eighteenth century. Both were physicians employed by the Levant Company, a British trading firm with interests throughout the Ottoman Empire. While many Europeans in the Middle East had little ability, let alone desire, to get beneath the surface of Arabic culture, the Russells possessed both. As medical practitioners, they had rare access to the homes, harems and bathhouses of the citizens of Aleppo. Their two-volume work, attributed to Alexander but to which both brothers contributed, describes the city and its monuments, the culture and customs of its residents and the natural history of the area. It also mentions diseases such as smallpox as well as evidence that protection by vaccination was a common and long-established practice throughout the Arab region well before it was developed in Europe. Through this and other examples, *The Natural History of Aleppo* provided an informed and objective view of Middle Eastern life at a time of general ignorance and attitudes of superiority in the West. It remained one of the main British sources of information about the region until the end of the eighteenth century.

Another traveller to get closer to Muslim culture than most Europeans was the renowned

CORNEILLE LE BRUYN

Dutch artist Corneille Le Bruyn spent nineteen years travelling through the Middle East in the late seventeenth century. His *Voyage to the Levant* contains more than two hundred engravings, including panoramic views such as this depiction of Jerusalem.

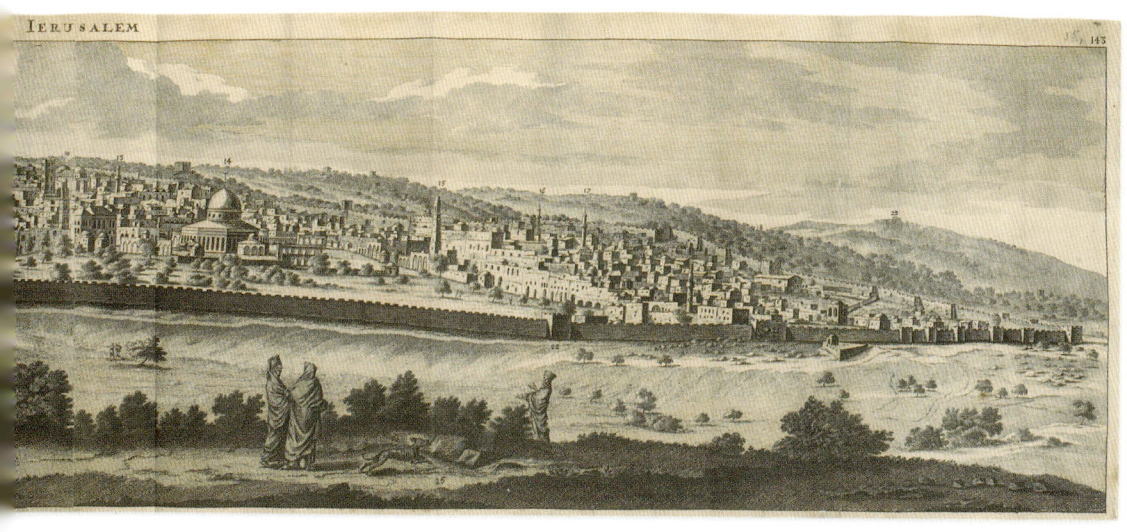

LEFT:
Corneille Le Bruyn
A Voyage to the Levant: or Travels in the Principal Parts of Asia Minor …
London, printed for Jacob Tonson and Thomas Bennet, 1702

FAR LEFT:
Richard Burton
Personal Narrative of a Pilgrimage to El-Medinah and Meccah
London, Longman, Brown, Green & Longmans, 1855–56

LEFT:
James Otto Lewis
The Aboriginal Portfolio
Philadelphia, JO Lewis, 1835–36

OPPOSITE:
James Rattray
Scenery, Inhabitants and Costumes of Afghaunistan
London, Hering & Remington, 1848

nineteenth-century British adventurer, orientalist and linguist Richard Burton. Throughout his military and diplomatic career, Burton travelled far and wide, from central Africa to Syria and from Iceland to Brazil. He also completed translations of *The Arabian Nights*, the *Kama Sutra* and *The Perfumed Garden*, all contentious at the time for their erotic allusions. Burton is probably most famous, however, for his daring pilgrimage in disguise to Mecca in 1853, as it is forbidden for non-Muslims to enter the holy city. He was not the first non-Muslim to participate in the Hajj, but his detailed account, *Personal Narrative of a Pilgrimage to El-Medinah and Meccah* (1855–56), made his journey the best documented.

Thirty years after Burton's controversial journey to Mecca, the Dutch orientalist Christiaan Snouck Hurgronje became the first European scholar to spend an extended period on the Arabian Peninsula—initially in the Dutch consulate at Jeddah, then for six months in Mecca in 1885. His two-volume work *Bilder-atlas zu Mekka* (1888–89) is a detailed study of Meccan society and includes views of the city and photographs of local dignitaries and pilgrims from as far away as Malaysia.

On the other side of the globe, travellers continued to explore the diverse cultures of the Americas. As the United States expanded west with the acquisition of French territories in 1803 and then Mexican-controlled lands north of present-day Mexico in 1848, American pioneers came into direct, and devastating, contact with the indigenous people of North America. The development of the railroad, the opening up of land to settlers and the slaughter of millions of buffalo had a severe impact on the ability of indigenous North Americans to move across their lands and hunt for food. During this time, a number of visitors to the area compiled and published books that attempted to capture indigenous life.

One such visitor was James Otto Lewis. A portrait painter, Lewis was commissioned to accompany government officials on a number of treaty expeditions in the Upper Great Lakes region during the 1820s. He undertook portraits of the individual chiefs who attended the treaty negotiations, as well as of some of their wives. Eighty of these portraits were reproduced as hand-coloured lithographs in his *Aboriginal Portfolio*, which was issued in ten monthly parts during 1835–36. At the time of publishing the tenth instalment, Lewis experienced financial difficulties and only a small number of sets were released. His work is therefore rare in number but also rare for its time in its dignified portrayal of indigenous North Americans as powerful individuals with both name and character rather than as anthropological types.

In an age of mass tourism and communication, it is difficult for us to appreciate the impact that such accounts had on their audiences. Many of these books, however, presented other cultures with the European biases of the day and now reveal as much about the society for which they were written as they do about their subjects.

JAMES RATTRAY

James Rattray was stationed in Afghanistan during the First Anglo-Afghan War of 1839–42. The hand-coloured plates in this volume are from his drawings done on the spot. They depict individuals from all parts of Afghan society as well as views of towns, buildings and monuments.

JOURNEYS
into the Past

It may be argued that the past is a country from which we have all emigrated. That its loss is part of our common humanity.

SALMAN RUSHDIE, *IMAGINARY HOMELANDS*

BOOKS ENABLE US TO JOURNEY INTO DISTANT PASTS. THEY TAKE US NOT ONLY TO THE TIMES IN WHICH THEY WERE WRITTEN, BUT THE PASTS OF WHICH THEY SPEAK.

The neoclassical era, in particular, was a period of fascination with the history and culture of Ancient Greece and Rome. The revival of classical learning had begun during the late Middle Ages with Europe's rediscovery of Greek and Latin texts. During the Renaissance, interest in Greek and Roman culture spread to influence art, architecture and literature. As archaeological sites began to be unearthed, artists and scholars travelled to these locations to study the temples, monuments and other evidence of these cultures for themselves. The books they produced upon their return documented their finds and inspired more artists and scholars to embark upon their own journeys of discovery.

From the late seventeenth until the early nineteenth century, the 'Grand Tour' emerged as a result of this new fascination with antiquity. It became a rite of passage for wealthy young men (and later women), particularly from the British Isles, to tour the European continent. Their time was spent visiting archaeological sites and being introduced to high society. After an absence of anywhere between six months and as many years, the 'grand tourist' would return with an impressive array of souvenirs, ranging from cameos and engravings to Greek vases, Roman statues and large and lavishly produced books.

Rome, with its abundance of classical ruins, was a popular destination. Ancient marvels such as the Colosseum, the Pantheon and the buildings and byways of the Roman Forum were recorded by local artists and these images sold as books, prints and paintings to this growing market. One artist whose work was avidly collected and carried home was Venetian-born Giovanni Battista Piranesi. Piranesi trained as an architect as well as an artist, and his plates capture the spectacular monumentality of Rome's ancient buildings. His images provided inspiration for neoclassical architects and designers throughout Britain and Europe.

Naples was another important stopover on the Grand Tour, largely due to its proximity to the recent excavations of the ancient cities of Herculaneum (unearthed from 1738) and Pompeii (from 1748). It was a sign of one's social status to secure an invitation to visit Sir William Hamilton, British Ambassador to the Court of Naples from 1764 to 1800. Hamilton studied the archaeology and geology of the region and

TOP:
Giovanni Battista Piranesi
Vedute di Roma
Paris, Francesco Piranesi, 1800

BOTTOM:
Sir Robert Ainslie
Views in Turkey
London, Robert Bowyer, 1810

OPPOSITE:
Thomas Major
The Ruins of Paestum, otherwise Posidonia, in Magna Graecia
London, T Major, 1768

amassed an enormous collection of Greek vases, Roman antiquities and geological specimens, many of which he later sold to the British Museum.

Hamilton had his collection of vases catalogued by French antiquarian Pierre d'Hancarville, and this record was published as four large volumes, *Antiquités Etrusques, Grecques et Romaines* (1766–67). Hamilton's *Campi Phlegraei: Observations on the Volcanos of the Two Sicilies* (1776, with a supplement in 1779) is a richly illustrated volume that documents the eruptions of Mount Vesuvius, the volcanic specimens and the excavations at Pompeii. Publications such as these encouraged tourists to visit the region and influenced artists and designers such as Jacques-Louis David, J-A-D Ingres and Josiah Wedgwood.

The eighteenth century was also the Age of Enlightenment, a time of great exploration and pursuit of knowledge. Significant works of classical history were published, notably Edward Gibbon's six-volume *History of the Decline and Fall of the Roman Empire* (1776–88). Throughout this period, major expeditions were undertaken by the French and the British to archaeological sites in Egypt, the Middle East and the Mediterranean. Artists and scientists were important members of these exploration parties, bringing back detailed accounts and depictions of these ancient sites. Such expeditions coincided with a golden age in book production, and there was a strong market for deluxe editions detailing these new-found wonders of the past.

When Napoleon Bonaparte embarked on his great scientific and military expedition to Egypt in 1798–99, he took with him around 170 scholars, scientists, artists and technicians. The team meticulously studied and documented the temples, statues and inscriptions of Ancient Egypt. One of the most significant discoveries was the Rosetta Stone, from which Jean-François Champollion would later unlock the secret to deciphering Egyptian hieroglyphic script. The archaeological findings of Napoleon's expeditionary forces were compiled by Edmé-François Jomard into the massive *Description de l'Egypte* (1809–28), comprising nine hundred plates bound in eleven 'elephant folio' volumes, nine volumes of text and three monumental volumes of double-sized engravings. The work would direct the attention of Europe to Ancient Egypt and help establish the field of Egyptology as we know it today.

RIGHT:
Pierre d'Hancarville
Antiquités Etrusques, Grecques et Romaines
Naples, William Hamilton, 1766–67

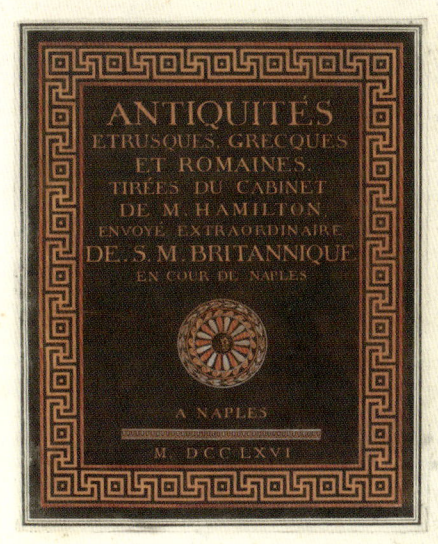

ATHANASIUS KIRCHER

Kircher's *Oedipus Aegyptiacus* is a remarkable early study of Ancient Egyptian hieroglyphic writing. A German Jesuit, Kircher has been compared to Leonardo da Vinci for his breadth of scholarship. He published texts in many scientific fields including medicine, geology, magnetism, acoustics and optics. He was also an authority in oriental studies and mastered many languages. Kircher developed a method of deciphering Egyptian hieroglyphic script that, while later discredited, remained an important source for Egyptologists such as Jean-François Champollion. With the rise of rationalism in the late seventeenth century, Kircher fell out of favour, but his work has re-emerged in recent years, and Kircher himself was given a cameo in Umberto Eco's 1994 novel *The Island of the Day Before*.

OPPOSITE:
William Hamilton
Campi Phlegraei: Observations on the Volcanos of the Two Sicilies
Naples, William Hamilton, 1776–79

ABOVE:
Athanasius Kircher
Oedipus Aegyptiacus
Rome, Vitalis Mascardi, 1652–54

ABOVE:
Edmé-François Jomard
Description de l'Egypte
Paris, Imprimerie de CLF
Panckoucke, 1821–28
(2nd edition)

RIGHT:
Karl Richard Lepsius
Denkmäler aus Aegypten und Aethiopien
Berlin, Nicolaische Buchhandlung, 1849–59

DAVID ROBERTS

The Scottish artist David Roberts arrived in Egypt in 1838 and from there travelled extensively throughout the Middle East. His *Holy Land: Syria, Idumea, Arabia, Egypt & Nubia* comprises three 'double-elephant' folios of lithographic plates depicting temples, columns and ruins of the region.

ABOVE, LEFT:
David Roberts
The Holy Land: Syria, Idumea, Arabia, Egypt & Nubia
London, FG Moon, 1842–49

ABOVE, RIGHT:
Giovanni Battista Belzoni
Narrative of the Operations and Recent Discoveries within the Pyramids, Temples, Tombs and Excavations in Egypt and Nubia
London, J Murray, 1820

Some years after the British defeat of Napoleon's Egyptian campaign, Italian engineer (and circus strongman) Giovanni Battista Belzoni travelled to Egypt in 1812 to propose to the Pasha, Mehmet Ali, a hydraulic scheme for the Nile. It was not adopted, but the British Consul General Henry Salt engaged Belzoni to remove the colossal bust of Rameses II from Thebes to the British Museum. Accompanied to Egypt by his wife Sarah, Belzoni also cleared the Temple of Abu Simbel of sand and was the first to enter the second pyramid at Giza. Belzoni recorded his discoveries in his lavishly illustrated *Narrative of the Operations and Recent Discoveries within the Pyramids, Temples, Tombs and Excavations in Egypt and Nubia* (1820). The volume also includes an essay described as 'Mrs Belzoni's trifling account of the women of Egypt, Nubia, and Syria'. This report is one of the earliest studies of domestic life in the region and could only have been undertaken by a woman because men were barred from visiting homes and other private spaces occupied by women.

In 1842, Egyptologist Karl Richard Lepsius was commissioned by King Frederick Wilhelm IV of Prussia to lead an expedition to Egypt and the Sudan. Modelled on the earlier Napoleonic expedition, a large team of scientists and artists studied and recorded the pyramids of Giza and the temples of Karnak and Luxor. Around 15 000 antiquities and casts were removed to the Egyptian Museum in Berlin, but Lepsius did leave behind a tribute to the Prussian king, carved into the stone above the entrance to the Great Pyramid of Giza and still visible today. Lepsius's massive twelve-volume work *Denkmäler aus Aegypten und Aethiopien* (Monuments from Egypt and Ethiopia, 1849–59) contains nearly nine hundred plates of drawings, plans and inscriptions, and was a primary source of information about Ancient Egypt until well into the twentieth century.

The past continues to be revealed to us through archaeological endeavour, scientific study and publishing, yet wars and pollution are increasingly taking their toll on the archaeological sites, monuments and artefacts that have been retrieved. While we race against time to discover, record and preserve our past, books live on as the evidence of peoples and cultures that have gone before us.

Terra AUSTRALIS

Touching the extent of these Regions newly discovered, grounding my judgment on that which I have seene with mine owne eyes ... The length therof is as great as all Europe & Asia ... the name of TERRA AUSTRALIS INCOGNITA may be blazoned and spread over the face of the whole world ...

PEDRO FENÁNDEZ DE QUIRÓS, *TERRA AUSTRALIS INCOGNITA*

THE PTOLEMAIC WORLD MAP OF THE LATE FIFTEENTH CENTURY DEPICTED A SPHERICAL EARTH MADE UP OF THREE CONTINENTS—EUROPE, AFRICA AND ASIA—JOINED IN THE SOUTH BY AN UNBROKEN EXPANSE OF LAND, NAMED *TERRA INCOGNITA*, WHICH CREATED A LAND-LOCKED INDIAN OCEAN. BUT EVEN AS EUROPEAN ARTISTS AND WRITERS WERE CONJURING IMAGINARY BEINGS IN THE UNKNOWN SOUTHERN HEMISPHERE, THE TASK OF ACCURATELY MAPPING THE WORLD'S OCEANS WAS UNDERWAY.

When Prince Henry the Navigator sent his Portuguese caravels beyond Cape Bojador on the African coast in 1434, he disproved the long-held belief that this point marked the furthest limit of the navigable ocean. Henry's caravels proved it was possible to sail down the coast of Africa and, more importantly, return. It took a further fifty years for Bartolomeu Dias to round the Cape of Good Hope, but a decade later Vasco da Gama's ships had reached India, forever dispelling the myth of a landlocked Indian Ocean. Christopher Columbus, sailing west from Spain in 1492 in search of the Indies, ran headlong into the Americas. By the time that Ferdinand Magellan, seeking a western route from Spain to the Spice Islands, sailed through the straits below South America and entered the Pacific in 1520, the true expanse of the world's oceans had at last been revealed to European cartographers.

By the 1530s, European world maps were showing an Indian Ocean linked to the Atlantic below Africa, and linking the Atlantic to the Pacific Ocean below the Americas. Already, the vast parameters of Ptolemy's southern continent were shrinking. But the concept of a southern continent was fixed in the European consciousness. Even after Magellan showed that the Pacific and Atlantic were joined, the land to the south of the Strait of Magellan, Tierra del Fuego, began to be conceived of as the northern tip of a vast southern continent. French cartographer Oronce Fine's map of 1531 depicted a great southern landmass, *Terra Australis*, to which he added the words 'newly discovered but not fully known' in reference to Magellan's Tierra del Fuego. Some years earlier, French navigator Paulmier de Gonneville claimed to have discovered *Terres Australes*, where he lived for several months during his voyage of 1503–04. The existence of Gonneville Land, which in reality was probably Brazil, held sway over the French imagination until the late eighteenth century, when several expeditions were dispatched, unsuccessfully, to rediscover it.

The exact shape and extent of the landmass *Terra Australis Incognita* varied on early maps, its scale generally dependent on the cartographer's imagination, as were other decorative features

Claes Jansz Visscher
Tabularum Geographicarum Contractarum
Amsterdam, CJ Visscher, 1649

RIGHT, TOP:
Ptolemy
Geografia
Venice, Vincentium
Valgrisium, 1562

RIGHT, BOTTOM:
Isaac Commelin, editor
Begin Ende Voortgangh, van de Vereenighde Nederlantsche Geoctroyeerde Oost-Indische Compagnie
Amsterdam, 1646

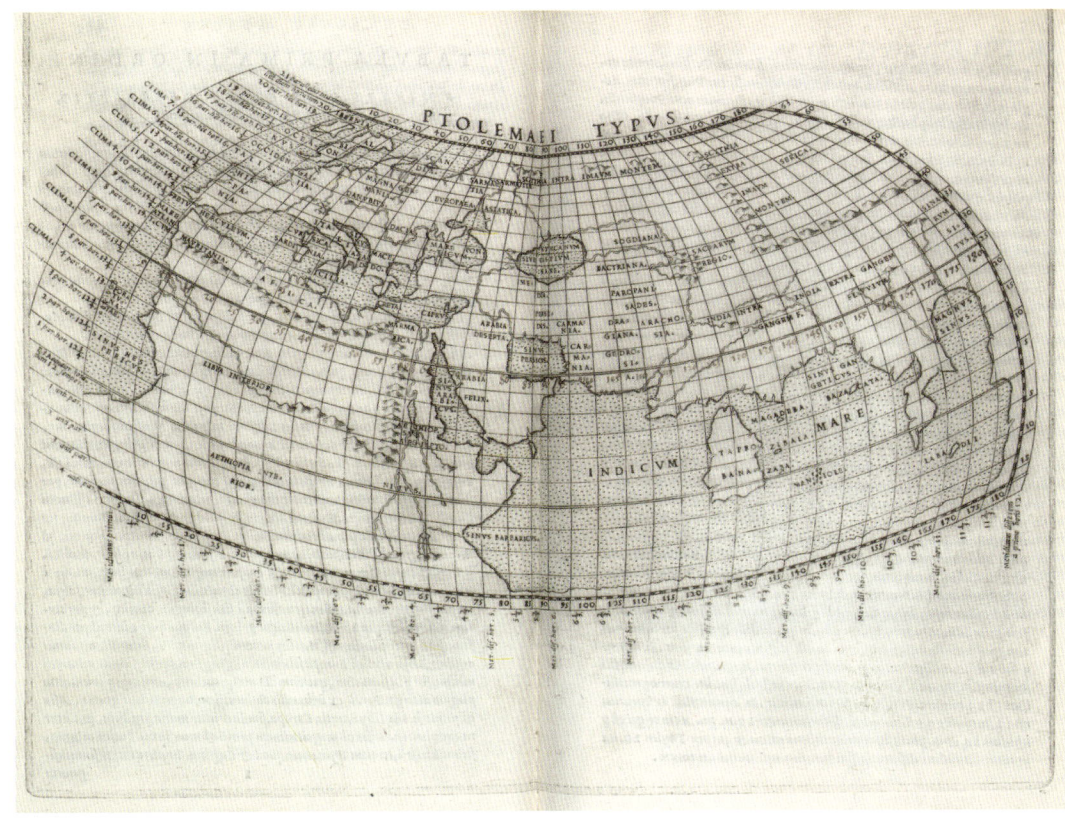

ISAAC COMMELIN

Dutch historian Isaac Commelin compiled this important collection of voyages, whose title literally translates as 'The Beginning and Ending of the Dutch East India Company'. It contains illustrated accounts of twenty-one Dutch voyages made between 1595 and 1640, including those by Cornelis Houtman, Jacob van Neck, Steven van der Hagen, Jacob Le Maire and others to the East Indies.

such as mermaids and sea monsters dotting the oceans. Marco Polo's account of his thirteenth-century travels from China to the Middle East, which included a six-month stay at Java Minor, proved a popular source of information for cartographers. Gerhard Mercator's world map of 1569 incorporated place names, often incorrectly cited, drawn from Marco Polo's travels—such as Beach and Maletur—onto his speculative southern continent below Java Major. Some cartographers, such as Abraham Ortelius in his atlas *Theatrum Orbis Terrarum* (1570), followed Mercator's lead, filling the Southern Hemisphere with an immense continent that circled the globe. Others remained content to trace a faint outline, a tantalising hint of the mysteries contained therein.

The series of world maps produced at the French port of Dieppe between the 1540s and 1560s remain exceptional for their uniform depiction of a large landmass known as Java la Grande, situated to the south of Java and separated from it by a narrow strait. The place names on these maps are believed to be of Portuguese origin, presumably derived from a common source such as a Portuguese world map. The consistency with which the landmass Java la Grande appears on these maps has led to the conjecture that its coastlines may reflect real rather than speculative knowledge. The resemblance of Java la Grande

BELOW:
Pierre Desceliers
World Map 1550 (detail)
London, Trubner & Co., 1885

BOTTOM:
Gerhard Mercator
Atlas Minor Gerardi Mercatoris
Amsterdam, 1610

PIERRE DESCELIERS

Pierre Desceliers's world map of 1550 is one of a series of maps, known as the Dieppe maps, produced by French cartographers at Dieppe between the 1540s and 1560s. The presence of Java la Grande, along with the Portuguese origin of many of the place names on the maps, led writers such as RH Major and George Collingridge to argue for a Portuguese discovery of Australia in the early sixteenth century.

GERHARD MERCATOR

This edition of Mercator's atlas was published by the Dutch cartographer Jocodus Hondius. He had purchased the plates of Mercator's atlas in 1604 from Mercator's grandson, and in 1606 and 1610, Hodius began reissuing the atlas in updated form, including this re-engraved pocket edition. Mercator's atlas had fallen out of fashion with readers in comparison with Ortelius's great atlas, and Hondius was largely responsible for the revival of Mercator's reputation. Hondius's reissue of the Mercator atlas proved immensely popular, and would eventually run to nearly fifty editions in the period up to 1641.

to the Australian continent has given rise to the claim that Portuguese navigators could have charted the east coast of Australia some 250 years before Captain James Cook's first voyage.

The world maps produced at Dieppe by Pierre Desceliers, Nicolas Desliens and others all show the coastline of Java la Grande joined to a large southern continent, *Terre Australle,* circling the globe. In the charts reproduced in Jean Rotz's *Boke of Idrography* (1542), however, the coastal outline of Java la Grande ends at a specific point in the southern oceans. Given Rotz's claim that his maps depicted only known coastlines, his charts provide the strongest evidence that some genuine local knowledge of the region informed the presence of Java la Grande on these maps.

By the second half of the sixteenth century, Portuguese mariners had charted the East Indies via their trade routes in the Indian Ocean and settlements at Goa, Hormuz and Malacca. The Spanish meanwhile carved out their own domain in the Pacific, establishing a trading post in the Philippines in the 1560s. New Guinea's northern coastline had been explored and was sometimes depicted on maps as joined to a large southern continent; at other times it was separated by a strait. Spanish navigator Álvaro de Mendaña,

sailing west from Peru in 1567, discovered the Solomon Islands, convinced that he had reached the outlying edges of the mythical *Terra Australis*. Because of the difficulty in determining longitude at the time, the islands effectively became lost to mariners and were not rediscovered for another two hundred years, when French navigator Louis-Antoine de Bougainville came across them. Mendaña would later lead a failed second expedition across the Pacific in 1595, which saw the Spanish establish a brief settlement on the island of Santa Cruz. Plagued by illness, the settlement was abandoned within months, and following Mendaña's death on the island, the survivors, led by Pedro Fenández de Quirós, sailed for the Philippines.

The Spaniard Quirós remained convinced that the massive continent of *Terra Australis* stretching across the Pacific to the Strait of Magellan lay within his reach. His expedition of 1605–06, sailing west from Peru, discovered a large landmass he believed to be the great southern continent and which he named *la Australia del Espíritu Santo*. In reality, Quirós had reached the largest group of islands in what was later named by Cook the New Hebrides. It was during the exploration of *la Australia del Espíritu Santo* that

Abraham Ortelius
Theatrum Orbis Terrarum
Antwerp, Ant. Coppenium
Diesth, 1574

JAN HUYGHEN VAN LINSCHOTEN

Linschoten's role as secretary to the Archbishop of Portuguese Goa in the 1580s provided him with the opportunity to travel extensively and collect information about the Far East. He also had access to detailed Portuguese charts of the region. His notebooks, first published in Amsterdam in 1596, would play an important role in facilitating Dutch expansion into the East Indies.

ABOVE, LEFT:
Jan Huyghen van Linschoten
Iohn Hvighen van Linschoten, His Discours of Voyages into ye Easte & West Indies
London, printed by John Wolfe, 1598

ABOVE, RIGHT:
Pedro Fenández de Quirós
Terra Australis Incognita, or a New Southerne Discoverie, Containing a Fifth Part of the World. Lately Found by Ferdinand de Quir
London, printed for John Hodgetts, 1617

OPPOSITE, TOP:
Joan Blaeu
Nova et Accuratissima Totius Terrarum Orbis Tabula
Amsterdam, J Blaeu, 1664

OPPOSITE, BOTTOM:
Willem Lodewijcksz
Prima Pars Descriptionis Itineris Navalis in Indiam Orientalem
Amsterdam, ex officina Cornelii Nicolai, 1598

the ships of the expedition became separated, and Luis Váez de Torres, continuing westwards, made his celebrated passage through the straits that bear his name.

After Quirós returned to Madrid in 1607, he spent his final years issuing memorials, some fifty in all, to the King of Spain describing his discoveries and petitioning for funds to return and explore the great southern continent he claimed to have discovered. His eighth memorial, translated into English in 1617 as *Terra Australis Incognita, or a New Southerne Discoverie, Containing a Fifth Part of the World. Lately Found by Ferdinand de Quir*, proclaimed the extraordinary size of this new continent: 'The length thereof is as great as all Europe & Asia'.

The Dutch move into the East Indies began in the late 1500s. Dutchman Jan Huyghen van Linschoten was in the employ of the Portuguese at Goa during the 1580s, and his account of the geography and natural history of the East Indies, published as *Itinerario, Voyage ofte Schipvaert van Jan Huygen van Linschoten* (1596), played an important role in Dutch expansion into the region by providing sailing directions that would avoid contact with the Portuguese. The first Dutch trading expedition to the East Indies, led by Cornelis Houtman, took place in 1595. The arrival of Houtman's four ships in Java, Madura and Bali signalled the end of the Portuguese monopoly on the lucrative spice trade.

The establishment of the VOC (Vereenigde Oostindische Compagnie), or East India Company, in 1602, and its monopoly on Dutch trade in the Pacific and Indian oceans, ensured the Dutch would be the dominant European presence in the region throughout the seventeenth century. In this they were assisted by the outstanding maps and atlases produced by Dutch cartographers of the period. The engraved maps of Willem Blaeu, Jan Jansson, Hendrik Hondius, Frederick de Wit and others, with their decorative borders depicting costumed figures and topographic views, were intentionally designed as both utilitarian and lavish productions.

In 1606, soon after the rise of the VOC, the tiny Dutch ship *Duyfken* made the first recorded European landfall on the Australian coast. Exploring the south coast of New Guinea and failing to find a passage through the Torres Strait, the *Duyfken* turned south and sailed down the western side of Cape York Peninsula, charting more than 300 kilometres of coastline.

The adoption of a new route by the Dutch to the East Indies after 1610 virtually guaranteed Dutch contact with the west Australian coastline. Instead of hugging the African coast, Dutch captains were advised to sail directly east after rounding the Cape of Good Hope, sailing as far as the longitude of the Sunda Straits before heading north for Batavia (now Jakarta). The difficulty

JOAN BLAEU

Joan Blaeu inherited his father Willem's printing business upon his death in 1638 and turned it into the largest European printing press of the seventeenth century. In the same year, he was appointed chief cartographer for the Dutch East India Company. From the mid 1630s to the 1660s, he progressively issued his multi-volume great world atlas *Theatrum Orbis Terrarum* or *Atlas Novus*, the largest and most expensive publication of its time. In 1672, a massive fire devastated the business, bringing to a close one of the great periods in cartographic history.

WILLEM LODEWIJCKSZ

Lodewijcksz sailed with Cornelis Houtman in 1595 as part of the first Dutch voyage to the East Indies. His journal was published by Cornelis Claesz less than a year after Houtman's return to Amsterdam. The voyage, financed by the Verre Company, produced little by way of profit but signalled the end of Portuguese domination of trade in the region.

of establishing longitude at sea led to a series of unintended landings on the Australian coast. Between 1616, when Dirk Hartog aboard the *Eendracht* landed in the vicinity of Shark Bay, and 1629, when the *Batavia* was wrecked on Houtman's Abrolhos, the Dutch could lay claim to having charted much of the western and south-western coastline of the Australian continent.

While the standard route for VOC ships to the East Indies was across the Indian Ocean, the private venture undertaken by Willem Cornelis Schouten and Jacob Le Maire in 1615 instead crossed the Pacific in search of a new route to the Indies. The voyage, funded by the newly formed Australische Compagnie, sought to challenge the VOC's monopoly on the spice trade, but also to seek out the rich lands of *Terra Australis* that Spanish navigator Quirós claimed to have discovered on his Pacific voyage. As all but VOC ships were banned from the Strait of Magellan, they sailed further south, rounding Cape Horn, which they named after one of their ships, the *Hoorn*, lost in a fire at Patagonia. The land they sighted to the south-east of Tierra del Fuego, which was later shown by Hendrik Brouwer in 1643 to be an island, they named Staten Landt, believing it to be the edge of a great southern continent. Their voyage across the Pacific provided important information for Dutch cartographers but failed to find any trace of Quirós's continent. When they arrived in Java, Schouten and Le Maire were immediately arrested for breaching the VOC's monopoly on the Indies trade.

The question whether Australia's coastline, in part charted by the Dutch, was connected to a much larger southern landmass was finally addressed in 1642, when the VOC sent Abel Tasman with two ships to discover 'the southern portion of the world'. Sailing at a latitude of roughly 44 degrees, Tasman's course took him below the Australian coastline, confirming it as separate from any larger southern continent. After touching upon the southern coast of Tasmania, he sailed east and charted the west coast of New Zealand. Despite the fact that, henceforth, Australia, or New Holland as the Dutch named it, would appear distinct from any depiction of *Terra Australis Incognita* on seventeenth-century maps, it remained a possibility that the coast of New Zealand was part of a larger continent stretching across to South America. To this end, Tasman named it Staten Landt, in the belief that it might have been connected to the land sighted by Schouten and Le Maire off South America on their earlier voyage.

By the time Tasman completed his second voyage in 1644, having charted the north-western coastline of Australia, the iconic Dutch map of New Holland was fixed. The findings of his voyages were first incorporated into Joan Blaeu's world map of 1645–46. Showing the western half of the continent, from Cape York Peninsula in the north to the south-western coastline, and part of Tasmania, it would be reproduced unchanged on European maps for more than a century, until the time of Cook's voyages.

While the long-held belief in *Terra Australis Incognita* persisted well into the eighteenth century, it was as if the confidence with which earlier cartographers had drawn it had been shaken. Increasingly, throughout the seventeenth century, European cartographers adopted the practice of including only known, rather than speculative, coastlines on their maps.

FREDERICK DE WIT

Based on an earlier map by Dutch cartographer Pieter Goos, this sea chart of South-East Asia, published by Frederick de Wit in his maritime atlas *Orbis Maritimus*, depicts the Dutch sphere of influence in the region at that time. It includes the known northern and western coastlines of Hollandia Nova based on early Dutch discoveries up to and including the voyages of Abel Tasman in 1642–44.

JORIS VAN SPILBERGEN

Spilbergen, an admiral with the Dutch East India Company, escorted Willem Cornelis Schouten and Jacob Le Maire back to Europe after their arrest in Java for breaching the VOC's monopoly on trade in the East Indies. Le Maire died on the return journey, and Spilbergen drew on his journals to publish one of the earliest accounts of Le Maire's voyage across the Pacific in 1615–17. Spilbergen's book included a plate of Patagonia showing Dutch sailors measuring the skeleton of a Patagonian estimated to be more than 3 metres in length.

ABOVE:
Frederick de Wit
Orientaliora Indiarum Orientalium
Amsterdam, c. 1675

OPPOSITE:
Joris van Spilbergen
Oost Ende West-Indische Spiegel
Leiden, 1619

A CLOSER Look

On the 31st, in the morning, we weighed anchor, having a fine breeze from the s.e. left the coast of New Zealand, and steered our course toward New Holland ...

SYDNEY PARKINSON, *A JOURNAL OF A VOYAGE TO THE SOUTH SEAS*

THE THREE GREAT VOYAGES OF CAPTAIN JAMES COOK TO THE PACIFIC USHERED IN A NEW ERA OF EXPLORATION. TAKING ADVANTAGE OF DEVELOPMENTS IN MARITIME TECHNOLOGY, SUCH AS JOHN HARRISON'S CHRONOMETER FOR DETERMINING LONGITUDE, COOK WAS ABLE TO CHART THE MANY ISLANDS AND COASTLINES THROUGHOUT THE PACIFIC OCEAN WITH ACCURACY UNDREAMT OF BY EARLIER NAVIGATORS.

Unlike European expansion into the East Indies, which was founded upon commercial imperatives, Cook took with him teams of scientists and artists, intent on documenting first-hand the peoples and landscapes of the Pacific. The artwork of Sydney Parkinson, William Hodges and John Webber, reproduced in both official and unofficial accounts of Cook's voyages, provided Europeans with an unparalleled visual narrative of the region.

The Age of Enlightenment in Europe brought with it an enthusiasm for cataloguing and classifying the world's knowledge and wonders. In 1735, Swedish botanist Carl Linnaeus had laid out a new set of principles for the classification of the natural world. In France, by the 1750s, philosopher Denis Diderot was at work on his great *Encyclopédie*, a vast compendium that sought to organise the world's knowledge along ordered lines. At the same time, the French natural historian Georges Louis Leclerc, Comte de Buffon, was issuing his forty-four volume *Histoire Naturelle, Générale et Particulière* (1749–1804), an unprecedented attempt to document and describe the natural world. These same principles of classification began to be applied to a newly developed interest in ethnography. In part, Cook's voyages were a natural outcome of this process of inquiry, and inaugurated a new cycle of European voyages concerned as much with science as with strategic or commercial considerations.

The official reason for Cook's first voyage in the *Endeavour* of 1768–71 was to observe the transit of Venus from Tahiti. The island had first been encountered in 1767 by the English navigator Samuel Wallis, who named it King George Island. The following year it was visited by French navigator Louis-Antoine de Bougainville, who, unaware of Wallis's visit, named it 'Nouvelle-Cythère' after the mythical island and birthplace of Aphrodite, the Greek goddess of love. Bougainville's account of the free-spirited Tahitians would do much to foster the ideal of the 'noble savage' and the utopian dreams of French philosophers such as Jean-Jacques Rousseau.

Cook spent three months on Tahiti carrying out astronomical observations, after which he sailed south, as instructed by the British Admiralty, in search of a continent whose fabled existence was the real reason for the voyage. However, after sailing south to 40 degrees latitude and failing to find any signs of a large continent, Cook sailed east and circumnavigated both islands of New Zealand, thereby proving it was not part of a larger landmass as had been suggested. Cook then sailed to the east coast of Australia, charting it for the first time from Tasmania to Cape York Peninsula and naming it New South Wales.

Cook's second voyage of 1772–75 was his greatest. By sailing further into Antarctic waters than

BELOW:
Sydney Parkinson
A Journal of a Voyage to the South Seas, in His Majesty's Ship, the Endeavour
London, printed for Stanfield Parkinson, the editor, 1773

BOTTOM:
James Cook
A Voyage towards the South Pole, and Round the World
London, printed for W Strahan and T Cadell, 1777

any previous navigator, he dispelled the age-old dream of *Terra Australis*. His vast sweeps across the Pacific added enormously to European knowledge of the region, and artist William Hodges's views of Tahiti, Easter Island, the Marquesas Islands, Tonga and the New Hebrides became the basis for a new, romantic vision of the South Seas.

Having solved the problem of *Terra Australis* for cartographers, Cook set out to find the mythical North-West Passage between the Pacific and Atlantic oceans. It was on this third voyage, in the *Resolution*, that he came upon the Hawaiian Islands, or Sandwich Islands as he named them, the first European to do so. Heading north, he explored the west coast of America, accurately charting it from California to the Bering Strait. It was on his return visit to Hawaii that Cook was killed as a result of a dispute about the theft of one of the *Resolution*'s longboats.

After Cook's great voyages, the English appeared to lose interest in scientific exploration of the Pacific, instead focusing their attention on the establishment of a penal settlement in New South Wales. The journals and accounts of officers of the First Fleet, including those of Governor Arthur Phillip, John White and John Hunter, published in London

SYDNEY PARKINSON

Parkinson was chief artist on Cook's first voyage, during which he completed some 950 botanical drawings for botanists Joseph Banks and Daniel Solander, along with several hundred topographic and ethnographic sketches. Parkinson died at sea in January 1771, and his journal was subsequently published in London by his brother Stanfield.

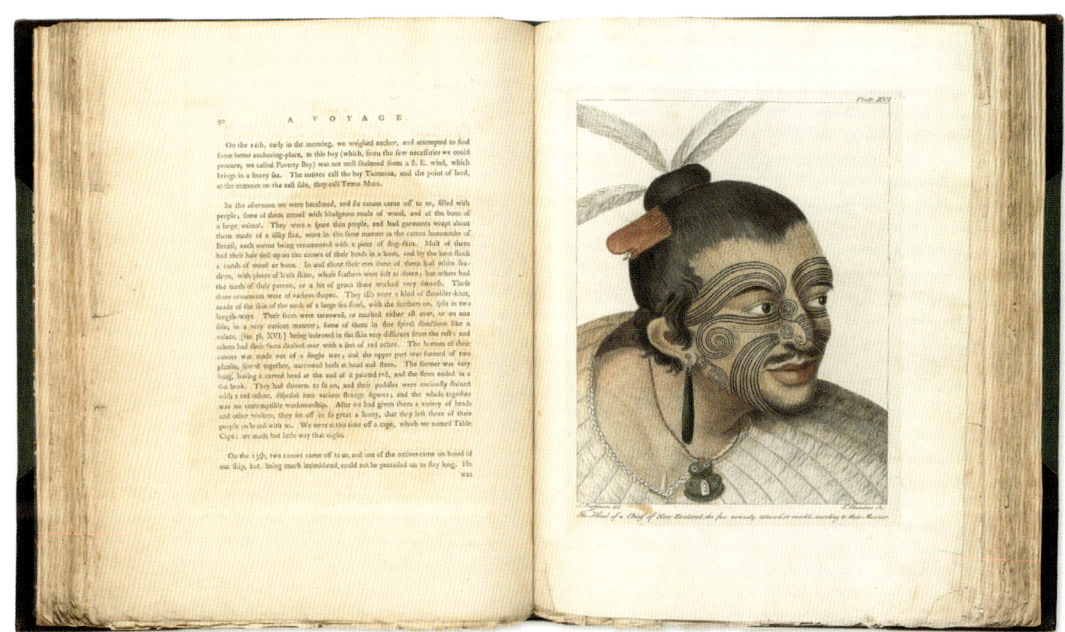

COOK'S SECOND VOYAGE

The British Admiralty had commissioned John Hawkesworth to write the official account of James Cook's first voyage in the *Endeavour*. Dissatisfied with the results, Cook undertook the task of writing the account of his second voyage himself. The work includes numerous engravings of Pacific scenes, many romanticised, after the drawings and paintings of William Hodges, principal artist on the voyage.

COOK'S THIRD VOYAGE

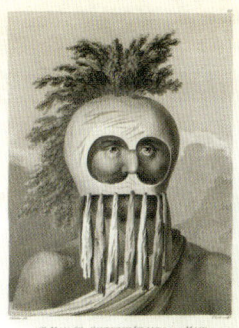

The official account of Cook's third voyage comprised three volumes of text and a magnificent 'atlas' of engraved views after the drawings of John Webber, chief artist on the voyage. Supervision of the official published accounts was undertaken by Lord Sandwich, drawing on the journals of Cook, as well as the journals of James King who, along with John Gore, succeeded Cook as expedition leader after Cook's death in Hawaii.

LEFT:
James Cook
A Voyage to the Pacific Ocean, Undertaken … for Making Discoveries in the Northern Hemisphere …
London, G Nicol and T Cadell, 1784

BELOW:
John White
Journal of a Voyage to New South Wales
London, printed for J Debrett, 1790

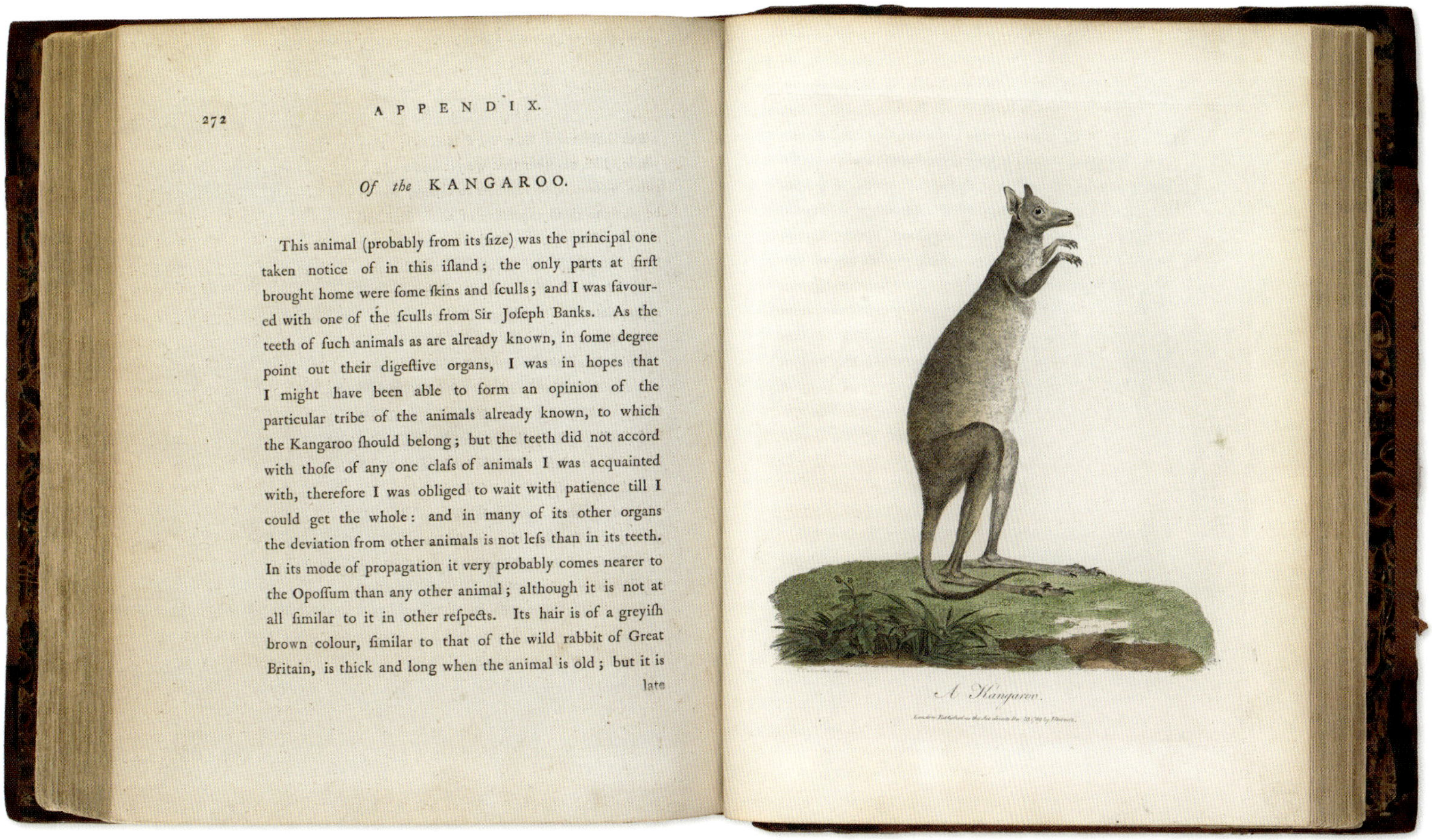

272 APPENDIX.

Of the KANGAROO.

This animal (probably from its ſize) was the principal one taken notice of in this iſland; the only parts at firſt brought home were ſome ſkins and ſculls; and I was favoured with one of the ſculls from Sir Joſeph Banks. As the teeth of ſuch animals as are already known, in ſome degree point out their digeſtive organs, I was in hopes that I might have been able to form an opinion of the particular tribe of the animals already known, to which the Kangaroo ſhould belong; but the teeth did not accord with thoſe of any one claſs of animals I was acquainted with, therefore I was obliged to wait with patience till I could get the whole: and in many of its other organs the deviation from other animals is not leſs than in its teeth. In its mode of propagation it very probably comes nearer to the Opoſſum than any other animal; although it is not at all ſimilar to it in other reſpects. Its hair is of a greyiſh brown colour, ſimilar to that of the wild rabbit of Great Britain, is thick and long when the animal is old; but it is late

A Kangaroo.

JOHN WHITE

John White was chief surgeon with the First Fleet when it sailed in 1787–88. His published account of the new colony of New South Wales was the first to give a detailed description of the natural history of the area. White was an enthusiastic amateur natural historian and spent his free hours in the colony recording the plants and animals of the region. He was assigned a number of convicts who were competent draughtsmen, most notably the artist Thomas Watling, and he sent their sketches and finished watercolours, along with specimens of animals and birds, back to England for inclusion in his book.

LA PÉROUSE

The disappearance of La Pérouse's ships after leaving Botany Bay in March 1788 was one of the great navigational mysteries of the period. It would not be resolved until 1826, when English sailor Peter Dillon established that the two ships, *La Boussole* and *L'Astrolabe*, had been wrecked off Vanikoro, one of the Santa Cruz group of islands. French navigator Dumont D'Urville visited the island in 1828, erecting a monument there to La Pérouse.

Jean-François de Galaup de La Pérouse
Voyage de La Pérouse Autour du Monde
Paris, Imprimerie de la République, 1797

in the first years of the settlement, provided Europe with its earliest detailed views of the continent.

In the absence of British interest, it was left to other nations, particularly the French, to fill in the cartographic gaps left by Cook and to continue the task of making a detailed record of the region. The French navigator Jean-François de Galaup La Pérouse charted the northern Pacific regions between 1785 and 1787. While at the Kamchatka Peninsula, he received further instructions to proceed to New Holland to report on the British colony being established there. La Pérouse sailed into Botany Bay in January 1788, just a few days after the arrival of the British First Fleet, and despite initial concern, relations proved cordial between the two nations. After departing Botany Bay on 10 March 1788, La Pérouse and his ships vanished, initiating one of the great navigational mysteries of the age. La Pérouse's practice of dispatching journals and sketches back to France during the course of the voyage ensured that some records from the expedition survived to be published in Paris. The magnificent atlas volume that accompanied *Voyage de La Pérouse Autour du Monde* (1797), with its natural history illustrations and topographic views of Kamchatka, Manila and Easter Island, would provide a template for the great wave of French publications on the Pacific that appeared over the following half century.

The many French voyages to the Pacific undertaken between 1790 and 1840 were ambitious state-sponsored ventures. While they no doubt had an eye on commercial opportunity, their primary purpose was to carry out extensive scientific surveys, and the naturalists and artists on board took back with them vast repositories of notes, specimens and drawings, later to be published in illustrated accounts.

Any ideas France might have had of emulating the British settlement in New South Wales were thwarted by political instability back home. When the expedition led by D'Entrecasteaux left France in 1791, ostensibly in search of the whereabouts of La Pérouse, it was at the behest of Louis XVI. Two years later, when the ships limped into Batavia, minus their leader, who had died from dysentery off the coast of New Guinea, the crew learned that Louis had been guillotined and that France was in the second year of the First Republic and at war with the rest of Europe.

The voyage of Nicolas Baudin in 1800–03 was begun under Napoleon's regime, and its focus on the coasts of Australia and New Guinea coincided with Matthew Flinders's detailed survey of the Australian coastline in the *Investigator*. Baudin's dallying in Tasmania robbed him of the opportunity to be the first to chart the unknown southern coast, and when his ships met Flinders at Encounter Bay in April 1802, the French could only lay claim to having been the first to chart some 300 kilometres of the coastline. Flinders's subsequent detainment at Mauritius on his return voyage, however, allowed the French to publish the first complete map of Australia, which appeared in naturalist François Peron's account of the voyage in 1811. The vignette on the title page of the historical atlas showed kangaroos and emus grazing in Empress Josephine's gardens at Malmaison in Paris, while the map of Australia's southern coastline was littered with revolutionary names under the banner 'Terre Napoleon'. Flinders's complete map of Australia did not appear until 1814, when it was published in his *Voyage to Terra Australis*.

LABILLARDIÈRE

French Admiral Bruny D'Entrecasteaux was commissioned in 1791 to lead an expedition to investigate the disappearance of navigator Jean-François de Galaup La Pérouse. Although failing to find any trace of La Pérouse, the expedition proved to be an important voyage of discovery, compiling detailed charts and scientific information relating to Australia, in particular Tasmania, and the Pacific region. D'Entrecasteaux died at sea on the return voyage in 1793. The account of the voyage by the naturalist Jacques de Labillardière attracted widespread interest and appeared in four different English translations in the same year as its publication in Paris.

TOP:
Jacques-Julien Houtou de Labillardière
Relation du Voyage à la Recherche de La Pérouse
Paris, HJ Jansen, Imprimeur-Libraire, 1800

ABOVE AND FOLLOWING PAGES:
François Péron
Voyages de Découvertes aux Terres Australes
Paris, dirigé par J Hilbert, 1807–11

FRANÇOIS PÉRON

Naturalist François Péron sailed with Nicolas Baudin to Australia and the Pacific in 1800–03. Baudin died on the return voyage, in September 1803, and it fell to Péron to prepare the results of the voyage for publication. His atlas of historical views is one of the finest publications ever issued on Australia. It includes a number of portraits of Aboriginal people from Tasmania and New South Wales, engraved after drawings by Nicolas-Martin Petit, one of the official artists on the voyage. It also contains the first printed map of the entire continent, pre-dating Matthew Flinders's map by several years.

N. Petit del. — J. Milbert direx. — B. Roger sculp.

TERRE DE DIÉMEN.

OURIAGA.

De l'Imprimerie de Langlois

NOUVELLE-HOLLANDE.

COUR-ROU-BARI-GAL.

It wasn't until the Bourbon Restoration of 1814 that France mounted its next voyage to the Pacific. Louis-Claude de Freycinet's circumnavigation of the globe, carried out between 1817 and 1820, included visits to Shark Bay on the west Australian coast, and to the British colony at Port Jackson, where he and his officers became the first Frenchmen to cross the Blue Mountains by the newly opened road. Freycinet's wife, Rose, accompanied him on the voyage, an act deemed illegal at the time. Though she appears in a number of watercolours made by Jacques Arago, artist on the voyage, she is erased from these same engraved plates in the published account *Voyage Autour du Monde* (1824–44). In a romantic gesture, Freycinet inserted his wife's name surreptitiously into his publication, attached to a chart of a small island discovered east of the Navigator's Archipelago in the Pacific, 'which I named Rose Island, from the name of someone who is dear to me'.

France, of course, was not alone. Spain mounted an ambitious expedition to the Pacific in 1789, but then buried the results when its leader, Alejandro Malaspina, fell foul of the authorities. Russian interest was spurred on by an expanding fur trade with Alaska, and Ivan Kruzenshtern's first Russian circumnavigation of the globe in 1803–06 generated detailed accounts and charts of the north-west Pacific. Otto von Kotzebue's subsequent voyage to the Pacific in 1815–18 provided important descriptions of Alaska, California, Hawaii and Micronesia. By the time the United States Exploring Expedition set sail on its great scientific circumnavigation in 1838, the young Charles Darwin had already completed his work as naturalist on the *Beagle* and had begun formulating the theories that would turn our understanding of the natural world on its head.

The exhaustive nature of the scientific collecting engaged in during these voyages is staggering. The botanists on Cook's *Endeavour* voyage, Joseph Banks and Daniel Solander, returned to England with more than 30 000 plant specimens, of which some 1400 species were new to science. Naturalist Georges Cuvier described the scientific collections brought back to France by the Baudin expedition as comprising more than 100 000 samples of animals, 'both great and small'. Spanish botanist Luis Née, sailing with Malaspina, wrote of his astonishment upon encountering the plant life at Port Jackson in 1793: 'He who knows what it is to study flora will be able to judge of the extent of my observations when he learns that in 27 days I collected more than 1000 plants of a new kind and of each plant various species'.

Publishers were quick to capitalise on the interest aroused by these voyages, and a voracious reading public, eager for accounts of faraway places, generated a tide of popular travel literature. In the same way, governments, keen to promote their national achievements, allocated funds for the production of deluxe illustrated books detailing the scientific results of expeditions. The published account of Dumont d'Urville's second voyage to the south polar regions in 1837–40 would run to twenty-three volumes of text, accompanied by seven folio atlases of lithographic views and natural history drawings.

These many illustrated books documenting scientific voyaging in the late eighteenth and early nineteenth centuries provide first-hand evidence of the responses of Europeans to new worlds. European artists, so far from home, sketched the peoples and landscapes, the plants and animals they encountered in the vast expanses of the Pacific. In drawing upon their own experiences to record the unfamiliar, they began the slow process of making real the age-old cartographers' dream of unknown southern lands.

FREYCINET

The complete publication of Louis-Claude de Freycinet's voyage was published as nine volumes of text and four folio atlases. The atlases contain around 320 engraved plates, partly derived from original paintings and drawings made on the expedition by the two official artists, Jacques Arago and Alphonse Pellion, and partly from the natural history specimens collected on the voyage. Arago also published his own account, *Promenade Autour du Monde*, in 1822.

KRUZENSHTERN

Kruzenshtern's voyage was the first Russian circumnavigation of the globe. Although undertaken to foster the fur trade of the Pacific coast and to open up trade links with China and Japan, its major contribution lay in its detailed accounts and charting of the north-west Pacific coastlines. Kruzenshtern's account of the voyage, which comprised three volumes of text and a folio atlas of charts and views, was published in Russian and German language editions in St Petersburg in 1810–13.

ABOVE:
Louis-Claude de Freycinet
Voyage Autour du Monde
Paris, Chez Pillet Aîné,
Imprimeur-Libraire,
1824–44

OPPOSITE:
Ivan Fedorovich Kruzenshtern
Atlas K Puteshestvie Vokrug Sveta
St Petersburg, Izdatel'stvo, Morskaya tipografiya
God izdaniya, 1813

The NATURAL World

The world is the work of Nature and, at the same time, the embodiment of Nature herself.
PLINY THE ELDER, *NATURAL HISTORY*

THE DEPICTION OF THE NATURAL WORLD GOES BACK TO THE EARLIEST PHASES OF HUMAN CIVILISATION. HORSES, BISON, MAMMOTHS AND WILD GOATS WERE PAINTED ONTO CAVE WALLS SUCH AS THOSE AT LASCAUX IN NORTHERN FRANCE AROUND 15 000 BCE. REFERENCES TO THE MEDICINAL PROPERTIES OF PLANTS WERE CONTAINED IN SUMERIAN AND BABYLONIAN TEXTS, AND IN EGYPTIAN AND EARLY CHINESE LITERATURE.

Aristotle wrote *Historia Animalium* (On the History of Animals) and other works that attempted to classify some five hundred kinds of animals, while his student Theophrastus produced an early treatise on botany, *Historia Planturum*. Pliny the Elder, before his death during the eruption of Vesuvius in 79 CE, compiled thirty-seven books on natural history that drew widely upon Greek and Roman sources.

Early botanical writers were primarily interested in cures and remedies. The most influential was Pedanius Dioscorides, a Greek physician practising in Rome in the first century CE. His travels as a surgeon with the Roman army allowed him the opportunity to collect specimens extensively, and his manuscript herbal *De Materia Medica*, written in Greek, presented more than five hundred plants, describing their medicinal properties. Unlike many classical scholars, whose writings waited until the Renaissance to be rediscovered, Dioscorides's herbal remained in circulation in Europe throughout the Middle Ages and was the standard pharmacopoeia at that time. The earliest surviving manuscript, known as the *Vienna Dioscorides*, was produced in the sixth century CE in Constantinople for presentation to Juliana Anicia, daughter of the emperor.

The first printed edition of Dioscorides's *De Materia Medica* appeared in Latin in 1478 and formed the basis for other early printed herbals, many of whose writers were chiefly concerned with identifying and commenting upon those plants known to Dioscorides. The illustrations included in these books were generally stylised woodcuts copied from earlier manuscript versions, with little regard for botanical accuracy. Otto Brunfels, often called the father of botany, revolutionised the subject by extending upon classical knowledge and featuring botanical illustrations drawn from life. His *Herbarum Vivae Eicones* (1530–32) presented a catalogue of plants from the Strasbourg region, many unknown to Dioscorides, and was illustrated by Hans Weiditz, a pupil of Dürer. Weiditz's botanical woodcuts, the result of direct observation of plants, broke with previous tradition and were an important influence on the later herbals by Leonhard Fuchs and Hieronymus Bock. Weiditz's figures have been criticised, however, for the emphasis he placed on illustrating a particular specimen, with all its flaws. Fuchs's *De Historia Stirpium* (1542), on the other hand, sought to iron out a specimen's blemishes, creating a more generalised or ideal example of a plant species. His illustrations also

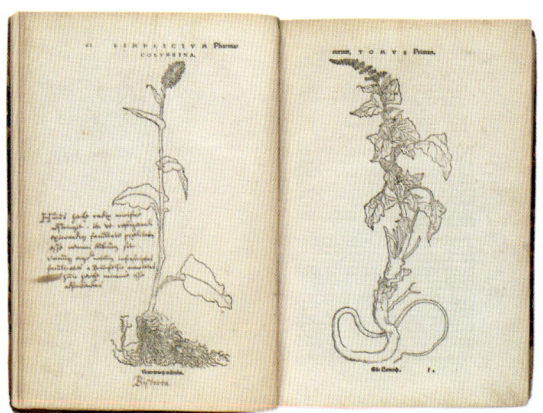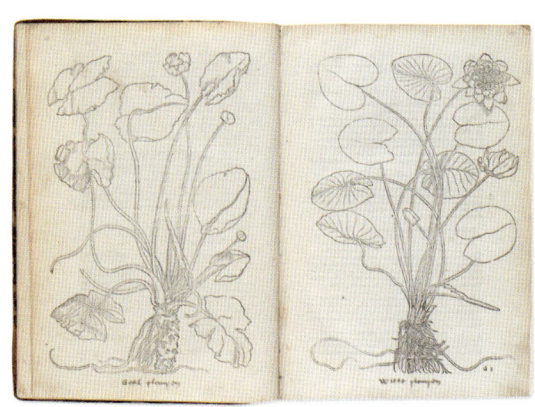

LEONHARD FUCHS

Botanist Leonhard Fuchs is generally regarded as the third father of German botany, after Otto Brunfels and Hieronymous Bock. He is best known for his 1542 herbal *De Historia Stirpium Commentarii Insignes* (Notable Commentaries on the History of Plants), published the following year in German as *New Kreüterbuch*. It contains more than five hundred woodcut figures, drawn from life by artist Albrecht Meyer. Of these, more than a hundred plants were illustrated for the first time.

PIETRO ANDREA MATTIOLI

This edition of Mattioli's herbal was edited by Joachim Camerer the Younger (1534–1598), a German physician who was among the earliest botanists to feature illustrations drawn from nature. The woodcuts used in this edition were originally created by Konrad Gesner, who had been preparing a massive *Historia Plantarum* before his death in 1565. The woodcuts were acquired by Camerer, who used them in the present work, supplementing them with his own. Like Brunfels and Fuchs, his emphasis on illustrations taken from nature was important in the development of a more scientific approach to botanical illustration.

TOP:
Otto Brunfels
Herbarum Vivae Eicones
Strasbourg, J Schoft,
1530–32

BOTTOM, LEFT:
Leonhard Fuchs
New Kreüterbuch
Basel, Michael Isingrin,
1543

BOTTOM, RIGHT:
Pietro Andrea Mattioli
De Plantis Epitome Utilissima
Frankfurt, 1586

sought to represent the seasonal changes in plant features, an important innovation at the time.

The herbals of Italian botanist Pietro Mattioli again built on the work of Dioscorides. He identified the five hundred or so plants originally described by Dioscorides, adding his own commentary and incorporating observations of new plants. His *Commentarii*, printed in Italian in 1544, quickly became the standard book on medical botany for European physicians in the second half of the sixteenth century, with some sixty editions appearing in many languages. Because they served a popular and practical rather than a scientific purpose, it was common for herbals to be published in the vernacular rather than in Latin.

As with botanical motifs, the representation of animals was a common feature in books of the Middle Ages, a practice that led to the rise in popularity of the medieval bestiary. These illustrated manuscripts of animals, both real and fabulous, were generally accompanied by moral texts and functioned symbolically rather than as attempts to describe the natural world. The scientific study of animals began with the Swiss naturalist Konrad Gesner's *Historiae Animalium* or 'History of Animals' (1551–58). Although his book was compiled from classical and medieval texts, Gesner corresponded widely with a network of scholars and travellers, obtaining information and specimens. He emphasised direct observation, describing each animal by its appearance and behaviour, and then by its cultural or symbolic meaning. Gesner's work provided the basis for Edward Topsell's *The Historie of Foure-footed Beastes* (1607) and John Johnston's *Historiae Naturalis de Quadrupedibus* (1657).

The large influx of plant and animal specimens making their way back to Europe as a result of voyages to the Americas and the East Indies brought about the need for a more systematic approach to the classification of the natural world. While there had been pioneers in the field, most notably British botanist John Ray, it was the system of taxonomy devised by Swedish naturalist Carl Linnaeus that came to be accepted. Linnaeus, in his *Systema Naturae* (1735), divided the natural world into three kingdoms—animal, vegetable and mineral—and he later devised the method for formulating a scientific name for species that is still used today.

Linnaeus's proposed groupings of plants or animals according to shared characteristics led to an increased need for natural history illustrators

JOHN JOHNSTON

The illustration in Johnston's book is modelled on the well-known woodcut by Albrecht Dürer. In May 1515, a rhinoceros from India was brought by ship to Portugal, the first such animal to be seen in Europe for more than a thousand years. From there a description and sketch were sent on to Dürer, who created his woodcut without ever having seen the animal. The rhinoceros was sent by the King of Portugal from Lisbon to Rome later that same year as a gift to Pope Leo X but was lost at sea in a shipwreck. It is testament to its power that Dürer's image was copied by natural history artists for almost three hundred years.

ABOVE:
John Johnston
Historiae Naturalis de Quadrupedibus
Amsterdam, Joannem Jacobi fil. Schipper, 1657

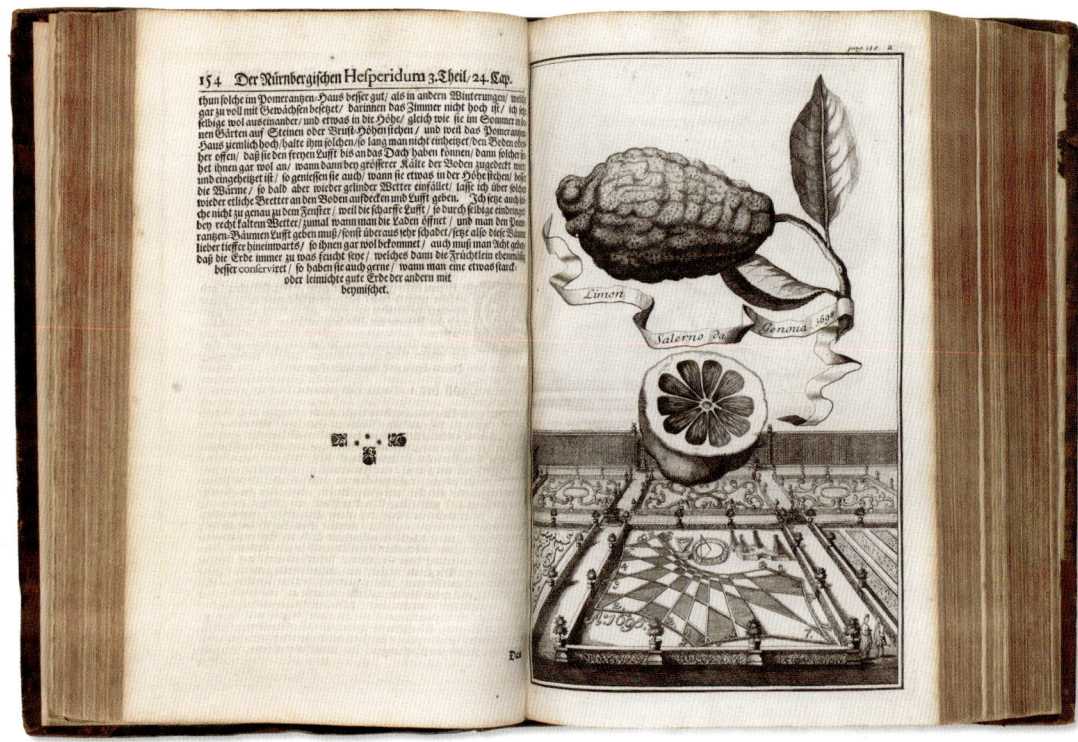

ABOVE:
Johann Volckamer
Nürnbergische Hesperides
Nuremberg, 1708–14

BELOW:
Christoph Jacob Trew
Hortus Nitidissimis Omnem per Annum Superbiens Floribus
Noribergae, 1750–72

JOHANN VOLCKAMER

By the seventeenth century, the growing of citrus fruits was highly fashionable among the aristocracy in Europe. During winter, the plants were housed in specially built glasshouses, or 'orangeries', and then moved outdoors during summer. The term 'Hesperides' was often used to refer to citrus at this time. Drawn from Greek mythology, it alluded to the golden apples guarded by the nymph-daughters of Hesperides. Volckamer's detailed depictions of prized fruits float rather incongruously above the formal European estates and houses where they were grown.

CHRISTOPH JACOB TREW

Christoph Trew was a distinguished physician of Nuremberg with an avid interest in botany. After coming across the botanical drawings of the young German artist Georg Ehret, he became a lifelong friend and patron of the artist. His publication *Hortus Nitidissimis* was devoted to the beauty of flowering plants and included more than forty designs by Ehret, considered one of the finest flower painters of the eighteenth century, along with work by other artists.

to reflect these subtle variations in their work. Copperplate engraving, developed in the late sixteenth century, allowed for a much finer rendering of detail than the earlier use of woodcut illustration and became the dominant illustrative medium for natural history books. The eighteenth and nineteenth centuries saw a surge in the publication of deluxe books on flora and fauna featuring hand-coloured engravings by the great natural history artists of the day. The German-born botanical artist Georg Ehret collaborated with Linnaeus on the influential *Hortus Cliffortianus* (1738), a record of the flora of the estate of Georg Clifford in the Netherlands. Clifford was a governor of the Dutch East India Company, and his herbarium was full of botanical curiosities from around the world. Ehret's work was the first to illustrate Linnaeus's sexual system of plants, focusing on the reproductive organs of plants. He spent his later life in England, where he contributed illustrations to numerous botanical books, including Christoph Jacob Trew's *Hortus Nitidissimis* (1750–86) and Alexander Russell's *Natural History of Aleppo* (1756).

One of the most curious natural history works of the period was Louis Renard's *Poissons, Ecrevisses et Crabes de Diverses Couleurs et Figures Extraordinaires* (1719). Renard was an enterprising Amsterdam publisher and bookdealer, who also dabbled in clandestine activities for the British. Though he never left the Netherlands, he compiled and published a bizarre collection of illustrations of fish and crustaceans of the East Indies. A direct product of Dutch colonialism, the work's coloured engravings were based on drawings commissioned by colonial governors of the Moluccas and the provinces of Ambon and Banda. The book took almost thirty years to produce, and only a hundred copies were printed. A second, equally small, edition was issued by publishers Reinier and Josué Ottens in 1754. While the colours of the illustrated specimens are exaggerated, giving them an oddly surreal character, many of the fish are identifiable species, aside from a few fanciful inventions, such as an illustration of a mermaid, said to have been caught off the coast of Borné in the province of Ambon.

Louis Renard
Poissons, Ecrevisses et Crabes de Diverses Couleurs et Figures Extraordinaires
Amsterdam, Chez Reinier and Josué Ottens, 1754

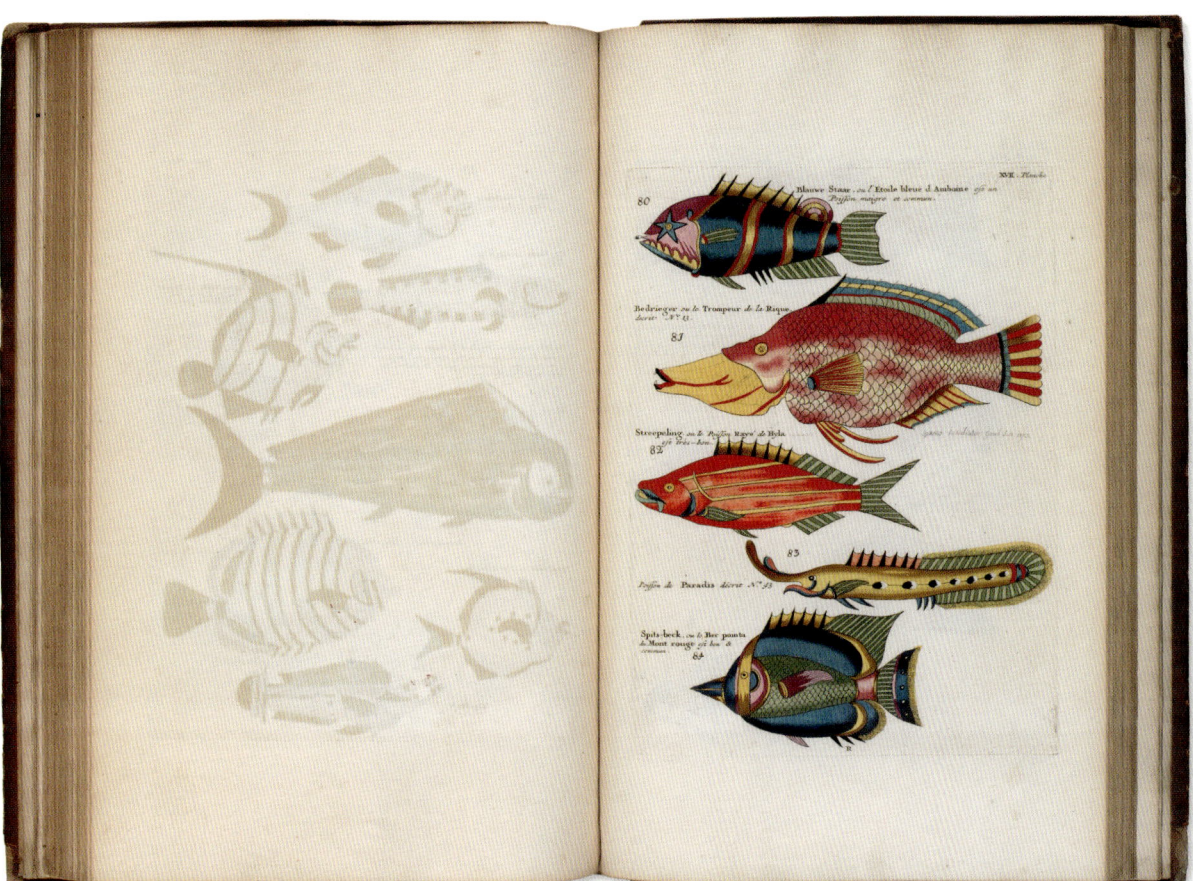

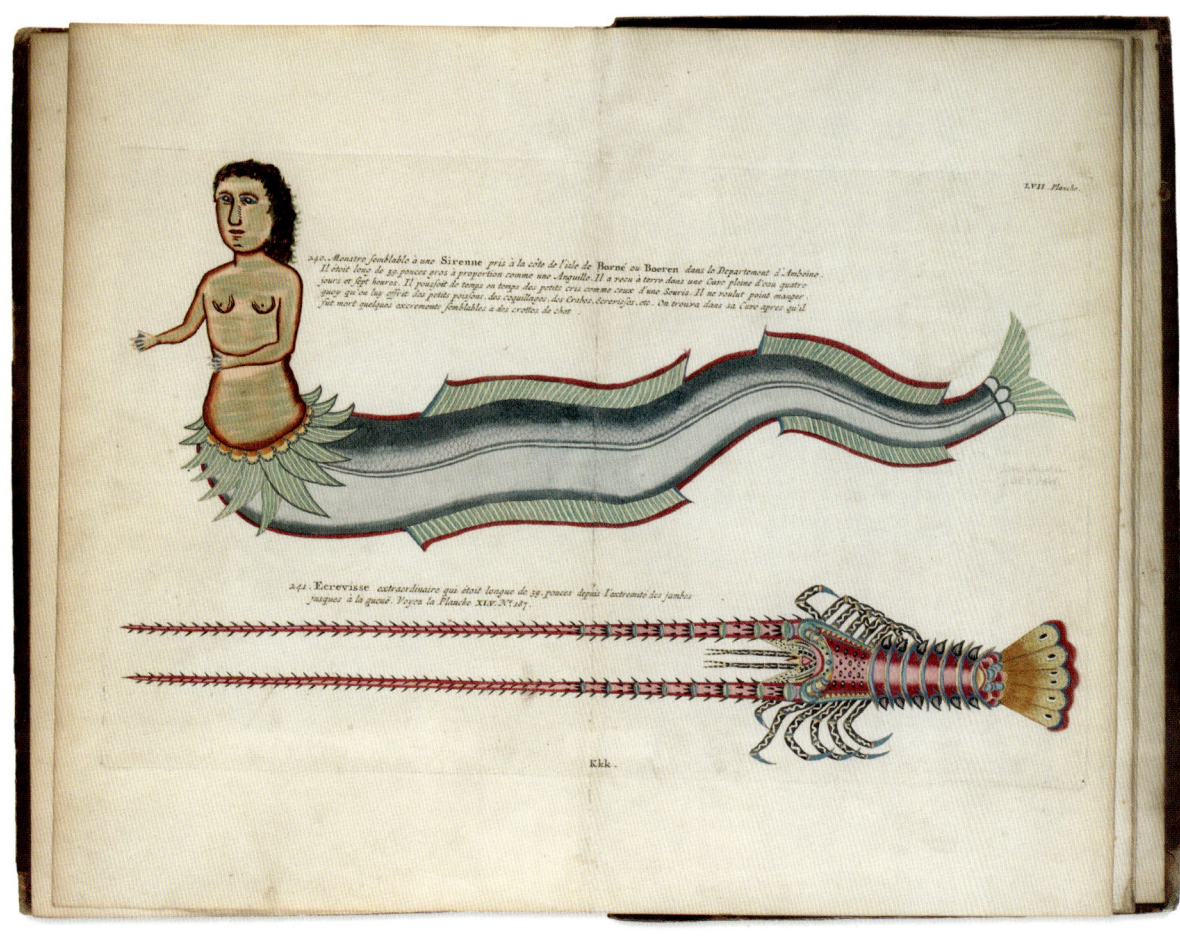

Amaryllis Formosissima   *Amaryllis Lys St. Jacques*

ROBERT JOHN THORNTON

The Temple of Flora is the third volume of Robert Thornton's work, *New Illustration of the Sexual System of Carolus von Linnaeus*. Inspired by Swedish botanist Carl Linnaeus, whose system of plant classification revolutionised botany, Thornton's approach ranged from objective study to affectionate sentimentality. He set many of his closely observed depictions of specimens within broader landscapes. Determined to produce a work that would surpass the scholarship of German botanical texts and the artistry of those from France, Thornton employed the finest British artists and printmakers of his day.

ABOVE, LEFT:
Robert John Thornton
The Temple of Flora, or Garden of the Botanist, Poet, Painter and Philosopher
London, printed for the publisher by T Bensley, 1799–1807

ABOVE, RIGHT:
Ferdinand Bauer
Illustrationes Florae Novae Hollandiae
London, 1813

OPPOSITE:
Pierre-Joseph Redouté
Les Liliacées
Paris, 1802–15

The late eighteenth century saw an increase in the number of wealthy subscribers and patrons able to support a growing market for ever more ambitious illustrated botanical books. When the Empress Josephine established a garden of rare plants at her newly acquired home at Malmaison in 1798, she commissioned botanical artist Pierre-Joseph Redouté, who had previously enjoyed the patronage of Marie Antoinette, to make a pictorial record of the plants. This commission led to a number of deluxe publications, in which Redouté employed the newly developed method of stipple engraving to great effect, including the celebrated *Les Liliacées* (1802–15), *Jardin de la Malmaison* (1803–05), *Description des Plantes Rares Cultivées à Malmaison* (1812–17) and *Les Roses* (1817–24). Redouté also contributed illustrations to Jacques de Labillardière's *Novae Hollandiae Plantarum Specimen* (Paris, 1804–06), the first major florilegium of Australian botany based on specimens collected by the D'Entrecasteaux expedition.

Not all attempts to attract subscribers to large-scale publishing ventures were successful. Ferdinand Bauer, who accompanied Matthew Flinders on his circumnavigation of Australia in the *Investigator* in 1801–05, began issuing his *Illustrationes Florae Novae Hollandiae* in London in 1813. However, he was able to attract only twenty-three subscribers and, after issuing fifteen plates, he abandoned the work and returned to his native Austria. Similarly, Robert Thornton's *The Temple of Flora* (1799–1807) was an immensely costly work to produce, and when it failed to recoup expenses, he was financially ruined. While Thornton's work has little botanical value by today's standards, the sheer luxuriousness and opulence of its coloured plates, many by artist Peter Henderson, has ensured its long-term renown as one of the finest botanical books of the period.

Two of the most successful nineteenth-century natural history entrepreneurs were American bird painter John James Audubon and British publisher John Gould, both of whom specialised in ornithology. Audubon is remembered for a single work, the large 'double-elephant' folio *Birds of America*, issued in parts to subscribers between 1827 and 1838. John Gould, on the other hand, published some forty folio volumes of hand-coloured lithographs sold by subscription, including the *The Birds of Europe* (1832–37), *The Birds of Australia* (1840–48) and *The Birds of Great Britain* (1862–73). All told, he published more than three thousand lithographs, executed by a variety of artists, including his wife Elizabeth. Gould also completed one major non-ornithological work, *The Mammals of Australia*

(1845–63), undertaken after his visit to Australia with his family in 1838–40.

The visual styles of Audubon and Gould could not be more contrasting. Audubon's life-size depictions of birds are full of drama and the frontier landscapes of the United States. Gould's rendering of the male and female of each species appear, by turn, delicate and restrained. Despite the fact that both men engaged in the wholesale slaughter of birds to obtain specimens for their work—common ornithological practice at the time—they both contributed enormously to the growth of nineteenth-century scientific knowledge of the natural world. This is perhaps nowhere more evident than in their illustrated descriptions of species now extinct, such as Audubon's Carolina parrot and Gould's thylacine (Tasmanian tiger), both casualties of encroaching human settlement.

By the late nineteenth century, the great cycle of natural history publishing had come to an end. The rising cost of producing such deluxe books made them a less attractive proposition for publishers. As well, new and cheaper printing technologies, such as chromolithography and photolithography, brought about a decline in the quality of natural history publications. Despite this, the art of drawing and painting nature is still considered, in many cases, superior to photography, and artists are regularly employed to illustrate new species or natural history collections today.

BELOW, LEFT:
John James Audubon
The Birds of America
London, published by the author, 1827–38

BELOW, RIGHT:
John Gould
Synopsis of the Birds of Australia and the Adjacent Islands
London, John Gould, 1837–38

BOTTOM, LEFT:
Celia E Rosser and Alexander S George
The Banksias
London, Academic Press and Clayton, Victoria, Monash University, 1981–2001

BOTTOM, RIGHT:
Banks' Florilegium
London, Alecto Historical Editions in association with the British Museum, 1981–88

JOHN GOULD'S BIRDS

This first publication on Australian birds by ornithologist John Gould contained basic descriptions of 168 species that were available to him in London, either from his own collection or in museums. The work was issued in four parts in 1837–38 and included seventy-three hand-coloured lithographic plates drawn by his wife, Elizabeth Gould. She subsequently contributed eighty-four lithographs to his monumental *The Birds of Australia* (1840–48), before her death following the birth of her sixth child in 1841.

JOHN JAMES AUDUBON

John James Audubon was born in Haiti and raised in France, and emigrated to America at the age of eighteen. He demonstrated an early interest in natural history and, after a failed business venture, decided to devote himself to a survey of North American birds. From then until his death he was constantly at work observing, collecting and painting specimens. In 1826, he travelled to London, seeking commercial partners and selling subscriptions for his proposed publication. For the work, his life-size paintings were transferred to copper plates, printed, then hand coloured. A complete set of *Birds* comprises 435 'double-elephant' folio plates, issued in eighty-seven parts over eleven years.

THYLACINUS CYNOCEPHALUS.

JOHN GOULD'S MAMMALS

Gould travelled to Australia with his wife and family in 1838, intent on studying the local bird species for his projected *The Birds of Australia*. During his eighteen-month stay he also became interested in the local fauna and, back in London, issued this three-volume work on Australian mammals. The majority of the lithographs for *Mammals* were produced by the artist Henry Richter, who also produced more than a thousand lithographs for Gould's later works.

ABOVE:
John Gould
The Mammals of Australia
London, the author,
1845–63

The capacity of the artist to render an ideal form, based on an understanding of nature, is something the mechanical shutter of the camera can never fully replicate. A recent example has been Celia Rosser's ambitious project to illustrate all known species of the Australian genus *Banksia*, a task on which she worked exclusively for twenty-five years. Her life-size watercolours, which took approximately three months each to complete, were published in three large volumes that harked back to the great natural history books of the nineteenth century.

But the most important link to the natural history books of the past came with the publication of Joseph Banks's *Florilegium* in the 1980s. When Banks returned to London from Cook's voyage in the *Endeavour*, his intention had been to publish the botanical results of the expedition. To this end, Banks had copperplates prepared by eighteen artists, at his own expense, between 1771 and 1784, based on Sydney Parkinson's original sketches made on the voyage. Banks's work, however, remained unpublished, and it was not until 1988 that all 738 botanical illustrations were printed for the first time directly from the original copperplates, arguably the most ambitious natural history publication ever undertaken.

The book, the idea of a book or the image of a book, is a symbol of learning, of transmitting knowledge... I make my own books to find my own way through the old stories.
ANSELM KIEFER, *HEAVEN AND EARTH*

Books are valued not only for their content, but as objects of beauty and fine craft. Artists have been involved in the production of books from the earliest times. They have determined the look and the shape of books, through processes ranging from paper making and illustration to design and binding.

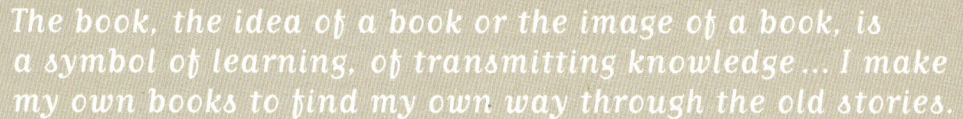

PART IV THE ARTIST AND THE BOOK

THE ART
of the Book

*After this to a bookseller's and bought,
for the love of the binding, three books ...*
SAMUEL PEPYS, *DIARY*, 1660

WITH THE EVOLUTION OF THE BOOK, A NUMBER OF ARTS AND CRAFTS HAVE DEVELOPED ALONGSIDE ITS PRODUCTION. WHILE THE PRIMARY PURPOSE OF BOOKBINDING IS TO PROTECT A BOOK'S CONTENTS, THE ART OF FINE BINDING ALSO TRANSFORMS IT INTO AN OBJECT OF BEAUTY.

A range of processes, styles and materials have developed throughout the world to suit the differing natures of books in various cultures. In the West, this history began in the first century CE with the move away from the scroll and the development of the codex form of pages between covers that we now recognise in the shape of our books today.

Once books took on this new form—the earliest using pages of papyrus—new ways of protecting their fragile contents had to be found. By the fourth century, leather covers were being used by the Christian Copts in Egypt, as evidenced by the 1945 discovery at Nag Hammadi of a cache of manuscripts from that era. Over subsequent centuries, leather bindings were introduced to both Christian Europe and the Islamic Near East. Parchment and fine-grade vellum (sheep- and calfskin respectively) became the most common materials for book pages in Europe, and to protect them, front and back covers made from wooden boards were added. These helped to keep the pages flat, as animal skin tends to curl and buckle with changes in temperature and atmosphere. Islamic bindings developed an additional panel or flap that extended from the back cover and wrapped around and protected the front edge (known as the fore-edge) of a book's pages.

While materials and decorative styles varied, the basic principles of bookbinding changed little in Europe until the industrial revolution. The binding process was undertaken in two major stages: forwarding (in which pages were assembled and attached to a cover) and finishing (in which the covers and page edges were decorated). Groups, or gatherings, of pages were sewn together using either thread or leather thongs. These were in turn attached to the wooden board covers, creating the distinctive horizontal bands across a book's spine that we today associate with traditional bindings. The book was then generally wrapped in an outer covering. The majority of European medieval bindings that have survived are of leather and either unadorned or decorated with 'blind' embossed or stamped designs. A small number of sacred texts were given highly decorated covers, tooled and encrusted with precious gems, ivory, silver or gold.

The bindings of many medieval books also incorporated various elements known as 'furniture'. These included metal clasps used to hold the covers of a book together so that its vellum pages did not buckle. Generally made of iron, brass or bronze, though sometimes of silver or gold, these clasps were often highly decorative. Metal studs known as 'bosses' were also used to protect leather bindings from the wear and tear

LEFT:
Eighteenth-century bookbinding
From **Denis Diderot, editor**
Encyclopédie, ou, Dictionnaire Raisonné des Sciences, des Arts et des Métiers
Paris, Chez Briasson, David l'Aîné, Le Breton, Durand, 1751–72

BELOW:
Antiphonal
Paris, c. 1350

of books being stored flat on shelves or on lecterns. Another important feature of many medieval bindings was a sturdy metal chain, up to 2 metres long, that attached a book to a shelf or reading table. This prevented theft and reflects the value that books were accorded.

Like so many other aspects of the history of the book, the event that would dramatically change bookbinding in Europe was the introduction of the printing press in the 1450s. Whereas manuscripts had been individually made and bound to order, books were now printed in editions of several hundred, and a printer had no guarantee of selling them all. A printed book was generally sold with the leaves protected in a simple paper or vellum wrapper. It was then taken to a binder to be bound in a style and material suited to the taste and finances of its new owner. Exceptions were standard works such as prayer books and school texts. A publisher could be assured of selling the print run of such titles because they were acquired for use rather than prestige, so they were often finished in simple leather bindings suitable for daily use. Books also became smaller at this time, as the primary market shifted from institutions to individuals, who wanted their books to be portable.

The introduction of paper in the mid fifteenth century also changed various aspects of bookbinding. Paper became the primary material for book pages because it was cheaper and better to print on than vellum. In turn, wooden board covers were no longer required to hold a book in shape; they were usually replaced by boards made from layers of paper pasted together.

Binding leathers were now tanned using dyes from vegetable and other plant matter. They were decorated by cut work, in which patterns were incised into the leather, and by panel stamping the dampened leather on a press using wooden or metal blocks carved or cast with intricate designs or biblical and allegorical scenes. A significant innovation at this time was gold tooling. It had developed in the Islamic world in the thirteenth century, and the technique was imported into Europe in the fifteenth century via major trading centres such as Venice. Islamic bindings were distinctive in their use of geometric designs that often comprised a central motif and ornamentation in each corner of the cover. Bookbinders in Europe also began to edge the pages of books in gold and then to decorate them with abstract designs through a process of incising or impressing known as goffering. While leather remained the dominant material for book coverings, some books were bound with fabrics such as velvets, silks and satins.

Binders did not attach their names to their work at this time, but the work of a particular binder or workshop can sometimes be identified through the use of symbols such as a dragon or unicorn on the binding.

One of the greatest bibliophiles in sixteenth-century Europe was Jean Grolier de Servières. French born of Italian descent, Grolier spent different periods of his life residing in Italy and France, serving as ambassador to Pope Clement VII and later as one of France's four treasurers. A lover of fine books, he became a friend and patron of the great Venetian printer Aldus Manutius. Grolier amassed a library of three thousand books, many of which he had bound by the finest binders of the day, generally in a delicate and understated geometric design. The style now bears his name, as do several societies dedicated to fine books. Grolier was also one of the first collectors to have the titles of his books tooled onto their spines. Before the sixteenth century, titles were often applied in ink to the fore-edge, as books until that time tended to be stored with their pages facing outwards.

GEOFROY TORY

This volume is a rare example of an original French binding from the Renaissance. It is bound in black calfskin that has been elaborately decorated with blind tooling. The *pot cassé*, or broken urn, motif visible in the tooling was often used by the printer and publisher Geofroy Tory to signify his work.

LEFT:
Horae in Laude Beatiss, Virginis Mariae, ad Usum Romanum (Book of Hours)
Paris, Geofroy Tory, 1531

RIGHT:
Almanach Royale
Paris, 1785

ABOVE:
A Specimen Book of Pattern Papers Designed for and in use at the Curwen Press
London, published for the Curwen Press by The Fleuron Ltd, 1928

LEFT:
Roland Dorgelès
Montmartre Mon Pays
Paris, Marcelle Lesage, 1928
Binding by
L Alexandrova

CURWEN PRESS

The Curwen Press, established in 1863 by the Reverend John Curwen, was originally a press for printing music. By the 1920s, Curwen's grandson Harold had expanded the press's activities to include the production of high-quality, limited edition books. Many of these were illustrated by young contemporary artists of the time such as Paul Nash, Edward Bawden and Eric Ravilious. This specimen book contains a selection of pattern papers used by the Curwen Press for bookbindings. The papers illustrated here are by Nash, who also provided the introductory text.

THE WORLD of the BOOK | 177

BELOW, LEFT:
François Couperin
Oeuvres Complètes de François Couperin
Paris, Éditions de l'Oiseau-Lyre, 1932–33

BELOW, MIDDLE:
Pablo Picasso
Carmen sur le Texte de Prosper Mérimée
Paris, La Bibliothèque Française, 1949

BELOW, RIGHT:
Charles Baudelaire
Les Fleurs du Mal
Chamonix, France, Jean Landru, 1946

LES FLEURS DU MAL

The design for this binding was created by Roger Carle. It loosely evokes the form of a flower, in reference to the book's title ('Flowers of Evil').

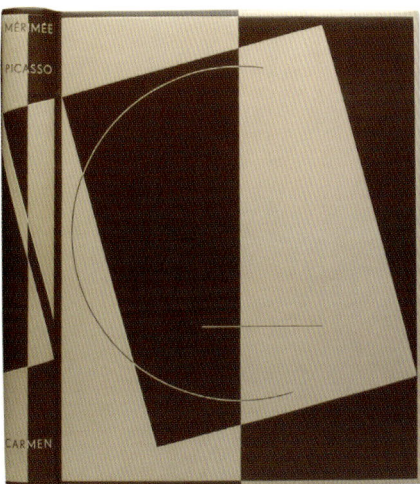
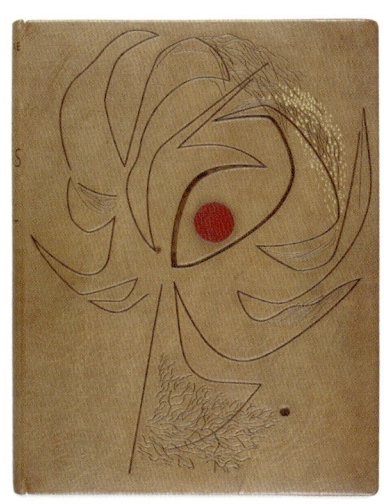

ÉDITIONS DE L'OISEAU-LYRE

Éditions de l'Oiseau-Lyre (Lyrebird) was founded by Australian music patron Louise BM Dyer in Paris in 1932 and continues to operate from Monaco and Melbourne. Dyer was committed to the support of both early and new French music, for which she was awarded the Légion d'Honneur in 1934. This deluxe twelve-volume publication of the complete works of François Couperin was her first major project and continues to be recognised for its fine production as well as its musical scholarship.

Until the mid sixteenth century, Italy was at the forefront of bookbinding in Europe. Around this time, however, French binders developed a greater refinement of decorative processes, using increasingly fine goat- and calfskins that enabled binding of exceptional detail and beauty. New decorative processes included onlays and inlays, in which thin pieces of different-coloured leathers were applied to or set into the leather of a book's cover.

Throughout the seventeenth and eighteenth centuries, European binders developed more detailed forms of ornamentation such as *dentelle*—lace borderwork using fine motifs in gold. Decorative borders popular in the French Empire period used motifs from ancient Egyptian, Greek and Roman art, signifying Napoleon's desire to emulate imperial Rome.

In the nineteenth century, bookbinding changed dramatically once more, this time with the industrial revolution. New mechanised methods of book production brought with them mass binding processes, the use of cheaper and often inferior materials, and the introduction of cloth in place of leather as a standard binding. In an effort to restore the traditional crafts of fine bookbinding, lawyer, designer and amateur binder Thomas J Cobden-Sanderson started the Doves Bindery in 1893. A friend of Arts and Crafts founder William Morris, Cobden-Sanderson established his bindery primarily for the limited edition books produced by Morris's Kelmscott Press and later those produced by his own Doves Press. One of Cobden-Sanderson's pupils was Douglas Cockerell, who would go on to become an influential master binder in the twentieth century.

Throughout the past hundred years, binding styles have reflected changing tastes and artistic movements such as Art Nouveau and Art Deco and have ranged from the ornate to the minimal.

An art long associated with book production is that of marbling, a method of decorating paper with abstract patterns. Chinese records indicate that the marbling process was practised there as far back as the tenth century. From around the twelfth century, artisans in Japan developed a particular style of marbling known as *suminagashi*, which translates as 'ink floating'. *Sumi*, or ink, was delicately floated onto the surface of very still water. Patterns were created by blowing gently across the water surface or manipulating it with a stylus or strand of human hair. A sheet of paper was then carefully placed on the surface and the ink patterns transferred.

ANN MUIR

Prominent British marbler Ann Muir has been making traditional hand-marbled paper in south-west England since 1983. Her papers are recognised for their complexity and design innovation and are used by bookbinders, fine presses and publishers worldwide. The one illustrated here suggests a sense of three-dimensionality and movement through the use of bold colour and sweeping form.

Ann Muir
Harvesting Colour: the Year in a Marbler's Workshop
Oldham, UK, Incline Press, 1999

By the fifteenth century, another form of marbling, known as *ebrû*, was practised in Persia and Turkey. Using oil or gouache paints rather than ink, intricate patterns suggestive of clouds or veins of marble could be created with a stylus, brush or comb. By 1600, marbling had spread to Europe via trade centres such as Venice, which itself became and remains a major centre for the production of marbled papers. Used primarily in the production of endpapers and 'half-bindings' on book covers, marbling was also used to decorate the fore-edges of ledgers and account books so that surreptitious removal of pages could be detected by subsequent irregularities in the marble pattern. Other decorative papers used in Europe included those block printed with patterns or scenes, and paste papers in which objects were pressed into or dragged across papers coated in a mixture of pigment and paste.

A sense of magic or mystery surrounded the process of marbling for centuries, and practitioners were keen to preserve the secrets of their trade. Guilds were established and apprentices were only trained in certain aspects of the craft so that they would not know the complete process until they themselves were established artisans. All this changed, however, when the English marbler Charles Woolnough published his book *The Art of Marbling* in 1853. Woolnough's book outlined in detail the ingredients and techniques of marbling and, in the process, caused howls of protest from marblers throughout Europe. Books by other authors swiftly followed, and by the end of the nineteenth century, the secrets of marbling were widely known. By this time, however, the demand for handcrafted marbling in the West had diminished as book production and binding became increasingly mechanised.

It is only in recent decades that the fine art of marbling has been revived by artists and binders involved in the production of high-quality books, especially as part of the private press movement. Today, artists such as Karli Frigge and Ann Muir continue to explore the creative possibilities of traditional marbling practices. And individual artist-binders today are also developing new forms of expression through the combination of centuries-old bookbinding techniques with materials found in our twenty-first-century world.

FEATHER AND PREY

Nick Doslov is one of the great master bookbinders working in Australia today. He combines age-old techniques with innovative ideas to preserve and extend the art of bookbinding. For more than twenty years, artist Peter Lyssiotis has collaborated with Doslov in the production of artists' books. Using the finest materials available and traditional handcrafts, these books are works of art for their bindings as well as their contents.

TOP:
Peter Lyssiotis
Feather and Prey
Melbourne, Masterthief Enterprises, 1997
Binding by Nick Doslov, Renaissance Bookbinding

BOTTOM:
Paul Wenz
Jim et Jack
Sydney, Bookbinding Exhibitions Australia, 2005
Binding by Yoko Ueno, Japan

THE BOOK
in Edo Japan

If we think of books as 'the mirror of the culture' of a nation, those that display pictorial art must be of special relevance. In Japan ... artists gave their view of the world, expressed their philosophy and expounded their theories of style in books and albums.

JACK HILLIER, *THE ART OF THE JAPANESE BOOK*

FROM CALLIGRAPHY TO THE MAKING OF FINE PAPERS, WOODBLOCK PRINTING AND BINDING, JAPAN IS RENOWNED FOR ITS BOOKS. THE HISTORY OF BOOK PRODUCTION IN PRE-MODERN JAPAN IS CHARACTERISED BY THE REFINEMENT OF THIS TRADITIONAL CRAFT OVER MANY CENTURIES AND BY THE CREATION AND USE OF HIGH-QUALITY MATERIALS.

While mechanical printing and binding processes have become the norm in contemporary Japan, traditional Japanese book arts continue to be practised by skilled artisans and appreciated by collectors worldwide.

The first books to appear in Japan were *kansubon*, which were horizontal handscrolls. This scroll format was introduced from China and was the primary book form in Japan from the fifth to ninth century. A significant category of Japanese book scrolls was *emakimono*, picture scrolls that presented a narrative through sequential images. Technologies of paper making were also developed in China and most likely introduced to Japan via Korean traders and then Buddhist monks. Early records indicate that paper was being made in Japan by 610, and by the eighth century coloured papers were in production. By the fourteenth century, Japanese paper makers were producing papers using materials distinctive to different regions. Some of these incorporated decorative elements such as pressed flowers, leaves and flecks of silver or gold added to the surface or embedded in the paper.

The scroll form continued to be used for manuscript works after the introduction of woodblock printing from China around the eighth century. For the next thousand years, printing tended to be used primarily for Buddhist texts, while secular and literary works were still produced as manuscripts. All this would change during the Edo period.

The Edo, or Tokugawa, period (1600–1868) began when the Tokugawa shogunate seized control of the country and established its capital at Edo, now Tokyo. Over subsequent decades, the ruling shoguns introduced policies that restricted access to the rest of the world. Japanese citizens who left the country were not permitted to return. Foreign communication was via trade with China and Korea, and with the Dutch East India Company who had a base on the island of Dejima at Nagasaki. Under Tokugawa rule, the Edo period was a time of relative peace and economic prosperity in which the arts and industry flourished.

New markets for culture developed at this time. While the traditional warrior class system placed samurai at the top and merchants at the bottom, a new balance of economic power blurred these divisions during the Edo period. Powerful feudal lords remained across the country, but the fortunes of many samurai declined with land redistribution and decreased revenue. A new urban class (*chōnin*), which cut across traditional divisions, developed in the cities of Edo, Osaka and Kyoto, and artisans and merchants found

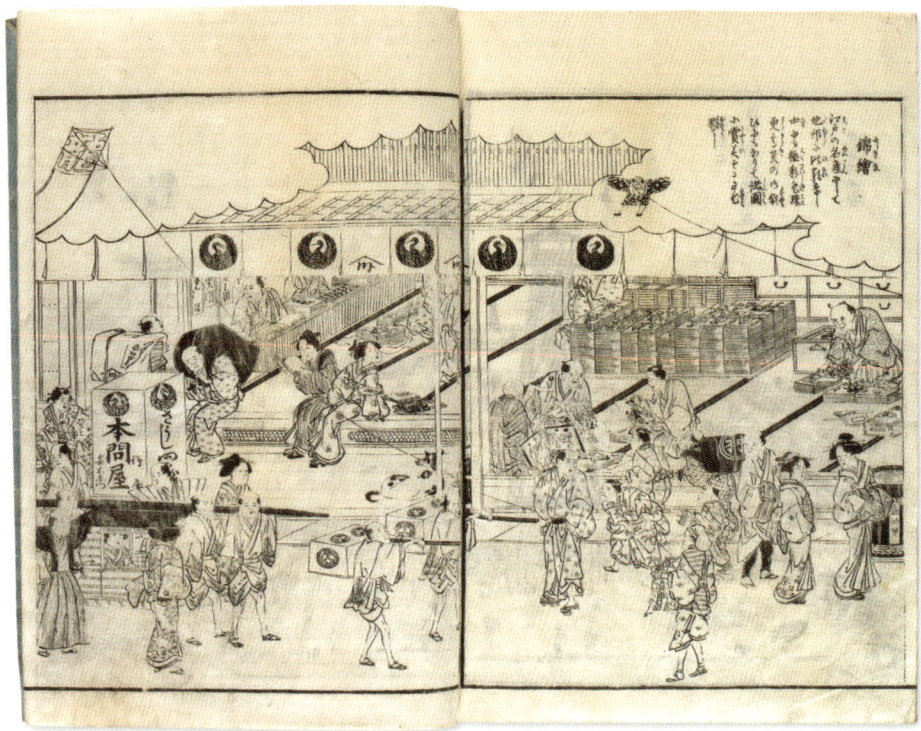

EDO MEISHO ZUE

Travel within Japan was very popular during the Edo period. *Meisho zue* were illustrated guidebooks that provided detailed information about the history and significance of sites to be visited as well as useful tips about nearby accommodation and restaurants. This plate by Hasegawa Settan is from one of the most comprehensive guides to the famous places and monuments of the city of Edo, now Tokyo. It depicts the bookshop of Tsuruya Kiemon, a leading Kyoto publisher who had a branch in Edo.

LEFT:
Edo meisho zue
Edo (Tokyo),
Subaraya Ihachi,
1834–36

OPPOSITE, TOP:
Kawamura Bunpō
Kinpaen gafu
Kyoto, Hishaya Magobē,
1811 (c. 1820 printing)

OPPOSITE, BOTTOM:
Katsushika Hokusai
Katsushika shinsō gafu
Tokyo, Matsumura Magokichi, 1890

new markets for their products. With an increasingly wealthy class denied access to the avenues of high culture controlled by the court or the samurai class, new forms of art and entertainment developed in the burgeoning pleasure districts of the major cities. Two cultural forms in particular arose at this time—*kabuki* theatre and *ukiyo-e* printmaking. While today we generally associate *ukiyo-e* with prints, either in single sheets or in series, it was through the medium of the book that *ukiyo-e* first developed and had its largest audiences.

Ukiyo-e literally means 'pictures of the floating world'. As a term, it came to refer in Edo Japan to notions of transience and an attitude of living for the moment. While the newly wealthy urban classes would never gain acceptance into established society, they could live out their fantasies in the pleasure districts and surround themselves with beautiful things. Picture books and prints were not only affordable but they also depicted and reflected the joys of this 'floating world'.

As demand grew, book production became an increasingly commercial enterprise, and new printing and binding processes that would enable the production of thousands of copies of a popular title were developed. The technologies of printing with moveable type were known from earlier contact with Jesuit missionaries and with Korean traders, but woodblock printing remained the common process until the end of the Edo period.

Woodblock printing was preferred for a range of practical and aesthetic reasons. It required little capital outlay compared with the large presses needed for printing with metal type. Hand-carved blocks of script offered aesthetic advantages, as they could more closely approximate the venerated art of calligraphy than could moveable type. Woodblock printing also facilitated the production of illustrated works because pictures and text could be carved from the same block. The blocks could then be retained or sold to other publishers for the later reprinting of popular works. Books of great quality were in demand, and many from the period were produced by highly trained artisans who used the best materials.

As the commercial publishing industry became increasingly competitive during this period, good-quality illustrations, often produced in colour using multiple woodblocks, gave publishers an edge over their competitors. Printers perfected registration techniques that enabled the printing of complex images with many colours. They also introduced the deluxe processes of blind embossing, lacquering and printing with special materials such as gold leaf and mica. Whereas book illustration was not seen as a respected practice for artists in China, it developed as an important and highly regarded form of employment in Japan. Well-known artists such as Suzuki Harunobu, Torii Kiyonaga, Kitagawa Utamaro, Utagawa Toyokuni, Utagawa Kunisada, Katsushika Hokusai and Utagawa Hiroshige were regularly commissioned to produce book illustrations, their names often promoted along with the work's author.

The choice of papers and wood, from which to carve the blocks, was particularly important to ensure both quality work and the capacity for mass production. Softwood was easier to carve than hardwood, but printing quality degraded after fewer copies had been printed. The wood most commonly used was cherry, a hardwood that allowed for the production of works of great detail and that had a long printing life. Printers used *washi*, papers made from natural fibres. The *kōzo* (mulberry) plant, in particular, was used to create papers that were durable and flexible but also light and translucent. The characteristics of these papers in turn influenced the styles of bindings developed for woodblock-printed books.

The *orihon*, or concertina, book form had been introduced from China for use in the production of Buddhist texts. Its popularity decreased over time, however, as it required sturdy paper that caused wear and tear on the printing blocks. Another form introduced from China was the *detchōsō*, or 'butterfly binding', in which sheets were printed on one side and folded, the folds being stitched together to create a spine.

The most popular form for printed books during the Edo period was the *fukuro-toji*,

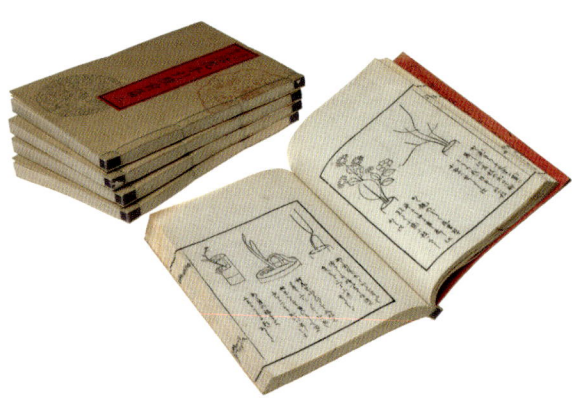

YOSHIO YASUMASA

This is an example of *fukuro-toji*, or 'bag' binding. The design on the cover is based on the chrysanthemum, one of the three national flowers of Japan and the emblem of the imperial family. This five-volume manual instructs practitioners in the techniques and styles of the Seizan school of ikebana, or flower arranging. Ikebana involves the arrangement of three primary stems that represent heaven, man and earth.

ANSEI KENMONSHI

Natural disasters were popular subjects for books in Edo Japan. This three-volume work documents the devastating effects of the great Ansei earthquake that rocked Edo (Tokyo) in 1855, killing more than ten thousand people and destroying most of the city either directly or through the subsequent fire. The plate shown here depicts the devastation of a section of the Yoshiwara, or pleasure district, of the city.

TOP:
Yoshio Yasumasa
Seizan goryū ikebana tebikigusa
Kyoto, Otani Jinbē, 1800
(later printing)

RIGHT:
Ansei kenmonshi
c. 1857

OPPOSITE:
Nakabayashi Chikudō
Yūsai kachō gafu
Kyoto, Fujii Magobē, 1831

or 'bag' binding, brought to Japan from China in the Muromachi period (1333–1568). In this style of binding, the sheets were folded with the printed side out and the spine stab-stitched at the loose edges to create pages of a double thickness. This enabled the use of translucent papers that were gentle on the printing blocks and also avoided the problem of ink showing through from one side of a sheet to the other. It did, however, require the left- and right-hand plates of a double-spread image to be printed on two separate blocks, alongside the corresponding halves of the preceding and following images. Artists became masters at working with the gap created between the left and right halves, leading the eye from one side to the other with compositional devices.

Book covers were generally made from coarse but sturdy material that was then covered with a finer paper. The colour of this outer paper was often specific to a particular genre, such as *aohon*, or 'blue books', for children and *kibyōshi*, or 'yellow backs', which were popular satirical novelettes. Covers were embossed or printed in several colours. One work would often consist of a number of volumes, kept together in a specially made case.

Even though literacy rates were relatively high in Edo Japan, the complexities of the written language challenged many readers and in turn ensured a great demand for illustrative works. These ranged from *e-iribon* (texts with illustrations) to *ehon* (picture books) and *gafu* (drawing books). Each of these was divided into a wide array of sub-genres. For example, a sub-genre of *ehon* was *gesaku* ('jestful writings'), which in turn was divided into *yomihon* (reading books), *sharebon* (witty books), *kokkeibon* (comic books) and the very popular *kibyōshi* mentioned earlier.

Subject matter was equally diverse. Street scenes, portraits of famous courtesans and kabuki actors, and the stories and scandals acted out in the theatres and brothels of the pleasure district were particularly popular. Other genres included scientific, botanical, travel, historical and literary works as well as books illustrating the work of famous painters (especially *kachō-ga*, 'flower and bird paintings'), drawing and ikebana manuals, and kimono pattern books.

The reproduction in printed books of paintings and drawings by famous Japanese artists made their work accessible to audiences who could not afford the originals, and to artists who wished to

NAKABAYASHI CHIKUDŌ

Kachō-ga, or the depiction of flowers and birds, has long been an important and popular genre in Japanese art. The placement of a particular bird with a type of flower can suggest a season in nature or make a poetic allusion. Nakabayashi Chikudō was a member of the Nanga school, and his *kachō-ga*, as well as his landscapes, were highly regarded.

learn particular techniques. For example, *Gazu hyakkachō* (Paintings of One Hundred Flowers and Birds) reproduced the work of the seventeenth-century painter Kanō Tan'yū, an important artist of the Kanō school. The Kanō school adopted the traditional painting styles of the Chinese masters and included the artists most favoured by the Tokugawa shogunate. First published in 1729 after Tan'yū's death, the reproductions of his works were undertaken by one of his followers, Sekichūshi Morinori, and were printed alongside information and instructions for artists. Art manuals and books on artists from other schools, such as the Nanga school (based on the Chinese school of amateur scholar-artists) and the Maruyama-Shijō school of naturalist painting, were also popular.

Of the various schools of Japanese print-making, the *ukiyo-e* artists are the most celebrated throughout the world today. And of these, the most famous, particularly in the West, is Katsushika Hokusai. A printmaker, book illustrator and painter, Hokusai lived for a remarkable eighty-nine years and was known for his eccentricity as well as his prolific output. Late in life he described himself as 'the old man mad about drawing'. He studied many schools of Chinese and Japanese art as well as western theories of perspective, synthesising elements of all of them into his unique works. Hokusai is renowned for his many depictions of Mount Fuji, such as those in his three-volume illustrated book *Fugaku hyakkei* (One Hundred Views of Mount Fuji) published between 1834 and around 1842.

In addition to creating landscape paintings and prints of sublime beauty, Hokusai produced works that depicted everyday life. He lived among the merchants, artisans and entertainers of the city of Edo, observing and depicting their lives with humour and affection. His fifteen-volume *Hokusai manga*, or 'random and whimsical sketches' (1814–78), contains, among other things, numerous studies of people, animals, gods and ghosts. Hokusai's influence was extensive and inspired European artists, who adopted the *Japonisme* style later in the nineteenth century as Japanese culture became more known in the West.

Tokugawa rule began to decline in the early nineteenth century. Around this time, Japan also increased its contact with other cultures beyond its borders. After the arrival of Commodore Matthew Perry of the US Navy, Japan formalised a new relationship with the West with the signing of the Treaty of Kanagawa in 1854. In 1868, the Meiji Restoration returned power to the imperial family. As Meiji rule moved swiftly to modernise Japan and expand trade with the West, book production changed dramatically with the introduction of industrial printing presses and new artistic influences. Japanese woodblock prints and illustrated books from the Edo period, however, continued to be as prized as they are today. They are collected and studied worldwide as examples of a golden era of Japanese art and book production.

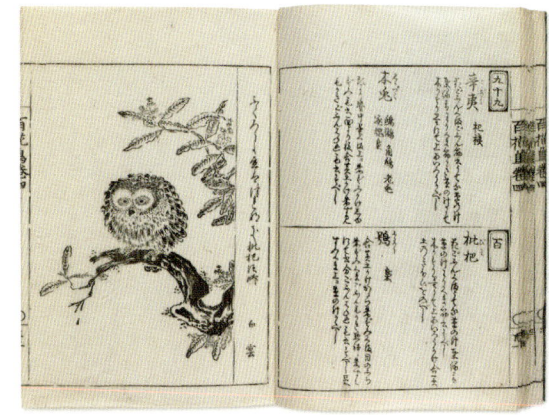

NESUMI TAKENOSUKE

This book is a catalogue of decorative patterns for children's *furisode*, or long-sleeved kimonos. Pattern books such as this were produced from the seventeenth century onwards, a high point in the art of the kimono. They reflect the importance of, and great interest in, all aspects of dress in Japan, as markers of social standing and of artistic excellence. As living standards improved during the Edo period, more people could afford luxury items such as custom-made kimonos. As a result, many artists turned to the design of kimono fabrics and other accessories.

MARUYAMA ŌKYO

The tonal gradations created in brush and ink painting have been achieved here by printing with *sumi*, a type of black ink made from charcoal and traditionally used in painting and calligraphy. Maruyama Ōkyo was a renowned painter and founder of the Kyoto-based Maruyama-Shijō school of naturalist painting.

OPPOSITE, TOP:
Kanō Tan'yū
Gazu hyakkachō
Osaka, Kagaya Zenzo,
1729 (1814 printing)
Woodcuts by Sekichūshi
Morinori

OPPOSITE, MIDDLE:
Nesumi Takenosuke
*Somemoyo hinagata:
nakadachi kodachi*
Osaka, Maekawa Zenbē,
1891

OPPOSITE, BOTTOM:
Maruyama Ōkyo
Ōkyo gafu
Kyoto, Tanaka Jiemon,
1850 (1891 printing)

RIGHT:
Katsushika Hokusai
Fugaku hyakkei
Nagoya, Katano Tōshirō,
1834–35 (1876 printing)

BOTTOM:
Katsushika Hokusai
Hokusai manga
Tokyo, Yoshikawa
Hanshichi, 1814–78
(later printing)

The WORLD of the BOOK | 187

The Artist as ILLUSTRATOR

In reading books, as in looking at pictures, one must admire what is beautiful with assurance—without doubt, without hesitation.
VINCENT VAN GOGH, LETTER TO THEO

WHILE ARTISTS HAVE ALWAYS PLAYED A ROLE IN THE PRODUCTION OF BOOKS, FROM EARLY MANUSCRIPTS THROUGH TO MODERN DUST JACKET ILLUSTRATION, IT HAS GENERALLY BEEN THE CASE THAT THIS ROLE HAS BEEN SUBSERVIENT TO THE TEXT OR OVERALL DESIGN OF THE BOOK. ILLUSTRATIONS HAVE MAINLY ACTED AS AN ACCOMPANIMENT, HELPING TO ELUCIDATE A BOOK'S THEMES BY PROVIDING A VISUAL NARRATIVE THAT BOTH FOLLOWS THE TEXT AND IS DEPENDENT UPON IT FOR ITS EXISTENCE.

Since the development of printing, and its associated illustrative techniques such as woodcut, engraving and lithography, there have been books or particular editions that are valued for their illustrations alone, rather than any other content. The reputation of such works generally rests on the stature of the artist contributing the original designs. Giovanni Battista Piranesi's dark and detailed engravings of archaeological sites throughout Italy were made available to wider audiences through their compilation into printed volumes.

For German artist Albrecht Dürer, the making of books was a logical extension of his work as a printmaker. As a young man, Dürer learned his craft in the workshop of Michael Wolgemut, one of the leading German artists and book illustrators of the day, employed by printer Anton Koberger to execute woodcuts for the *Liber Chronicarum* or 'Nuremberg Chronicle' (1493). Dürer went on to produce a number of books of his woodcuts based on religious themes, including *Life of the Virgin* (1511) and *Large Passion* (1511). His first book, *The Apocalypse* (1498), published in both Latin and German vernacular editions, depicted the dramatic revelations of St John the Divine. While this was a popular subject with fifteenth-century wood engravers, the expressive power of Dürer's woodcuts set a new standard for the illustrated book. By printing the text onto the reverse side of the woodcuts, Dürer elevated the pictorial component of the book above that of its traditional supporting role.

Artists were regularly called upon to illustrate popular and enduring texts, such as those by Virgil or Dante. One commonly illustrated text was the fables of Aesop. According to the Greek historian Herodotus, Aesop was a slave and storyteller in sixth-century BCE Greece, and his moral tales involving animals remained a favourite with printers and publishers. Johann Zainer issued an edition at Ulm in 1476, and William Caxton printed an English version in 1482. The French poet Jean de La Fontaine's versions of the fables first appeared in 1668, and these became the basis for one of the great illustrated books of the eighteenth century, Jean-Baptiste Oudry's *Fables Choisies* (1755–59). Oudry, director of the royal tapestry works at Beauvais, originally produced the designs for the 275 engravings of La Fontaine's fables between 1729 and 1734. But it was not until 1751, when the drawings were acquired by French financier Montenault, that publication was realised. Montenault thought that Oudry's designs were too 'free and loose' for engravers to follow and accordingly had them redrawn by Charles-Nicolas Cochin before engaging forty-two engravers to complete the copper plates. Such was the cost of this exercise that the first three volumes left Montenault in financial straits, and the fourth and final volume only appeared in 1759 through the assistance of a royal grant. One of the most striking elements of Oudry's illustrations is his pictorial rendering of the French countryside, which appears to prefigure the later ascendency of plein-air painting. Oudry's landscapes are imbued with such presence that they seem to hold as central a place in the narrative as the many animals that inhabit the book's pages. Equally notable are the decorative tailpieces, designed by flower painter Jean-Jacques Bachelier, used to fill the page at the end of each fable. In an age of sumptuous books, Oudry's *Fables Choisies* represents the pinnacle of eighteenth-century French book illustration.

In some cases, the later critical success of an artist or illustrator overshadows a book's original author. In the case of Robert Blair's volume of verse *The Grave*, it is almost entirely due to the presence of William Blake's engravings that the book continues to generate interest. Blair was a Scottish clergyman and poet, best known for 'The Grave', a morbid contemplation of death and the solitude of the grave. It was first published in 1743, and by 1798 had appeared in forty-nine editions. For the 1808 edition, publisher Robert Cromek commissioned original illustrations from William Blake. However, after raising £1800 from subscribers, including artists Samuel Palmer, Henri Fuseli and John Flaxman, Cromek turned Blake's finished designs over to the more fashionable engraver Louis Schiavonetti, who was paid £600 for his work. Blake, who received a mere £20 for his designs, would later describe Cromek as 'A petty, Sneaking Knave who loves the Art but 'tis the Art to Cheat'. Despite Schiavonetti's role in producing the engravings, the completed illustrations remain entirely Blakean.

A previous commission Blake received had also ended badly. In 1795, Richard Edwards engaged Blake to illustrate a new edition of *The Complaint, and the Consolation, or, Night Thoughts* by Edward Young, a popular meditative poem on 'life, death & immortality', first published in 1742–45. Blake originally produced 537 watercolours, intending to engrave two hundred of these for the work.

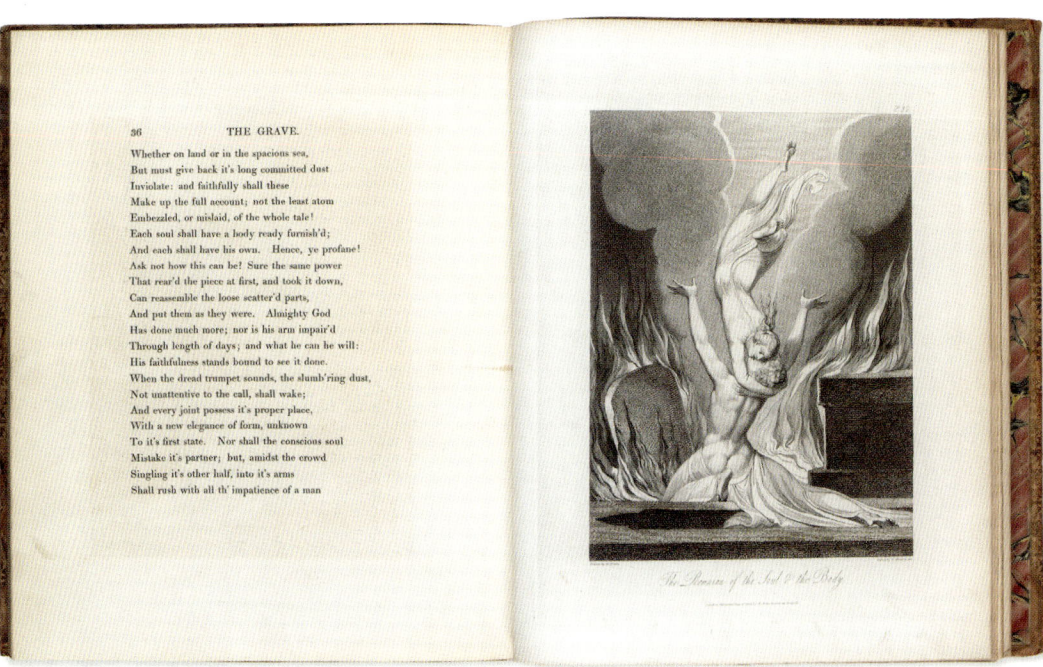

TOP:
Jean de La Fontaine
Fables Choisies,
Mises en Vers
Paris, printed by Charles-Antoine Jombert, 1755–59
Illustrated by
Jean-Baptiste Oudry

BOTTOM:
Robert Blair
The Grave: a Poem
London, printed by
T Bensley for the
proprietor, R Ackermann,
1813
Illustrated by William Blake

OPPOSITE:
Albrecht Dürer
'The Four Horsemen
of the Apocalypse'
From *The Apocalypse*
Nuremberg, 1498
Collection: National
Gallery of Victoria,
Melbourne

LEFT:
Dante (Dante Alighieri)
The Vision of Hell
London, Cassell, Petter & Galpin, 1866
Illustrated by Gustave Doré

OPPOSITE:
JMW Turner
Liber Studiorum
London, JMW Turner, 1807–19

The first volume published included forty-three of Blake's engravings but was a commercial failure, convincing Edwards to abandon the project.

Aside from such commissions from publishers, the bulk of Blake's artistic energies went into the production of illustrated editions of his own books of poems, such as *The Marriage of Heaven and Hell* (1790–93) and *Jerusalem* (1804–20). For these works, Blake wrote the text directly onto copper plates and printed the text and illustrations together as relief etchings—a technique he said was revealed to him in a dream by his dead brother, Robert. Influenced by the tradition of illuminated manuscripts, Blake managed to unify his visionary poems and illustrations in entirely new and daring ways. Though little read in his day, Blake's work is now central to the history of the illustrated book.

The great English landscape artist JMW Turner published his *Liber Studiorum*, or 'Book of Studies' between 1807 and 1819, in part inspired by Claude Lorrain's *Liber Veritatis*, produced in the mid seventeenth century. In this ambitious work, Turner set out to describe the six categories of landscape: historic, mountainous, pastoral, marine, architectural and epic pastoral. Of the hundred images planned, seventy-one were published. Turner was closely involved in the production of the book and etched the preliminary designs onto the plates himself. His innovative decision to use mezzotint, a process developed in the Netherlands in the 1640s but little used in books before the eighteenth century, enabled engravers to render dramatic contrasts of light and shade.

One of the most prolific of the nineteenth-century illustrators was French artist Gustave Doré, whose editions of classic texts by Dante, Milton and Cervantes were widely and popularly reproduced. His illustrated edition of the Bible proved so popular in England that it led to a major exhibition in London in 1867 and to the opening of the Doré Gallery in New Bond Street. His illustrations were predominantly reproduced as wood engravings, and such was his output for books and magazines that more than forty wood-cutters were allegedly required to keep pace with it. At their best, Doré's scenes are full of dramatic intensity and darkness. French poet Théophile Gautier went on to acclaim them for the vitality they brought to chimeras and nightmares, and for their capacity to render the monsters of fantasy.

LEFT:
Oscar Wilde
Salome: a Tragedy in One Act
London, John Lane, The Bodley Head, 1907
Illustrated by Aubrey Beardsley

Yet, to the end of his life, Doré remained disappointed at the refusal of the fine art establishment in France to accept him as a painter rather than as an illustrator.

The notoriety of artist Aubrey Beardsley rests largely on his fin de siècle decadence, inspired by Art Nouveau fashion of the period. In his short life, he produced a large number of illustrations for books and journals. He was most notably associated with *The Yellow Book*, the illustrated quarterly he helped found in 1894, but he also contributed to magazines such as *The Savoy* and *The Studio*. Unlike his contemporary William Morris, who emphasised traditional printing techniques, Beardsley was willing to engage with newer reproductive processes, such as photographic line block. This was a cheaper printing method that guaranteed his work the widest possible circulation. Beardsley's daring and stylised illustrations proved popular with publishers, and he was commissioned to create work for well-known erotic texts such as *Lysistrata* and Oscar Wilde's *Salome*. Wilde's drama *Salome* was written in French and first published in Paris in 1893, being performed there by Sarah Bernhardt after having been banned in London by the Lord Chamberlain. The first English edition appeared in London in 1894, translated by Lord Alfred Douglas and illustrated by Beardsley. Wilde was of the opinion that Beardsley's graphics overwhelmed the text, while the publishers who commissioned the artwork demanded a reduction of what they perceived as the grotesque nudity of the plates. Wilde's comment on Beardsley's designs was typically Wildean: 'They are cruel and evil and so like dear Aubrey who has a face like a silver hatchet with grass-green hair'. Beardsley's *Salome* added to Wilde's notoriety, and contributed to Beardsley being banned from *The Yellow Book*.

The onset of the twentieth century saw a rise in the number of deluxe illustrated books published, particularly in France, as entrepreneurial art dealers such as Ambrose Vollard, Daniel-Henry Kahnweiler and later Albert Skira took advantage of the commercial opportunities afforded by a widening pool of collectors interested in modern art. Vollard was the first to exhibit Vincent van Gogh, and his gallery on Rue Lafitte in Paris, which opened in 1903, was home to the works of Paul Cézanne, Pablo Picasso, Henri Matisse and others. In 1900, he issued his first publication, *Parallèlement*, a collection of poems by Paul Verlaine, illustrated by Impressionist artist Pierre Bonnard. Following on from William Morris's emphasis on the fundamental features of the book—design, typography, paper—Vollard and other publishers began to issue books featuring original prints by the leading artists of the day, including Picasso, Georges Rouault and André Derain. These illustrations were sometimes paired with texts by contemporary writers, such as Guillaume Apollinaire, but more often with classical texts, such as Picasso's edition of Prosper Mérimée's *Carmen* (1949) or Marc Chagall's illustrated edition of La Fontaine's fables (1952). These works commonly became known as *livres d'artiste* or *éditions-de-luxe*, and were integral to the development of the modern artist's book.

The French tradition of *livres d'artiste* carried over to the magazines of the period. Along with the many Surrealist productions, most notably Albert Skira's *Minotaure* of the 1930s, it was perhaps *Verve* magazine that set the trend. Publisher Efstratios Teriade, who had previously worked as artistic director on *Minotaure* and later published Henri Matisse's groundbreaking *Jazz* (1947), began issuing the magazine in December 1937. Its first cover was specially designed by Matisse, and during its long run until 1960, the lavishly designed magazine featured illustrations by Chagall, Bonnard, Picasso, Georges Braque

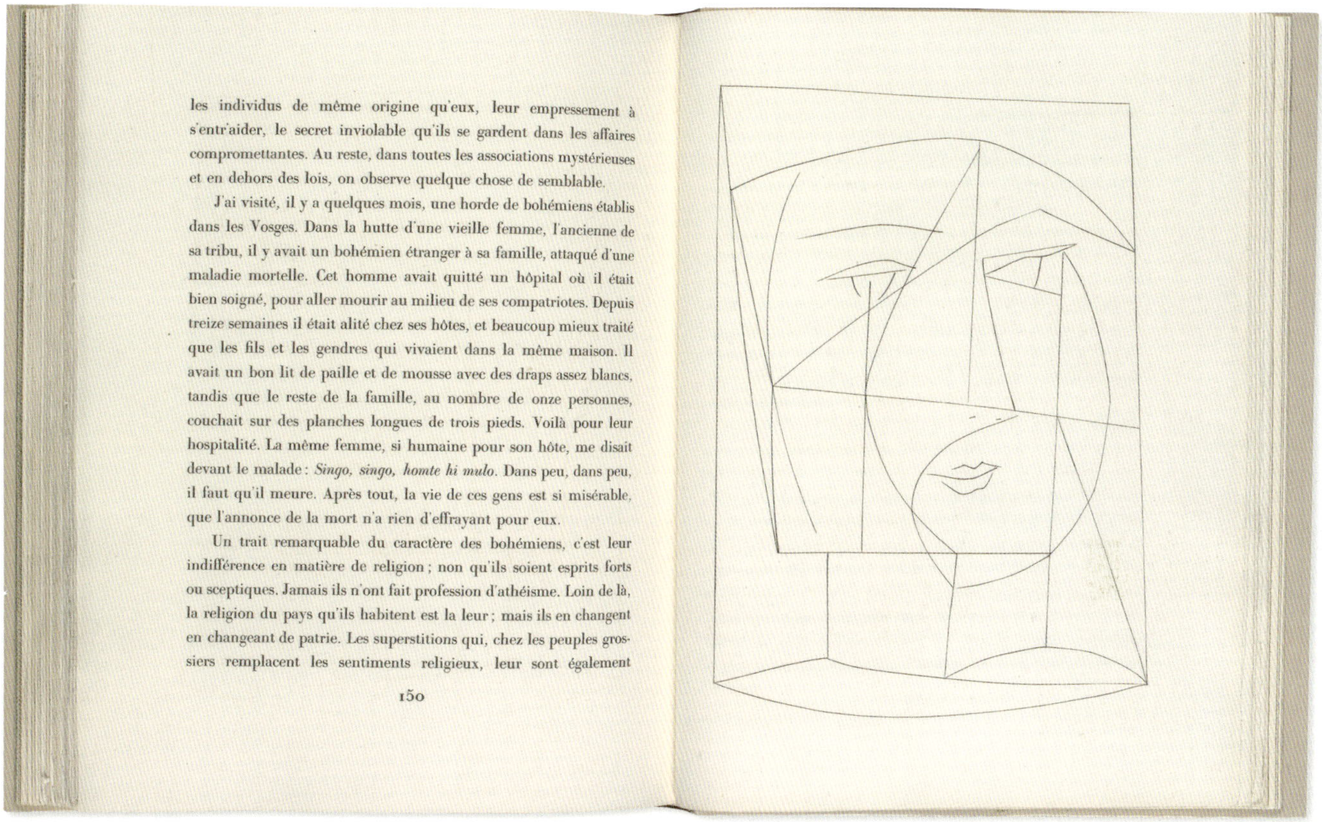

les individus de même origine qu'eux, leur empressement à s'entr'aider, le secret inviolable qu'ils se gardent dans les affaires compromettantes. Au reste, dans toutes les associations mystérieuses et en dehors des lois, on observe quelque chose de semblable.

J'ai visité, il y a quelques mois, une horde de bohémiens établis dans les Vosges. Dans la hutte d'une vieille femme, l'ancienne de sa tribu, il y avait un bohémien étranger à sa famille, attaqué d'une maladie mortelle. Cet homme avait quitté un hôpital où il était bien soigné, pour aller mourir au milieu de ses compatriotes. Depuis treize semaines il était alité chez ses hôtes, et beaucoup mieux traité que les fils et les gendres qui vivaient dans la même maison. Il avait un bon lit de paille et de mousse avec des draps assez blancs, tandis que le reste de la famille, au nombre de onze personnes, couchait sur des planches longues de trois pieds. Voilà pour leur hospitalité. La même femme, si humaine pour son hôte, me disait devant le malade : *Singo, singo, homte hi mulo.* Dans peu, dans peu, il faut qu'il meure. Après tout, la vie de ces gens est si misérable, que l'annonce de la mort n'a rien d'effrayant pour eux.

Un trait remarquable du caractère des bohémiens, c'est leur indifférence en matière de religion ; non qu'ils soient esprits forts ou sceptiques. Jamais ils n'ont fait profession d'athéisme. Loin de là, la religion du pays qu'ils habitent est la leur ; mais ils en changent en changeant de patrie. Les superstitions qui, chez les peuples grossiers remplacent les sentiments religieux, leur sont également

150

RIGHT, TOP:
Pablo Picasso
Carmen sur le Texte de Prosper Mérimée
Paris, La Bibliothèque Française, 1949

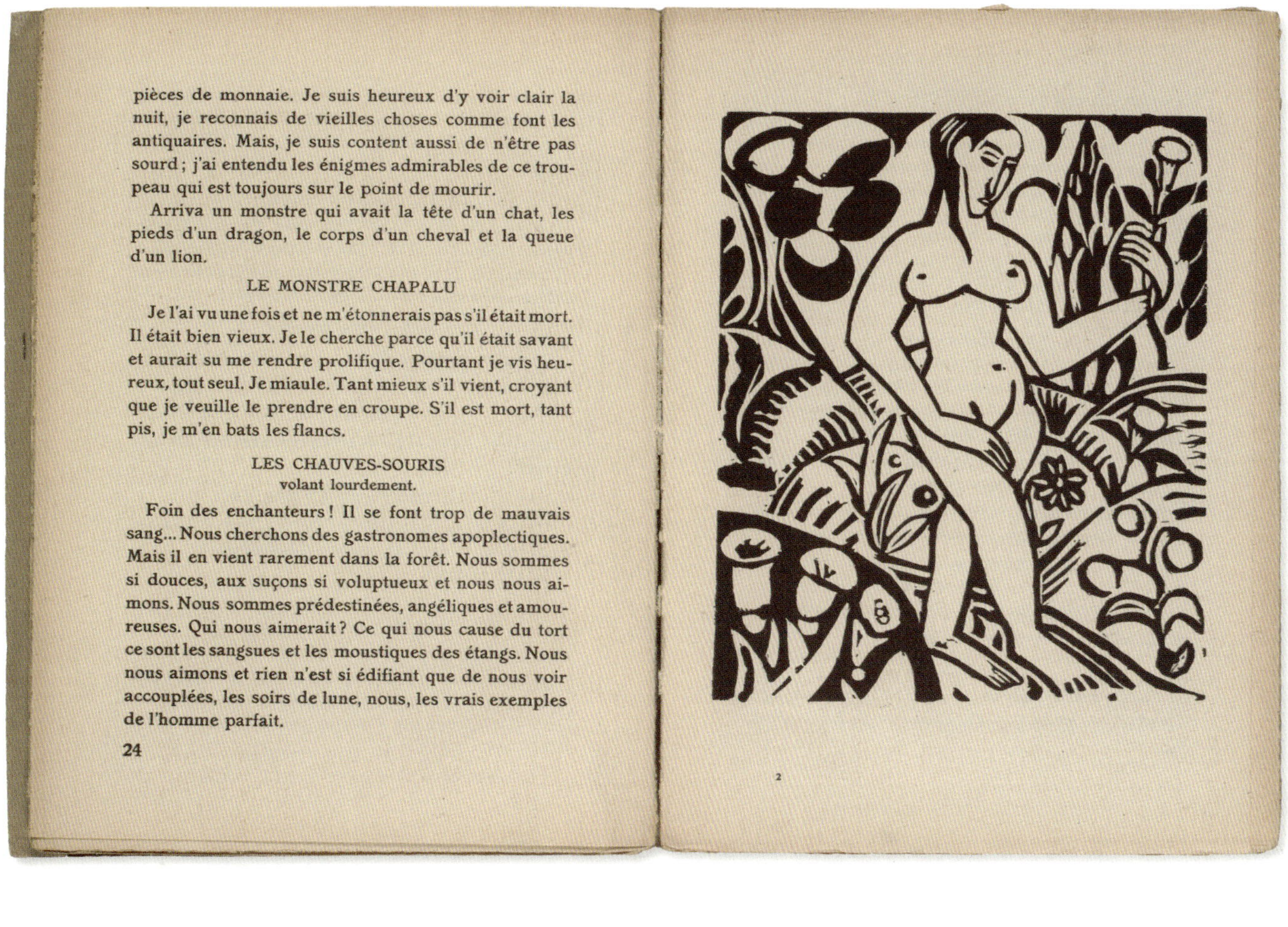

pièces de monnaie. Je suis heureux d'y voir clair la nuit, je reconnais de vieilles choses comme font les antiquaires. Mais, je suis content aussi de n'être pas sourd ; j'ai entendu les énigmes admirables de ce troupeau qui est toujours sur le point de mourir.

Arriva un monstre qui avait la tête d'un chat, les pieds d'un dragon, le corps d'un cheval et la queue d'un lion.

LE MONSTRE CHAPALU

Je l'ai vu une fois et ne m'étonnerais pas s'il était mort. Il était bien vieux. Je le cherche parce qu'il était savant et aurait su me rendre prolifique. Pourtant je vis heureux, tout seul. Je miaule. Tant mieux s'il vient, croyant que je veuille le prendre en croupe. S'il est mort, tant pis, je m'en bats les flancs.

LES CHAUVES-SOURIS
volant lourdement.

Foin des enchanteurs ! Il se font trop de mauvais sang... Nous cherchons des gastronomes apoplectiques. Mais il en vient rarement dans la forêt. Nous sommes si douces, aux suçons si voluptueux et nous nous aimons. Nous sommes prédestinées, angéliques et amoureuses. Qui nous aimerait ? Ce qui nous cause du tort ce sont les sangsues et les moustiques des étangs. Nous nous aimons et rien n'est si édifiant que de nous voir accouplées, les soirs de lune, nous, les vrais exemples de l'homme parfait.

24

2

RIGHT, BOTTOM:
Guillaume Apollinaire
L'Enchanteur Pourrissant
Paris, Éditions de la Nouvelle Revue Française, 1921
Illustrated by André Derain

BELOW:
Verve
vol. 1, no. 1
Paris, 1937
Cover design by
Henri Matisse

and Man Ray, along with articles and prose by Ernest Hemingway, James Joyce, André Malraux, Jean-Paul Sartre and Albert Camus. The inclusion in *Verve* of original lithographs influenced the later, long-running art review *Derrière le Miroir*, issued by Aime Maeght in Paris. Beginning in 1946, each issue of Maeght's review, intentionally designed as a large-format art object, was devoted to the work of a single artist and included an essay by a prominent poet or writer, such as Samuel Beckett, Louis Aragon, René Char or Pierre Reverdy. Like *Verve*, each issue featured original lithographs by artists including Fernand Léger, Joan Miró, Alexander Calder, Antoni Tàpies and Chagall.

The first half of the twentieth century was a period of innovation in the history of artists and illustrated books. The collaborative marriage of major artists and writers engineered by publishers of deluxe *livres d'artiste* reached new heights with works such as Matisse's *Jazz* or *A Toute Épreuve* by Paul Eluard and Miró. Artists were no longer merely illustrating texts; they were engaging with words at the point of design, integrating text and images in new and innovative ways. In Germany, Expressionist artists like Ernst Barlach and Ernst Ludwig Kirchner looked to the early German gothic woodcut tradition to bring a heightened intensity to their illustrated books. Some artists, like Franz Masereel, dispensed with text altogether. His wordless novels made up of woodcuts, such as his paean to the metropolis *La Ville* (1925), seem to prefigure the contemporary graphic novel.

Increasingly, the tradition of the deluxe illustrated book began to merge with the contemporary artist's book. Rapid advances in publishing technologies in the second half of the twentieth century also saw the rise of a new generation of graphic designers—Alan Fletcher, Milton Glaser, David Carson—who adapted the

OPPOSITE:
Verve
vol. 8, nos 29–30
Paris, 1954
Artwork by
Pablo Picasso

LEFT:
Derrière le Miroir
no. 206
Paris, Maeght Éditeur,
1973
Artwork by
Valerio Adami

BOTTOM:
Derrière le Miroir
no. 231
Paris, Maeght Éditeur,
1978
Artwork by
Joan Miró

OPPOSITE, ABOVE:
André Frénaud
La Nourriture du Bourreau
Losne, France,
Thierry Bouchard, 1983
Illustrated by
Antoni Tàpies

OPPOSITE, BELOW:
James Joyce
Ulysses
San Francisco,
Arion Press, 1988
Illustrated by
Robert Motherwell

typographic and visual experiments of an earlier avant-garde to produce innovative book and magazine work that inhabited the corporate world as comfortably as it did an earlier tradition of fine art illustration.

Perhaps the enduring illustrated books are those that combine the imagination of great artists with that of great writers. In the exceptional works of William Blake, the two were one and the same. In the modern era, we think of the pairing of Georges Braque with St John Perse, or Jasper Johns with Samuel Beckett. The Arion Press, established by Andrew Hoyem in 1974 in San Francisco, is one of the major presses retaining an ongoing commitment to the tradition of limited edition books with original art. In 1988, the press issued an ambitious publication that combined the work of one of the greatest twentieth-century writers in the English language, James Joyce, with one of the great postwar American artists, Robert Motherwell. Having first read *Ulysses* at twenty years of age, Motherwell retained a fascination with the text through his long career and regularly drew upon Joyce's work for the titles of his paintings and drawings. The Arion Press edition comprises 838 pages of letterpress with forty etchings by Motherwell. It is unlikely that anyone will read Joyce's novel in this form, but the substantial and overwhelming presence of the finished edition, issued in 150 copies, evokes the essence of the modern illustrated book, in this case neither a singular work of art nor a work of prose, but instead a book that is indefinably other.

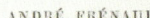

ANDRÉ FRÉNAUD

La nourriture du bourreau

Poèmes suivis d'une Note

Eau-forte de
ANTONI TÀPIES

THIERRY BOUCHARD
GASTON PUEL
1983

MIDNIGHT

(THE Mabbot street entrance of night-
town, before which stretches an uncobbled tramsiding set with skeleton tracks, red and green will-o'-the-wisps and danger signals. Rows of flimsy houses with gaping doors. Rare lamps with faint rainbow fans. Round Rabaiotti's halted ice gondola stunted men and women squabble. They grab wafers between which are wedged lumps of coal and copper snow. Sucking, they scatter slowly. Children. The swancomb of the gondola, highreared, forges on through the murk, white and blue under a lighthouse. Whistles call and answer.)

THE CALLS
Wait, my love, and I'll be with you.

THE ANSWERS
Round behind the stable.

(A deafmute idiot with goggle eyes, his shapeless mouth dribbling, jerks past, shaken in Saint Vitus' dance. A chain of children's hands imprisons him.)

THE CHILDREN
Kithogue! Salute!

THE IDIOT
(Lifts a palsied left arm and gurgles.) Grhahute!

THE CHILDREN
Where's the great light?

471

IN THE BEGINN

GOD CREATED THE HEAVEN AND THE EAR
THE EARTH WAS WITHOUT FORM, AND
DARKNESS WAS UPON THE FACE OF THE D
SPIRIT OF GOD MOVED UPON THE FACE OF T
¶ And God said, Let there be light : & there was light. And Go
that it was good : & God divided the light from the darkness.
the light Day, and the darkness he called Night. And the e
morning were the first day. ¶ And God said, Let there be a fi
midst of the waters, & let it divide the waters from the waters.
the firmament, and divided the waters which were under the f
the waters which were above the firmament : & it was so. An
firmament Heaven. And the evening & the morning were t
¶ And God said, Let the waters under the heaven be gathere
one place, and let the dry land appear : and it was so. And Go
land Earth; and the gathering together of the waters called he
saw that it was good. And God said, Let the earth bring forth
yielding seed, and the fruit tree yielding fruit after his kind,
itself, upon the earth : & it was so. And the earth brought fort
yielding seed after his kind, & the tree yielding fruit, whose se
after his kind : and God saw that it was good. And the evening
were the third day. ¶ And God said, Let there be lights in th
the heaven to divide the day from the night; and let them be fo
seasons, and for days, & years : and let them be for lights in th
the heaven to give light upon the earth : & it was so. And God
lights; the greater light to rule the day, and the lesser light to ru
made the stars also. And God set them in the firmament of the
light upon the earth, and to rule over the day and over the nig
the light from the darkness : and God saw that it was good. A
and the morning were the fourth day. ¶ And God said, Let th
forth abundantly the moving creature that hath life, and fov
above the earth in the open firmament of heaven. And God
whales, & every living creature that moveth, which the waters
abundantly, after their kind, & every winged fowl after his kir

William Morris and the PRIVATE PRESS Movement

I have always been a great admirer of the calligraphy of the Middle Ages, and of the earlier printing which took its place.

WILLIAM MORRIS, A NOTE ON HIS AIMS IN FOUNDING THE KELMSCOTT PRESS

WHEN WILLIAM MORRIS FOUNDED THE KELMSCOTT PRESS IN 1891, HE HAD A CLEAR IDEA AS TO ITS PURPOSE. IN AN ESSAY HE WROTE SEVERAL YEARS LATER, HE STATED:

I began printing books with the hope of producing some which would have a definite claim to beauty, while at the same time they should be easy to read and should not dazzle the eye, or trouble the intellect of the reader by eccentricity of form in the letters.

Morris was one of the founders of the Arts and Crafts movement in Great Britain. As early as 1861, he had established the firm of Morris, Marshall, Faulkner & Co. with his friends Dante Gabriel Rossetti, Edward Burne-Jones, Ford Madox Brown and Philip Webb, with a view to promoting a revival of traditional crafts, including stained glass, tapestry and wallpaper design. It was in keeping with this aspiration that Morris developed his interest in a return to the craft of fine printing, focusing on the principal elements of the book—paper, ink, typography, illustration and binding.

The mechanisation of the printing and publishing industry brought about by the introduction of the steam-driven press in the early 1800s had seen publishers increasingly abandon many of the book design principles of the past. While mechanised printing enabled the mass production of books and their distribution to broader audiences, the increased competition for sales that arose from this led to the use of cheaper, and poorer, grades of production materials.

In looking to revive the craft of the book, Morris, as always, looked to the past, finding inspiration in medieval manuscripts and the work of fifteenth-century printers. Rather than the cheaper illustrative process of lithography favoured by publishers, he advocated the use of woodcuts as a means of integrating text and image on the page. He looked to the early typeface designers, such as Nicolaus Jenson, and the use of the hand press over the machine press. Morris had been inspired, in part, by a lecture he attended in 1888 by Emery Walker, a master printer and engraver who used the occasion to rail against the poor quality of Victorian typography compared with the beautiful books produced by fifteenth- and sixteenth-century printers. To gain the quality he desired, Morris insisted on the use of handmade paper, which he obtained from a paper mill at Little Chart in Kent, and suitable black inks from the German firm Jaenecke.

Morris set up his Albion hand press, along with a small press for taking proofs, in a rented cottage near his home at Kelmscott Manor, in Hammersmith on the banks of the Thames, in 1891. The previous year he had designed the first of his typefaces, Golden type, based on the fifteenth-century Roman type of Nicolaus Jenson, specifically from his 1476 printing of Livy's *Historia Naturalis*. The new typeface was intended for use in producing the press's first book, *The Golden Legend*, a medieval collection of saints' lives, but difficulties in securing the right paper led to delays, and the book was not issued until 1892 as the Kelmscott Press's seventh publication.

Morris's next typeface was a Gothic one based on the typefaces of early German printers Peter Schoeffer, Anton Koberger and Günther Zainer.

OPPOSITE AND ABOVE:
Geoffrey Chaucer
The Works of Geoffrey Chaucer
Hammersmith, UK, printed by William Morris at the Kelmscott Press, 1896

Morris named it Troy, after the first Kelmscott book in which it featured, *The Recuyell of the Historyes of Troye* (1892), a reprint of the first book printed in English around 1473 by William Caxton. The decorated borders, initials and motifs featured in Kelmscott publications reflected Morris's prolonged investigations into illuminated manuscripts and early printed books, and his belief in the book as a work of art. In this he was ably supported by friends and colleagues, most notably Burne-Jones, who designed many of the illustrations for the books, and William H Hooper, principal wood engraver for the press.

Morris's masterwork was Kelmscott's ambitious printing of *The Works of Geoffrey Chaucer*, completed in June 1896 just months before his death. Along with fellow student Burne-Jones, Morris had first discovered Chaucer in the 1850s at Exeter College, Oxford, and he began planning an edition of Chaucer shortly after establishing the Kelmscott Press. By late 1891, he had begun designing his third typeface, Chaucer, in preparation for this edition, having decided that his Troy type, cut in 18 point, was too large for the project. Between 1892 and 1895, Burne-Jones worked on the designs for the eighty-seven wood engravings featured in the book. The decorative borders and the initial letters were designed by Morris. The edition was completed on 2 June 1896, and comprised 425 copies, selling for £20 each, as well as thirteen copies printed on vellum.

The Kelmscott Press continued for a further two years after Morris's death, overseen by the press's secretary Sydney Cockerell, who issued the fifty-third and final Kelmscott book, *A Note by William Morris on His Aims in Founding the Kelmscott Press*, in 1898. For Morris, the principles of good design and practice were the foundation of all his endeavours, whether tapestry, wallpaper design or books. His essay 'The Ideal Book' (1893) acknowledged that although the illustrated book is not absolutely necessary to man's life, 'it gives us such endless pleasure, and is so intimately connected with the other absolutely necessary art of imaginative literature that it must remain one of the very worthiest things towards the production of which reasonable men should strive'.

Diana White
The Descent of Ishtar
London, Eragny Press,
1903

Dante Gabriel Rossetti
The Blessed Damozel
London, Hacon & Ricketts, 1898

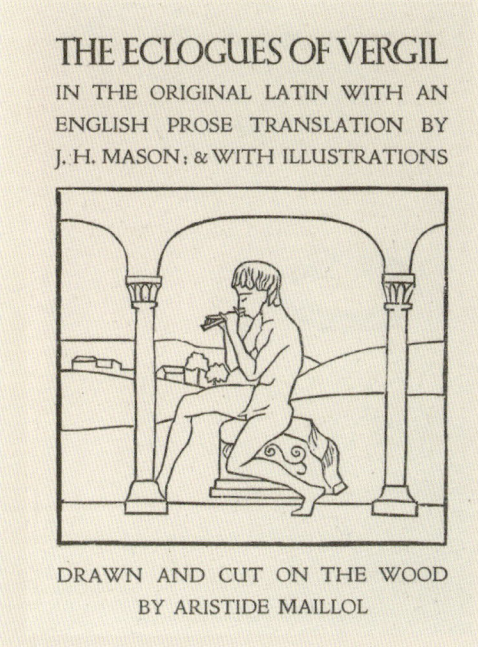

The Eclogues of Vergil
London, published in England for the Cranach Press by Emery Walker Limited, 1927

While Morris's Kelmscott Press was not the first private press to operate in the modern era—the Reverend Charles Daniel had begun issuing books on his miniature Albion press in the late 1870s—it can reasonably be said that Morris founded the modern private press movement. After he began issuing his Kelmscott books, a number of similar presses started up in Great Britain and Europe. Lucien Pissaro, son of Impressionist painter Camille Pissaro, set up the Eragny Press with wife Esther in London in 1894, producing more than thirty books before closing the press in 1914. Charles Ricketts founded the Vale Press in 1896, and in the following eight years published more than forty books, most in collaboration with master printer Charles McCall at the Ballantyne Press. The Ashendene Press was established by CH St John Hornby in 1895 and continued publishing until 1935. CR Ashbee, a pioneer of the Arts and Crafts movement, founded the Essex House Press in London in 1898. When the Kelmscott Press closed in that year, Ashbee purchased Morris's two Albion presses and took on a number of the Kelmscott printers, eventually producing some eighty titles. In Germany, Count Harry Kessler started the Cranach Press in 1913, drawing on the talents of English and French artists and designers. His first commission was for French sculptor Aristide Maillol to produce a series of woodcuts for an edition of Virgil's *Eclogues,* with title and initials designed by English typographer Eric Gill. Delayed by the war, it did not appear until 1926 in Germany and 1927 in England.

All of these presses followed, to a greater or lesser degree, Morris's championing of good book design, in particular the focus on typography and traditional illustrative processes. However, while beholden to Morris's ideals, the history of the twentieth-century private press movement was not without its own innovators. Thomas J Cobden-Sanderson, who established the Doves Press with Emery Walker in 1900, reacted against what he saw as Morris's overly decorative approach to book design. His typefaces, though similarly based on those of fifteenth-century typographer Nicolaus Jenson, were lighter in feel than Morris's. Moreover, the books were issued without illustration or ornament, relying solely on the beauty of the type and page layout for their impact. The Doves Press edition of *The English Bible*, published in five volumes (1903–05), is rightly considered a typographic masterpiece. After a dispute, Walker withdrew from the partnership in 1909. When Cobden-Sanderson closed the press in 1916, he threw the press's type, punches and matrices off a bridge into the Thames, thus bringing the story of one of the most important early presses to an abrupt and dramatic end.

LEFT:
Friedrich Wolters
Herrschaft und Dienst
Berlin, Der Einhorn Presse, 1909

OPPOSITE:
The English Bible
Hammersmith, UK, Doves Press, 1903–05

IN THE BEGINNING

GOD CREATED THE HEAVEN AND THE EARTH. ¶ AND THE EARTH WAS WITHOUT FORM, AND VOID; AND DARKNESS WAS UPON THE FACE OF THE DEEP, & THE SPIRIT OF GOD MOVED UPON THE FACE OF THE WATERS. ¶ And God said, Let there be light: & there was light. And God saw the light, that it was good: & God divided the light from the darkness. And God called the light Day, and the darkness he called Night. And the evening and the morning were the first day. ¶ And God said, Let there be a firmament in the midst of the waters, & let it divide the waters from the waters. And God made the firmament, and divided the waters which were under the firmament from the waters which were above the firmament: & it was so. And God called the firmament Heaven. And the evening & the morning were the second day. ¶ And God said, Let the waters under the heaven be gathered together unto one place, and let the dry land appear: and it was so. And God called the dry land Earth; and the gathering together of the waters called he Seas: and God saw that it was good. And God said, Let the earth bring forth grass, the herb yielding seed, and the fruit tree yielding fruit after his kind, whose seed is in itself, upon the earth: & it was so. And the earth brought forth grass, & herb yielding seed after his kind, & the tree yielding fruit, whose seed was in itself, after his kind: and God saw that it was good. And the evening & the morning were the third day. ¶ And God said, Let there be lights in the firmament of the heaven to divide the day from the night; and let them be for signs, and for seasons, and for days, & years: and let them be for lights in the firmament of the heaven to give light upon the earth: & it was so. And God made two great lights; the greater light to rule the day, and the lesser light to rule the night: he made the stars also. And God set them in the firmament of the heaven to give light upon the earth, and to rule over the day and over the night, & to divide the light from the darkness: and God saw that it was good. And the evening and the morning were the fourth day. ¶ And God said, Let the waters bring forth abundantly the moving creature that hath life, and fowl that may fly above the earth in the open firmament of heaven. And God created great whales, & every living creature that moveth, which the waters brought forth abundantly, after their kind, & every winged fowl after his kind: & God saw that it was good. And God blessed them, saying, Be fruitful, & multiply, and fill the waters in the seas, and let fowl multiply in the earth. And the evening & the morning were the fifth day. ¶ And God said, Let the earth bring forth the living creature after his kind, cattle, and creeping thing, and beast of the earth after his kind: and it was so. And God made the beast of the earth after his kind, and cattle after their kind, and every thing that creepeth upon the

ABOVE:
Geoffrey Chaucer
The Canterbury Tales
London, Golden Cockerel
Press, 1929–31

OPPOSITE:
Jas H Duke
Dada Kampfen um Leben und Tod: a Prose Poem
Katoomba, Wayzgoose Press, 1996

The English engraver and typographer Eric Gill played an important role in the history of twentieth-century private presses. As well as his work for the Cranach Press in Germany, Gill's association with typographer Stanley Morison led to his design of the Perpetua typeface in 1925, followed by the Gill Sans typeface, for which he is best known. This was based on Edward Johnston's work for the London Underground lettering, with which Gill assisted. The modernist design of Gill Sans typeface was used on the covers of prewar Penguin books and was later adopted by the British Broadcasting Corporation.

Gill also played a major role in the publications of the Golden Cockerel Press. It was originally founded by Harold Midgley Taylor in 1920 but was taken over in 1924 by Robert Gibbings after Taylor was forced to sell due to ill health. Gibbings was a wood engraver who had illustrated some of the press's early books, and he began to commission Gill to design wood engravings for a number of Golden Cockerel titles, including *The Song of Songs* (1925) and *Troilus and Criseyde* (1927). Dissatisfied with the Caslon type he had inherited from Taylor, Gibbings decided Golden Cockerel should have its own type. He commissioned Gill to design what became the Golden Cockerel type, described by Gill as 'a heavy closely massed type suitable for use with modern wood engravings'; it was first used in AE Coppard's *The Hundredth Story* (1931).

Under Gibbings's stewardship, Golden Cockerel produced some of the finest private press books of the period, drawing upon the talents of major English artists and wood engravers such as Gill, Paul Nash, Agnes Miller Parker and David Jones. Gill's masterpieces for the press included *The Four Gospels* (1931) and *The Canterbury Tales* (1931). For the latter, which took two and a half years to complete, Gill drew upon the medieval manuscript tradition of using figurative borders to provide satirical commentary on the text.

While the escalating costs of producing books by hand led to a decline in the number of major private presses operating in the second half of the twentieth century, the ideal of the perfect book as set out by Morris provided inspiration to printers worldwide. From its base in Paris, John Crombie's Kickshaws Press continues to issue typographically playful books. The Fleece Press, Gregynog Press and Old Stile are still active in Great Britain, as are Walter Hamady's Perishable Press, Julie Chen's Flying Fish Press and hundreds of others in the United States. In Australia, the leading private press is the Wayzgoose Press, founded in 1985 by Jadwiga Jarvis and Mike Hudson at their home in the Blue Mountains, New South Wales. To date, they have produced more than twenty books and thirty broadsides, including an ambitious series of large-scale concertina books featuring the work of contemporary Australian poets. *Dada* (1996), a hand-printed version of Jas H Duke's experimental sound poem, draws upon the Russian and German avant-garde books of the 1920s and ranks as one of the finest private press books of recent years.

In the same way that Morris reacted against the decline in the quality of production standards brought about by the industrial revolution, some printers have reacted to the rise of the computer in publishing. The recent shift to electronic publishing has brought about a renewed interest in the use of letterpress and hand printing. In the face of the media's constant refrain that we are facing 'the death of the book', private press publishing, with its emphasis on the fundamental craft of book production and good design as practised by the earliest printers, is a continuing reminder of the book's long and varied history, and of its capacity to adapt and survive in a changing world.

LIFE AND DEATH
IN BERLIN
WINTER 1918-19

H	H	H	B	J	H	M
A	U	E	A	U	E	E
U	L	A	A	N	R	H
S	S	R	D	G	Z	R
M	E	T	E		F	I
A	N	F	R	G	E	N
N	B	I		R	L	G
N	E	E		O	D	H
	C	L		S	E	O
	K	D		Z		E
						C
						H

CONFRONT THE
SPIRIT OF THE TIME

which was

Everything seems to be vibrating. Defending the ground foot by foot. Through the standing corn. Ro ut and disintegration. **Lost a Total War Totally**. A drag ging anticlimax. We are at the limit of our powers. It will be an immense struggle that will begin at one point continue at another and take a long time. Only a 1000 calories a day. Parties of all arms of the enemy are through our reserve line. Dying of half measures. It was a manoeuvre of the battlefield. But an immediate ar mistice. The reserves must be put in where the attack is progressing not where it is held up. Unconditional surrender. But not the blockade. Difficult question is what to do next. What would they do with it. No annexations and no indemnities. It was still dark. The craters nearly touching. To illumine the darkness. There was champagne for dinner. It is the day of the chosen people. The battle is won.

which was with DADA

the Greatness and fall of deutschland in 5 storeys 3 gardens 1 tunnel 2 lifts and a door shaped so much romantic silence the Dada bomb or only a bad harvest can save us and comrades of both sexes soldiers with out insignia of rank murder the moonlight the reins of Dada Government the syphilis you swine red capsules three patent medicines the stages are filling up with kings poets and faust impersonators for everything Lenin a little chemist also with a monocle the soul could only show itself in actions enthusiasm for the **Self** *die neue Zeit beginnt mit dem Todesjahr des OBERDADA* flirting with prayers incense when it does not prefer to build its cardboard cannon for even the most revolting because I love you I quarrel with you the tailor's flower *Was ist nun der* **Dadaismus**? A crowbar to release seeking to bring **the Armed Forces** into contempt and distributing indecent publications sliced open by the howitzers of Noske the character of a musical notation who every hour snatch capture of Fiume a Dadaist masterstroke the face of the ruling class the world's greatest work of reference the tatgers tat ters of the bodies out of the frenzied characters the **President of the Globe the President** but efforts to abolish **Art** that sentimental resistance to the times with **Everyman His Own Football** instead of wreathes for the Prxsldentrx makes words into individuals in word an image to be against this manifesto is to be a Dadaist.

ARTISTS' Books

If all the elements or activities which contribute to artists' books as a field are described what emerges is a space made by their intersection ...
JOHANNA DRUCKER, *THE CENTURY OF ARTISTS' BOOKS*

THE IDEA OF ARTISTS MAKING, RATHER THAN MERELY ILLUSTRATING, BOOKS IS A PHENOMENON OF THE TWENTIETH CENTURY AND BEYOND. THE FOUNDATIONS OF THIS PRACTICE LIE IN THE DELUXE *LIVRES D'ARTISTE*, PUBLISHED BY AMBROSE VOLLARD AND OTHERS IN THE EARLY TWENTIETH CENTURY. THESE FEATURED LITHOGRAPHS AND ETCHINGS BY LEADING ARTISTS OF THE DAY, OFTEN COMBINED WITH WELL-KNOWN OR CLASSIC TEXTS.

In the same way, French poet Stéphane Mallarmé's experimental typographic poem 'Un Coup de Dés Jamais n'Abolira le Hasard', published in 1897, influenced the later thinking of artists and writers on the design and visual layout of text on the page. Intriguingly, Vollard himself had planned to publish an edition of Mallarmé's poem, to be illustrated by Odilon Redon, but the project was abandoned after the poet's death in 1898.

Most *livres d'artiste* were conceived by entrepreneurial art dealers or editors rather than by artists. But during the first half of the twentieth century, some artists began to break free of the *livres d'artiste* tradition, integrating text and image in radical new ways. Henri Matisse's 1947 masterpiece *Jazz*, made while in his seventies, combined his own playful calligraphic text with a suite of prints based on his cut-outs. Sonia Delaunay's *pochoir* stencil designs for Blaise Cendrars's poem 'La Prose du Transsibérien et de la Petite Jehanne de France' (1913) evoked the fragmented consciousness of the poet's experience of his 1904 train trip across Siberia. Conceived as the first 'simultaneous' book, the 2-metre-long concertina was a landmark in the development of the modern artist's book.

What then defines an artist's book? To date, there has been no formal consensus, but perhaps this is as it should be. In the most rudimentary definition, artists' books are books made by artists. Critic Johanna Drucker argues that artists' books can be considered the quintessential twentieth-century art form, appearing in every major movement of art and literature. She, too, acknowledges that a single definition remains elusive, believing that the concept is best expressed not as something rigid but as an activity encompassing a 'number of different disciplines, fields, and ideas'—fine press, book arts, conceptual art, concrete poetry, performance art, experimental music and the tradition of the illustrated book among others. Artists' books, she believes, exist 'at the intersection of, but just beyond the limits of, any of these individual fields of activity'. And while, as Drucker again notes, 'it's easy enough to state that an artist's book is a book created as an original work of art, rather than a reproduction of a pre-existing work', such a definition raises as many questions as answers, not least among them—what is an original work of art?

The rise of the avant-garde in the years before and after World War I saw an explosion of

LEFT:
Angela Cavalieri
INRI
Melbourne, 2005
(edition of six copies
and two artist's proofs)

OPPOSITE, TOP:
Peter Lyssiotis
Feather and Prey
Melbourne, Masterthief
Enterprises, 1997 (edition
of ten copies)

OPPOSITE, BOTTOM:
**Angela Cavalieri
and Peter Lyssiotis**
–1316
Melbourne,
Masterthief Enterprises,
2004 (edition of ten copies
plus two artist's proofs)

book-related activity by artists, including the typographic experiments of Filippo Marinetti and the Italian Futurists, the Dada publications of Tristan Tzara, Kurt Schwitters and others, the proliferation of Surrealist books and magazines, and the radical typographic and formal designs of El Lissitzky, Alexander Rodchenko and the Russian Constructivists.

While the history of artists' books in the twentieth century is a relatively recent field of study, and one that is still in flux, there is a widespread perception that the books of American photographer Ed Ruscha are seminal to the development of the modern artist's book. In particular, Ruscha's *Twenty-six Gasoline Stations* (1962) heralds a radical new way of thinking about artists and books. The sheer banality of the black-and-white photographs of gas stations Ruscha encountered driving along Route 66 from Los Angeles to Oklahoma City harks back to Marcel Duchamp's tongue-in-cheek irony, while the inexpensive format of his book prefigures the proliferation of 1960s multiples and the adoption by artists of newer technologies such as photocopying as a means of democratising art outside galleries.

But it would be unfair to mark out Ruscha's work as the starting point of a new paradigm for the contemporary artist's book. His work can be seen as part of a continuum of artists using the book as a flexible and conceptual medium with which to investigate their own artistic practices. In the 1950s, German artist Dieter Roth began exploring the format and structure of books. In his works, the physical experience of handling and turning the pages becomes part of the intimate process of 'reading'. The work of Roth and Ruscha, generally produced using photo-mechanical print technology and often issued in editions of hundreds of copies, was in direct contrast to the expensive, limited edition productions typical of the *livres d'artiste* tradition. For both, the making of books was not a peripheral activity in relation to their work as artists; it was central to their vision of art practice.

In recent years, the production of artists' books has grown dramatically to encompass all manner of mediums and formats, from fine press editions to inexpensive multiples to altered or sculptural books to installations. Their contents can embrace narrative, history, conceptual ideas, abstraction, politics or autobiography. The books made by artist Peter Lyssiotis since the early 1980s have drawn upon a number of these strands. His earliest books, such as *Journey of a Wise Electron* (1981), were produced by offset in editions upwards of a thousand copies and reflected his interest in narrative photography and collage. Increasingly, however, his work began to incorporate elements of fine press tradition, with the use of letterpress and high-quality papers and binding to create limited edition books exploring a variety of themes, from the private language of the subconscious to the harsh realities of global politics. In *Feather and Prey* (1997), produced in an edition of ten copies, the white space of the page surrounds and almost overwhelms the text and images, evoking the disturbing silence of dreams. *The Products of Wealth* (1997), designed as a direct homage to the Russian Constructivist book of the 1920s, is a manifesto setting out Lyssiotis's long-held interest in political photomontage, in particular the work of German artist John Heartfield.

Artists have drawn upon their own life stories, constructing narratives of migration and separation. Angela Cavalieri's *Quattro Pagine* (1999) renders the physicality of the words *'quattro pagine'* as a series of abstract linocuts that explore the stark materiality of letter forms. The phrase in English literally means 'four pages' but can also be used colloquially to refer to a few pages from a life. Her book highlights the beauty and abstract quality of the words while at the same time hinting at an autobiographical narrative. Cavalieri's expressed interest lies in exploring the art of storytelling in a visual form, combining text and images drawn from literary, religious and historical sources. Her growing interest in Italian church architecture and symbolism, developed during a residency at the British School of Rome in 2003, can be seen in *INRI* (2005), a large concertina book of linocuts that examines the individual letters of the Italian word *'crocifissione'* (crucifixion). Her collaborative book with Peter Lyssiotis, *–1316* (2004), is a response to Dante's *Divine Comedy* and takes its title from the year Dante probably completed the *Inferno*. Dante's circles of hell become the starting point for an investigation into the circle as a geometric form, similar in intent to the investigations of Russian artist Kasimir Malevich into the square.

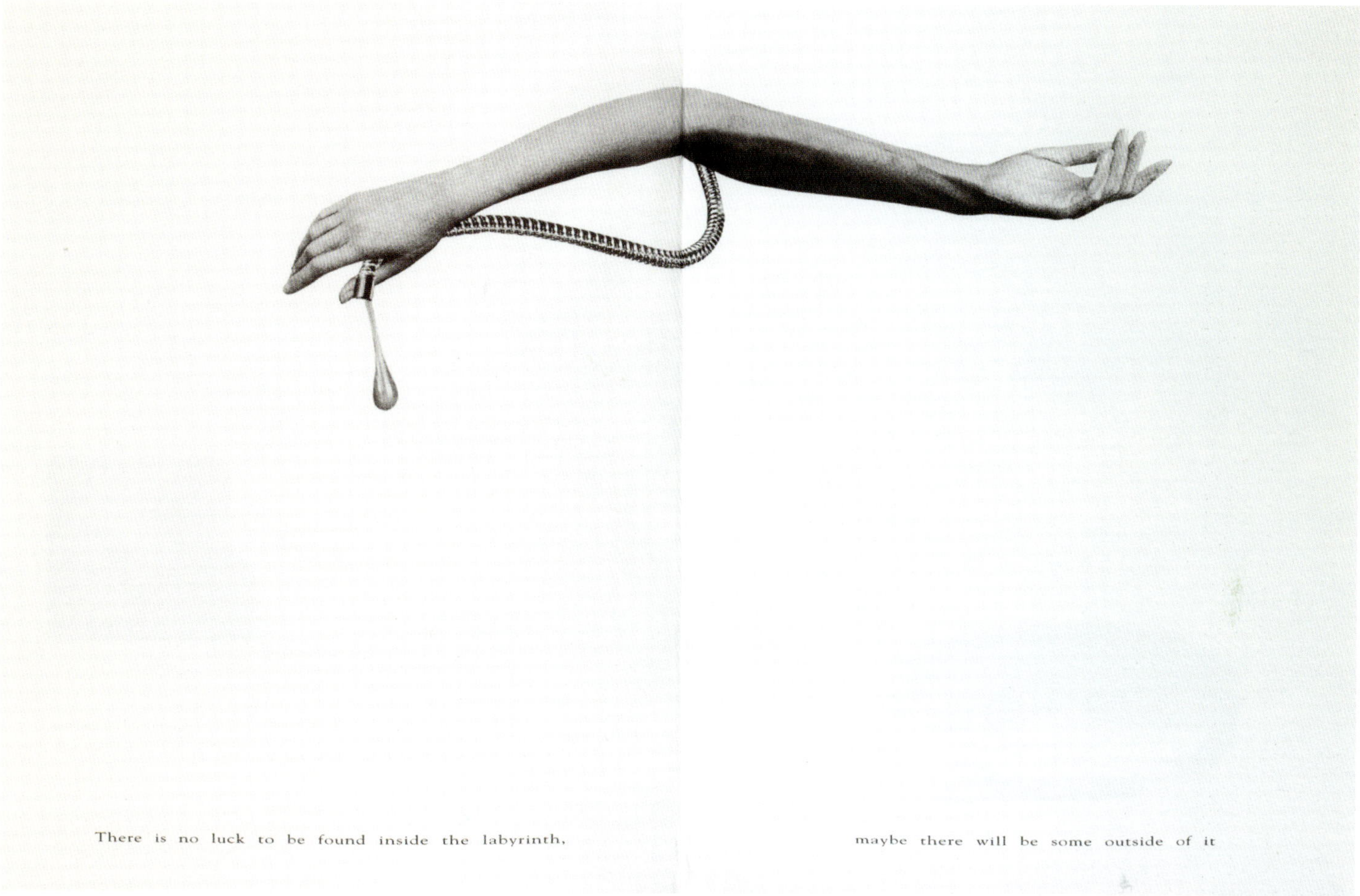

The WORLD of the BOOK | 213

There is no luck to be found inside the labyrinth, maybe there will be some outside of it

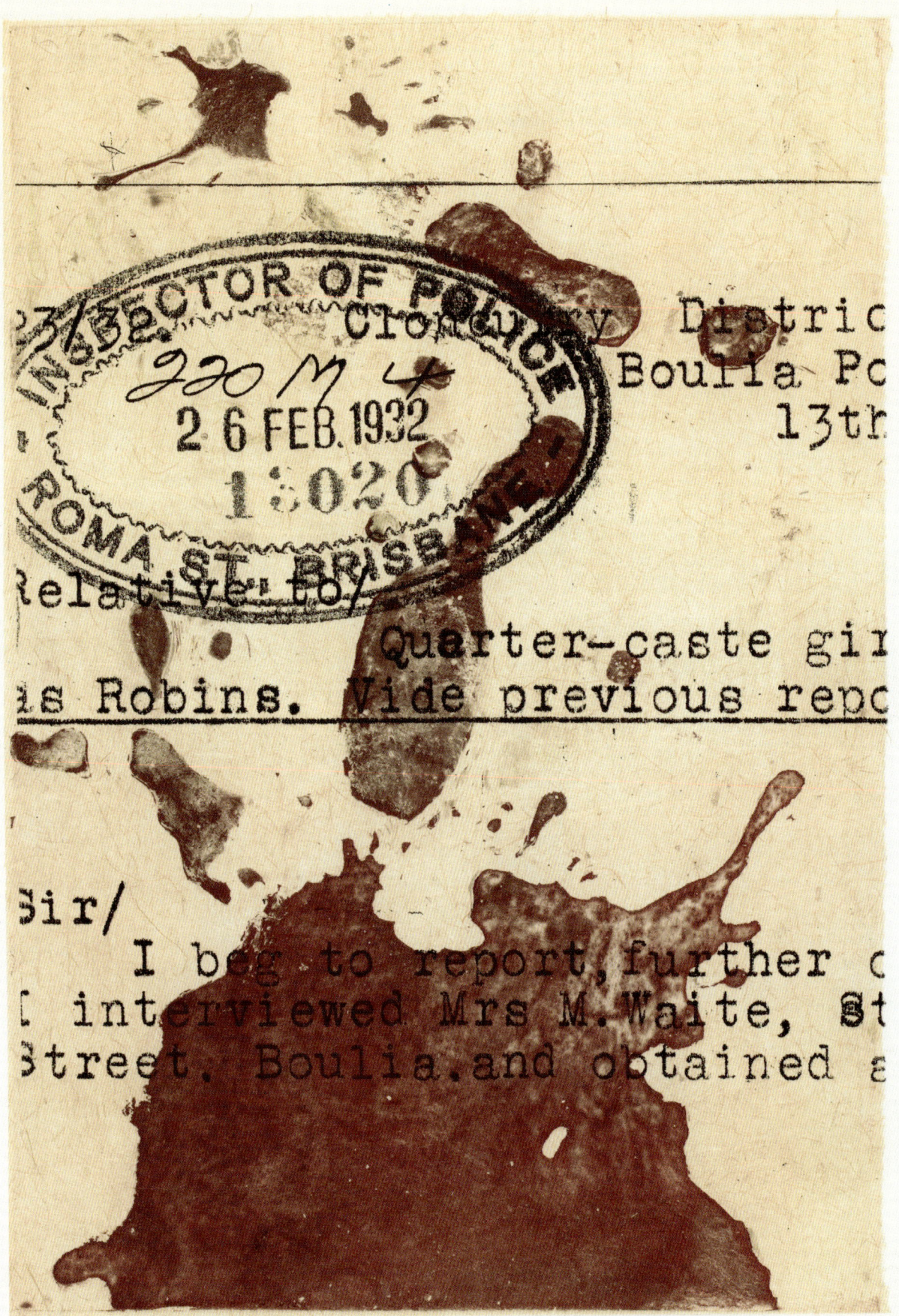

LEFT:
Judy Watson
a preponderance of aboriginal blood
Brisbane, numero uno publications, grahame galleries + editions, 2005
(edition of five copies)

OPPOSITE:
Bruno Leti and Chris Wallace-Crabbe
Drawing
Melbourne, Centre for the Development of Artists' Books, 1994
(edition of forty-five copies)

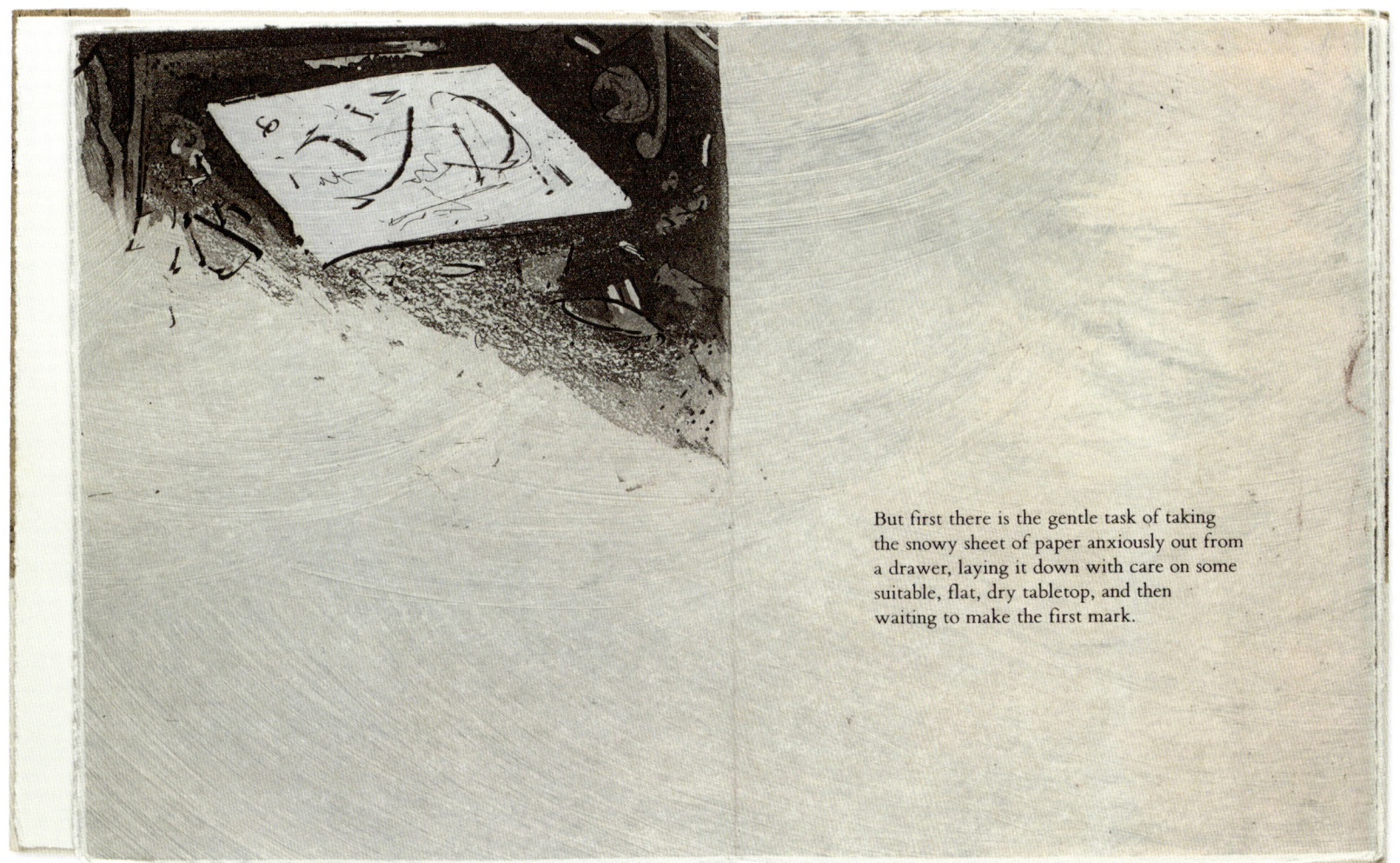

> But first there is the gentle task of taking the snowy sheet of paper anxiously out from a drawer, laying it down with care on some suitable, flat, dry tabletop, and then waiting to make the first mark.

The artist's book has proven itself an ideal medium for collaborative projects. Artist Bruno Leti's collaborations with poet Chris Wallace-Crabbe have yielded a series of books reflecting their ongoing dialogue about the process of making art. For the work *Iron Age* (1996), Leti printed a series of images directly from rusted and weathered scraps of metal he found during a visit to Clunes in central Victoria in 1995. The sheets of metal, which reminded him of etching plates, produced rich and textured abstract shapes, to which he added aquatint as a means of accentuating the rust colours. Wallace-Crabbe's accompanying poem, inspired by these 'wafers of old iron', conjures 'an entire landscape from assembled horizontals'. The finished book becomes a meditation on randomness and time, an excavation of the ages. Aside from his collaborations with writers, Bruno Leti has produced books in the form of personal travel notes, such as *Notations of a Journey* (1992) and *New York Travel Journal* (1996); others, such as *Recorded Movements in Time* (1991) or *Drawing* (1994), seem to trace the patterns and journeys of the most fundamental element of drawing—the line. Bruno Leti's work grows out of a personal dialogue with poets living and dead, one book giving rise to another.

In contrast to two-dimensional pictorial works, the form of the book as a series of pages lends itself to the development of narrative sequences. In the very act of turning the pages, the reader moves through time. There is the accumulation of detail. For some artists, the format provides scope to document personal narratives and histories. Judy Watson's journey to her grandmother's country in north-east Queensland in 1990 to research her family history had a profound impact on her work as an artist. As a direct descendant of the Waanyi clan, Watson, in her art, has increasingly drawn upon her Aboriginal heritage. Her artist's book *a preponderance of aboriginal blood* (2005) reproduces government documents housed in the Queensland State Archives, including electoral enrolment statutes that relate to the classification of 'full-blood' Aborigines, who were ineligible to vote, and 'half-caste' Aborigines, who were entitled to vote. Fragments of these documents have been printed, overlaid with images of blood. Watson has stated that she felt compelled to make this work after attending a lecture by Loris Williams and Margaret Reid on 'Indigenous Australians and the Right to Vote in Queensland'. The use of the phrase 'a preponderance of Aboriginal blood' during the lecture was the catalyst for this powerful work, which, in her own words, expresses an outrage that 'my own family especially my wonderful Grandmother, Grace Isaacson, were subjected to this sort of treatment and classification by the white authorities in this country'.

216 | ARTISTS' Books

Allan Mitelman
Ko-Ko
Townsville,
Lyre-Bird Press, and
Melbourne, Zimmer
Editions, 2000
(edition of thirty copies)

BELOW:
Kylie Stillman
Pine, Eleven Years Old
Melbourne, 2004
(unique work)

RIGHT:
Nicholas Jones
Medallion
Melbourne, 1999
(unique work)

BOTTOM:
Jonathan Tse
Portrait of an Australian
Robertson, Queensland, 1998
(edition of ten copies and two artist's proofs)

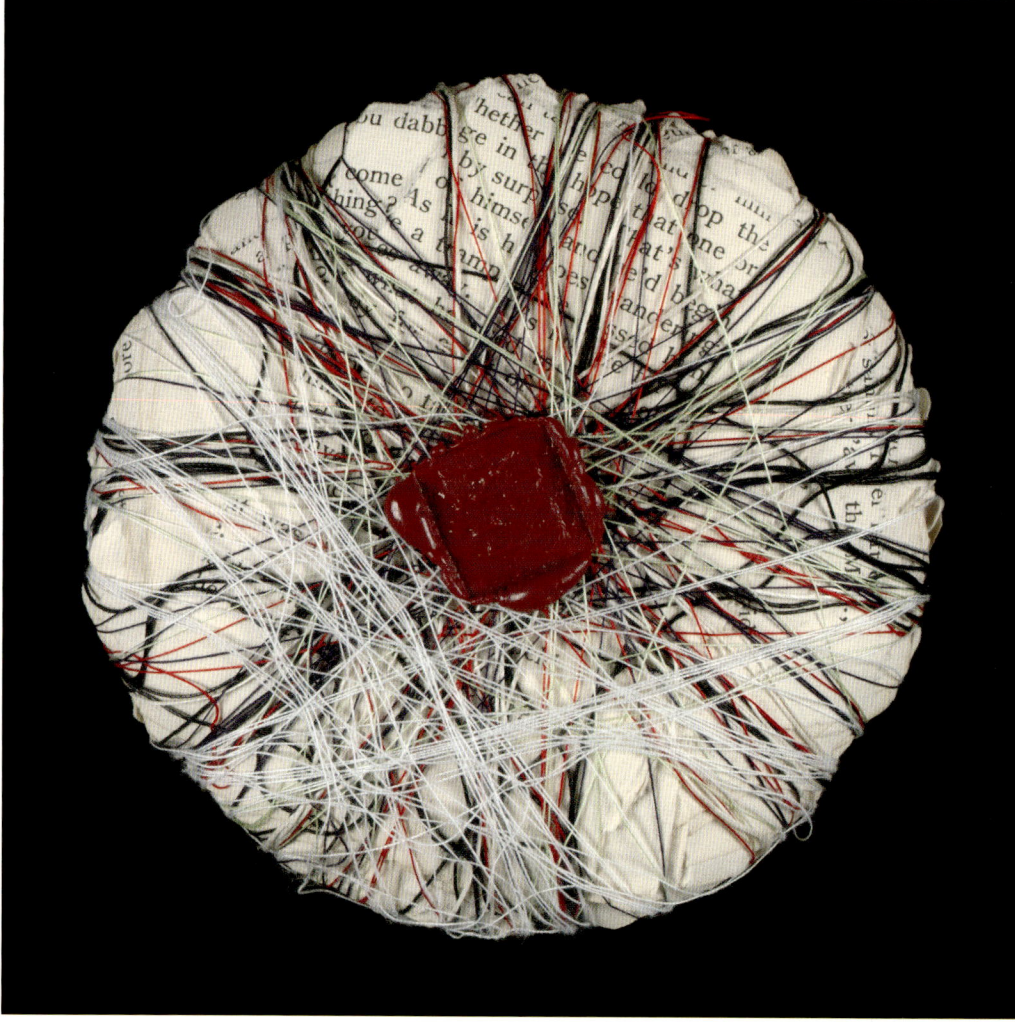

The beauty inherent in a book's form has often been revealed by artists who change and modify books. Nicholas Jones's altered books are made with surgical precision, as he rips, tears, cuts and folds them into new shapes. His work attempts to highlight the beauty of the book through a process of changing it. Instead of considering the book as a vehicle for narrative or ideas, we are instead confronted by the abstract quality of the book's shape. Its original text is almost irrelevant to the final sculptural form, except as a fragmented pattern that peers out from beneath the finished folds or cuts. Jones's father was a surgeon, and it is the very implements of that trade—scalpel, surgeon's needle—that he uses to alter books. The act of defacement is the process whereby Jones renews the physical form of a book, divesting it of its original intent and allowing the viewer to 'read' it in an entirely new way.

The means at an artist's disposal for making books now encompass the entire spectrum of reproductive technologies, from traditional printmaking through to offset, photocopy or digital reproduction. The finished work, whether unique or multiple, may take the form of a codex, a scroll, an altered book, a sculpture or something else entirely. Defining the modern artist's book is therefore an increasingly redundant proposition. In the same way that Marcel Duchamp conferred the status of 'art work' on an everyday porcelain urinal purely on the basis that he, as an 'artist', defined it as such, then so too does a book become an artist's book if so defined by the artist.

While the shift to electronic text has challenged the book's hegemony, it has at the same time liberated the book from its traditional role as primary carrier of information. In a world of bits and bytes, the book has been freed up to revert to its iconic status as 'book', a three-dimensional solid object capable of conveying a diverse array of meanings. The book's form carries within it the entire history of words and ideas, and the contemporary artist is free to draw upon that history while at the same time renewing it, constructing physical objects that go to the heart of our personal and cultural relationship with books.

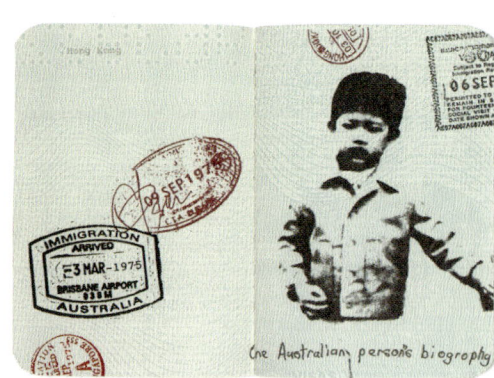

JONATHAN TSE

Jonathan Tse's book, printed in the form of an Australian passport, sets out the personal milestones of the artist's life to date using family portraits, school photos, an image of a suburban house. Tse's family migrated to Australia from Hong Kong in 1975, and his book visually recounts a personal and family journey of migration, remembered at a time when political attitudes in Australia led many to question the notion of identity and what it means to be Australian.

The WORLD of the BOOK | 219

MILAN MILOJEVIC

Milan Milojevic explores notions of cultural identity through his prints and artist's books. *Borges Bestiary* refers to the mythological creatures described by Jorge Luis Borges in his *Book of Imaginary Beings*. Milojevic has created his beasts by digitally combining elements from woodcut illustrations found in Konrad Gesner's sixteenth-century *Historiae Animalium*. Milojevic has said of his work, 'The notion of the hybrid creature provides a metaphor for me to investigate my own identity—that of a first generation Australian of German Yugoslav descent'.

RICHARD TIPPING

The four volumes of *The Sydney Morning* published to date reflect Richard Tipping's ongoing interest in iconic Australian signs and logos, as featured in his 1982 photographic book *Signs of Australia*. The series of concrete poems, rendered in silkscreen, are at once both playful and political in their appropriation of the advertising logos and signs that daily surround us.

ABOVE, LEFT:
Richard Tipping
The Sydney Morning
Newcastle, Thorny Devil Press, 1989–94
(four volumes: editions vary between fifty and sixty copies)

TOP:
Milan Milojevic
Borges Bestiary
Hobart, 2000
(edition of ten copies)

DESIGNING Books

At the root of it, design is a language just as French and German are languages. Whilst some people are able to understand design fluently, there are those who just use phrase-books.
NEVILLE BRODY, *THE GRAPHIC LANGUAGE OF NEVILLE BRODY*

THE ROLE OF ALL BOOKS IS TO COMMUNICATE. WHILE THE WORDS AND THE IMAGES FORM THE MESSAGES TO BE CONVEYED, GRAPHIC DESIGN IS THE VEHICLE BY WHICH THIS IS DONE. DESIGN HAS ALWAYS PLAYED A PART IN THE CREATION OF A BOOK, WHETHER THROUGH THE CHOICE OF TEXT SIZE AND STYLE, THE LAYOUT OF A PAGE OR THE PLACEMENT OF AN IMAGE. SUCH JUDGEMENTS INFLUENCE THE CHARACTER AND AESTHETICS OF A BOOK AS WELL AS THE EASE WITH WHICH ITS CONTENT CAN BE READ AND UNDERSTOOD.

The look of text itself is a major element in the design of all books. From the development of the first alphabets in ancient times through to the scripts that are regularly used around the world today, the desire for regularity, clarity and beauty has informed the design of the written word.

Some of the earliest surviving examples of book design in the West can be found in Celtic manuscripts from the seventh and eighth centuries. Illuminated manuscripts throughout medieval and Renaissance Europe continued to be adorned with decorated initials and borders, detailed miniatures and full-page illustrations of religious scenes. Text was carefully laid out on evenly spaced lines and was written in a fine script.

The design of books in Europe changed rapidly in the mid fifteenth century with the introduction of printing. The first printed books imitated the appearance of manuscript books, most likely to assure the book-buying public that a printed book was as authoritative, if not as ornate, as a manuscript version. The first printers tended to use type modelled on traditional Gothic scripts. As the demand for and acceptance of printed books quickly grew, however, publishers increasingly used individually cast letters to produce books in a range of new styles, layouts and types. The engraver and printer Nicolaus Jenson is recognised today for his Roman typeface, which influenced type for centuries to come. Jenson also designed new Greek and Gothic fonts, which gave a fresh look to earlier text styles, and was one of the first to develop trademarks, the precursors to today's multinational corporate logos.

Venetian master printer Aldus Manutius employed typeface designer Francesco Griffo, who designed a number of typefaces, including the first italic font. One of Griffo's earliest typefaces was designed for a book by Pietro Bembo. Versions of Bembo, a Roman typeface, are still popular today after more than five hundred years. Manutius's 1499 edition of *Hypnerotomachia Poliphili* by Francesco Colonna is considered one of the most beautiful books to have survived from the Renaissance. With Griffo's Bembo type laid out in either harmonious grids or replicating forms such as a classical urn, each spread is a masterpiece of graphic design.

The sixteenth to eighteenth centuries were witness to many important developments in

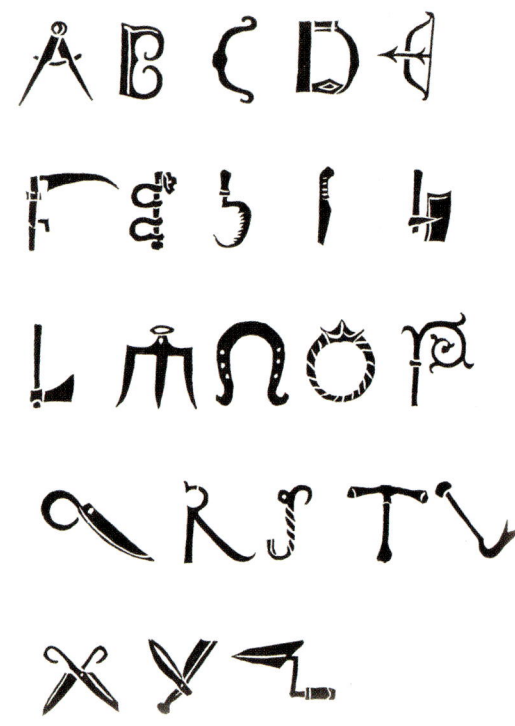

type and graphic design throughout Europe. Typeface designers of the time included Claude Garamond (from France), John Baskerville (from England) and Giambattista Bodoni (from Italy), all of whose typefaces continue to be used today. France in particular was a major centre for book production at this time, with advances in typography and design combining with printing and bookbinding of the highest quality and using the finest materials.

As it had done with the introduction of moveable type, graphic design underwent another major development with the industrial revolution and the introduction of the steam-driven press. Throughout the nineteenth century, other major developments included the introduction of mechanised typesetting and new methods of image reproduction. The rise in the number of printing firms and the number of books produced annually meant that competition for readers was fierce.

As printers strove to offer greater diversity and visual impact than their competitors, new illustrative processes and typefaces were developed. These included new 'fat' and 'bold' fonts and large-scale wooden type that would command attention in posters, handbills and magazines. The first sans serif typeface, a style with no serifs (extensions) for individual letters, also appeared at this time. Designed by William Caslon IV in 1816 and called Two Lines English Egyptian, its modest arrival gave no indication of the impact that sans serif typefaces would have on graphic design in the twentieth century.

In the Victorian era, typography became increasingly ornate, with shadows and decorative elements offered in a range of styles. The Victorian taste for excess was also accommodated through new reproductive processes such as chromolithography, which utilised a separate stone or plate for each colour, enabling images to be printed affordably in an array of rich colours.

The Arts and Crafts movement, led by William Morris, emerged as a reaction against the excesses of the Victorian era and the loss of traditional artisan crafts with the mechanisation of book production. Morris designed three typefaces for use at his Kelmscott Press—Golden, Troy and Chaucer—their names alone reflecting Morris's evocation of a past age. The press closed in 1898, two years after Morris's death, but his influence on graphic design continues to this day.

From the 1890s, virtually every decade has witnessed new artistic styles and movements in graphic design. Many European books and magazines published at the turn of the century were in the Art Nouveau and *Japonisme* styles so

ABOVE, LEFT:
Francesco Colonna
Hypnerotomachia Poliphili
Venice, Aldus Manutius, 1499
Typography by Francesco Griffo

ABOVE, RIGHT:
'Fantastic Alphabet'
From **Geofroy Tory**
Champ Fleury
New York, Grolier Club, 1927
(Reproduction of 1529 edition)

OPPOSITE, TOP ROW:
Initials designed by Michael Burghers for Oxford University Press, late seventeenth century
From *Alphabet and Image* no. 7
London, Shenval Press, May 1948

OPPOSITE, MIDDLE ROW:
Initials designed by Eric Gill for the Golden Cockerel Press, c. 1930
From *Alphabet and Image* no. 7
London, Shenval Press, May 1948

OPPOSITE, BOTTOM ROW:
Initials designed by Aubrey Beardsley for
Sir Thomas Malory
Le Morte d'Arthur
London, JM Dent, 1927

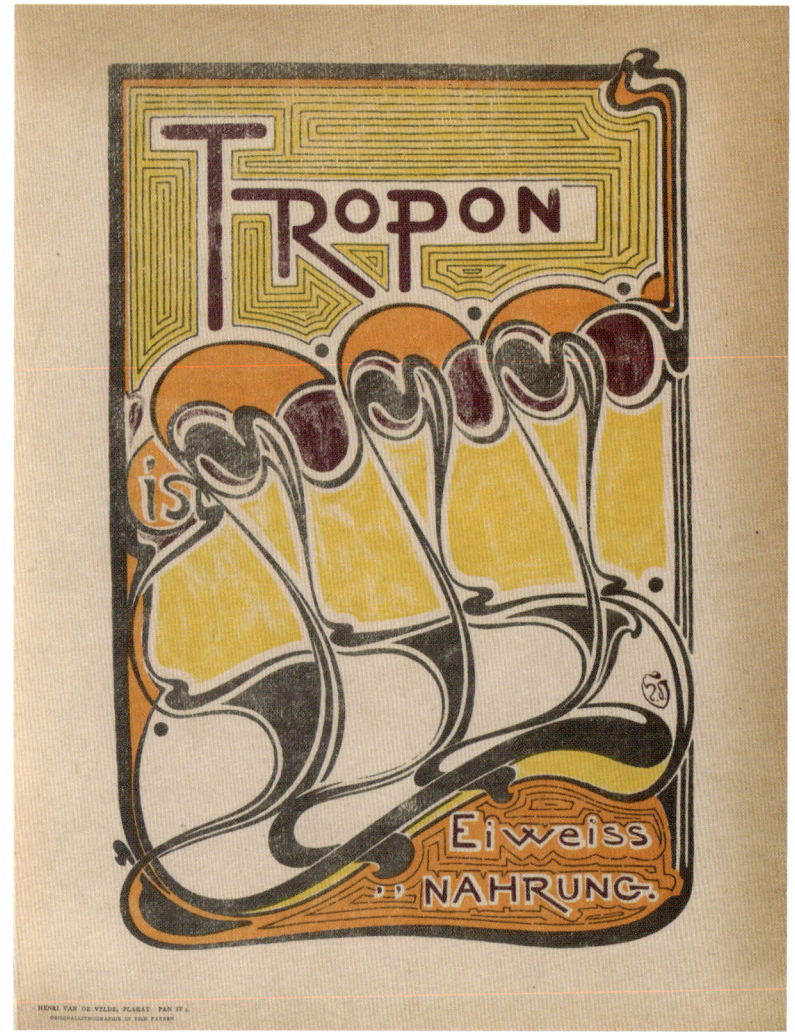

LEFT:
'Tropon' by Henri van de Velde
From *Pan*
Berlin, 1898

RIGHT:
'The Kiss' by Peter Behrens
From *Pan*
Berlin, 1898

popular at the time. Graphic elements incorporated organic forms such as vine tendrils and peacock feathers and used flat planes of colour as epitomised by Japanese *ukiyo-e* woodblock prints. Art magazines such as *The Studio* and *Pan* promoted new design to audiences throughout Europe and featured the work of influential artists, particularly Aubrey Beardsley, Walter Crane and Peter Behrens.

The twentieth century ushered in a period of great change and upheaval in all areas of life, from the introduction of new forms of transportation to the redrawing of the European map as a result of war. Art and design reflected these developments with the rise of movements including Cubism, Futurism and Vorticism. Within typography, sans serif typefaces came to the fore, championed by the avant-garde as embodying the spirit of the modern age. Sans serifs were traditionally seen to be too difficult to read in large blocks of text and were therefore generally used for headings and short pieces. Designers such as Peter Behrens began to challenge these accepted principles by setting whole pages of text in sans serif. One of the most significant, and most recognised, sans serifs developed at this time was the Railway type, commissioned exclusively for the London Underground in 1916 from the renowned Arts and Crafts calligrapher Edward Johnston.

The Vorticist art journal *Blast* (1914) is today considered one of the great examples of modernist design and typography. Founded by the painter and writer Wyndham Lewis, its impact extended far beyond its short life of only two issues. Within its pages of radically arranged type and linocuts, it characterised aspects of contemporary life as either 'blessed' or 'blasted' according to the Vorticist view.

Other artistic movements to shape the design of books in the first decades of the twentieth century were the anti-art Dadaist movement, Surrealism and Russian Suprematism and Constructivism. Type was increasingly used as bold and abstract form as much as for conveying the meaning of its text. El Lissitzky was a major figure in Russian

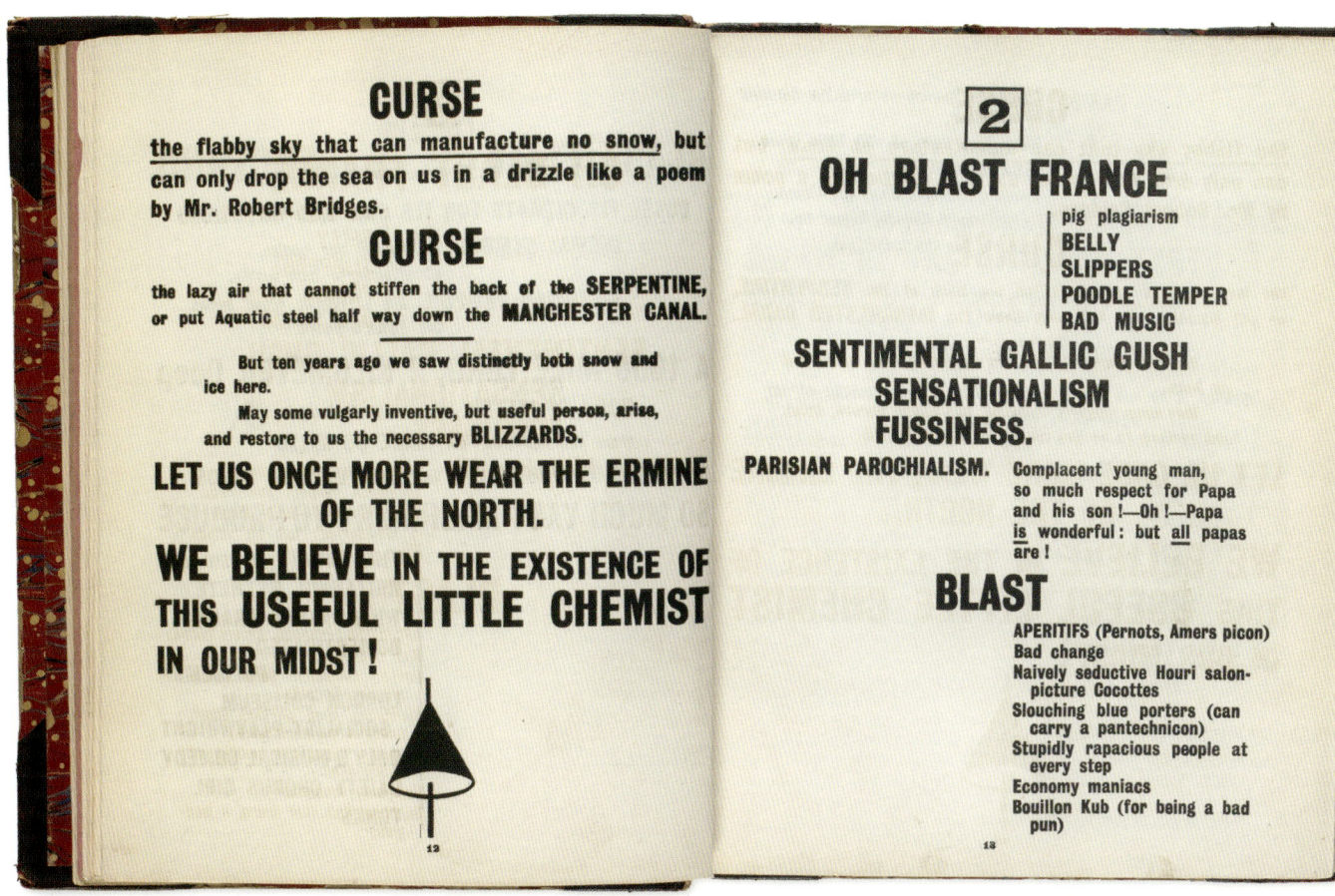

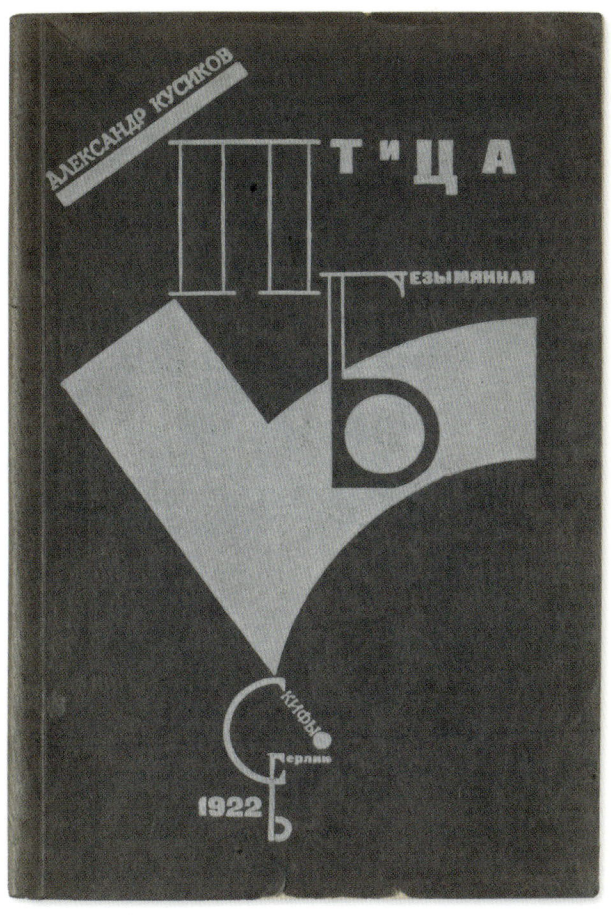

TOP:
Wyndham Lewis, editor
Blast: a Review of the Great English Vortex
no. 1
London, John Lane, 1914

BOTTOM, LEFT:
El Lissitzky and Hans Arp
Die Kunstismen 1914–1924
Erlenbach-Zurich, Eugen Rentsch, 1925
Cover design by El Lissitzky

BOTTOM, RIGHT:
Aleksandr Kusikov
Ptitsa Bezymiannaia: Izbrannye Stikhi 1917–1921
Berlin, Skify, 1922
Cover design by El Lissitzky

art and design in the 1920s, and his *Die Kunstismen 1914–1924* (The Isms of Art), edited with Hans Arp, is a significant example of book design of the period. Lissitzky used all aspects of a page, enlarging or emphasising traditionally minor elements, such as image numbers and white space, and setting text within dynamic geometric grids.

With the rise of new commodities as well as illustrated magazines, the first decades of the twentieth century were also a time in which commercial art came to the fore. Artists and designers presented the latest trends in interior decoration, shopfront display, architecture and fashion in portfolios, handbooks and trade journals. The portfolios produced throughout the 1920s by the Parisian publisher Albert Lévy, such as L-P Sézille's *Devantures de Boutiques* (1927), exemplify the work of the time. Lévy used the *pochoir* stencilling method to reproduce original artwork by some of the leading artists, designers and architects of the day. This process was very popular during the Art Nouveau and Art Deco periods as it could produce flat planes of dynamic colour and crisply delineated outlines.

Typeface design also underwent significant development during the 1920s and 1930s. Major creators of the period included the Bauhaus-inspired designer Jan Tschichold, who designed a range of sans serif fonts, including Sabon, and expounded his modernist theories in his seminal *Die Neue Typographie* (1928). A major force in British type design at this time was Eric Gill, whose influential Gill Sans and Perpetua series of fonts have remained popular ever since their introduction.

Another milestone in typography at this time was Stanley Morison's Times New Roman, developed in 1931 for, and named after, *The Times* newspaper of London. A serif typeface, Times New Roman was heralded for its readability at a time when sans serifs were beginning their ascendancy. Morison wrote that Times New Roman must be 'worthy of *The Times*—masculine, English, direct, simple, not more novel … and absolutely free from faddishness and frivolity'.

The period from 1930s to the 1950s was characterised by bold new graphic styles, expressed particularly in poster and magazine art. The American magazine *Harper's Bazaar* employed some of the great artists and designers of the era, such as Russian-born French designer Erté (Romain de Tirtoff), who designed hundreds of fashion illustrations and covers between 1915 and 1937. As the Hollywood movie industry became a dominant force in popular culture, advertising posters and film credits by major figures such as Saul Bass established the direction for much graphic design of the 1950s. The so-called 'Swiss Design' movement from Switzerland and Germany generated a new range of important sans serif fonts at this time, including Univers by Adrian Frutiger, Optima by Hermann Zapf and Helvetica by Edouard Hoffman and Max Miedinger.

The youth and anti-establishment movements of the 1960s and 1970s ushered in a new wave of graphic expression. From the immediacy of the May 1968 street protests in Paris and the subsequent work of the Grapus artists' group to Andy Warhol's pop aesthetic and the psychedelia of Haight-Ashbury's music- and drug-inspired subcultures, text and image found new forms in the posters, album covers and magazines of the time.

The underground magazine *Oz* embodied much of the counterculture of the 1960s. It was founded in Sydney in 1963 by university students Richard Neville, Richard Walsh and Martin Sharp. After Neville and Sharp moved to London in 1966, they joined forces with fellow Australian Jim Anderson to publish *Oz* there from the following year. With its parodies of prominent political figures, its strong anti-Vietnam War stance and its celebration of sex and drugs, *Oz* was often the centre of controversy and, on two occasions, the subject of obscenity trials. Martin Sharp was responsible for much of the design, typography and layout of *Oz*, using new materials such as metal foils and fluorescent inks to create his original artwork. Sharp's cover illustration of a psychedelic Bob Dylan is one of his most famous and is an icon of its time.

OPPOSITE, FAR LEFT:
L-P Sézille
Devantures de Boutiques
Paris, Editions Albert Lévy,
1927
Artwork by
Francis Jourdain

OPPOSITE, TOP RIGHT:
Development of Gill Sans
typeface by Eric Gill
From *Alphabet and Image*
no. 6
London, Shenval Press,
January 1948

OPPOSITE, BOTTOM RIGHT:
'Experiments with Letters'
by Robert Brazil
From *Motif 7*
London, Shenval Press,
1961

RIGHT:
Oz
no. 7
London, Oz Publications
Ink Ltd, 1967
Artwork by Martin Sharp

ROBERT SMITH

PROFILE FIONA RUSSELL POWELL PHOTOGRAPHS DEREK RIDGERS

A SUITABLE CASE for Treatment

HE IS A VERY LOQUACIOUS POP STAR. ENDLESSLY QUOTABLE, HE IS ENDLESSLY QUOTED; A BRAZENLY WAYWARD SOUL FOR AN AUDIENCE OF TIMIDLY WAYWARD SOULS. BEHIND THIS FACADE, IS HE JUST AS CONFUSED?

"We can't make it. We are ready to die when we are born. We are the patsies. And I hate the intellectual freak who realises all this and condescends to it and makes himself seemingly superior because he feels he just doesn't belong and therefore is." (Charles Bukowski)

"I look inside myself and see my heart is black" (Jagger/Richard)

HE STARTS OFF BY picking half a lemon (his favourite fruit) out of the fridge and sucking on it and this slurping is driving me up the wall because I'm speeding but I can't say anything because he's a popstar with a capital P just like the Pope, so I smile politely whereas I'd rather wring his fucking neck. What's worse is that this intellectual slob knows that I know that he knows because nothing passes unseen before the candid blue gaze buried in a pudding face.

At Fiction Records' headquarters which is a house but not a home near Baker Street, Robert Smith arrives late as usual in his "Russian junkmobile" (a jeep) and wants to sit outside because it's a sunny day. How strange . . . That's one of my preconceptions squashed right away (at least I have the grace to admit it). I would have preferred to stay in a nice cool dark room and so the tables are turned. And keep on turning for two-and-a-half hours.

I'm not being bossy, just practical when I ask to *please* take your hands away from your mouth because I can't hear what you're saying. Poor Robert — everything's upside down. Interview time — turn your insides out. Actually, if the truth be known, the surgeon would find him in perfect health, his father-confessor would find his soul fully-clothed because, to Robert, life's just a never-ending story. The Cure proffer and thrive on lies. I don't mind being spun a yarn or two as long as it doesn't turn into a blanket. This little fly has got a brain; he manages to pull a few legs and never jumps into the web. Robert's really into role-playing, as you can see. Not only at work, but also at home in his recently acquired flat in Maida Vale with his one and only-ever girlfriend Mary.

"A lot of that role-playing is sort of true. I made a video of us the other week. I left a video-camera in the corner of the room and after a couple of hours you forget that it's on and I was quite horrified at the amount of rubbish we say to each other. It's like listening to mental people.

THE FACE 43

carmine st.

The year is 1979. And 1942. At a small neighborhood pool in Greenwich Village, a movie crew is time-tripping 30-odd years into the past to film "Raging Bull," the story of boxer Jake LaMotta. A gang of skinny, shirtless kids holler from a rooftop as the cameras follow Robert DeNiro (playing LaMotta). He buys a soda at the concession stand, and sits at a picnic table with the actor playing LaMotta's brother. Around the pool, women in one-piece bathing suits relax in chaise lounges, and local Mafia hoods in tropical shirts play cards. DeNiro has eyes for only one: the platinum blonde who sits at pool's edge, luxuriantly paddling her long legs in the cool water. The camera moves in for a close-up of her legs...and director Martin Scorsese calls,

COLORS

Promoted as a 'magazine about the rest of the world', *Colors* is sponsored by the Italian fashion company Benetton, which has developed a reputation for its provocative advertising campaigns. The magazine was established in 1991 by creative director Oliviero Toscani and Hungarian-American designer Tibor Kalman (as editor-in-chief), and quickly became known for its bold layouts of striking graphics and political statements. In one controversial issue, digital manipulation was used to present well-known contemporary figures such as Queen Elizabeth and Pope John Paul II as members of ethnic minorities.

OPPOSITE, TOP:
The Face
no. 66
London, The Face,
October 1985
Art direction and design
by Neville Brody
Photograph by
Derek Ridgers

OPPOSITE, BOTTOM:
Beach Culture
no. 5
San Juan Capistrano, CA,
Surfer Publications,
February – March 1991
Art direction by
David Carson
Photography by
Pat Blashill

RIGHT:
Colors Magazine
no. 9
Rome, Benetton Group,
December 1994 –
February 1995

Although the 1960s and 1970s were a time of great social change, nothing would revolutionise graphic design more than the introduction of the computer and desktop publishing in the mid 1980s. The most influential of these developments were the Apple Macintosh computer and Pagemaker, the first desktop publishing software program. Many predicted the death of the design profession and of graphic design itself when it seemed that what had previously been done by a range of artists, designers, artisans and technicians could now be seemingly achieved by a single operator with the right skills and equipment. Rather than the demise of graphic design, however, the digital age has witnessed an explosion of innovation and experimentation in design and typography.

Each year has seen the arrival of new computers, scanners and printers, all with more memory, speed, colours and capabilities, and all at more affordable prices and more compact than previous models. At the same time, each subsequent generation of page layout, photographic and type software has enabled greater potential for complexity, flexibility and manipulation of word and image.

Throughout the 1980s, magazines were an important avenue for experimentation and the presentation of new developments in graphic design and typography. Two magazines that were groundbreaking in their respective fields were *Emigre* and *The Face*. Graphic design magazine *Emigre* was first published in San Francisco in 1984. Produced by Dutch-born designer Rudy Vanderlans in partnership with Czechoslovakian-born typographer Zuzana Licko, *Emigre*'s adventurous layouts featured a seemingly endless array of font styles made possible by digital means.

Under the art directorship of designer and typographer Neville Brody, music and popular culture magazine *The Face* was at the cutting edge of British design. Brody's design aesthetic embodied the postmodern by boldly combining elements from previous eras with his own new typefaces, and merging the handmade with the computer-generated. Through his innovative work on album covers, books, magazines and newspapers, Brody has continued to influence the direction of graphic design over subsequent decades. In 2006, he oversaw the redesign of *The Times* newspaper and the creation of a new bespoke font, Times Modern.

One of the most influential designers of the 1990s was American surfer and designer David Carson. Beginning with *Transworld Skateboarding* in 1983, Carson designed and art directed a number of seminal youth culture and music magazines including *Beach Culture, Surfer* and *Ray Gun*. Carson rejected traditional approaches to typesetting with their grid-based formats in favour of unconventional layouts that were more expressive of an article's content. While some criticised Carson's designs, dismissing them as unreadable, his overlapping, cropping and merging of type and his placement of photographs sideways or upside-down had an enormous impact on contemporary graphic design.

BELOW, LEFT:
Dale Nason
Defective Part
no. 1
Melbourne, c. 2003

BELOW, RIGHT:
McSweeney's Quarterly Concern
no. 9
San Francisco, 2002

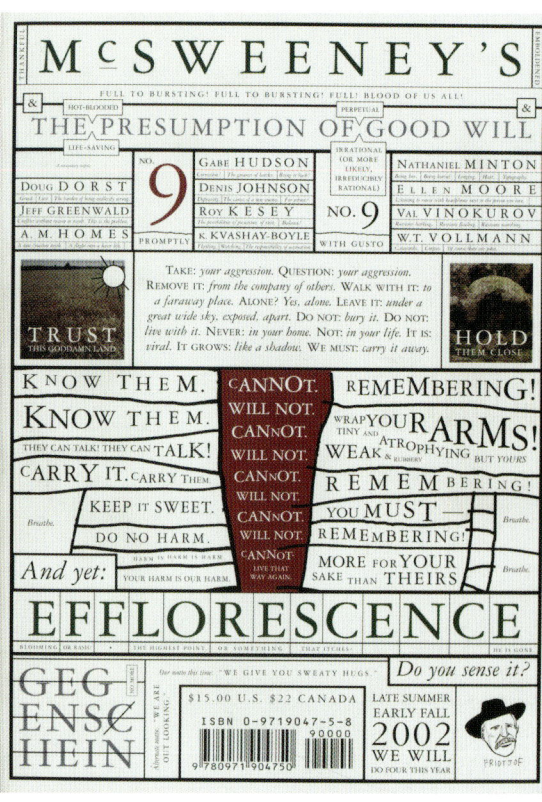

As books and magazines have become increasingly lavish with new developments in design and printing, an alternative graphic form to flourish in the digital era has been the 'zine' or do-it-yourself magazine. Zines offer an affordable alternative for writers, artists and designers who do not have access to, or do not wish to be part of, mainstream publishing. Zine design can more correctly be understood as anti-design, a rejection of the slick finish achievable through digital design in favour of the rawness propounded by movements such as punk in the 1970s. This approach is particularly evident in the 'ransom-note' style of designers such as Jamie Reid, most famous for his album covers and posters for the Sex Pistols. Generally low-budget and distributed through specialist networks, zines have emerged as a popular medium for personal expression on a range of topics as diverse as music, politics, poetry and television. In recent years, the more traditional format of the photocopied and stapled zine has been joined by e-zines, online versions that take advantage of the opportunities for self-publishing made possible by the internet.

When the digital era began to revolutionise not only the appearance of information but also the ways in which it is stored and retrieved, many predicted that it would cause the demise of books. More than twenty years after these predictions were first made, however, the book as we know it still exists. In a world in which information can be scanned, retrieved and downloaded electronically, millions of readers continue to prefer their words and pictures to come printed on a page and packaged between the covers of a book. Rather than witnessing the decline of the book, we are experiencing its renaissance as a dynamic and ever-changing form.

Perhaps in answer to those forecasting the end of the book, publishers are increasingly issuing books to be desired, collected and enjoyed as artworks or objects, as well as to be read. And they are commissioning book designers to develop exciting new forms of book construction, shape and packaging for the conveyance of image and text into the future. We, as readers, will continue to celebrate our relationship with books, old and new.

McSWEENEY'S

McSweeney's is an independent US literary journal edited by writer Dave Eggers. Since its first issue in 1998, it has won many literary and design awards for its support of new writing and its adventurous design. Eggers designs most of the issues but also occasionally engages guest designers, such as the artist and graphic novelist Chris Ware. As stated on the *McSweeney's* website, 'we try to make each issue very different from the last. One issue came in a box, one was Icelandic, and one looks like a pile of mail'.

The WORLD of the BOOK

VISIONAIRE

Since 1991, Visionaire has challenged traditional definitions of the book or magazine through its limited edition art and fashion publications. Each issue features a specific theme and is conceived and developed by a collaborative team of invited artists, fashion designers, photographers and art directors, who are given freedom to design the format and packaging, as well as the content, of that issue. Contributors have included Karl Lagerfeld, Mario Testino, Sam Taylor-Wood, Bruce Weber, Sofia Coppola and Philippe Starck. The packaging of individual issues has ranged from more traditional portfolios to a jewellery box, a battery-operated lightbox, a travel bag, a case of perfume vials and, as shown here, a puzzle.

ETISOPPO

Etisoppo is a 'super-mini-card-style-artbook' produced by Japanese-born artist and designer Jun Tagami, who now resides in Sydney. The images are contributed by a range of artists based predominantly in Sydney but with a strong connection to Asia. *Etisoppo*'s title ('opposite' spelt backwards) makes reference to the directions in which text is read in different cultures. With its format of individual cards within an acrylic holder, *Etisoppo* acts both as a magazine and a mini gallery. The lack of binding encourages viewers to interact by mixing and matching the images and ensures that there is no one hierarchy or reading.

ABOVE, LEFT:
Visionaire 30: the Game
New York, Visionaire,
1999
Image: Patricia Piccinini,
Sheen – 1.00.613–3
(detail), 1998

ABOVE, RIGHT:
Etisoppo Infinity
no. 6
Sydney, 2004
Jun Tagami, creative director and editor
Images by Jun Tagami, Chad Edwards and Mayumi Takami

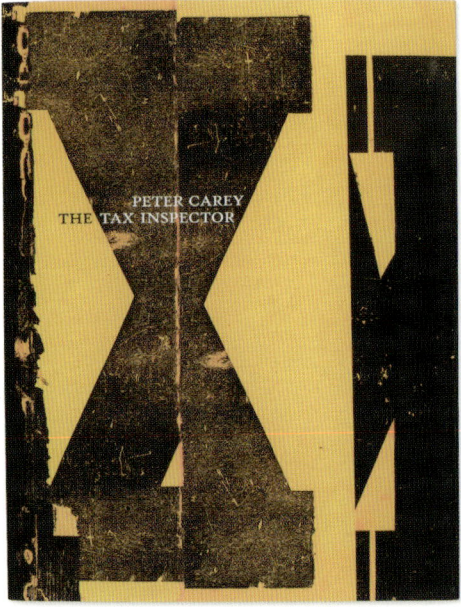

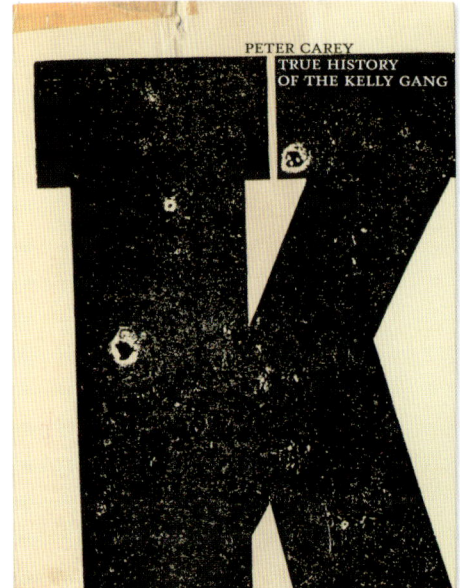

JENNY GRIGG

In recent years, book cover design has witnessed a return to traditional typography and the handmade over computer-generated imagery. Examples of this approach are Jenny Grigg's award-winning cover designs for the University of Queensland Press reissue of Peter Carey's works in 2001. The individual letters created from large wooden type suggest a past era of letterpress printing but also, as noted by Carey himself, the conceptual work of twentieth-century artists such as New Zealand painter Colin McCahon.

Jenny Grigg
Cover design for works by Peter Carey
Brisbane, University of Queensland Press, 2001

TOP:
Kat Macleod
Bird
Melbourne, 3 Deep Design, 2002

BOTTOM:
Chip Kidd
Cover design for James Ellroy, *White Jazz*
New York, Alfred A Knopf, 1992

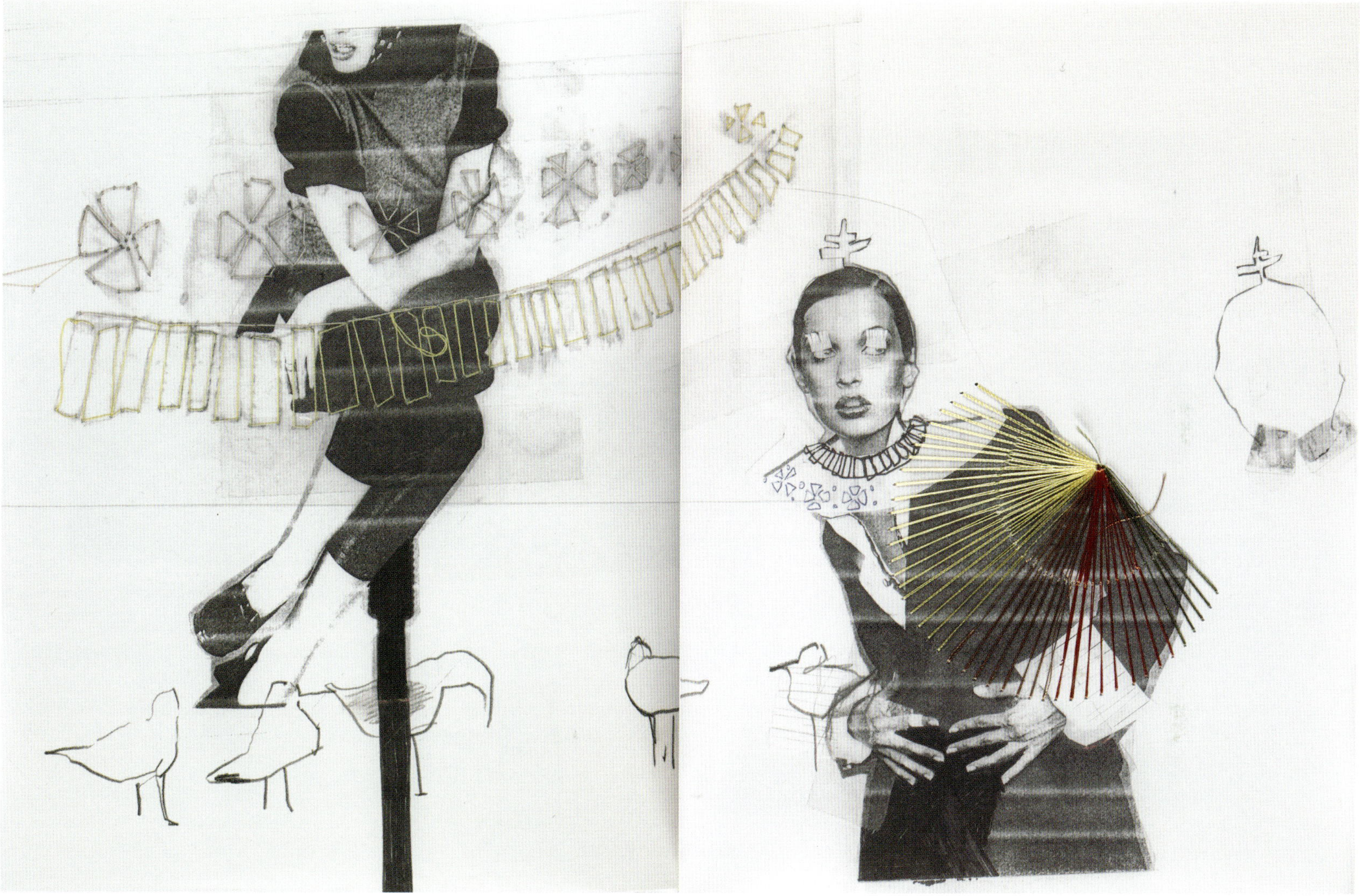

The WORLD *of the* BOOK | 233

CHIP KIDD

Chip Kidd is internationally recognised for his book jacket designs for Alfred A Knopf over the past fifteen years. He designs jackets for works by major contemporary writers including Cormac McCarthy, Haruki Murakami, James Ellroy, Peter Carey, Anne Rice, Orhan Pamuk, John Updike and Donna Tartt. James Ellroy, quoted in Kidd's *Book One: Work: 1986–2006*, said of the design for *White Jazz*, a novel about police corruption, 'Chip Kidd frames the front cover in pristine white—a color at once stark, innocent, and inviting. Centered in that white expanse: an LAPD patrol car door shot full of holes. The potential book buyer/reader has been presented with a statement and a challenge—forceful, simple, elegant. Read this book!'

3 DEEP

The publishing credo of Melbourne-based design firm 3 Deep declares that 'despite the advances in communication and the emergence of electronic media, the book still exists as a critical cultural artefact'. Their award-winning *Bird* was the first book to be fully conceived, designed and produced by the group, who have gone on to establish a profile for their innovative art and design publishing. With artwork by Kat Macleod, *Bird* explores relationships between birds, the female form and fashion. The book has been created as a work of art and includes embroidery on some of the seven specialty papers used throughout.

Picture credits

PART I: BOOKS AND IDEAS

p. 29 *Sefer Torah* and *Yad*: Courtesy of the Jewish Museum of Australia, Melbourne.

p. 30 Qur'an fragment: © The Trustees of the Chester Beatty Library, Dublin, CBL Is 1494; Photographer: Roy Hewson.

p. 49 Marshall McLuhan and Quentin Fiore, *The Medium is the Massage*: Used by permission of Penguin Books Ltd. Germaine Greer, *The Female Eunuch*: © 1971 Germaine Greer. By permission of HarperCollins Publishers Ltd.

PART II: THE BOOK AND THE IMAGINATION

p. 54 Murasaki Shikibu, *Genji monogatari utaejo*: © The Trustees of the Chester Beatty Library, Dublin, CBL J 1041; Photographer: Roy Hewson.

p. 72 Wyndham Lewis (ed.), *Blast*: © By kind permission of the Wyndham Lewis Memorial Trust.

p. 73 Wyndham Lewis, *Apes of God*: © By kind permission of the Wyndham Lewis Memorial Trust. Virginia Woolf, *The Waves*: © The Estate of Vanessa Bell, courtesy of Henrietta Garnett.

p. 76 Covers of titles by Ezra Pound and Samuel Beckett courtesy of Faber and Faber Ltd.

p. 77 Samuel Beckett, *Imagination Dead Imagine*: Courtesy of Calder Publications Limited. Sculpture © Alberto Giacometti / ADAGP. Licensed by VISCOPY, Sydney 2007.

pp. 78–85 All Penguin covers used by permission of Penguin Books Ltd, with the exception of Paul Auster, *The New York Trilogy* © 1990 by Penguin Books, used by permission of Penguin, a division of Penguin Group (USA) Inc.

p. 88 Allen Ginsberg, *Howl and Other Poems*: Courtesy of City Lights Books. William Burroughs, *The Naked Lunch* (1959): Courtesy of Olympia Press. William Burroughs, *Naked Lunch* (1962): Courtesy of Grove/Atlantic Inc. William Burroughs, *The Naked Lunch* (1964): Courtesy of Calder Publications Limited.

p. 89 Jack Kerouac, *On the Road* (1958): Cover artwork by Len Deighton. Used by permission of Andre Deutsch.

p. 90 Jack Kerouac, *The Dharma Bums*: © Jack Kerouac, 1958. Courtesy of Pan Macmillan, London, UK. Jack Kerouac, *The Subterraneans*: Used by permission of HarperCollins Publishers.

p. 91 Jack Kerouac, *Scattered Poems* and Jack Kerouac, *Book of Dreams*: Courtesy of City Lights Books. William Burroughs, *Early Routines*: Courtesy of Cadmus Editions.

p. 94 Hergé, *Les Aventures de Tintin: les Cigares du Pharaon*: © Hergé/Moulinsart 2007.

p. 95 John Dixon and Maurice Bramley, *The Phantom Commando*: Courtesy of Horwitz Publications, Sydney.

p. 96 Stanley Pitt, *Silver Starr*: Courtesy of Luke Pitt.

p. 97 Covers for titles by Marc Brody, Carter Brown and Paul Valdez reproduced courtesy of Horwitz Publications, Sydney. Covers for Larry Kent titles reproduced courtesy of Cleveland Publishing Co., Sydney.

p. 98 KT McCall, *The Lady's a Decoy*: Courtesy of Horwitz Publications, Sydney.

p. 99 Robert Crumb, 'Mr Natural': Courtesy of Bloomsbury Publishing, UK.

p. 100 Shō Makura and Takeshi Okano, *Jigoku sensei nūbē*: © 1993 by Shō Makura and Takeshi Okano / SHUEISHA Inc.

p. 101 Tezuka Osamu, *Buddha*: © Tezuka Productions.

p. 102 Patricia Martinelli and Mario Gomboli, *Il Grande Diabolik: per la Testa di Diabolik*: Courtesy of Astorina SRL. Daniel Clowes, *Ice Haven*: Copyright © 2001, 2005 by Daniel G Clowes. Used by permission of Pantheon Books, a division of Random House, Inc.

p. 103 Art Spiegelman, *Maus II*: © 1991 by Art Spiegelman. Used by permission of The Wylie Agency. Chris Ware, *Jimmy Corrigan*: Used by permission of The Random House Group Ltd.

p. 110 AA Milne, *Winnie-the-Pooh*: Illustration by Ernest H Shepard. Used by permission of Curtis Brown. Wilf Reeves and Olga Miller, *The Legends of Moonie Jarl*: Courtesy of Glen Miller.

p. 111 Maurice Sendak, *Where the Wild Things Are*: Used by permission of The Random House Group Ltd. Jean de Brunhoff, *Babar's Travels*: Jean de Brunhoff, *Le Voyage de Babar* © Librairie Hachette 1939. Shaun Tan, *The Lost Thing*: Courtesy of Shaun Tan and Hachette Livre Australia.

PART III: EXPLORING THE WORLD

P. 168 *Banks' Florilegium*: Courtesy of Alecto Historical Editions.
Celia E Rosser and Alexander S George, *The Banksias*: Courtesy of Celia E Rosser and Monash University.

PART IV: THE ARTIST AND THE BOOK

P. 176 *A Specimen Book of Pattern Papers*: Courtesy of The Curwen Studio.
P. 177 François Couperin, *Oeuvres Complètes*: Courtesy of Éditions de l'Oiseau-Lyre SAM.
P. 178 Ann Muir, *Harvesting Colour*: Courtesy of Ann Muir and Incline Press.
P. 179 *Feather and Prey*: Courtesy of Nick Doslov of Renaissance Bookbinding and Peter Lyssiotis.
Jim et Jack: Courtesy of Yoko Ueno. Photographer: Chris Chen.
P. 191 Albrecht Dürer, *The Apocalypse*: Courtesy of the National Gallery of Victoria, Melbourne. Felton Bequest 1956.
P. 195 Pablo Picasso, *Carmen*: © Pablo Picasso / Succession Picasso. Licensed by VISCOPY, Sydney 2007.
Guillaume Apollinaire, *L'Enchanteur Pourrissant*: © André Derain / ADAGP. Licensed by VISCOPY, Sydney 2007.
P. 196 *Verve*, nos 29–30: © Pablo Picasso / Succession Picasso. Licensed by VISCOPY, Sydney 2007.
P. 197 *Verve*, no. 1: © Henri Matisse / Succession Matisse. Licensed by VISCOPY, Sydney 2007.
P. 198 *Derrière le Miroir*, no. 206: © Valerio Adami / ADAGP. Licensed by VISCOPY, Sydney 2007.
Derrière le Miroir, no. 231: © Successió Miró / ADAGP Magritte, Miró, Chagall. Licensed by VISCOPY, Sydney 2007.
P. 199 André Frénaud, *La Nourriture du Bourreau*: © Antoni Tàpies / VEGAP. Licensed by VISCOPY, Sydney 2007.
James Joyce, *Ulysses*: Courtesy of Arion Press. Robert Motherwell © Dedalus Foundation / VAGA. Licensed by VISCOPY, Sydney 2007.
P. 208 *The Canterbury Tales*: Used by permission of The Estate of Eric Gill.
P. 209 Jas H Duke, *Dada Kampfen um Leben und Tod*: Courtesy of Wayzgoose Press and the Estate of Jas H Duke.
P. 212 Angela Cavalieri, *INRI*: Courtesy of the Artist.
P. 213 Peter Lyssiotis, *Feather and Prey*: Courtesy of the Artist.
Angela Cavalieri and Peter Lyssiotis, *–1316*: Courtesy of the Artists.
P. 214 Judy Watson, *a preponderance of aboriginal blood*: Courtesy of the Artist and grahame galleries + editions.
P. 215 Bruno Leti and Chris Wallace-Crabbe, *Drawing*: Courtesy of the Artist and the Author.
PP. 216–17 Allan Mitelman, *Ko-Ko*: Courtesy of the Artist and Lyre Bird Press and Zimmer Editions.
P. 218 Kylie Stillman, *Pine, Eleven Years Old*: Courtesy of the Artist and Utopia Art Sydney.
Nicholas Jones, *Medallion*: Courtesy of the Artist.
Jonathan Tse, *Portrait of an Australian*: Courtesy of the Artist.
P. 219 Milan Milojevic, *Borges Bestiary*: Courtesy of the Artist.
Richard Tipping, *The Sydney Morning*: Courtesy of the Artist.
P. 223 Initials designed by Eric Gill for the Golden Cockerel Press: Used by permission of The Estate of Eric Gill.
P. 225 Wyndham Lewis (ed.), *Blast*: © By kind permission of the Wyndham Lewis Memorial Trust.
P. 226 Eric Gill, Gills Sans typeface: Used by permission of The Estate of Eric Gill.
P. 227 *Oz*: Courtesy of Martin Sharp.
P. 228 *The Face*, no. 66: Courtesy of Research Studios, London. Photograph courtesy of Derek Ridgers.
Beach Culture, no. 5: Courtesy of David Carson.
P. 229 *Colors Magazine*, no. 9, pp. 84–5: Courtesy of *Colors Magazine*.
P. 230 *Defective Part*, no. 1: Courtesy of Dale Nason.
McSweeney's, no. 9: Courtesy of McSweeney's.
P. 231 *Visionaire 30: the Game*: Copyright Visionaire, image copyright Patricia Piccinini.
Etisoppo, no. 6: Courtesy of Jun Tagami, Chad Edwards and Mayumi Takami.
P. 232 Jenny Grigg cover designs for works by Peter Carey: Courtesy of Jenny Grigg.
P. 233 Kat Macleod, *Bird*: Courtesy of 3 Deep Design.
Chip Kidd cover design for James Ellroy, *White Jazz*: Courtesy of Random House, Inc.

Further reading

THE INFORMATION CONTAINED IN THIS BOOK HAS BEEN DRAWN FROM A BROAD RANGE OF GENERAL AND SPECIALISED SOURCES. THE FOLLOWING LIST IS INTENDED AS BOTH A RECORD OF SOME OF THE KEY BOOKS CONSULTED AND A GUIDE FOR THOSE READERS WISHING TO EXPLORE THE SUBJECT FURTHER.

Aitken, Richard, *Botanical Riches: Stories of Botanical Exploration*, Melbourne, The Miegunyah Press in association with State Library of Victoria, 2006.

Atkinson, Geoffrey, *The Extraordinary Voyage in French Literature,* New York, Columbia University Press, 1920.

Baines, Phil, *Penguin by Design: a Cover Story 1935–2005,* London, Allen Lane, 2005.

Baker, Colin, *Qur'an Manuscripts: Calligraphy, Illumination*, London, British Library, 2007.

Bartram, Alan, *Five Hundred Years of Book Design*, London, British Library, 2001.

Battles, Matthew, *Library: an Unquiet History*, New York, Norton, 2003.

Birkett, Dea, *Spinsters Abroad: Victorian Lady Explorers*, Oxford, Blackwell, 1989.

Black, Jeremy, *The British Abroad: the Grand Tour in the Eighteenth Century,* New York, St Martin's Press, 1992.

Blackwell, Lewis, *20th-Century Type*, rev. edn, New Haven, Yale University Press, 2004.

Bland, David, *A History of Book Illustration: the Illuminated Manuscript and the Printed Book*, 2nd edn, London, Faber, 1969.

Bloom, Harold, *The Western Canon: the Books and School of the Ages*, New York, Harcourt Brace, 1994.

Blunt, Wilfrid, and William T Stearn, *The Art of Botanical Illustration*, rev. edn, Woodbridge, UK, Antique Collectors' Club in association with Royal Botanic Gardens, Kew, 1994.

Bovey, Alixe, *Monsters & Grotesques in Medieval Manuscripts*, London, British Library, 2002.

Bragg, Melvyn, *12 Books that Changed the World,* London, Hodder & Stoughton, 2006.

—— *The Adventure of English: the Biography of a Language*, New York, Arcade, 2004.

Bright, Betty, *No Longer Innocent: Book Art in America, 1960–1980*, New York, Granary Books, 2005.

Brown, Yu-Ying, *Japanese Book Illustration*, London, British Library, 1988.

Bury, Stephen, *Artists' Books: the Book as a Work of Art, 1963–1995*, Aldershot, UK, Scolar Press, 1995.

Cassen, Lionel, *Libraries in the Ancient World,* New Haven, CT, Yale University Press, 2001.

Cave, Roderick, *The Private Press,* 2nd edn, New York, RR Bowker, 1983.

Davies, Martin, *The Gutenberg Bible*, London, British Library, 1996.

De Hamel, Christopher, *The Book: a History of the Bible*, London, Phaidon, 2001.

—— *The British Library Guide to Manuscript Illumination: History and Techniques*, London, British Library, 2001.

—— *A History of Illuminated Manuscripts*, 2nd edn, London, Phaidon, 1994.

—— *Scribes and Illuminators*, Toronto, University of Toronto Press, 1992.

Doubleday, Richard B, *Jan Tschichold, Designer: the Penguin Years*, New Castle, DE, Oak Knoll Press and Aldershot, UK, Lund Humphries, 2006.

Drucker, Johanna, *The Century of Artists' Books*, 2nd edn, New York, Granary Books, 2004.

Eisenstein, Elizabeth L, *The Printing Revolution in Early Modern Europe*, 2nd edn, Cambridge, Cambridge University Press, 2005.

Eisler, William, and Bernard Smith, *Terra Australis: the Furthest Shore*, Sydney, International Cultural Corporation of Australia, 1988.

Ellman, Richard, *James Joyce,* new and rev. edn, New York, Oxford University Press, 1982.

Fausett, David, *Writing the New World: Imaginary Voyages and Utopias of the Great Southern Land,* Syracuse, NY, Syracuse University Press, 1993.

Febvre, Lucien, and Henri-Jean Martin, *The Coming of the Book: the Impact of Printing 1450–1800,* new edn, London, NLB, 1976.

Finkelstein, David and Alistair McCleery, *An Introduction to Book History*, New York, Routledge, 2005.

Franklin, Colin with John R Turner, *The Private Presses*, 2nd edn, Aldershot, UK, Scolar Press, 1991.

Füssel, Stephan, *Gutenberg and the Impact of Printing*, Aldershot, UK, Ashgate, 2003.

Glaister, Geoffrey Ashall, *Encyclopedia of the Book*, 2nd edn, London, British Library and New Castle, DE, Oak Knoll Press, 1996.

Gove, Philip Babcock, *The Imaginary Voyage in Prose Fiction,* New York, Columbia University Press, 1941.

Gravett, Paul, *Manga: Sixty Years of Japanese Comics*, London, Laurence King, 2004.

Harthan, John, *The History of the Illustrated Book: the Western Tradition*, London, Thames & Hudson, 1981.

Head, Dominic, ed., *The Cambridge Guide to Literature in English*, 3rd edn, Cambridge, Cambridge University Press, 2006.

Hibbert, Christopher, *The Grand Tour*, London, Methuen, 1987.

Hillier, Jack, *The Art of the Japanese Book*, London, Sotheby's, 1987.

Hooker, JT, ed., *Reading the Past: Ancient Writing from Cuneiform to the Alphabet*, Berkeley, University of California Press and British Museum, 1990.

Howgego, Raymond John, *Encyclopedia of Exploration*, Potts Point, NSW, Hordern House, 2003–2006.

Hunt, Peter, ed., *Children's Literature: an Illustrated History*, Oxford, Oxford University Press, 1995.

Johnson-Woods, Toni, *Pulp: a Collector's Book of Australian Pulp Fiction Covers*, Canberra, National Library of Australia, 2004.

Jubert, Roxane, *Typography and Graphic Design: from Antiquity to the Present*, Paris, Flammarion, 2006.

Jury, David, *Letterpress: the Allure of the Handmade*, Mies, Switzerland, RotoVision, SA, 2004.

Katz, Bill, *Dahl's History of the Book*, 3rd edn, Metuchen, NJ, Scarecrow, 1995.

Kenner, Hugh, *The Pound Era,* London, Faber, 1972.

Kilgour, Frederick G, *The Evolution of the Book*, New York, Oxford University Press, 1998.

Kornicki, Peter, *The Book in Japan: a Cultural History from the Beginnings to the Nineteenth Century*, Leiden, the Netherlands, Brill, 1998.

Levarie, Norma, *The Art and History of Books*, 2nd edn, London, British Library and New Castle, DE, Oak Knoll Press, 1995.

Lewis, Jeremy, *Penguin Special: the Life and Times of Allen Lane,* London, Viking, 2005.

Loxley, Simon, *Type: the Secret History of Letters*, London, IB Tauris, 2004.

Manguel, Alberto, *A History of Reading*, New York, Viking, 1996.

Manion, Margaret M, and Vera F Vines, *Medieval and Renaissance Manuscripts in Australian Collections*, Melbourne, Thames & Hudson, 1984.

Marks, PJM, *The British Library Guide to Bookbinding,* London, British Library, 1998.

Martin, Henri-Jean, *The History and Power of Writing*, Chicago, University of Chicago Press, 1994.

May, John, *The Gutenberg Revolution: the Story of a Genius and an Invention that Changed the World*, London, Review, 2003.

McKendrick, Scot, and Kathleen Doyle, *Bible Manuscripts: 1400 Years of Scribes and Scripture*, London, British Library, 2007.

McMurtrie, Douglas C, *The Book: the Story of Printing & Bookmaking*, 3rd rev. edn, London, Oxford University Press, 1943.

Meggs, Philip B, and Alston W Purvis, *Meggs' History of Graphic Design*, 4th edn, Hoboken, NJ, John Wiley and Sons, 2006.

Morgan, Bill, and Nancy J Peters, *Howl on Trial: the Battle for Free Expression*, San Francisco, City Lights Books, 2006.

National Library of Australia, *Treasures from the World's Great Libraries*, Canberra, National Library of Australia, 2001.

Newland, Amy Reigle, ed., *The Hotei Encyclopedia of Japanese Woodblock Prints*, Amsterdam, Hotei Publishing, 2005.

Olmert, Michael, *The Smithsonian Book of Books*, Washington, DC, Smithsonian Books, 1992.

Parkinson, Richard, *Cracking Codes: the Rosetta Stone and Decipherment*, Berkeley, University of California Press, 1999.

Pearson, David, *English Bookbinding Styles, 1450–1800: a Handbook*, London, British Library and New Castle, DE, Oak Knoll Press, 2005.

Peters, FE, *The Voice, the Word, the Books: the Sacred Scripture of the Jews, Christians and Muslims,* London, British Library, 2007.

Peterson, William S, *The Kelmscott Press: a History of William Morris's Typographical Adventure*, Oxford, Oxford University Press, 1991.

Phillips, Lisa, *Beat Culture and the New America, 1950–1965,* New York, Whitney Museum of American Art in association with Flammarion, Paris, 1995.

Rice, Tony, *Voyages of Discovery: Three Centuries of Natural History Exploration*, London, Scriptum Editions in association with the Natural History Museum, London, 2000.

Robinson, Andrew, *The Story of Writing*, rev. edn, London, Thames & Hudson, 2007.

Ryan, John, *Panel by Panel: a History of Australian Comics*, Stanmore, NSW, Cassell Australia, 1979.

Saunders, Gill, *Picturing Plants: an Analytical History of Botanical Illustration*, Berkeley, University of California Press in association with the Victoria and Albert Museum, 1995.

Schodt, Frederik L, *Manga! Manga!: the World of Japanese Comics*, Tokyo, Kodansha International, 1983.

Speake, Jennifer, ed., *Literature of Travel and Exploration: an Encyclopedia*, New York, Fitzroy Dearborn, 2003.

Staikos, Konstantinos Sp., *The History of the Library in Western Civilization*, New Castle, DE, Oak Knoll Press and 't Goy-Houten, the Netherlands, Hes & De Graaf Publishers BV and Athens, Kotinos Publications, 2004–2005.

Steinberg, SH, *Five Hundred Years of Printing*, rev. edn, London, British Library and New Castle, DE, Oak Knoll Press, 2001.

Stockwell, Foster, *A History of Information Storage and Retrieval*, Jefferson, NC, McFarland, 2001.

Suarez, Thomas, *Early Mapping of the Pacific*, Singapore, Periplus, 2004.

Tahan, Ilana, *Hebrew Manuscripts: the Power of Script and Image,* London, British Library, 2007.

Twyman, Michael, *The British Library Guide to Printing: History and Techniques*, Toronto, University of Toronto Press, 1998.

Watson, Steven, *The Birth of the Beat Generation: Visionaries, Rebels, and Hipsters, 1944–1960*, New York, Pantheon Books, 1995.

Weiner, Stephen, *Faster than a Speeding Bullet: the Rise of the Graphic Novel*, New York, NBM, 2003.

Whalley, Joyce Irene, and Tessa Rose Chester, *A History of Children's Book Illustration*, London, John Murray in association with the Victoria and Albert Museum, 1988.

Williams, Glyndwr, and Alan Frost, eds, *Terra Australis to Australia*, Melbourne, Oxford University Press, 1988.

Wolfe, Richard J, *Marbled Paper: Its History, Techniques and Patterns,* Philadelphia, University of Pennsylvania, 1990.

Index

Note: References in italics are to illustrations, captions or text within illustration panels.

a

Aa, Pieter van der, *Icones Arborum, Fruticum et Herbarum*, *120*, 121
The Aboriginal Portfolio (James Otto Lewis), 130, *130*
Action Comics (comic book series), 94
Adami, Valerio, *198*
Aeneid (Virgil), 55
Aesop's Fables, 106, 189
Afghanistan, accounts of, *131*
Age of Enlightenment, 39, 45, 136, 151
Ainslie, Sir Robert, *Views in Turkey*, *134*
Akkadian language, 3
Alcuin, 10–11
Aldine Press, 23; *see also* Manutius, Aldus
Alembert, Jean Le Rond d', 39
Alice's Adventures in Wonderland (Lewis Carroll), 106, 109, *109*
Allais, Denis Vairasse d', *L'Histoire des Severambes*, 66, 68, *68*
Almanach Royale, 175
Alphabet and Image, 223
alphabet books, 105
altered books, 218
anatomical atlases, *37*
ancient civilisations, 132–9
Andersen, Hans Christian, 106
animals, scientific study of, 163
Ansei kenmonshi, *184*
antiphonals, *11*, *174*
Antiquités Etrusques, Grecques et Romaines (Pierre d'Hancarville), 136, *137*
The Apes of God (Wyndham Lewis), 71, *73*
The Apocalypse (Albrecht Dürer), 189, *191*
Apollinaire, Guillaume, *L'Enchanteur Pourrissant*, 195
Apple Macintosh computers, 229
Arabian Peninsula, accounts of, 130
Arabic calligraphy, 30, 32
Arad, Ron, *85*
Arago, Jacques, *158*

archaeological expeditions, 136
Arion Press, 198
Aristotle, *Historia Animalium (On the History of Animals)*, 161
Armitage, Audrey, *98*
art magazines, 224
Art Nouveau style, 222, 224
The Art of Marbling (Charles Woolnough), 178
art of the book, 172–9
Arthurian legends, 14, 56
artists and illustrators, 109, *152*, 188–99; of scientific voyages, *152*, 154, *156*, 158, *158*
artists' books, 210–19
Arts and Crafts movement, 201, 222
Ashbee, CR, 205
Ashendene Press, 205
astronomy, 115–16, 122, *123*
Atlas Coelestis (John Flamsteed), 122, *123*
Atlas K Puteshestvie Vokrug Sveta (Ivan Fedorovich Kruzenshtern), *158*, 159
Atlas Minor Gerardi Mercatoris (Gerhard Mercator), *144*
atlases, 36; *see also* world maps
Audubon, John James, *168*; *Birds of America*, 167–8, *168*
Augsburg (Germany), 23
Australia: Blaeu's map of, 148; charting of coastline, 127, 144, 146, 151; Dutch map of, 148; first printed map of, *156*; first recorded use of term, 66; natural history of, *153*
Australische Compagnie, 148
Autobiography of Alice B Toklas (Gertrude Stein), 76

b

Babar the Elephant books (Jean de Brunhoff), 110
Babar's Travels (Jean de Brunhoff), *111*
Baines, Phil, 82, *83*
Banks, Joseph, 158; *Florilegium*, 168, 169
The Banksias (Celia E Rosser & Alexander S George), 168, 169
banning of books, 43, 73
Batavia (Dutch ship), 148

Batman: the Dark Knight Returns (Frank Miller), 103
battledores, 105, *106*
Baudelaire, Charles, *Les Fleurs du Mal*, 177
Baudin, Nicolas, 155
Bauer, Ferdinand, *Illustrationes Florae Novae Hollandiae*, 167, *167*
Beach, Sylvia, 73
Beach Culture magazine, *228*
Beardsley, Aubrey: illustrations and initials for *Le Morte d'Arthur*, *57*, *223*; *Salome* (Oscar Wilde), 194; *The Yellow Book*, 194
Beat literature, 86–91; and postwar youth culture, 90; prose style, 88
'Beatnik' archetype, 88
bebop music, 88
Beckett, Samuel, 75; *Imagination Dead Imagine*, *77*; *Waiting for Godot*, 76, *76*
Begin Ende Voortgangh, van de Vereenighde Nederlantsche Geoctroyeerde Oost-Indische Compagnie (Isaac Commelin), 143
Behrens, Peter, 'The Kiss', *224*
Bell, Andrew, 40
Belzoni, Giovanni Battista, *Narrative of the Operations and Recent Discoveries ...*, 139, *139*
Beowulf (epic poem), 56
Bhagavad-Gita ('Song of the Lord'), 27, 53
Bible: first printed editions, 32; German edition, *33*; King James Bible, 33, *33*; Koine Greek editions, 32; Martin Luther's edition, 32; New Testament, 32; Old Testament, 32; translation and interpretation of, 32; Tyndale's translations, 32–3; Vulgate, 32
bibliographies, 36
bibliophiles, 174
Bilder-atlas zu Mekka (Christiaan Snouck), 130
Bird (Kat Macleod; 3 Deep Design), *233*
Birds of America (John James Audubon), 167–8, *168*
Birds of Australia (John Gould), 167, *168*
Birds of Europe (John Gould), 167

Birds of Great Britain (John Gould), 167
'blackletter' script, 14
Blaeu, Joan, 148; *Nova et Accuratissima Totius Terrarum Orbis Tabula*, *147*; *Theatrum Orbis Terrarum (Atlas Novus)*, *147*, 148
Blahnik, Manolo, 85, *85*
Blake, William, 190: engravings for *The Complaint, and the Consolation, or, Night Thoughts* (Young), 190, 193; engravings for *The Grave* (Blair), 190, *190*; *Jerusalem*, 193; *The Marriage of Heaven and Hell*, 193
Blashill, Pat, *228*
Blast: a Review of the Great English Vortex (Wyndham Lewis), 71, *72*, 224, *225*
The Blessed Damozel (Dante Gabriel Rossetti), *205*
block books, 19
Boethius, *De Musica*, 10
Bonaparte, Napoleon, expedition to Egypt, 136
'Bonfires of the Vanities', 43
book collecting, 17
book design, 220–33; at introduction of printing, 221
book illustration in Japan, 182
Book of Dreams (Jack Kerouac), *91*
Book of Hours (*Horae*), 11, *12–13*, 14, *17*; calendars, 14; contents of, 14; *Horae in Laude Beatiss, Virginis Mariae, ad Usum Romanum*, *25*, *175*; *see also* prayer manuals
Book of Kells, 10
book trade, 11–12, 14
bookbinding: cover decoration, 174; decorative processes and ornamentation, 177; edging of pages, 174; gold tooling, 174; impact of printing press, 174; Islamic bindings, 174; Italian and French, 177; marbling of paper, 177–8; mechanised production, 177; pattern papers, *176*; prayer books and school texts, 174; process, 173; Renaissance French, *175*
books for entertainment, 14
Books of the Dead, 4, 27

Bordon, Benedetto, 24
Borges Bestiary (Milan Milojevic), *219*
botanical descriptions and illustrations, 161, *162*, 164
Bougainville, Louis-Antoine de, 144, 151
Brant, Sebastian, *The Ship of Fools* (Das Narrenschiff; Stultifera Navis), 58
Brazil, Robert, 'Experiments with Letters', *226*
Breydenbach, Bernhard von, *117*, 121; *Peregrinatio in Terram Sanctam*, 116, *117*, 121
Brody, Marc, 97, 99; see also Williams, WH
Brody, Neville, *228*, 229
Brown, Carter, 97, 99; see also Yates, Alan
Brown, Ford Madox, 201
Brunfels, Otto, *Herbarum Vivae Eicones*, 161, *162*
Brunhoff, Cécile de, *111*
Brunhoff, Jean de, 110; *Babar's Travels*, *111*; *L'Histoire de Babar* (The Story of Babar), *111*
Buck Rogers in the Year 2429 AD (comic strip; Philip Francis Nowlan & Dick Calkins), 94
Buck Rogers Special (comic series), *95*
Buddha (Tezuka Osamu), *100*, *101*
Buddhism, 27–8
Buddhist literature, 27–8
Burghers, Michael, *223*
Burne-Jones, Edward, 201, 203
Burroughs, William, 90; *Early Routines*, *91*; *Junkie, Confessions of an Unredeemed Drug Addict*, 88; *The Naked Lunch*, 88, *88*
Burton, Nathan, *84*
Burton, Richard, *Personal Narrative of a Pilgrimage to El-Medinah and Meccah*, 129–30, *130*, *130*

c

calligraphy, Arabic, 30, 32
Camerer, Joachim the Younger, *162*
Campi Phlegraei: Observations on the Volcanos of the Two Sicilies (Sir William Hamilton), 136, *136*

The Canterbury Tales (Geoffrey Chaucer), 23, 56, 59, *208*; Golden Cockerel edition, 208
Canton (China), 127
The Cantos (Ezra Pound), 76, *76*
Carey, Peter, cover designs by Jenny Grigg, *232*
caricature illustrations, 93
Carle, Roger, *177*
Carmen sur le Texte de Prosper Mérimée (Pablo Picasso), *195*
Carolingian script, *10*, 10–11
Carroll, Lewis (Rev Charles Dodgson), *Alice's Adventures in Wonderland*, 106, 109, *109*
Carson, David, *228*, 229
cartoons: political, 93; see also comics and pulp fiction
Caslon, William IV, 222
Cassady, Neal, 88, 90
Cavalieri, Angela: *INRI*, 212, *212*; –*1316*, 212, *213*
Caxton, William, 20; printer's device, *21*; printing of *Aesop's Fables*, 106; printing of *Le Morte d'Arthur*, 56; printing of *Myrrour of the World*, 21, 23; printing of *The Canterbury Tales*, 56, 59; printing quality, 23; publishing in English, 23; *Receuils des Histoires de Troye*, 23; translation of texts, 23
Cendrars, Blaise, 'La Prose du Transsibérien et de la Petite Jehanne de France', 211
censorship, 43, 73, 87, 88
Cérémonies et Coutumes Religieuses de Tous les Peuples du Monde, 28
Cervantes, Miguel de, *Don Quixote*, 59, *59*
chained books, 174
Champollion, Jean-François, 4, 136
Le Charivari (French satirical magazine), 93
Chaucer, Geoffrey: *The Canterbury Tales*, 56, 59, *208*; *The Workes of Geffray Chaucer*, *57*; *The Works of Geoffrey Chaucer*, *202*, 203
children's books, 104–11; see also picture books
China, accounts of, 127

Chinese picture writing, 7
Chinese poetry and philosophy, 53
Chinese script, 7
Christianity, 9, 28, 32–3
Christie, Agatha, *The Mysterious Affair at Styles*, 80
The Christmas-Box, or, the Golden Play-Thing for Little Children, 105
City Lights Books, 87
City Lights bookstore (San Francisco), 87
Civilization and Its Discontents (cover design David Pearson), *83*
classification of natural world, principles of, 151, 163–4
clay tablets/tokens, 3, 7
A Clockwork Orange (cover design David Pelham), *82*
Clowes, Daniel: *Ghost World*, 102; *Ice Haven*, 102
Cobden-Sanderson, Thomas J, 177, 205
Cochin, Charles-Nicolas, 190
Cockerell, Douglas, 177
Code of Hammurabi, 4
codex, 9, 173
Colonna, Francesco, 24, 221; *Hypnerotomachia Poliphili*, 24, *222*
Colors magazine, *229*
Columbus, Christopher, 141
Comelius, Johann Amos, *Orbis Sensualium Pictus* (The Visible World in Pictures), 105–6
comic artists, 99
comic book series: *Buck Rogers*, 95; *Famous Funnies*, 94; *Mad*, 99; *The Phantom Commando*, 95; self-censorship, 99; *Silver Starr*, 96; *Spider-Man*, 99; *Tintin*, 94; see also manga
comic strips, 93–4; *Buck Rogers in the Year 2429 AD*, 94; 'Golden Age', 94; *Hogan's Alley*, 93; *Tarzan*, 93–4
comics and pulp fiction, 92–103
Commelin, Isaac, *143*; *Begin Ende Voortgangh, van de Vereenighde Nederlantsche Geoctroyeerde Oost-Indische Compagnie*, *143*

Commentarii (Pietro Andrea Mattioli), 163
commercial art, 226
The Complaint, and the Consolation, or, Night Thoughts (Edward Young; illus by William Blake), 190, 193
Confessions of a Sinner (cover design Catherine Dixon), *83*
Cook, Capt James, 151; second voyage, 151–2, *152*; third voyage, *153*; *A Voyage to the Pacific Ocean, Undertaken …*, *153*; *A Voyage towards the South Pole, and Round the World*, *152*
Copernicus, Nicolaus, *De Revolutionibus Orbium Coelestium* (On the Revolutions of the Celestial Spheres), 45
costume books, 127
The Costume of China (George Henry Mason), *127*
Couperin, François, *Oeuvres Complètes de François Couperin*, 177
cover design, 79, 80–5, *81*, *232–3*
cover designers, examples of work: Ron Arad, *85*; Phil Baines, *83*; Manolo Blahnik, *85*; Nathan Burton, *84*; Catherine Dixon, *83*; Germano Facetti, *81*, 81–2; Jim Friedman, *84*; Fuel (Stephen Sorel & Damon Murray), *85*; Kate Gibb, *84*; Jenny Grigg, *232*; Chip Kidd, *233*; Ruslana Lyzchicko, *84*; Romek Marber, *81*; David Pelham, *82*; Sheila Perry, *81*; Hans Schmoller, *81*; Andrew Smith, *84*; Paul Smith, *85*; Art Spiegelman, *85*; Sam Taylor-Wood, *85*; Jan Tschichold, 81, *81*
Cranach, 205
Crane, Walter, *Puss in Boots*, 107
Crombie, John, 208
Crome Yellow (Aldous Huxley), *80*
Cromek, Robert, 190
Cruikshank, George, 106
Crumb, Robert, 99; 'Mr Natural' *(Odds and Ends)*, *99*
cuneiform tablet, *4*
cuneiform writing, 3; decipherment of, 4

Curwen Press, *176*
Cuvier, Georges, 158

d

da Vinci, Leonardo: *Traitté de la Peinture de Leonard de Vinci*, 46
Dada Kampfen um Leben und Tod: a Prose Poem (Jas H Duke), 209
Daniell, Thomas, *Oriental Scenery: Twenty-Four Views in Hindoostan*, *128*
Dante: *La Divina Commedia* (Divine Comedy), 55–6; *The Vision of Hell*, *192*
Darwin, Charles, 158; *On the Origin of Species by Means of Natural Selection*, 45, *47*
Das Kapital: Kritik der Politischen Oekonomie (Karl Marx), *47*
de Beauvoir, Simone, *Le Deuxième Sexe* (The Second Sex), *48*
De Dissectione Partium Corporis Humani (Charles Estienne), *37*
De Humani Corporis Fabrica (Andreas Vesalius), *37*
De Materia Medica (Pedanius Dioscorides), 161
De Re Metallica (Georgius Agricola), 36, *37*, 39
De Revolutionibus Orbium Coelestium (On the Revolutions of the Celestial Spheres; Nicolaus Copernicus), 45
Decline and Fall (Evelyn Waugh), *80*
La Découverte Australe par un Homme-Volant (Restif de la Bretonne), *69*
Defective Part (Dale Nason), *230*
Defoe, Daniel, *The Life and Strange Surprizing Adventures of Robinson Crusoe*, 64
Delaunay, Sonia, 211
deluxe illustrated books, 194
Denkmäler aus Aegypten und Aethiopien (Karl Richard Lepsius), *138*, 139
D'Entrecasteaux, Bruny, 154, *155*
Derain, André, *195*
Derrière le Miroir (Aime Maeght), *197*, *198*

Desceliers, Pierre, World Map 1550, *144*
The Descent of Ishtar (Diana White), *204*
Description de l'Egypte (Edmé-François Jomard), *136*, *138*
Description des Plantes Rares Cultivées à Malmaison (Pierre-Joseph Redouté), 167
destruction of books, 43, 73
detchōsō (Japanese 'butterfly binding'), 182
Le Deuxième Sexe (The Second Sex; Simone de Beauvoir), *48*
Devantures de Boutiques (L-P Sezille), *226*
d'Hancarville, Pierre, *Antiquités Etrusques, Grecques et Romaines*, 136, *137*
The Dharma Bums (Jack Kerouac), 87, *90*
Dialogo Sopra i Due Massimi Sistemi del Mondo, Tolemaico e Copernicano (Dialogue Concerning the Two Chief World Systems, Ptolemaic and Copernican; Galileo Galilei), 45
Dias, Bartolomeu, 141
dictionaries of English language, 40
A Dictionary of the English Language (Dr Samuel Johnson), 40, *40*
Diderot, Denis, *Encyclopédie, ou, Dictionnaire Raisonné des Sciences, des Artes et des Métiers*, 38, 39, 151, 174
Dioscorides, Pedanius, *De Materia Medica*, 161
La Divina Commedia (Divine Comedy; Dante), 55–6, *56*
Dixon, Catherine, 83
Dodgson, Rev Charles; see Carroll, Lewis
Don Quixote (Miguel de Cervantes), 59, *59*
Doré, Gustave, *192*, 193–4
Dorgelès, Roland, *Montmartre Mon Pays*, 176
Doslov, Nick, *179*
Doves Bindery, 177
Doves Press, *The English Bible*, 205, *207*
Doyle, A Conan, *The Hound of the Baskervilles*, 80
Drawing (Bruno Leti & Chris Wallace-Crabbe), 215, *215*
Dreadful Summit (cover design Germano Facetti), *81*
Drucker, Johanna, 211
Duke, Jas H, *Dada Kampfen um Leben und Tod: a Prose Poem*, 209
Dulac, Edmund, *Sindbad the Sailor and Other Stories From the Arabian Nights*, 108
Dunn, Des R, 99
Dürer, Albrecht, 23; *The Apocalypse*, 189, *191*
d'Urville, Dumont, 158
Dutch East India Company, 125, 146, 181
Duyfken (Dutch ship), 146
Dyer, Louise BM, *177*

e

e-iribon (Japanese illustrated books), 184
e-zines, 230
Early Routines (William Burroughs), *91*
East Indies: accounts of, 146; exploration of, 144; maps and atlases depict, 146; new route to, 147, 149
ebrû (marbling technique), *178*
The Eclogues of Vergil, 205
Éditions de l'Oiseau-Lyre, *Oeuvres Complètes de François Couperin*, 176
éditions-de-luxe, 194
Edo meisho zue, *182*
Edo (Tokugawa) period (Japan), 181
Eggers, Dave, *230*
Egypt, accounts of, 136, 139
Egyptian hieroglyphic script, 4, 5, *137*
Egyptology, 136, *137*, 139
Ehret, Georg, *Hortus Cliffortianus*, 164, *164*
Eisner, Will, *A Contract with God and Other Tenement Stories*, 100
electronic publishing, 208
elementary schools, 105
Eliot, TS: 'The Waste Land', 71; *The Waste Land*, 73

Ellroy, James, *White Jazz*, *233*
emakimono (Japanese books), 100, 181
embellished initials and letters, 9
Emigre magazine, 229
Empty Mirror (Allen Ginsberg), *91*
L'Enchanteur Pourrissant (Guillaume Apollinaire), *195*
Encyclopædia Britannica, 40, *41*
encyclopedia: Arabic, 35; Greek and Roman, 35
Encyclopédie, ou, Dictionnaire Raisonné des Sciences, des Artes et des Métiers (Denis Diderot), *38*, 39, 151
L'Encyclopédie Méthodique ou par Ordre de Matières par une Société de Gens de Lettres, de Savants et d'Artistes, 39, *174*
The English Bible (Doves Press), 205, *207*
Epic of Gilgamesh, 4
epics, 53
Eragny Press, 205
Erté (Romain de Tirtoff), 226
Essex House Press, 205
Estienne, Charles, *De Dissectione Partium Corporis Humani*, *37*
Etisoppo, 231
European expeditions of discovery, 124–31, 140–8
Evans, Edmund, 109

f

fables, 106
Fables Choisies, Mises en Vers (de La Fontaine; illus by Jean-Baptiste Oudry), 189–90, *190*
The Face magazine, 228, 229
Facetti, Germano, *81*, 81–2
fairytales, 106
Famous Funnies (comic book series), 94
'Fantastic Alphabet' (Geofroy Tory), *222*
The Farewell Party (cover design Andrzej Klimowski), *82*
A Farewell to Arms (Ernest Hemingway), *80*
Feather and Prey (Peter Lyssiotis), *179*, 212, *213*

The Female Eunuch (Germaine Greer), 47, 49, *49*
Ferlinghetti, Lawrence, 87
Fine, Oronce, 141
Finnegan's Wake (James Joyce), 75
Fiore, Quentin, *The Medium is the Massage*, 49
Flamsteed, John, *Atlas Coelestis*, 122, *123*
Les Fleurs du Mal (Charles Baudelaire), *177*
Flinders, Matthew, *Voyage to Terra Australis*, 155
Florilegium (Joseph Banks), *168*, 169
Foigny, Gabriel de: *Sehr Curiöse Reise-Beschreibung Durch das-Neu-Entdeckte Südland*, *67*; *La Terra Australe Connue*, 66
Foster, Harold (Hal), *Tarzan* (comic strip), 93–4
Foxe's Book of Martyrs (*Actes and Monuments of these Latter and Perillous Days, Touching Matters of the Church;* John Foxe), 32
Frénaud, André, *La Nourriture du Bourreau*, 199
Freud, Sigmund, *Gesammelte Schriften* (Collected Writings), 47
Freycinet, Louis-Claude de, 158; *Voyage Autour du Monde*, 158
Freycinet, Rose, 158
Friedman, Jim, *84*
Fuchs, Leonhard: *De Historia Stirpium Commenetearii Insignes*, 161, *162*, 163; *New Kreütterbuch*, *162*
Fuel (Stephen Sorel & Damon Murray), 85, *85*
Fugaku hyakkei (Katsushika Hokusai), *187*
fukuro-toji (Japanese 'bag' binding), 182, 184, *184*
'furniture' (bookbinding), 173–4
Fust, Johann, 19, 20

g

Galilei, Galileo: *Dialogo Sopra i Due Massimi Sistemi del Mondo, Tolemaico e Copernicano* (Dialogue Concerning the Two Chief World Systems, Ptolemaic and Copernican), 45

Gama, Vasco da, 141
Gazu hyakkachō (Paintings of One Hundred Flowers and Birds, Kanō Tan'yū), 186, *186*
Gedenkwaerdige Gesantschappen (Memorable Embassies; Arnoldus Montanus), 125, *126*
Gekiga ('dramatic pictures'), 100
Genji monogatari (Tale of Genji; Murasaki Shikibu), 53, 54, 55
Geographia (Ptolemy), 115, *143*
George, Alexander S, *The Banksias*, 168
Gesammelte Schriften (Collected Writings; Sigmund Freud), 47
Gesner, Konrad: *Historiae Animalium*, 121, 163, *219*; *Historiae Plantarum*, *162*
Ghost World (Daniel Clowes), *102*
Gibb, Kate, *84*
Gibbings, Robert, 208
Gibbon, Edward, *History of the Decline and Fall of the Roman Empire*, 136
Gibson, Walter B, *The Shadow* series, 94
Gill, Eric, 205, 208, *223*, 226
Ginsberg, Allen: *Empty Mirror*, *91*; *The Fall of America: Poems of these States 1965–1971*, 90; 'Howl', 87; *Howl and Other Poems*, 88
Girodias, Maurice, 88
Golden Cockerel Press, 208; *The Canterbury Tales*, 208
Gonneville, Paulmier de, 141
gospel books, 10
Gothic script, 11
Gould, John: *Birds of Australia*, 167–8, *168*; *Birds of Europe*, 167–8; *Birds of Great Britain*, 167–8; *The Mammals of Australia*, 167–8, *169*; *Synopsis of the Birds of Australia and the Adjacent Islands*, 168
'Grand Tour', 133
Il Grande Diabolik, *102*
Grant, Maxwell; *see* Gibson, Walter B
graphic design, 220–33; computers and desktop publishing, 229; digital age, 229; industrial revolution, 222; role in book, 221; 1960s and 1970s, 226; 1930s to 1950s, 226; text design, 221

graphic novel, 100, 103
The Grave (Robert Blair; engravings by William Blake), 190
Greek classics, editions of, 23
Greene, Graham, *It's a Battlefield*, 80
Greer, Germaine, *The Female Eunuch*, 47, 49, *49*
Griffo, Francesco, 23, 24, 221; *Hypnerotomachia Poliphili*, 24, *222*
Grigg, Jenny, *232*
Grimm, Jacob & Wilhelm, *Kinder- und Hausmärchen* (Childhood and Household Tales; German Popular Stories), 106
Grindlay, Robert Melville, *Scenery, Costumes and Architecture Chiefly on the Western Side of India*, 128
Guest in the House (cover design Germano Facetti), *81*
Gulliver's Travels (Jonathan Swift), 63
Gutenberg, Johann, 19–20, *20*
Gutenberg Bible, 19–20, *20*, 32

h

Haas, Charles, *The Beat Generation* (movie), 90
Hall, Bp Joseph, *Mundus Alter et Idem*, 63, *64*
Hamilton, Sir William, 133, 136; *Campi Phlegraei: Observations on the Volcanos of the Two Sicilies*, 136, *136*
Hammett, Dashiell, *The Thin Man*, 80
Haring, Don, 99
Harry Potter series (JK Rowling), 110
Hartog, Dirk, 148
Hawaiian Islands, 152
Hemingway, Ernest, *A Farewell to Arms*, 80
Henderson, Peter, 167
Henry the Navigator, Prince, 141
herbals, illustrations in, 161, 163
Herbarum Vivae Eicones (Otto Brunfels), 161, *162*
Hergé; *see* Remi, Georges
The Hermit, or, the Unparalled Sufferings and Surprising Adventures of Mr Philip Quarll,

an Englishman (Peter Longueville), 64, 66
Herrschaft und Dienst (Friedrich Wolters), *206*
Hevelius, Johannes, *Selenographia*, 122, *122*
Hindu literature, 27
L'Histoire des Severambes (Denis Vairasse d'Allais), 66, 68, *68*
Histoire Naturelle, Générale et Particuliére (Georges Louis Leclerc), 151
Histoires ou Contes du Temps Passé (Charles Perrault), 106
Historia Animalium (On the History of Animals; Aristotle), 161
Historia Naturalis (Pliny 'the Elder'), 35
Historia Plantarum (Theophrastus), 161
De Historia Stirpium Commenetarii Insignes (Leonhard Fuchs), 161, *162*, 163
Historiae Animalium (Konrad Gesner), 121, 163
Historiae Naturalis de Piscibus et Cetis (John Johnston), *121*
Historiae Naturalis de Quadrupedibus (John Johnston), 121, *121*, 163, *163*
The Historie of Foure-footed Beastes (Edward Topsell), *121*, 163
The History of Four-Footed Beasts and Serpents (Edward Topsell), 121, *121*
History of Little Goody Two-Shoes (John Newbery), 106
History of the Decline and Fall of the Roman Empire (Edward Gibbon), 136
History of the Horn-book, 106
The Hobbit (JRR Tolkien), 56
Hodges, William, 152
Hogan's Alley (The Yellow Kid; comic strip, RF Outcault), 93
Hogarth Press, 71, 73; *see also* Woolf, Leonard; Woolf, Virginia
Hokusai, Katsushika, 100; *Fugaku hyakkei* (One Hundred Views of Mount Fuji), 186, *187*; *Hokusai manga* ('random and whimsical sketches'), 186, *187*; *Katsushika shinsō gafu*, *183*

Hokusai manga (Katsushika Hokusai), *186*, *187*
Holy Land, accounts of, 129
Holy Land: Syria, Idumea, Arabia, Egypt & Nubia (David Roberts), *139*
Homer, *The Iliad*, 55
Hondius, Jocodus, *144*
Hooke, Robert, *Micrographia*, 122, *122*
Hooper, William H, 203
Horae in Laude Beatiss, Virginis Mariae, ad Usum Romanum (Book of Hours), *25*, *175*
'horn books', 105, *106*
Hornby, CH St John, 205
Hortus Cliffortianus (Carl Linnaeus, Georg Ehret), 164
Hortus Nitidissimis Omnem per Annum Superbiens Floribus (Christoph Jacob Trew), 164
The Hound of the Baskervilles (A Conan Doyle), *80*
The House of the Arrow (cover design Romek Marber), *81*
'Howl' (Allen Ginsberg), 87
Howl and Other Poems (Allen Ginsberg), *88*
Hoyem, Andrew, 198
Hudson, Mike, 208
Humanism, 17
Humanist script, 17
Hurgronje, Christiaan Snouck, *Bilder-atlas zu Mekka*, 130
Huxley, Aldous, *Crome Yellow*, *80*
Hypnerotomachia Poliphili, 24, *24*, 221, *222*

i

I Am Prepared to Die (Nelson Mandela), *48*
Ice Haven (Daniel Clowes), *102*
Icones Arborum, Fruticum et Herbarum (Pieter van der Aa), *120*
The Iliad of Homer, 55
illuminated manuscripts, 8–17, 221
illuminators, 24
illustrated books, collaboration with artists and writers, 197, 198, 215
Illustrationes Florae Novae Hollandiae (Ferdinand Bauer), *167*, *167*
illustrations: accompaniment to text, 189
illustrators of books for children, 106
imaginary voyages in literature, 62–9
Imagination Dead Imagine (Samuel Beckett), *77*
Index Librorum Prohibitorum (Index of Prohibited Books), 43, 45
India, accounts of, *128*
INRI (Angela Cavalieri), 212, *212*
'insular manuscripts', 10
internet as source of knowledge, 40
Iohn Hvighen van Linschoten, His Discours of Voyages into ye Easte & West Indies (Jan Huyghen van Linschoten), *146*
Iron Age (Bruno Leti & Chris Wallace-Crabbe), 215
Islam, 28, 29, 30–2
Islamic manuscripts, 11
The Isle of Pines, or, a Late Discovery of a Fourth Island near Terra Australis (Henry Neville), 64, 66, *66*
Italy, accounts of, 136
Itinerario, Voyage ofte Schipvaert van Jan Huygen van Linschoten naar Ost (Jan Huyghen van Linschoten), 146
It's a Battlefield (Graham Greene), *80*

j

Janeway, James, *Token for Children*, 105
Japan: accounts of, *127*; class system, 181–2; Dutch traders' accounts of, 125; Edo period books, 180–7; printing technologies, 182; printmaking, 182
Japanese books: covers, 184; *detchōsō* ('butterfly binding'), 182; *emakimono*, 181; *fukuro-toji* ('bag' binding), 182, 184; genres, 184; illustrated, 184; *kansubon*, 181; *orihon*, 182; reproductions by famous artists, 184, 186
Japanese comics *(manga)*, 99–100
Japanese script, 7
Japonisme style, 222, 224
Jardin de la Malmaison (Pierre-Joseph Redouté), 167
Jarvis, Jadwiga, 208
Java la Grande, 143–4, *144*

Jazz (Henri Matisse), 211
Jenson, Nicolaus, 23, 221
Jerusalem (William Blake), 193
Jimmy Corrigan, the Smartest Kid on Earth (Chris Ware), *103*
Johnson, Dr Samuel, *A Dictionary of the English Language*, 40
Johnston, Edward, 224
Johnston, John, 121; *Historiae Naturalis de Piscibus et Cetis*, *121*; *Historiae Naturalis de Quadrupedibus*, 121, 163, *163*
Jomard, Edmé-François, *Description de l'Egypte*, 136, *138*
Jones, Nicholas, *Medallion*, 218
Josephine, Empress, 167
Jourdain, Francis, 226
A Journal of a Voyage to the South Seas, in His Majesty's Ship, the Endeavour (Sydney Parkinson), 152
Journey of a Wise Electron (Peter Lyssiotis), 212
Joy and Josephine (cover design Hans Schmoller), *81*
Joyce, James: *Finnegan's Wake*, 75; *Ulysses*, 73, 74, *75*, 198, *199*; *Work in Progress*, 75
Judaism, 28–30

k

kabuki theatre, 182
Kachō-ga (Japanese flower and bird illustration), 185
Kalman, Tibor, *229*
Kanō school, 186
Kanō Tan'yū, 186; *Gazu hyakkachō*, *186*
kansubon (Japanese books), 181
Katsushika Hokusai, 100; *Fugaku hyakkei*, 186, *187*; *Hokusai manga*, 186, *187*; *Katsushika shinsō gafu*, *183*
Kawamura Bunpō, *Kinpaen gafu*, *183*
Kelmscott Press, 201, 203; *A Note by William Morris on His Aims in Founding the Kelmscott Press*, 203; *see also* Morris, William
Kenner, Hugh, 76
Kerouac, Jack: *Book of Dreams*, 91; *The Dharma Bums*, 87, 90, *90*; 'Essentials of Spontaneous Prose', 88; *On the Road*, 88, *89*; *Scattered Poems*, 91; *The Subterraneans*, 90; *The Subterraneans* (film version), 90; *Tristessa*, 90, *90*
Kessler, Count Harry, 205
kibyōshi (Japanese literary genre), 100
Kickshaws Press, 208
Kidd, Chip, *233*
kimono fabric design, 186
King, Martin Luther, 49
Kircher, Athanasius, *Oedipus Aegyptiacus*, 137
'The Kiss' (Peter Behrens), *224*
Ko-Ko (Allan Mitelman, Lyre-Bird Press), 216–17
Koberger, Anton, 23, *33*; *Liber Chronicarum* (Nuremberg Chronicle), *22*, 23; *Schatzbehalter*, 22, 23
Koelhoff, Johann, 20
Kotzebue, Otto von, 158
Kruzenshtern, Ivan Fedorovich, *Atlas K Puteshestvie Vokrug Sveta*, 158, *159*
kufic script, 30
Die Kunstismen 1914–1924 (El Lissitzky), *225*
Kusikov, Aleksandr, *Ptitsa Bezymiannaia: Izbrannye Stikhi 1917–1921*, *225*

l

La Fontaine, Jean de, 106, 189, *190*
La Pérouse, Jean-François de Galaup de, 154, *155*; *Voyage de La Pérouse Autour du Monde*, 154
Labillardière, Jacques-Julien Houtou de: *Novae Hollandiae Plantarum*, 167; *Relation du Voyage à la Recherche de La Pérouse*, 155
landscape art, 193
Lane, Allen: launch of Penguin paperbacks, 79
languages: Akkadian, 3; English, 59; Italian, 56; Latin, 23; vernacular, 14, 23, 163
Lao-tzu, *Tao-te Ching*, 53
Larry Kent series, *97*, 99
Lascaux, cave paintings, 161
Le Bruyn, Corneille, *A Voyage to the Levant: or Travels in the Principal Parts of Asia Minor*, 128–9

Le Maire, Jacob, 148
Leclerc, Georges Louis, *Histoire Naturelle, Générale et Particuliére*, 151
The Legends of Moonie Jarl (Olga Miller & Wilf Reeves), 110
Lepsius, Karl Richard, *Denkmäler aus Aegypten und Aethiopien*, 138, *139*
Leti, Bruno, *Drawing*, 215, *215*
Lévy, Albert, 226
Lewis, James Otto, *The Aboriginal Portfolio*, 130, *130*
Lewis, Wyndham, 224; *The Apes of God*, 71, *73*; *Blast: a Review of the Great English Vortex*, 71, *72*, 224, *225*
Liber Chronicarum ('Chronicle of the World', Nuremberg Chronicle; Hartmann Schedel, Anton Koberger), *22*, 23, 36, *36*, 64, 116, *117*
Liber Studiorum (JMW Turner), 193, *193*
Library of Alexandria, 34
Licko, Zuzana, 229
The Life and Strange Surprizing Adventures of Robinson Crusoe (Daniel Defoe), 64
Light in August (cover design Hans Schmoller), *81*
Les Liliacées (Pierre-Joseph Redouté), *166*, 167
Linnaeus, Carl, 151; *Hortus Cliffortianus*, 164; *Systema Naturae*, 163
Linschoten, Jan Huyghen van: *Iohn Hvighen van Linschoten, His Discours of Voyages into ye Easte & West Indies*, 146; *Itinerario, Voyage ofte Schipvaert van Jan Huygen van Linschoten naar Ost*, 146
Lissitzky, El, 224, *225*, 226; *Die Kunstismen 1914–1924*, 224, *225*, 226
literary foundations, 52–61
lithographs, 196
lithography and Arabic script, 32
livres d'artiste, 194, 197, 211
Lodewijcksz, Willem, *Prima Pars Descriptionis Itineris Navalis in Indiam Orientalem*, 147
longitude, 148
Longueville, Peter, *The Hermit, or, the Unparalled Sufferings and Surprising Adventures of Mr Philip Quarll, an Englishman*, 64, 66
The Lost Thing (Shaun Tan), *111*
Luther, Martin, 32, *44*
Lyre-Bird Press, 216–17
Lyssiotis, Peter: *–1316*, 212, *213*; *Feather and Prey*, 179, 212, *213*; *Journey of a Wise Electron*, 212; *The Products of Wealth*, 212
Lyzchicko, Ruslana, *84*

m

Macfarquhar, Colin, 40
Macleod, Kat, *Bird*, *233*
Mafatih al-Ulum (Arabic encyclopedia), 35
Magellan, Ferdinand, 122, 141
maghribi script, *31*
Mahabharata (Indian epic), 27, 53
Maillol, Aristide, 205, *205*
Major, Thomas, *The Ruins of Paestum, otherwise Posidonia, in Magna Graecia*, 135
The Making of Americans (Gertrude Stein), 75, *75*
Makura, Shō, *Jigoku sensei nūbē*, *100*
Mallarmé, Stéphane, 'Un Coup de Dés Jamais n'Abolira le Hasard', 211
Malory, Sir Thomas: *The Canterbury Tales*, 56, *57*; *Le Morte d'Arthur … (The Birth, Life and Acts of King Arthur …)*, 56, *57*
The Mammals of Australia (John Gould), 167–8, *169*
Mandela, Nelson, *I Am Prepared to Die*, *48*
manga (Japanese comics), 99–100; cinematic techniques, 100; origins, 100; sales in the West, 103; term first coined, 100
manuscript production, 14, 17
manuscripts, survival of, 17
Manutius, Aldus, 23–4, 221, *222*; *Hypnerotomachia Poliphili*, 24, *24*, 221
Mao Zedong, *Quotations from Chairman Mao Tse-Tung* ('The Little Red Book'), 47, *49*
maps: *see* world maps
Marber, Romek, *81*, *84*
marbling of paper, 177–8
Mari, clay tablet collection, *4*
The Marriage of Heaven and Hell (William Blake), 193
Martin, Peter, 87
Martinelli, Patricia, *Il Grande Diabolik*, *102*
Maruyama Ōkyo, *Ōkyo gafu*, *186*
Maruyama-Shijō school of painting, *186*
Marx, Karl, 49; *Das Kapital: Kritik der Politischen Oekonomie*, 47, *47*
Mason, Maj George Henry, *The Costume of China*, 127, *127*
Matisse, Henri, *197*; *Jazz*, 211
Mattioli, Pietro Andrea: *Commentarii*, 163; *De Plantis Epitome Utilissima*, *162*
Maus II: a Survivor's Tale: and Here my Troubles Began (Art Spiegelman), 103, *103*
Mayan inscriptions, *7*
McCall, KT, *The Lady's a Decoy*, *98*; *see also* Armitage, Audrey; Watkins, Muriel
McLuhan, Marshall, *The Medium is the Massage*, 49, *49*
McSweeney's literary journal, *230*
Mecca, accounts of, 130
Medallion (Nicholas Jones), *218*
Mediaeval Sinhalese Art (Ananda K Coomaraswamy), *28*
medicinal properties of plants, 161
medieval bestiary, 163
The Medium is the Massage (Marshall McLuhan), 49, *49*
Meiji Restoration, 186
meisho zue, *182*
Mercator, Gerhard, 143; *Atlas Minor Gerardi Mercatoris*, *144*
Merian, Matthäus, 121
Meurs, Jacob van, 125, *127*
Meyer, Albrecht, 162
Micrographia (Robert Hooke), 122, *122*
Middle East, accounts of, 129
Miller, Frank: *Batman: the Dark Knight Returns*, 103
Miller, Olga, *The Legends of Moonie Jarl*, 110
Miller, William, *The Costume of Great Britain*, 127, *129*
Milne, AA, *Winnie-the-Pooh*, 109–10, *110*
Milojevic, Milan, *Borges Bestiary*, *219*
Milton, John, *Paradise Lost: a Poem in Twelve Books*, 60, *61*
miniature books, *40*
mining and metallurgy, references on, 36, 39
Miró, Joan, *198*
Mitelman, Allan, *Ko-Ko* (Lyre-Bird Press), 216–17
modernist literature, 70–7
monastic scribes, 9
monstrous beings, accounts of, 116
Montanus, Arnoldus, *Gedenkwaerdige Gesantschappen* (Memorable Embassies), 125, *126*
Montmartre Mon Pays (Roland Dorgelès), *176*
Morison, Stanley, 208, 226
Morris, William, 222; Kelmscott Press, 201, 203; 'The Ideal Book', 203; typefaces, 201, 203; *The Works of Geoffrey Chaucer*, *202*, 203, *203*
Le Morte d'Arthur (Sir Thomas Malory), *57*, 223
Mother Goose: The Old Nursery Rhymes (illustrator Arthur Rackham), *109*
Mother Goose's Melody (John Newbery), 106
Motherwell, Robert, 198, *199*
Muir, Ann, *Harvesting Colour: the Year in a Marbler's Workshop*, 178
Mundus Alter et Idem (Bp Joseph Hall), 63, *64*
Murasaki Shikibu, *Genji monogatari* (Tale of Genji), 53, *54*, 55
Murder Plan Six (cover design Sheila Perry), *81*
Muslim culture, accounts of, 129–30
Muslim scholarship, 11
Myrrour of the World (William Caxton), *21*, 23

The Mysterious Affair at Styles (Agatha Christie), *80*
myths and legends, 56

n

Nakabayashi Chikudō; *Yūsai kachō gafu*, *185*
The Naked Lunch (William Burroughs), 88, *88*
Naples, accounts of, 133
Narrative of the Operations and Recent Discoveries … (Giovanni Battista Belzoni), 139, *139*
narratives: oral origins of, 53; reinterpretation of, 53
Nason, Dale, *Defective Part*, *230*
natural history, 160–9
The Natural History of Aleppo (Alexander Russell), 129, *129*
Née, Luis, 158
neoclassical era, 133
Nesumi Takenosuke, *Somemoyo hinagata: nakadachi kodachi*, *186*
Die Neue Typographie (Jan Tschichold), 226
Neville, Henry, *The Isle of Pines, or, a Late Discovery of a Fourth Island near Terra Australis*, 64, 66, *66*
Neville, Richard, 226
The New-England Primer, 105, *106*
New Hebrides, 146
New Illustration of the Sexual System of Carolus von Linnaeus (Robert John Thornton), *167*
New Kreüterbuch (Leonhard Fuchs), *162*
New Zealand, 148, 151
Newbery, John: *History of Little Goody Two-Shoes*, 106; *A Little Pretty Pocket-Book*, 106; *Mother Goose's Melody*, 106
Newton, Isaac, *Philosophiae Nataualis Principia Mathematica* (The Mathematical Principles of Natural Philosophy), 45, *45*
Night Flight (Antoine de Saint-Exupéry), *80*
'95 Theses' (Martin Luther), *44*
Nineveh, library of clay tablets, 4
Nippon: Archiv zur Beschreibung von Japan (Philipp Franz von Siebold), *127*

North America, accounts of, 130
North-West Passage, 152
La Nourriture du Bourreau (André Frénaud), *199*
Nova et Accuratissima Totius Terrarum Orbis Tabula (Joan Blaeu), *147*
Novae Hollandiae Plantarum (Jacques-Julien Houtou de Labillardière), 167
Nuremberg Chronicle (*Liber Chronicarum*), 22, 23, 36, *37*, 64, 116, *117*
Nuremberg (Germany), 23
nursery rhymes, 106

o

obscenity, American law on, 88
Oedipus Aegyptiacus (Athanasius Kircher), *137*
Okano, Takeshi, *Jigoku sensei nūbē*, *100*
Oeuvres Complètes de François Couperin (Éditions de l'Oiseau-Lyre), *177*
Ōkyo gafu (Maruyama Ōkyo), *86*
On Art and Life (cover design David Pearson), *83*
On the Origin of Species by Means of Natural Selection (Charles Darwin), 45, *47*
Opera (Virgil), 56
'oracle bones' (Chinese script), 7
Orbis Maritimus (Frederick de Wit), *148*
Orbis Sensualium Pictus (The Visible World in Pictures; Johann Amos Comelius), 105–6
Oriental Scenery: Twenty-Four Views in Hindoostan (Thomas Daniell), *128*
Orientaliora Indiarum Orientalium (Frederick de Wit), *148*
orihon (Japanese books), 182
ornithological books, 167–8
Ortelius, Abraham, *Theatrum Orbis Terrarum*, 36, *36*, 116, *118–19*, 143, *145*
Oudry, Jean-Baptiste, *Fables Choisies, Mises en Vers* (de La Fontaine), 189–90, *190*
*Our Exagmination Round his Factification for Incamination

of Work in Progress*, 75
Outcault, RF, *Hogan's Alley* (*The Yellow Kid*), 93
Oxford English Dictionary, 40
Oz magazine, 226, *227*

p

Pacific Ocean: French voyages to, 154, 158; Russian voyages to, 158; Spanish voyages to, 158
Pagemaker, 229
paper: choice of in Japan, 182; first used for books in Europe, 174; handmade, 201; scroll format, 28
paper making, 11; Chinese and Japanese techniques, 28, 181
paperback books, 78–85
papyrus, 7, *7*, 9, 27
Paradise Lost: a Poem in Twelve Books (John Milton), 60, *61*
Parallèlement (Ambrose Vollard), *194*
parchment, 9, 173
Parkinson, Sydney, *A Journal of a Voyage to the South Seas, in His Majesty's Ship, the Endeavour*, 152
Pearson, David, *83*
Pelham, David, *82*
Pellion, Alphonse, *158*
Penguin Books: cover design, 79, 81–5; first paperback books, 79; Great Ideas series, 82; Harmondsworth premises, 79; imprints, 79, 81; King Penguin series, 82; 'Penguin Composition Rules', 81; Penguin Designer Classics, 85; Penguin Graphic Classics, 85; penguin logo, 79; Pocket Penguin paperbacks, 82, 85; typography and cover design, 82
Péron, François, *Voyages de Découvertes aux Terres Australes*, 155, *155*, 156–7
Perrault, Charles, *Histoires ou Contes du Temps Passé*, 106
Perry, Sheila, *81*
Personal Narrative of a Pilgrimage to El-Medinah and Meccah (Richard Burton), 129–30, *130*
Petrarch, Francesco, 17
Pfister, Albrecht, 20

The Phantom Commando (comic series), 95
Philippines, exploration of, 144
Philosophiae Nataualis Principia Mathematica (The Mathematical Principles of Natural Philosophy; Isaac Newton), 45
Phoenician alphabetic script, 4–6
Phoenician civilisation, 4
Picasso, Pablo, *196*; *Carmen sur le Texte de Prosper Mérimée*, *177*, *195*
Pine, Eleven Years Old (Kylie Stillman), *218*
Piranesi, Giovanni Battista, 133, 189; *Vedute di Roma*, *134*
Pisan Cantos (Ezra Pound), 76
Pissaro, Lucien, 205
Pitt, Stanley, *Silver Starr* (comic book series), *96*
De Plantis Epitome Utilissima (Pietro Andrea Mattioli), *162*
Planudes, Maximos, 115
Plato's academy, 34
Pliny 'the Elder', 116, 161
pochoir stencilling, 226
poetry, 53–6, 71, 87
Poissons, Ecrevisses et Crabes de Diverses Couleurs et Figures Extraordinaires (Louis Renard), 164, *165*
pop-up books, 106
Pope, Alexander, translations of *Iliad* and *Odyssey*, 55
Portrait of an Australian (Jonathan Tse), *218*
Portraits and Prayers (Gertrude Stein), 75, *75*
poster and magazine art, 226
Pound, Ezra: *The Cantos*, 76, *76*; *Pisan Cantos*, 76; *Section: Rock–Drill 85–95 de los Cantares*, 76
prayer manuals, 15; *see also* Psalters
a preponderance of aboriginal blood (Judy Watson), *214*, 215
Prima Pars Descriptionis Itineris Navalis in Indiam Orientalem (Willem Lodewijcksz), *147*
primers, 105
printed books: development of, 18–25; impact on bookbinding, 174
printing: block technology, 28; borders, initials and

ornamentation, 23; casting individual letters, 19; colour photographic processes, 109; computers, impact on, 208; copperplate engraving, 164; earliest-known examples, 28; early moveable type, 19; Gutenberg specimens, 19; hand-coloured engraving, 164; impact of Arts and Crafts movement, 201; introduction in Europe, 17; Islamic technologies, 32; Japanese technologies, 182; mathematical and geometrical diagrams, 23; mechanisation, 201; mezzotint, 193; moveable type, 19; origins in China and Korea, 19; photographic line block, 194; revolution in, 24; stipple engraving, 167; woodblock, 182; woodcuts, 201
private ownership of books, 10
private presses, 200–9
The Products of Wealth (Peter Lyssiotis), 212
Project Gutenberg, 24
psalters, *10*, 14
Ptitsa Bezymiannaia: Izbrannye Stikhi 1917–1921 (Aleksandr Kusikov), *225*
Ptolemy: *Almagest,* 115–16, *116*; *Geographia,* 115, *143*; theory of great southern continent, 63; world map, 115
Pu Qua, 127
publication dates, fictitious, 69
pulp fiction and comics, 92–103; Australian popularity, 99; crime fiction, *98,* 99; French and Italian genres, 94; pulp fiction covers, 1950s, *97*; *The Shadow,* 94
Punch (British satirical magazine), 93
Puss in Boots (Walter Crane), *107*

q

Quirós, Pedro Fenández de, 144, 146; *Terra Australis Incognita …,* 146, *146*
Quotations from Chairman Mao Tse-Tung ('The Little Red Book'; Mao Zedong), 47, *49*
Qur'an, 28, 29, 30, *30*, *31*, 32; Arabic language for worship, 30; central role in Islam, 30; cover for, *31*; *hafiz* (memorising entire text), 30

r

Rackham, Arthur, *Mother Goose: The Old Nursery Rhymes,* 109
Ratdolt, Erhard, 23
Rattray, James, *Scenery, Inhabitants and Costumes of Afghaunistan,* 30, 130, 131
Rawlinson, Henry, 4
Rayhan script, *30*
Receuils des Histoires de Troye (William Caxton), 23
Redouté, Pierre-Joseph: *Description des Plantes Rares Cultivées à Malmaison,* 167; *Jardin de la Malmaison,* 167; *Les Roses,* 167; *Les Liliacées, 166,* 167
Reeves, Wilf, *The Legends of Moonie Jarl,* 110
Reid, Jamie, 230
Relations de Divers Voyages Curieux (Melchisédech Thévenot), *126,* 127
religious texts, 26–33; *see also* sacred books
Remi, Georges: *Les Aventures de Tintin: les Cigares du Pharaon,* 94; *Tintin* comic strip series, *94*
Renaissance Europe: explosion of knowledge, 116; and printing revolution, 24; rediscovery of classical texts, 133
Renard, Louis, *Poissons, Ecrevisses et Crabes de Diverses Couleurs et Figures Extraordinaires,* 164, *165*
Restif de la Bretonne, Nicolas Edmé, *La Découverte Australe par un Homme-Volant,* 69, *69*
Reuwich, Erhard, *117,* 122
Richter, Henry, *169*
Ricketts, Charles, 205
Ridgers, Derek, *228*
Rieu, EU, 81
Roberts, David, 129; *The Holy Land: Syria, Idumea, Arabia, Egypt & Nubia,* 139
Rome, accounts of, 133
'A Room of One's Own' (Virginia Woolf), 73
Les Roses (Pierre-Joseph Redouté), 167
Rosetta Stone, 4, 6, 136
Rosser, Celia E, *The Banksias,* 168, 169
Rossetti, Dante Gabriel, 201; *The Blessed Damozel,* 205
Roth, Dieter, 212
Rowling, JK, Harry Potter series, 110
The Ruins of Paestum, otherwise Posidonia, in Magna Graecia (Thomas Major), *135*
Ruscha, Ed, *Twenty-six Gasoline Stations,* 212
Russell, Alexander, *The Natural History of Aleppo,* 129, *129*
Russell, Patrick, 129

s

sacred books, 26–33; Bible, 28, 32, 33; Qur'an, 28–9, 30, 31, 32; Torah, 28–30
Saint-Exupéry, Antoine de, *Night Flight,* 80
Salome: a Tragedy in One Act (Oscar Wilde; illus Aubrey Beardsley), 194, *194*
Sayers, Dorothy L, *The Unpleasantness at the Bellona Club,* 80
Scattered Poems (Jack Kerouac), *91*
Scenery, Costumes and Architecture Chiefly on the Western Side of India (Robert Melville Grindlay), *128*
Scenery, Inhabitants and Costumes of Afghaunistan (James Rattray), 30, 130, *131*
Schatzbehalter (Stephan Fridolin), *22,* 23
Schedel, Hartmann, 36; *Liber Chronicarum* (Nuremberg Chronicle), *22,* 23, 36, *36,* 64, 116, *117*
Schmoller, Hans, 81, *81*
Schoeffer, Peter, 20
Schouten, Willem Cornelis, 148
scientific enterprise, 122, 158
Scriptores Historiæ Augustæ, 16, *17*
scriptoria, 9
scripts: Carolingian, *10,* 10–11; demotic, 4; Egyptian hieroglyphic, 4, *5, 137*; Gothic ('blackletter'), 11, 14; Humanist (Roman), 17; Irish, 10; Italian, 10; italic, 23; Japanese, 7; *kufic,* 30; *maghribi, 31*; *Rayhan, 30*; Sumerian, 3–7
Section: Rock–Drill 85–95 de los Cantares (Ezra Pound), *76*
Seizan goryū ikebana tebikigusa (Yoshio Yasumasa), *184*
Selenographia (Johannes Hevelius), 122, *122*
Sendak, Maurice, *Where the Wild Things Are,* 110, *111*
Seriman, Zaccaria, *Viaggi di Enrico Wanton alle Terre Incognite Australi* (Voyage of Enrico Wanton to Terra Australis Incognita), 64, *65*
Servières, Jean Grolier de, 174
Seuss, Dr (Theodor Geisel), 110
The Shadow series ('Maxwell Grant' = Walter B Gibson), 94
Shakespeare, William: development of English language, 59; First Folio of plays, *60*; *Mr William Shakespeares Comedies, Histories and Tragedies …,* 60; Second Folio of plays, *60*
Sharp, Martin, 226, *227*
Shepard, Ernest H, 109–10, *110*
The Ship of Fools (*Das Narrenschiff; Stultifera Navis;* Sebastian Brant), 58
Siebold, Philipp Franz von, *Nippon: Archiv zur Beschreibung von Japan, 127*
Signs of Australia (Richard Tipping), *219*
Silver Starr (comic book series; Stanley Pitt), *96*
Sindbad the Sailor and Other Stories From the Arabian Nights (Edmund Dulac), *108*
Smellie, William, 40
Smith, Andrew, *84*
Smith, Paul, *85*
Solander, Daniel, 158
Solomon Islands, exploration of, 144
Somemoyo hinagata: nakadachi kodachi (Nesumi Takenosuke), *186*
South-East Asia, sea-chart of, *148*
Spanish Inquisition, 43
A Specimen Book of Pattern Papers

Designed for and in use at the Curwen Press, 176
Speculum Majus (The Great Mirror; Vincent of Beauvais), 36
Spiegelman, Art, 85, *85*; *Maus II: a Survivor's Tale: and Here my Troubles Began*, 103, *103*
Spilbergen, Joris van, *148*, 149
star charts, 115–16
Stein, Gertrude: *Autobiography of Alice B Toklas*, 76; *The Making of Americans*, 75, *75*; *Portraits and Prayers*, 75, *75*
Stillman, Kylie, *Pine, Eleven Years Old*, 218
The Subterraneans (Jack Kerouac), 90
Sumerian temples, 27
Sumerian script, 3–7
suminagashi (Japanese marbling technique), 177
Swift, Jonathan, *Travels into Several Remote Nations of the World* (Gulliver's Travels), 63
'Swiss Design' movement, 226
The Sydney Morning (Richard Tipping), *219*
Synopsis of the Birds of Australia and the Adjacent Islands (John Gould), 168

t

Tabularum Geographicarum Contractarum (Claes Jansz Visscher), *142*
Tagami, Jun, *231*
Tahiti, 151
A Tale of a Tub (cover design David Pearson), *83*
Tan, Shaun, *The Lost Thing*, 111
Tao-te Ching, (Lao-tzu), 53
Tàpies, Antoni, *199*
Tarzan (comic strip; Harold Foster), 93–4
Tasman, Abel, 127, 148
Taylor-Wood, Sam, 85, *85*
The Temple of Flora (Robert John Thornton), 167, *167*
Tenniel, John, 109, *109*
Teriade, Efstratios, 194
La Terra Australe Connue (Gabriel de Foigny), 66

'Terra Australis Incognita', 140–9; depicted on maps, 115, *141*, *143*; in literature, 62–9
Terra Australis Incognita … (Pedro Fenández de Quirós), 146, *146*
Tezuka Osamu, 100; *Buddha*, *100*, *101*
Theatrum Orbis Terrarum (Abraham Ortelius), 36, *36*, 116, *118–19*, 143, *145*
Theatrum Orbis Terrarum (*Atlas Novus*; Joan Blaeu), *147*
Theophrastus, *Historia Planturum*, 161
Thévenot, Melchisédech, *Relations de Divers Voyages Curieux*, 126, *127*
The Thin Man (Dashiell Hammett), 80
–1316 (Peter Lyssiotis & Angela Cavalieri), 212, *213*
Thornton, Robert John: *New Illustration of the Sexual System of Carolus von Linnaeus*, 167; *The Temple of Flora*, 167, *167*
3 Deep Design, *233*
Tierra del Fuego, 141
Tintin comic strip series (Georges Remi), 94
Tipitaka (Buddhist scripture), 27
Tipping, Richard: *Signs of Australia*, *219*; *The Sydney Morning*, *219*
To the Lighthouse (Virginia Woolf), 73
Token for Children … (James Janeway), 105
Tolkien, JRR, *The Hobbit*, 56
Topsell, Edward, *The History of Four-Footed Beasts and Serpents*, 121, *121*, 163
Torah, 28–30; *Sefer Torah*, *28*, *29*, 29, 30; transcription of, 29; translation and other editions, 30
Torres, Luis Váez de, 146
Tory, Geofroy, 24; 'Fantastic Alphabet', *222*; *Horae in Laude Beatiss, Virginis Mariae, ad Usum Romanum*, 25, *175*
Toscani, Oliviero, *229*
'toy books', 109
travel writing, 124–31; 'armchair travellers', 125; confusion of real and imagined, 122; by women, 125
Travels into Several Remote Nations of the World (Gulliver's Travels;

Jonathan Swift), 63
The Travels of Don Francisco de Quevedo: Through Terra Australis Incognita, 64, *65*
Très Riches Heures (Limbourg brothers), 14, *15*
Trew, Christoph Jacob, *Hortus Nitidissimis Omnem per Annum Superbiens Floribus*, 164
Tripitaka (Buddhist scripture), 27
Tristessa (Jack Kerouac), *90*
'Tropon' (Henri van de Velde), *224*
Tschichold, Jan, 81, *81*; *Die Neue Typographie*, 226
Tse, Jonathan, *Portrait of an Australian*, 218
Turner, JMW, *Liber Studiorum*, 193, *193*
Twenty-six Gasoline Stations (Ed Ruscha), 212
Tyndale, William, 32, 33
typeface designers, 221–2
typefaces: Bembo, 221; Chaucer, 203, 222; Gill Sans, 208, 226, *226*; Golden, 201, 222; Golden Cockerel, 208; Helvetica, 226; italic, 221; large-scale, 222; modelled on Gothic scripts, 221; Optima, 226; Perpetua, 208, 226; Railway, 224; Roman, 23, 221; 1920s, 1930s development, 226; sans serif, 222, 224; Times Modern, 229; Times New Roman, 226; Troy, 203, 222; Two Lines English Egyptian, 222; Univers, 226
typography, 24, 81, 82; experimental, 212
Tyssot de Patot, Simon, *Voyages et Avantures de Jacques Masse*, 69

u

Ueno, Yoko, *179*
ukiyo-e artists, 186
ukiyo-e printmaking (Japan), 182
Ulm (Germany), 23
Ulysses (James Joyce), 73, *74*, *75*, 198, *199*
United States Exploring Expedition, 158
universities and demand for books, 11

The Unpleasantness at the Bellona Club (Dorothy L Sayers), 80

v

Vale Press, 205
Vanderlans, Rudy, 229
Varro, Marcus Terentius, 35
Vedas (Hindu scripture), 27
Vedute di Roma (Giovanni Battista Piranesi), *134*
vellum, 173
Venice, printers in, 23–4
Verve magazine, 194, *196*, *197*
Viaggi di Enrico Wanton alle Terre Incognite Australi (Voyage of Enrico Wanton to Terra Australis Incognita; Zaccaria Seriman), 64, *65*
Vienna Dioscorides, 161
Views in Turkey (Sir Robert Ainslie), *134*
Vincent of Beauvais, 35–6; *Speculum Majus* (The Great Mirror), 36
A Vindication of the Rights of Woman (Mary Wollstonecraft), 47, *47*
Virgil: *Aeneid*, 55; *Eclogues*, 205
The Vision of Hell (Dante), *192*
Visionaire 30: the Game, *231*
Visionaire publications, 231
Visscher, Claes Jansz, *Tabularum Geographicarum Contractarum*, *142*
Volckamer, Johann, *Nürnbergische Hesperides*, 164
Vollard, Ambrose, 211; *Parallèlement*, 194
Voyage Autour du Monde (Louis-Claude de Freycinet), *158*
Voyage de La Pérouse Autour du Monde (Jean-François de Galaup de la Pérouse), *154*
Voyage de Robertson aux Terres Australes, 69
The Voyage Out (Virginia Woolf), 73
A Voyage to the Levant: or Travels in the Principal Parts of Asia Minor (Corneille Le Bruyn), *128–9*
A Voyage to the Pacific Ocean, Undertaken … (Capt James Cook), *153*
A Voyage towards the South Pole, and Round the World (Capt James Cook), *152*

Voyages et Avantures de Jacques Masse (Simon Tyssot de Patot), 69
Vulgate Bible, 32

w

Waiting for Godot (Samuel Beckett), 76, *76*
Walker, Emery, 201, 205
Wallace-Crabbe, Chris, *Drawing*, 215, *215*
Walsh, Richard, 226
Ware, Chris, 85; *Jimmy Corrigan, the Smartest Kid on Earth*, 103
'The Waste Land' (TS Eliot), 71
The Waste Land (TS Eliot), 73
Watkins, Muriel, *98*
Watson, Judy, *a preponderance of aboriginal blood*, 214, *215*
Waugh, Evelyn, *Decline and Fall*, 80
The Waves (Virginia Woolf), 73, *73*
Wayzgoose Press, 208
Webb, Philip, 201
Weiditz, Hans, 161
Wenz, Paul, *Jim et Jack*, 179
Where the Wild Things Are (Maurice Sendak), 110, *111*
White, Diana, *The Descent of Ishtar*, *204*
White, John, *Journal of a Voyage to New South Wales*, 153
White Jazz (James Ellroy; Chip Kidd), 233
Why I Am So Wise (cover design Phil Baines), *83*
Wilde, Oscar, *Salome: a Tragedy in One Act* (illus Aubrey Beardsley), 194, *194*
Williams, WH ('Marc Brody'), 99
Winnie-the-Pooh (AA Milne), 109, 110
Wit, Frederick de: *Orbis Maritimus*, 148; *Orientaliora Indiarum Orientalium*, 148
Wollstonecraft, Mary, *A Vindication of the Rights of Woman*, 47, *47*
Wolters, Friedrich, *Herrschaft und Dienst*, *206*
Wonders of the East, 116
woodcuts, 20
Woolf, Leonard, 71; see also Hogarth Press
Woolf, Virginia, 71; 'A Room of One's Own', 73; *To the Lighthouse*, 73; *The Voyage Out*, 73; *The Waves*, 73, *73*; see also Hogarth Press
Woolnough, Charles, *The Art of Marbling*, 178
The Workes of Geffray Chaucer (Geoffrey Chaucer), *57*
The Works of Geoffrey Chaucer (printer William Morris), *202*, 203, *203*
World Map 1550 (Pierre Desceliers), *144*
world maps, 36; development of, 141, 143; produced at Dieppe, 143, 144; Ptolemaic, 141
writing, origin and development of, 3–7
writing tools, wedge-shaped implements, 3
Wycliffe, John, 32

y

yad (Torah pointer), 29, *29*
Yates, Alan ('Carter Brown', 'Paul Valdez', 'Tex Conrad', 'Tod Conway'), 99
The Yellow Book (Aubrey Beardsley), 194
Yoshio Yasumasa, *Seizan goryū ikebana tebikigusa*, 184
Young, Edward, 79
youth culture and music magazines, 229
Yūsai kachō gafu (Nakabayashi Chikudō), 184

z

Zainer, Günther, 23
Zainer, Johann, 23
Zap Comix (Robert Crumb), 99
Zell, Ulrich, 20
'zine' or do-it-yourself magazines, 230

FOLLOWING PAGES:
Denis Diderot, editor
Encyclopédie, ou, Dictionnaire Raisonné des Sciences, des Arts et des Métiers
Paris, Chez Briasson, David l'Aîné, Le Breton, Durand, 1751–72
(Detail)

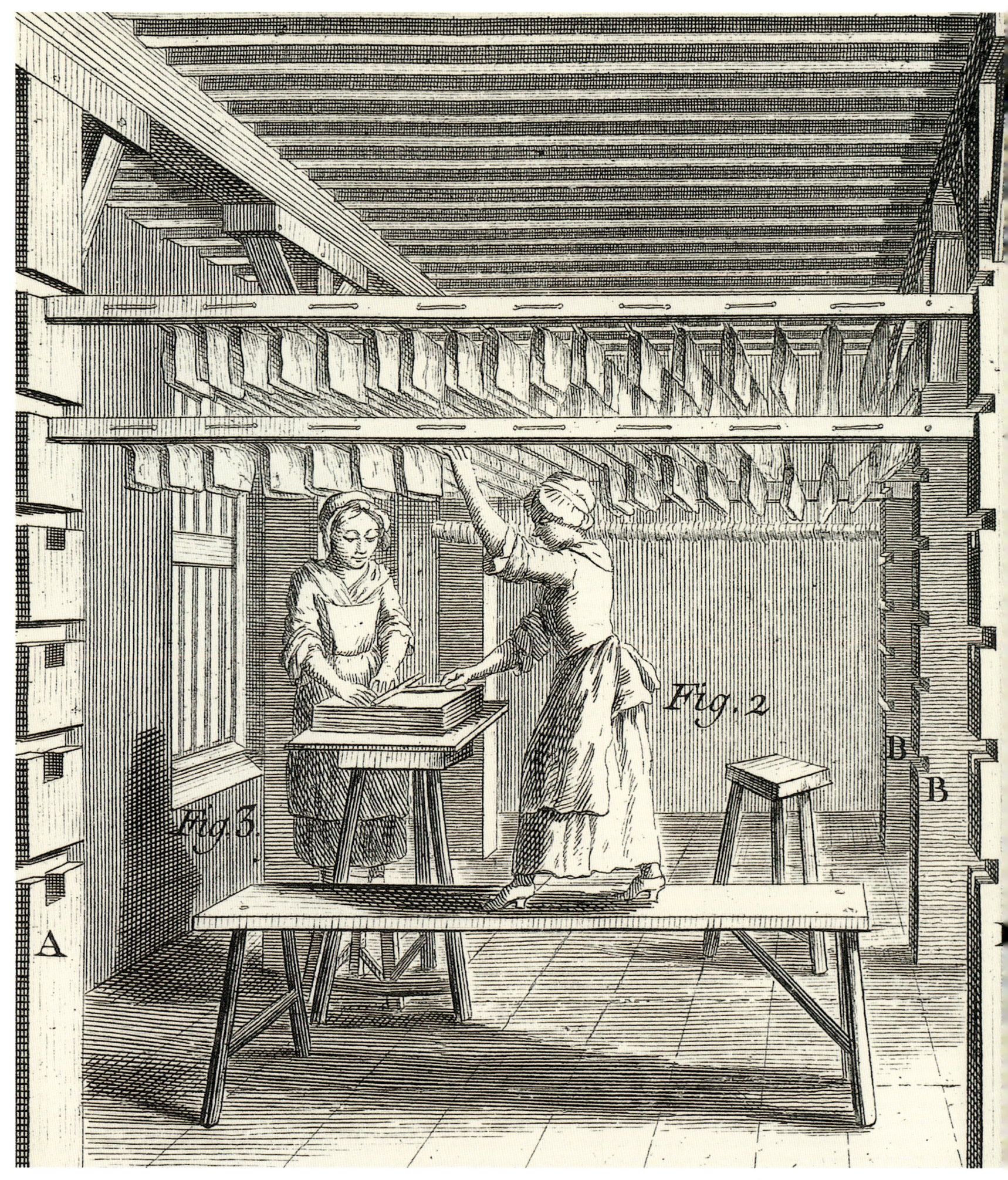

Fig. 1.

THE MIEGUNYAH PRESS

This book was designed and typeset by Pfisterer + Freeman.
The text was set in 10 point Adobe Garamond Pro
with 2¾ points of leading.
The text is printed on 128gsm matt art paper.
This book was edited by Bryony Cosgrove.